SIGNS OF WATER

ARTS IN ACTION

MOUNT ROYAL
UNIVERSITY
1910

SERIES EDITOR:
Jennifer Pettit, Dean, Faculty of Arts, Mount Royal University

Co-published with Mount Royal University
ISSN 2371-6134 (Print) ISSN 2371-6142 (Online)

This series focuses on illuminating, promoting, or demonstrating the fundamental significance of the Arts, Humanities, and Social Sciences to public well-being and contemporary society—culturally, spiritually, socially, politically, and economically—with the aim of raising awareness of the essential skills, perspectives, and critical understandings of societal issues these disciplines cultivate.

No. 1   *Understanding Atrocities: Remembering, Representing, and Teaching Genocide*
Edited by Scott W. Murray

No. 2   *Orange Chinook: Politics in the New Alberta*
Edited by Duane Bratt, Keith Brownsey, Richard Sutherland, and David Taras

No. 3   *Signs of Water: Community Perspectives on Water, Responsibility, and Hope*
Edited by Robert Boschman and Sonya L. Jakubec

UNIVERSITY OF CALGARY
Press

Edited by
ROBERT BOSCHMAN
& SONYA L. JAKUBEC

Signs *of* Water

*Community Perspectives on
Water, Responsibility, and Hope*

Arts in Action Series
ISSN 2371-6134 (Print) ISSN 2371-6142 (Online)

University of Calgary Press
2500 University Drive NW
Calgary, Alberta
Canada T2N 1N4
press.ucalgary.ca

LIBRARY AND ARCHIVES CANADA CATALOGUING IN PUBLICATION

Title: Signs of water : community perspectives on water, responsibility, and hope / edited by Robert Boschman & Sonya L. Jakubec.
Names: Boschman, Robert, 1961- editor. | Jakubec, Sonya L., editor.
Series: Arts in action ; no. 3.
Description: Series statement: Arts in action, 2371-6134 ; no. 3 | Includes bibliographical references.
Identifiers: Canadiana (print) 20210354240 | Canadiana (ebook) 20210354275 | ISBN 9781773852348 (softcover) | ISBN 9781773852355 (Open Access PDF) | ISBN 9781773852362 (PDF) | ISBN 9781773852379 (EPUB)
Subjects: LCSH: Water.
Classification: LCC GB661.2 .S54 2022 | DDC 553.7—dc23

The University of Calgary Press acknowledges the support of the Government of Alberta through the Alberta Media Fund for our publications. We acknowledge the financial support of the Government of Canada. We acknowledge the financial support of the Canada Council for the Arts for our publishing program.

Alberta Government   Canada   Canada Council for the Arts   Conseil des Arts du Canada

Copyediting by Francine Michaud
Cover image courtesy Robert Boschman
Cover design, page design, and typesetting by Melina Cusano

This book is dedicated
to the memory
of
Milton Born with a Tooth
(1958–2019)

Contents

Foreword

Robert William Sandford
Global Water Futures Chair, Water & Climate Security
Institute for Water, Environment and Health
United Nations University

The world is waking up to the fact that there has never been a time in history when it was more important, wherever you live, to know where the water you drink comes from; how much of it is used and for what purposes; and the condition in which it is returned to the river for downstream use of others. We are also waking up to the fact that water will be more ecologically precious than we can even begin to imagine in the future and that we must, for the sake of the future, value it as we never have before.

To that end, this is a book that actually fulfills the promise of embracing the widest range of awareness of water and culture not just regionally and nationally, but globally. It is truly multi- and transdisciplinary in perspective. The book demonstrates just how many ways a thoughtful observer can immerse themselves in water. In this book, water is viewed as a form of liquid modernity. The reader is invited to ponder the notion of the aquagenesis of human life while, at the same time, react to confront the challenges of the digital revolution, neoliberalism, and all of the anthropogenic hazards of this problematic century head on and to do so with self-deprecating wit, equanimity, and optimism.

If you savour posthuman political theory, there is a chapter in which you can lose yourself in metaphorical vampire contemplation of Detroit's neoliberal racialized liquidity. If music videos are your métier, there is a deep critique of the water scenes in Beyoncé's *Lemonade* album. In other chapters, less metaphorical and far blunter realities relate to access to clean water surface from cultural settings as widely diverse and geographically different as Northern Canada, the American west, the Amazon, Sub-Saharan Africa, and India. In one chapter you accompany the author on a walk through a graveyard in a remote Alberta First Nation. Many of those buried there died prematurely—a testament to the deteriorating health of local residents linked directly to alarming industrial impacts on the condition of their water supply. In Arizona, the reader is invited to bear witness to the consequences of irremediable damage to aquifers due to the breakdown of long-term intergenerational standards of care. In Brazil, we confront the gap between promise and practice with respect to the rights of Indigenous peoples. In Northwest Cameroon we confront the global issue of soil depletion and we are introduced to all the usual suspects that threaten the future in the absence of good governance. In another chapter we are uplifted by the enormous power of stories and story-telling to re-mind us of what we know from the past and how we must act if we are to have hope for the future.

While each of the chapters offers its own insights, the value of the book also resides in the comparative example offered through the rich, elaborate weaving of stories and the broad range of shared experiences related to how water informs our way of life. Pull on any thread in the fluid fabric that holds this book together and you will see that thread connected somehow to every other and all connect in some way to the link between water and culture. If you care about reliable drinking water supply, sus-tainable water management, hydro-ecological stability, the human right to water, Indigenous water issues, water and community, or how water is linked to climate change, this book cannot but bring you to the threshold of both optimism and outrage.

Ultimately, however, this is a book about hope. We now know what Indigenous peoples have known for thousands of years. We can reduce and moderate the threat of disruptive global change by protecting, restor-ing, and constantly rehabilitating natural system function. From this we see that this is not the end of the world. It is just the beginning of another. There is great power in realizing this, for it is at the local level—where we live—that we have the most power to bring about change and to act most effectively in service of where and how we live and who we love, now and in the future.

In sum, this book makes it clear that if we are to have any hope of addressing the threat of climate disruption in time, we need reconciliation—meaningful reconciliation—first with one another, and at the same time with the Earth. Such reconciliation would demand that we first restore local identity and humanity's sense of place and connection; that we restore truth; restore responsibility to human dignity, economic morality, and equality, and in so doing restore common purpose and a vision for the future of humanity and the planet. Of that message, I am sure that Milton Born with a Tooth, to whom this book is dedicated, would greatly approve.

Acknowledgements

We gratefully acknowledge the support provided by Mount Royal University that makes this book possible. We especially acknowledge and thank the Dean of the Faculty of Arts, Professor Jennifer Pettit, for recognizing the historical and environmental value attached to this project. Like Pettit, Connie Van Der Byl, Director of the Institute for Environmental Sustainability (IES) at MRU, has anchored parts of this volume with significant funding support. The chapter on Uranium City, especially, would not be possible without funding. This book has many moving parts and much study has gone into integrating those parts to create a structure that reflects organic wholeness and processes. The folks at the University of Calgary Press, particularly Brian Scrivener, Helen Hajnoczky, Alison Cobra, Melina Cusano, and Francine Michaud have been instrumental in implementing the design of this book. Funding from the Social Sciences and Humanities Research Council of Canada (SSHRC) has made *Signs of Water* a reality.

Introduction

Robert Boschman and Sonya Jakubec

Where life dwelled, water flowed through it.

> —Lynn Margulis, *Symbiotic Planet*: *A New Look at Evolution*

This book is concerned with community responses to water issues. In the fifteen chapters gathered here, contributors from multiple perspectives and disciplines from around the world weigh in on water: how it flows through human life in specific locations. Fifteen of the twenty-one writers gathered here are women; and all the research and documentation concern water at the community level, stemming from fieldwork, art, and collaborative experience across the Americas as well as in the EU, Africa, and Asia. Many contributors have worked in and studied particular communities and their relationships to water—with respect to, for example, access, facilitation, health, history, and politics—from rural northwest Cameroon to South Africa, the U.K., Japan, Brazil, India, Indonesia, and Canada. They also record the histories of a number of major river basins, including the Upper Xingu (Brazil), the Fraser (British Columbia), the Tambraparni (South India), the Mackenzie (Northwest Territories), and the St. Lawrence (Quebec). Most are deeply engaged with Indigenous communities struggling with a wide range of overlapping issues relating to water, such as rights, sanitation, pollution, and the long-term and on-going effects of colonization.

As demonstrated in these chapters, Indigenous peoples are raising their voices and being heard, and water especially ranks among their most pressing concerns. From Tucson, Arizona and Java, Indonesia, to northern Brazil, Alberta, northwest Cameroon, and South India, Indigenous communities are fighting everyday for healthy access to, and long-term viability of, both water and justice in the face of long and relentless histories of colonization, commodification, exploitation, and contamination.

Six interrelated approaches, all community-based approaches to knowing, thinking about, and working with water, frame this volume: immersions, formations, histories, interventions, responses, and implementation. In practice, of course, these approaches are used together throughout the book, as they do in the life of water itself (and indeed in our own lives), but we think it is clarifying to design the flow of chapters with various emphases, beginning with the existential and concluding with the infrastructural. Hence in this book the reader's experience begins with works by anthropologist Julie Laplante and literary scholar Michaela Keck, both of whom study water's immersive characteristics relative to human lives and communities—and moves gradually through politics, history, and art towards basic community actions culminating in Anna Frank's engineering essay regarding water harvesting. We begin with an anthropological quest and end with an infrastructural solution; and in doing so Laplante and Frank, like the other contributors in between, take us to many different human communities around the world. All are concerned deeply with water.

As an anthropologist, Laplante leads readers on a quest to study water as substance both natural and cultural: a water imaginary that is very human but also places us firmly in what we call *nature*. Reading Laplante, who travels to and lives in Quebec, Brazil, South Africa, and Java, we encounter water anew, as though for the first time. What is water? What is our relationship to and with it? As Julia Laplante reminds us, "We are also water" (p. 19).

Following Laplante's contribution, with the second chapter of Section I *Immersions*, is Michaela Keck's revealing work on the British nature writer Roger Deakin, a proponent of "wild swimming." Living and working in northern Germany, Keck studies the practice of swimming in and along rivers, gorges, and other waterways regardless of current social norms and prohibitions. Like Laplante, Keck resists the "objectification of water" (p. 20). Immersion (in this case, the practice of wild swimming) is inherently social and communal (p. 50): "being human means consisting of water" (p. 49). The portrait of Roger Deakin that emerges here is informed by the respective works of Bruno Latour and Tim Ingold, both of whom also impact Julia Laplante's anthropological quest to know water intimately. Neither Laplante nor Keck is interested in romanticizing water; both reject the idea of water as some pure substance, found for example in the ubiquitous plastic bottle that one buys and then abandons. As we discover reading Keck, wild swimmer Roger Deakin finds himself in conflict with regulatory forces concerned with private property and human health. Politics are inevitable.

American theorist C.R. Grimmer sees water as a political formation constructed and wielded by neo-liberalism so that water is perceived as neutral, pure, and a matter of choice. As the opening essay found in *Formations*, Section 2 of this book, Grimmer's chapter on the Detroit water shut-offs of 2013–2016 provides transitions from Keck's portrait of wild swimmer Roger Deakin. If Keck takes Deakin as her immersive figure, Grimmer takes the African-American multimedia artist Beyonce who, through *Lemonade*, immerses herself in water in a way seen by millions. Like Deakin's confrontation with the owners of the waterfront river where he wants to swim, "Can't you read the sign?," Beyonce reveals water's substantive historical and political reality. She evokes water's significant role in the histories of oppressed and exploited human communities. Water is anything but pure and apolitical. Like all the contributors to this volume, Grimmer makes clear that water is relational. When in the spring of 2013 Detroit Water and Sewage began to carry out 70,000 shutoffs in 730 days, the United Nations intervened (without success) to defend residents' human rights (p. 65). Water is not a commodity that is chosen and purchased but rather a right that is inherent and available to all people, as established by the UN in July 2010 (www.un.org/en/sections/issues-depth/water/).

Not only the United States but Canada should be meeting this right—the right to clean, healthy, and accessible water—to all citizens. Yet, as Denise L. Di Santo makes clear in chapter 4, in which she documents histories of contaminated water supply in both Tucson, Arizona, and Fort Chipewyan, Alberta, this is not the case. Indeed, Di Santo at the outset of her essay describes being warned by an Indigenous resident of Fort Chipewyan (through which the Athabasca River flows into Lake Athabasca) not to drink the water when she visits that community. In the wider context, Di Santo offers a detailed history of the formation of environmental justice in the United States and Canada over the last forty years (pp. 87–91), while placing both Fort Chip and Tucson in the foreground of this history. With their water sources (the Athabasca and Tucson basins) contaminated by industry, both communities have endured not only serious health impacts but also disrupted cultural traditions; and both have had to wage public and legal campaigns for acknowledgement and remedy.

Di Santo emphasizes repeatedly the issue of externalized costs, a potent theme arising throughout this collection. Such costs are too often borne by Indigenous communities and communities of colour. Even as C.R. Grimmer and Denise Di Santo both make this plain, their work is powerfully corroborated in chapter 5 by Marcella LaFever, Shirley Hardman, and Pearl Penner, authors of "Indigenous Stories and the Fraser River: Intercultural Dialogue for Public Decision-Making," which rounds out Section II, *Formations*. These three researchers have painstakingly recorded—and here in this book documented—the first-person stories of the Stó:lō and other First Nations elders testifying before the Cohen Commission of Inquiry into the Decline of Sockeye Salmon in the Fraser River (2012, http://publications.gc.ca/site/eng/432516/publication.html). Their chapter crucially emphasizes the centrality of Indigenous knowledge and stories. Indigenous voices are primary here; they come first, and their concerns about the Fraser River and Sockeye salmon are foremost in the reader's mind in this chapter. Through their storytelling before the Cohen Commission regarding the Fraser River and the human relation to salmon, "the Stó:lō [people of the river]" (p. 112) speak of the values needed to sustain not only the Fraser River system but any waterway: sharing, relations, and communication. Curating this collection, we hope, contributes to all three.

Sharing, relations, and communication seem obvious as ecological values for living sustainably with water, a human right. Would that we lived in a world where such values were instantly obvious and accepted as common sense, and did not have to be restated before a government commission organized on the decline of a fishery in a major, world-renowned river in Canada. The contradictions are alarming in a country frequently recognized as the best country in the world on a variety of metrics, including quality of life, and particularly those related to environment (https://www.usnews.com/news/best-countries/overall-rankings). Would that we lived in a world where water as a human right were a given and not contested by global corporations—Swiss Nestlé, for instance—which view it as a commodity to be acquired and sold for profit to consumers. In a world where sharing, relations, and communication were the norm regarding water, the problems addressed in *Histories*, Section III of this book, would not exist, at least not as direly as they do according to the four historical essays which follow the work of LaFever, Hardman, and Penner on the Fraser River.

We, as editors, have recognized the ways in which these authors' original scholarly work can be juxtaposed fruitfully with that of their Brazilian colleagues, Fernanda Viegas Reichardt, Andrea Garcia, and Maria Elisa de Paula Eduardo Garavello, who have no less painstakingly documented the historical and political water-related issues extant in the Upper Xingu River Basin, which is part of the Amazon River Basin, "the most extensive water network of the planet" with "nearly 60% of the Brazilian Indigenous population" (p. 156). During their research in the field, they travelled more than 24,000 kilometers, and their photographic images are compelling. Like other writers make clear in this book, the authors of this chapter draw close connections between water and traditional cultures, diversity, and biodiversity, and provide evidence to that end. Their call for the legal protection of the Upper Xingu regions in face of Brazil's ongoing frontier practices of deforestation is based on their integrated research work involving immersion and participation with and in the communities they encounter.

What they discover and report to readers syncs with the historical fieldwork of Henry Bikiwibili Tantoh in northwest Cameroon, who records a statement that applies to this book in various ways: "The water crisis that many communities face is progressively about how people, as individuals, and as part of a collective society, govern the availability, usage, and control over water resources and their benefits" (p. 203). Tantoh reports on how traditional communities living in continuous relation to the same water sources for epochs have, in recent historical times, seen that relation disrupted. The question here, again, is "how to dismantle the fortress of centralised management institutions and replace them with an all-inclusive system that is not the only protector and supporter, but also an enabler and liberator" (p. 188). And once again, this time in Sub-Saharan Africa, and in a country that Tantoh states is second only to "the Democratic Republic of Congo in terms of quantity of available water resources" (p. 196), readers encounter top-down water governance that is the legacy of colonialism. As a scholar of water stationed in the field in northwest Cameroon, Tantoh finds and articulates evidence paralleling and corroborating conditions related to water, as reported in the other chapters, that pertain to population, climate, drought, degradation, contamination, and lack of access. Repeatedly, he informs readers that local communities are excluded from governance in respect to the very water that sustains their existence. Cultural discontinuities are as harmful to human health and ecology as any other environmental malpractice. While Tantoh stresses that solutions must be local and sensitive to historical context, he also uses the term *polycentric* in relation to water governance that works for all.

In the chapter that follows, Arivalagan Murugeshapandian, working from archival sources, provides a history of the Tambraparni River basin in South India. Again, the impact of colonialism is clear. First the river is conquered through the colonial critique of Indigenous knowledge systems and practice concerning water sharing, irrigation, and fishing. Murugeshapandian employs the term "alarmist discourse" in his careful unfolding of the evidence. Such discourse makes way for new infrastructure—dams, reservoirs, and regulations; then the authorities "use the river system as a tool to take control of the forests from Indigenous peoples" (p. 220), even though (and perhaps even *because*) their ancient irrigation system throughout the basin worked well for centuries. What Arivalagan Murugeshapandian articulates here is a history of conflict between colonial and post-colonial governments and Indigenous fishers and farmers. Priorities are awarded to industries focused on water extraction and hydroelectric power requirements, while traditional farmers must literally beg for allotments to see their crops survive (p. 229). Likewise, Indigenous fishers are compelled to pay angling fees even as industrial aquaculture is established in the newly formed reservoirs (p. 232). Authoritarian dis-course sets the stage for new infrastructure projects that, once established, exclude and disenfranchise local and traditional peoples while empow-ering government-sanctioned industry.

A world away, but with a history that overlaps the time period Murugeshapandian covers, the Mackenzie River system in northern Canada undergoes its own alterations at the hands of colonial and post-col-onial governments. The longest river in Canada, the Mackenzie serves a vast complex of interrelated watersheds. Reg Whiten, the author of chapter 9, focuses on the Upper Kiskatinaw and Upper Peace basins to the south as well as the pristine Peel in the far north. Whiten's extensive experience in, and knowledge of, this region extends across the Mackenzie River sys-tem, significant parts of which fall under the terms of Treaty 8 (1899). He carefully documents the impacts on Indigenous nations within this large area. Like other contributors in this collection of essays, Whiten empha-sizes the significant role that grassroots exclusion has played in the rise of water-related issues in the Upper Kiskatinaw and Upper Peace basins. In recent decades, other water-related concerns have also developed across communities throughout this region. The ongoing construction of the Site C Dam on the Peace, despite opposition from First Nations and other activists, only reinforces Whiten's concerns about community exclusion. Through this continuing concern regarding top-down decision-making processes regarding river basins, Whiten forcefully foregrounds the Peel River basin, which falls under Yukon's 1993 Final Umbrella Agreement, and which in turn has been confirmed by the Supreme Court of Canada.

The fourth section of this collection, *Interventions*, constitutes the place where the voices of artists come to the fore on behalf of water. Our book on water is entitled *Signs of Water* for a host of reasons, the fore-most of which must be that the artist's production is no less important to community wellbeing in relation to water than that of the anthropologist's (with which this volume begins) or the engineer's (with which it ends). Canadian poet Richard Harrison, winner of the 2017 Governor General's Award for poetry, highlights in his meditative essay on water, culture, and environment how colonial culture—with its default emphasis on wheel-based technologies—has robbed itself (and those it has dominated) of opportunities to see community and life differently. Harrison, whose family home was hit hard in the 2013 flooding that inundated Calgary, Alberta, grieves over water. Specifically, he raises the problematic relationship between roads and water in ways that invoke other essays in our volume, such as the chapters on Brazil, the Fraser River, and the Mackenzie discussed above.

If Harrison at the close of chapter 10 imagines the wake of a boat he rides in, JuPong Lin and Devora Neumark suggest building a boat and offer a blueprint for such a project based on the craft of an actual boat builder. Their performance score composition, "Instructions for Being Water," is also offered here for inspiration and use. Using language that evokes Walt Whitman (who had much to say about water), they "lean towards each other and again outward. We invite new kinships" (p. 289). Visual artist Barbara Amos leads a similar collective called The Red Alert Project, and in her eponymously titled chapter 12, Amos demonstrates how her community work coincides with not only that of the Fierce Bellies Collective (created by Lin and Neumark), but the efforts of the Ghost River community, also located in Alberta, documented by Sharon Meier MacDonald in chapter 13. Both Amos and MacDonald, with their respective communities, have courageously opposed the watershed damage that is ongoing in this region, even in the unmitigated ruin that followed the great flooding of 2013. Both testify that they work at times under duress.

Sharon Meier MacDonald's chapter on the Ghost River watershed constitutes the opening piece in this volume's penultimate section, wherein two very different communities provide response models to critical water issues in their respective bioregions. In the aftermath of the 2013 flooding that swept through the Bow River watershed in southern Alberta, an event that awakened many Albertans to the reality of climate change, the Ghost River community located within this corridor came together to meet the crisis before them. Unfortunately, this meant facing industry, particularly the timber industry, which, at that time, was bent on clear-cutting even with the ecological disaster that had just unfolded with unprecedented fury. MacDonald's work documents this period when, dramatically, the people of the Ghost River region united, with First Nations and settlers alike working together.

Similarly, Bill Bunn and Robert Boschman, whose research is supported by a Social Sciences and Humanities Research Council grant, have twice visited the abandoned remains of Uranium City, once home to about 4,000 citizens. In the aftermath of Eldorado Mining Corporation's sudden eclipse of its uranium ore extraction and milling operations throughout this area in 1982, the community now holds about fifty people. As in the work of Reg Whiten (chapter 9), what is documented here through fieldwork, archival study, and interviews concerns the Treaty 8 (1899) region of Canada, which spans three provinces and a territory. It is here specifically, the ancient home of the Dene, where Bunn and Boschman begin their chapter focusing on Patrick Deranger, a Dene Elder who was born on the very land where Uranium City would later be established and because of which the Deranger family would be relocated. For Patrick Deranger, who died while this book was being written, the city's legacy was personal and complex, but among the many issues he faced water came first. It informs the Dene world view, and in this region the challenges are numerous given the intensive extraction and milling of uranium ore at multiple locations. With exceptions, as Bunn and Boschman have documented, these sites have not all been remediated. The most serious, Gunnar, an open-pit uranium operation from the mid-twentieth century that sits right on the shores of Lake Athabasca, is only now being attended to, at a cost to taxpayers of approximately $100 million CAD. That a project like Gunnar should never have happened in the first place is perhaps a point of contention to be debated by historians and environmentalists. What surely cannot be acceptable, however, is that a toxic field like Gunnar should be left behind for later generations to deal with and pay for. *Indeed, this region generally represents how colonialism and industry together create external costs as legacies to be borne by those who had nothing to do with their creation but must suffer and live with the consequences.* On many counts, the above statement stands for this volume, with its emphasis on communities forced to deal with the decisions of magnitude taken by others, who too often made no plans or provisions for consequences and impacts.

If Bunn and Boschman's chapter on Uranium City constitutes a kind of denouement to this volume, Anna Frank's chapter demonstrates how the science of infrastructural engineering can be deployed in ways that are anything but reckless. Frank brings to fruition here the theme of hopeful implementation and the successful search for good working results that can be found throughout these chapters, and which Robert Sandford observes in his Foreword. Moreover, with her careful historical context of the technology she describes, large-scale rain and flood water harvesting, Frank reveals how and why ancient water technologies, such as the qanat, actually worked. With an engineer's insight and a storyteller's sense of wonder, she lays down plans for how proven infrastructures such as the qanat can and will take us into the future as we deal with global climate change.

The editors of this book have also highlighted Frank's closing statement, "**We are on the brink of endless opportunities to learn more by consolidating science instead of breaking it apart into traditional silos,**" precisely because it calls on hope, vision, collaboration, and multidisciplinary action when we need these most crucially. Today is not a day for despair but for "investment and realization." This book is likewise a project that has been realized with hope and a multitude of visions, perspectives, and disciplines, all focused on human communities in their relation to water, essential to all life. This book is here for all to read, use, rely on, and most importantly perhaps, build on.

REFERENCES

Cohen, B. I. (2012, October). *Cohen Commission of inquiry into the decline of sockeye salmon in the Fraser River - final report.* Accessed March 1, 2020, from http://publications.gc.ca/site/eng/432516/publication.html

Margulis, L. (1998). *Symbiotic planet: A new look at evolution.* Basic Books.

United Nations. (2020). *The right to water.* Accessed March 1, 2020, from https://www.un.org/en/sections/issues-depth/water/

U.S. News and World Report. (2020). *Overall best countries ranking: 2020 ranking.* Accessed March 1, 2020, from https://www.usnews.com/news/best-countries/overall-rankings

I. IMMERSIONS:
From Water Imaginaries to Wild Swimming

Photo courtesy Robert Boschman

Introduction

So how might we know from water flowing through our bodies, sensing its gush, feeling its pressures and intensities as it speeds up and slows down, as it pushes against and within us, sometimes in excess?

—Julie Laplante, Chapter 1

No longer an element that is experienced by the senses or as an element that is itself an autonomous, living force, [water] has become the commodity referred to as H_2O, which is loathed as a potential health risk and, hence, managed and monitored according to its degree of purity.

—Michaela Keck, Chapter 2

This first section of *Signs of Water* is concerned with both the theoretical and real aspects of being in water—both the waters that flow inside us as well as those that an immersive swimmer such as Roger Deakin, following rivers, pursues. As authors Julie Laplante and Michaela Keck here state in their respective ways in chapters 1 and 2, humans themselves are made mostly of water, are conceived and develop in it. Our terrestrial lives—from birth to death—are contingent on, and soaked in, our beginnings in water; and humans share in such origins with many other life forms on (or better yet, in) this oceanic planet. In water lies the very proof some require that humans are of this world and not some other. We are in fact water beings. We die so quickly without it that the common equation made between water and life can be painfully real. How water can then be denied as a basic right and instead promoted as an extractive commodity to be sold would be laughable, were it not for the very fact that is successfully pursued by actual corporations with the rights of persons in law.

The term *immersion* is Latinate, used often to express the experience of plunging or being plunged into something. For example, in Anglophone parts of Canada, which we editors call home, French immersion refers to the experience of being schooled in the second official language listed in the Charter of Rights and Freedoms. Our constitution prods those in the English-only majority to plunge into French as though it were this other water body, deep and dark and unknown to many, in which swimming, metaphorically, is something else entirely. Yet the term *immersion*, when it is disambiguated, reveals *mer*, the French word for sea. In the chapters that follow, both Julie Laplante and Michaela Keck make detailed explorations from their respective disciplines—anthropology and literature—of the literal and figurative ramifications of water's immersive qualities. These chapters constitute in themselves an immersive experience.

If immersion in the real, substantive water of our world often means immersing oneself in others and in their stories and histories—as we shall see throughout this book—it also means encountering regulatory warnings in the form of signs. Hence, Roger Deakin's water politics, as Keck describes them at the close of this section, also set up our reading of C.R. Grimmer's portrait of Detroit and its own political and justice struggles over water in the first chapter of the section that succeeds Immersions.

—Robert Boschman and Sonya Jakubec, editors

Water Imagination in Anthropology: On Plant Healing Matters

Julie Laplante

For a dream to pursue itself with enough constance to give a written account, for it not to simply be the holiday of a fugitive hour, it needs to find its matter, there has to be a material element which gives it its own substance, its own rule, its specific poetic.

—Gaston Bachelard

In *L'eau et les rêves* (*Water and Dreams*), Bachelard (1942) shows how the form and matter of our imagining are two mutually constitutive aspects that we can never completely separate. Building on this foundation established by Gaston Bachelard, Illich makes a distinction between imagination as the source of form, and imagination as the wellspring of formless "stuff" (6). While attesting that what is watery in each place may vary, Illich suggests that "beneath the mass of images, verbal variations, moods, tactile experiences, and lights that shape water in our imagination, there is a stable, dense, slow, and fertile water stuff that obscurely vegetates within us" (6–7). I would like to suggest that this fertile water stuff is not hidden or "beneath," yet very much at the surface of the visible, the lived, and the felt or in the imagination that perdures. In line with Bachelard, I am interested in the intimate imagination of vegetative and material forces: image "as a plant which needs earth and sky, substance and form" (9). My interest is more specifically in water as element that nourishes everyday practices, one that we grow into and which grows into us, and thus becomes real. Water comes up through my research in ways of healing with plants. Plants pull water from the roots up the stem or trunk, transpiring and nourishing the leaves at the top. How might water be similarly enlivening anthropology?

My first objective is to tease out how water appears in anthropology as more than a metaphor and thus as real ways of understanding worlds; more specifically, I aim to show how water is never either only HO or H_2O, never pure, and thus more elemental than a compound. As such, I will pose a critique to both social and natural sciences, which take this idea of water as a beginning point and thus as a hard object with a prexisting form, rather than a fluid lively element that nourishes everyday thoughts and practices. Second, I write about how water comes up in my research in ways of healing with plants at two edges of the Indian Ocean as well as in the Amazon basin. It is both critique and analysis that leads to ways of thinking and healing with plant waters in terms of plasticities, intensities, and affects in worlds in flux. This suggested way forward goes against the grain, yet it goes along with water.

Poetics

The ice and snow cover yields into the gushing water of the river. It is mid-March and the sounds of the river have been muffled since November. At that time, every year, it always feels as if a new life surges to the surface, overflowing and freezing over itself before it breaks the ice to push through and with it more freely, raging furiously as if catching up with all it had to tell following a long silence. I live along the river, in a small park in the Laurentians in Quebec, Canada. Everyday, I walk along the river, usually going upstream and returning following it downstream. It is never the same, its flows, speeds, and intensities always slightly different, always nourishing thoughts, moods, and ideas in one way or another. As the river is especially high and extends itself out of its bed this spring, the whole province is currently facing an unprecedented flooding situation since May 2017. With snows melting and rain falling incessantly, the battle to contain water seems hopeless. Water in excess is moving forcefully through the strength of its flows, pressures, the intensities of its waves as it takes up speed infiltering places where it is otherwise unexpected. The extreme situation is framed as the result of "climate change," in this way appearing as an "external" cause, even if attributed internally to a certain kind of "industrial" human in what we have begun to call the "Anthropocene." The Anthropocene would be a new geological period following the Holocene. Its particularity is that it would be marked by a moment in which human activity is leaving a pervasive and persistent signature in form of geological deposits,[1] with the rise of temperature and sea levels being some of the major expressions of recent changes (Waters et al.). The local flooding situation framed within a broader "global ecological crisis" becomes a reminder that water is both life and also has profound limits on a much larger scale. The local flooding also expresses how water *is* movement and flux, namely what science and most of the Western world have tried to contain—and continue to do so—in all sorts of ways, generally opting to learn *about* the world in stasis. Against this current, I aim here to learn *from* the world in flux. The nuance between learning *about* the world and learning *from* it is discussed by Ingold, who specifies that you know as you go "not that you know by means of movement but that knowing *is* movement" (*The Life* 1). So how might we know *from* water flowing through our bodies, sensing its gush, feeling its pressures and intensities as it speeds up and slows down, as it pushes against and within us, sometimes in excess? Water will thus be discussed as an intimate copresence rather than a global bioresource or compound to control or know from the outside, which ultimate objectives lead to either conserve, preserve, or even protect. I hope to convey that this path of conservation, preservation, and protection might aim to contain water, while water itself keeps flowing. The idea of closed entities, whether objects or subjects, seems to be the matter of a certain kind of imagination interested in form, while, upon listening to water, open-ended life matters entwined constitute what is really going on and can also be imagined as a way forward. To achieve this, certain knots or lines caught up in objects imagined as separate forms need to be loosened and perhaps undone.

Some of the most difficult objects to undo are perhaps those of nature as opposed to culture. Descola undertook this task by suggesting that there are essentially four main ways life has been organized, which he calls ontologies (animism, totemism, analogism, and naturalism) albeit with only the latter doing so through a "Great Divide" between nature and culture. Naturalist ontology, which refers to positivist science, would be the most recent and unique, beginning with experimental science in the 16th century. In this ontological divide, it is only humans who are given culture while all other forms of life fall into nature. Paradoxically perhaps, culture is only given to the higher human form of life, and yet, at the same time, is relegated as secondary with contrast to nature. Latour suggests the nature/culture divide is a great political ploy of science, since what is nature (or how the world is "really" composed, namely of objects such as molecules, atoms, H_2O ... , which exist only in the laboratory) is made hierarchically, according to what is visible, lived, and felt and thus pertains to the realm of culture ("Another Way"). While Descola's solution to move across the nature/culture divide is to replace it with one of interior/exterior that can then apply to the other three ontologies as well, Latour's solution, resting on the Stengers-Despret normative argument, is to find a middle ground which moves transversally across the current disciplines as a plea for more articulation rather than less ("How to talk"). Haraway also offers a third way she calls the Chtulucene, inviting us to join and "become with" underground critters as well as other forms of life to reworld or amend the current trend to diminish places of refuge. With the suggested Chtulucene, Haraway is nuancing the discussion emerging across the disciplines suggesting we have entered the period of the "Anthropocene." While there have always been anthropogenic effects, the Anthropocene awakes us to its planetary and accelerated scale, bearing the risk to reify the human once again. It is, however, only a certain kind of human that is disturbing (destroying?) earth's motions rather than humanity as a whole. The Anthropocene is thus more specifically refering to the Capitalocene as a particular kind of human using Nature as resource who would follow the Plantationocene (which would have begun with agriculture and can be understood as a process of enslaving plants), with the Chtulucene being a suggestion as to how to "become with," perhaps as opposed to "against" Nature. To this we might add the Elementalocene that continues to move through us in more or less committing ways, with sounds and water, for instance, as powerful affects that overflow and can point a way forward, as

I will suggest with ways of becoming with water. In a similar spirit to find ways of understanding worlds or how to reconstitute them, Deleuze and Guattari had previously suggested ways of thinking in-between by bringing us to think affects (or nonhuman becomings of man) in a world in flux, an approach Ingold (*The Life*) also suggests by inviting us to consider humans as inhabitants rather than exhabitants. We are also water and it is this immanence that continues to escape us.

Yet another way this Great Divide has been understood is through *zoe* and *bios*, or what respectively distinguishes between the "natural" (simple fact of living) and the "political" (qualified life). Hannah Arendt and Michel Foucault upheld that in the 16th century, when experimentation arose, there was a rupture that would have shifted the importance formerly granted to *bios* to *zoe*. This means that, from the ancients to the moderns, what is "natural" comes to take precedence over what is "political." For Giorgio Agamben, this separation is thus of the same *polis*, being the very foundational philosophy of Aristotle proposing a hierarchy of lives, with the lowest form of life given to plants (for its nutritive function) when minerals is attributed no life, while water, together with air, earth, and fire, is one of the four known basic elements in Greek philosophy. In his genealogy of the concept of life, Agamben suggests that both before and after the 16th century, it is the same separation that is at play, that is, one that moves towards making bare life political.[2] For him, this is the anthropological machine, namely the machine that makes man distinguishable from animal, and consequently from other forms of life. It is upon making this "bare life" as the locus of our politics, or what we are accustomed to call biopolitics following these authors, that we act upon it as if it were an object. In turn, all forms of life are deemed amenable to scientific experimentation as well as to forms of governmentality. In the process, we have privileged the separation of humans from nature, with the consequence of turning much of its compositions into parts and commodities. Water, for instance, in this anthropological machine, can become a bioresource, HO or H_2O, which we can then contain, sell, control, contaminate as well as protect, conserve, or treat. Generally speaking, in the Western worlds, we have come to think of water in a pure form that perhaps exists nowhere. Defined at its molecular level, which is currently at the top of science's hierarchy of knowledge legitimacies, water becomes a dictionary entry: "a transparent, odorless, tasteless liquid, a compound of hydrogen and oxygen, H_2O, freezing at 32°F or 0°C and boiling at 212°F or 100°C, that in a more or less impure state constitutes rain, oceans, lakes, rivers, etc."[3] The idea of water as H_2O has, however, never been settled. Water has been made into such a molecular object or compound during the Chemical Revolution between 1760 and 1860; it is with early electrochemistry that water's compound nature was confirmed and, with early atomic chemistry, it first became HO and then H_2O, but without decisive empirical evidence (Chang). With the idea of water in a "pure" form, it only "appears" bluish when in thick layers, and movement is only given back to it upon reference to external qualifications. To overcome this objectification of water, we need to avoid thinking through separation and let go of the anthropological machine. To render inoperable the anthropological machine that has separated human from animal, vegetal, elemental, and ethereal, we need to think water not as H_2O, nor as "life" and its limit, but as full of life, animation, and intensity, as a number of anthropologists have suggested by turning to water as both metaphor and real ways of doing in anthropology.

Carse suggests that water has been taken for granted in anthropology; however, its presence acts pervasively as we find numerous metaphors throughout the discipline, some doing so more convincingly by bringing the matter of water to life. Marcel Mauss, sometimes called the father of French anthropology, suggests for instance that "we see [how things really are] in motion as an engineer sees systems, or as we observe octopuses and anemones in the sea" (181–182). He continues to say real-life human beings inhabit fluid reality in which nothing is ever the same, and this is also what the philosopher Henri Bergson is saying at about the same time. Picking up on this oceanic metaphor, Ingold suggests that "in this oceanic world, every being has to find a place for itself by sending out tendrils which can bind it to others" (*The Life* 11). As such, Ingold is taking this fluid reality out of the water to account for the ways we are immersed in the air and the world as inhabitants. Stefan Helmreich for his part does underwater anthropology literally or an "anthropology of sound" by diving to the seafloor, suggesting we understand seawater as "a lively and deadly element that swirls semiosis and substance together in an indivisible eddy" (*Sounding* xxvii). The oceanic metaphor thus rests in particular forms and materiality. Steinberg similarly suggests that we should engage the ocean "as a material space characterized by movement and continual reformation across all of its dimensions" (156). How then might we know water best by thinking and doing through such lines and movements, ebbs and flows, rather than beginning with objects (organisms) or components (biotic or abiotic) as is done through most research in ecosystems and ecology and as we think water as H_2O or as global water? These abstractions enable us to make up or construct water as a commodity in crisis, which is part of the problem rather than a solution. To the contrary, thinking with and immersing ourselves in water keeps bodies open-ended; it also enables us to pay attention to the space improvised as people and water entwine in motions to live and stay alive, thus bringing attention to the importance of keeping water alive and flowing as well.

Helmreich (*Sounding*) suggests we understand seawater imagery and metaphors in anthropology as having undergone three moments. In early anthropology, giving in examples scholars such as Malinowsky, Firth, Lévi-Strauss, and Margaret Mead, water would have been treated as atheoretical or a substance upon which to meditate. Second, in what Helmreich calls maritime anthropology, water would have become a more explicit substance to think with. Third, he suggests that it is only in recent social theory—with Gilroy, Bauman, and Sloterdijk, for example—that "scientific descriptions of water's form, molecular and molar, have become prevalent in figuring social, political, and economic forces and dynamics" (96). While seawater would have moved from an implicit to an explicit figure in anthropological accounts, attention to watery materiality would have paid more attention to "the form of water," perhaps thus missing out on its very substance. Numerous recent works pointing in this direction, however, do not quite succeed in letting water flow through their thoughts. For instance, in *Waterworlds: Anthropology in Fluid Environments*, Hastrup and Hastrup take up Bauman's idea of liquid modernity (liquid fear, liquid times, liquid worlds) while adding "fluid" to environments, but they do so from the outside. The authors also take the Anthropocene as a starting point without making the distinction that it is only a particular kind of human who is acting from hubris, namely the one who makes up the world into objects or resources as part of the Capitalocene, as discussed above. The authors are intrigued by Helmreich's proposition that nature "moves faster" than culture to allude to different speeds as we think in land-based idioms (*Sounding* 3). The question they ask on this point, however, is "why is that so, and how may it be measured?" (Hastrup and Hastrup 7), thus keeping with the nature/culture divide and slipping into an objectifying project that they seem to oppose, at least in part. They also later state that it is "people"—like Bauman, Helmreich, Tsing, and themselves—"who decide what is worth analysing and what is not … " (15). This odd comment attests to the externality of their position from the environments they aim to "know," thus perpetuating the very problem they wish to surpass, namely that water suggests passage through and in-between human and nonhuman life forms, not primacy of the subject (in "them" and "us" terms). In this way, Hastrup and Hastrup fall short of recognizing that the greatest pathology of Western thought is the idea of the subject, as suggested by Bateson, whom they ironically cite for his notion of flexibility yet without mentioning his main thesis which cuts across the subject-environment divide. It would not appear that it is they who decide what is worth analysing; yet, they could have left a place for water as presence and thus taken part in how things are imagined and come to the surface. This implies letting go of a quest to either measure or analyse: "analysis means taking something apart in order to understand it" (Capra 30). What is rather desperately needed are ways of understanding how things hang together, entangle, and create affects in-between, such as what happens when an excess of waters occurs. This is the route I aim to explore and it is one closer to what Deleuze and Guattari suggest with a world of flux, lines, taking up speed in the middle, with no beginning and no end, pulling and bending. It is not adding "flux" or fluidity to environments, yet it offers to understand lines of becoming as material-flux interwined with potentialities of taking lines of flight in a plane of immanence.

Similarly on the theme of flow within containment, Wagner's *The Social Life of Water* maintains an interest in developing more effective water governance. Taking obvious inspiration from Appadurai's *The Social Life of Things*, which pertains to global flows and seems to fit, the author extends the theme, borrowing from Latour. Upon doing so, however, Wagner does not take inspiration from Appadurai's theory of flows (*Modernity*), in the sense that people and things, he argues, entangle in all sorts of ways locally or become indigenized (or not). Further, Wagner contends in his introduction that the social and the ecological should be considered conjointly; however, it is the social that he aims to connect to water rather than the other way around. In other words, water is not penetrating the text. While it is stated that it is about "the ways in which social practices shape and are shaped by water" (Wagner 3), the text clearly reveals an interest in "the influence of water on our social lives" (6). Thus by keeping water on one side and humans or the social on the other in causal logic, it leads the author to want to add "agency"; upon undertaking Latour's actor-network theory, Wagner even ventures into making water into a commodity (or actor) upon which we can continue to govern. Treating water as an actor and giving it agency in only a limited fashion makes the whole discussion a little bit troubling : "we cannot assign intentionality to water as we conventionally define that term, but we can assign agency to it in ecological terms and therefore in socioecological terms" (8). However, who are we to assign agency? According to Ingold, this dilemma can only be resolved "by conjuring a magical mind-dust that, sprinkled among its constituents, is supposed to set them physically in motion" ("Materials" 11). Given Wagner's discussion at the beginning of the book's introduction of how we are mostly water, it is hard to grasp how objects and subjects, actors and agency are maintained as useful beginning points. This is again how I find the world in flux, without subjects and objects, the most interesting way forward.

Strang's work *Water: Nature and Culture* is perhaps the one that comes closest to achieving this. While her work on the entire story of human-water relations can appear thin because of its immense scope in time and space, it never *contains* water but rather lets it *permeate* through her words. Her very gentle critique is quite powerful. Essentially Strang highlights recent dams as the greatest calamity, contrasting them with Roman dams that continued to respect water by letting it flow (132), never aiming to control water with taps or closed pipelines. Further, she begins with water moving through us and all animate and nonanimate lifeforms, and ends with expressing the need for us to correspond with water as kin for any new kind of relation to emerge. Simple as it may sound, it is perhaps the most "sustainable" and worthwhile solution to consider.

The remainder of this chapter will explore ways people have found to think and do with water: namely thinking in winds understood as streams and currents as found in Javanese philosophy, and as done in the Cape and in the Amazon where I conducted fieldwork on ways of healing with plants. The effervescence of fresh liquid vegetal healing remedies reveals how keeping the flows going are vital and can be something one can hone.

Worlds in Flux

> There is indeed such a thing as measured, cadenced rhythm, relating to the coursing of a river between its banks or to the form of a striated space; but there is also a rhythm without measure, which relates to the upswell of a flow, in other words, to the manner in which a fluid occupies a smooth space.

> —Deleuze and Guattari

The Amazon basin is never fully contained, its tides moving up and down, filling its forests and draining its swamps, meandering East, disgorging its flows into the Atlantic Ocean. I aim to describe how water occupies ways of healing when I conducted fieldwork in the Amazon and at two extreme points of the Indian Ocean. More specifically I am interested in practices of taking fresh plant waters as remedy, and yet also to discern ill-being and dreams, to communicate with ancestors or with the cosmos, to know and to keep on going in life. Throughout these studies, plants and people are understood as passing through each other, both shaping and being shaped through waters. While I set out with interests in different medicine used as remedy, whether biopharmaceutically transformed or in their plant, animal, mineral, and elemental forms, I became interested in what emerges and matters in these processes. In 1992, my journey began in the Brazilian Amazon in the "Casa das Plantas Medicinais da Amazonia" (House of Medicinal Plants of Amazonia) in Belém de Parà, where an abundance of fresh plants stacked up on boats travelling downstream arrived on a daily basis to be sold at the Mercado-Ver-O-Peso in the port. Indigenous women travelling on those boats or arriving by foot with their liquified plant mixtures to share and sell most intrigued me. I soon began to imagine a way to do my doctoral studies upstream in Indigenous villages, highly attracted, like numerous anthropologists before me, to what I would find at the "source." The political situation made it difficult to obtain permits and, as I began my PhD in January 1998, I undertook at the same time training to become a volunteer for Médecins Sans Frontières (MSF or Doctors Without Borders). A foot in each path, I negotiated an official affiliation with MSF in their projects in the Brazilian Amazon, namely in the Medio Solimoes, doing some work as a volunteer as well as extending my stay as an anthropologist (Laplante, *Pouvoir guérir*). Both with this highly global and local entry into the deepest black rivers where Indigenous people live, my interests went, on the one hand, towards the lengthy process of turning plants into pills; on the other hand, I became fascinated with how biopharmaceuticals were tested locally in the *rami* (*banisteriopsis caapi*) hallucinogenic drink known by shamans to enable access to the wisdom of vegetal and cosmic worlds. Upon following this elaborate medicine-making trajectory in multiple directions, one of turning life into a commodity and the other of bringing a commodity into life, a few crucial things had escaped me at the time; one was sound and the other was water. In other words, I omitted to pay attention to the ephemeral and the elemental, which is typical in academia. It is only recently that sound's assumed ephemerality has been put into question (Samuels et al.); it is perhaps also only recently that the elemental has returned into academia as a way to address the presence of water as flow and flux. While sound and water escaped me academically, I grew into them and they into me, their intensities, plasticities, and affective presence undeniable, in particular as they passed through plants or plants through them.

Interested in how an Indigenous plant is transformed into a laboratory pill during my subsequent research in Cape Town, South Africa (2006–2010), I became aware of how powerful sounds were with relation to connecting with plants in healing. An *isangoma* (Xhosa healer in this case), who pointed to drums and invited me to a drum healing session to explain how a plant "works" (heals), awoke me to this (Laplante, *Becoming-Plant in India*). With a gesture of his arms, he indicated that a person needed to be (en)sounded to connect and heal with plants. He did not speak of water, although water was at the centre of the healing session in a big pot in which a dream plant (ubulawu) was mixed with a stick, its foam rising on the top attesting to the proper connection with the ancestors.[4] This experience led me to undertake my more recent study on jamu medicine in Java, Indonesia, directly through sound and movement (Laplante, *Jamu Stories*), with water taking up my attention more directly. Jamu medicine is a practice of healing with vegetal beverages prepared to heal and maintain vitality in human life. Mostly women prepare daily healing beverages with plants, rhizomes, and spices of all sorts to be drunk fresh while it is still in liquid form, and thus watered up. Jamu medicine makers spend numerous hours on a daily basis slowly and rhythmically washing, pounding, and mashing fresh rhizomes, leaning their whole upper body in a back and forth motion to extract their juices—for instance, rolling a volcanic stone cylinder onto fresh herbs placed on a stone tablet (*pipisan*) to obtain their precious liquids. These processes of entanglement in between humans and plants are explicitly designed to increase vitalities, unblock passages, even to enliven thoughts, practices, and places; the vegetal flows increase vitalities, cleanse bodily fluids, and adjust vital bodily movements (Laplante, *Devenir humain*; *Becoming-Plant: Jamu*). It is said these elixirs constitute just another fluid passing through bodies of winds and flows (Ferzacca), namely offering possibilities of healing and of staying healthy by unblocking passages. Javanese fluid ontologies and the notion of "rasa" (sensing) further enable humans to grasp ways of knowing water from the inside without breaking it up into parts that make it decohere.

Bodies in Java are fluid bodies of winds and flows which very much echoe Deleuze and Guattari's suggestion to think "Bodies without Organs" (BwO), or more precisely to problematize the organism as "leaving just enough to the body so as to let it reform each dawn" (160). For Ingold, who also takes inspiration from Merleau-Ponty (1964), bodies are never objects, for they are always flesh in motion. Should lines as imagined by Ingold (*The Life*) and Deleuze and Guattari always be in becoming, then so should bodies which are made of lines or knots of lines made up of forms and substances that entwine. Water moves through bodies, passes through them, immerses them, moves upwards, swirls, circulates through them in all sorts of directions, never fully contained. Jamu attends to the ways fluids occupy bodies, thus considers them as smooth space rather than objects or even subjects, of which fluid is contained. Taking this approach to the surrounding waters, Deleuze and Guattari follow Pierre Chaunu to suggest accordingly that it is from an extended confrontation at sea between the smooth and the striated during the course of which the striated progressively took hold.

Deleuze and Guattari suggest that the sea is both the archetype of smooth spaces and the first to have undergone gradual striation; its striation was taken to land, cities, and also air and to the stratosphere. Another way of understanding striation in the social sciences is with the Latourian notion of actor network (points that connect), smooth space being closer to Ingold's notion of meshwork (interweaving lines). I am not suggesting returning to an earlier system of navigation, but to a contemporary one as "the smooth always possesses a greater power of deterritorialization than the striated" (Deleuze and Guattari 480), to the image of the strategic submarine, or in the sense of enabling to find a line of flight from dominant grids. Water carries this potential, as does the air: that is, of continuously becoming smooth space again, and in a way that can be very powerful.

Cape Town, where I conducted my research in South Africa, is situated near the meeting of the Atlantic and Indian Oceans, the actual meeting of the currents moving seasonally between Cape Point and Cape Agulhas. On the Atlantic side of the Cape, the waters are icy-cold as per the northward flow of the Atlantic's Benguela current, which originates from the upwelling of water from the cold depths of the Atlantic Ocean against the west coast of the continent. The huge flow of warm water is the Agulhas current, which runs southward along the Indian Ocean shoreline of Southern Africa. The meeting of the waters appeals to the imagination, but also speaks to the tensions between Indigenous medicine and biomedicine. Practices coming from the West were cold and colonial, and they progressively rendered Indigenous medicine practices illegal from as early as the 1860s. Practices coming from the East, namely the Ayurvedic ones, were warm, enriching, and weaved into everyday practices with much more camaraderie. Within such everyday practices, weather lines offer a way to understand people's engagements with plants for healing in the Cape, namely in thinking through water's fluidities. The Agulhas "leak," peel off from the Indian Ocean, and form eddies increasing in strength and in warm salty waters pouring into the Atlantic Ocean. Recent studies suggest this leaking may have the effect of balancing "global warming," showing Indian Ocean worlds are necessary to Atlantic Ocean worlds.

The Indian Ocean is the smallest, youngest, and most physically complex of the world's three major oceans, covering approximately one-fifth of the total ocean area of the world.[5] Yogyakarta (Jogja), the city where I did my research in Java, is situated near the Indian Ocean's deepest point—the Sunda Deep of the Java Trench off the southern coast of Indonesia's Java island. Abram describes the Indonesian archipelago "as enlivened with indigenous animism appropriating Hindu Gods and goddesses by the more volcanic, eruptive spirits of the local terrain" (14–15). It is a terrain filled with such indeterminacies permeating Jogja's livelihoods; the city sits at the foot of one of the most active volcanoes on the island (Merapi) to the North. To the South lies one of the Indian Ocean's deepest points bringing all sorts of uncertainties of its own. The high cliffs of Java's southern coast are known for disasters often attributed to the South Sea Queen. Present-day fishermen from Java and from Bali still make a ceremony every year in her honour to appease her temper.[6] Jogja thus lies between the Merapi volcano to the north and the Indian Ocean to the south, a location that suggests, perhaps, a more in-depth movement of Ayurvedic medicine into Javanese everyday healing practices, ones currently emerging as Jamu. Traces of Jamu medicine from as early as the 8th century can be found in the Hindu Temple of Prambanan, near Jodja, but Jamu bloomed during the Mataram Kingdom from the late 16th to 18th century.

Jamu's healing practices, like those regrouped under the term *muti* (broadly indicating all South African Indigenous medicine), are set as contrasting lines to modern biopharmaceuticals often overshadowing their multiplicities as well as interweavings, as they too become watery and fluid as they move through and in between those who consume them. The idea of "water" or the ocean provides ways to grasp how these practices might move fluidly and with infinite possibilities of both undercurrents and breaking the surface: certain practices are made to rise to the surface in a certain way under particular circumstances, only to disappear again beneath the surfaces following different tempos and rhythms. Oceans meet with no fixed point or limitation of worlds, borders that dissipate further when we are fully immersed in the world of the everyday. It is only from afar that we can see such lines separating the oceans, and only from the inside that we can understand how oceans meet and mix, carrying things and people in and across them (Laplante, *Healing Roots*).

It is also upon thinking with water that I was able to understand how human-plant entanglements are prized and how the long hours spent preparing the elixirs contrast with how the customers drink it quickly, in a single shot, enabling the plant mixtures to meet and mix with human winds and flows. The turmeric and tamarind pressed with hands, the juice trickling down through the fingers, enables jamu makers to extract textured part of the rhizomes' and fruits' flesh to make the beverage with the right consistencies. The yellow-orange tincture left on the hands following this step, which is also accomplished through movement and rest, is known to be different if coming from meshing with fresh rhizomes or if it comes from chemical dye, expressing a higher value of the woman's copresence with the plants' colourful waters.

The movements in preparing jamu beverages are in fact similar to those of *Pencak Silat*, a popular martial art in Java, in particular, the hand movements pushing forwards and backwards, synchronizing between breath and motion and producing energy. Producing energy is to correspond breath with movement in kicks, yet also through firm movements of the arms, this action being done in preparing *jamu*, namely in attuning breathing with upper body motions. This combination enables one to "enter in correspondence" with fresh plants, which are also producing energy. The added value in the case of jamu, in contrast with *Pencak Silat*, is that it is energy entangling with plant lives, the latter also in motion and producing energy. Some of the jamu makers revealed that they both gain as well as put energies in their beverages through corresponding motions, making the beverages that much more powerful and connected to the customer they have in mind as they prepare the drink.

The idea of life forces that one can hone to mobilise an increased ability to sense, including with other life forms, is invested in doing jamu that treats a body of flows and winds:

> *Aliran* [flows, winds, literally translated as stream or current] in the socio-political realm organize and channel fluid political forces that are always on the verge of sluggish motility or even disorder. Aliran as Indonesian socio-political streams or currents described by Geertz [1959] and Anderson [1990] share similar characteristics with the embodied

aliran of fluids and winds, nerves and veins—channels of and for essential life-forces. These perspectives on the potential nature of aliran coincide with Javanese perspectives on and practices towards the body as a comprehensive pattern, a fragile kaleidoscopic structure, an organized and unorganized but potentially organizable integration that when operating smoothly signifies good health. (Ferzacca 118)

One of the healers Ferzacca met during his fieldwork combined massage with herbal and plant medicines she grows and processes herself. Her work is one of disentangling "channels and networks that allow for the smooth flow (*lancar*) of fluids, airs and winds—the currents (*aliran*) of life—and in the process revitalize the fluent and virtual pathos of self and omipresent ethos of identity" (119).

While some masseuses say their work is to loosen up entangled nerve networks, most masseuses see a functionalism of nerves (*saraf*), veins (*pembuluh darah*), bones (*tulang*), joints (*persendian*), muscle (*otot, urat*), breath (*napas*), winds (*angins*) and flows (*aliran*) as networked within a dynamic configuration of inner life force (*tenaga dalam*), natural life-force (*tenaga alam*), and social life-force (*tenaga lingkungan*)—a *badan mengalir*, or a body that flows—all of which are signified by *rasa*. (116)

Healing work done on the body is thus done on a body of *aliran* open to these life forces.

Jamu is often used to clear passages, channels, or blockages. "For many of the healing traditions breath (*nafas*) is an important sign and symptom of health and disease, for it is the essence of a fluid life" (Ferzacca 119). In its healing aspect, *pencak silat* can enable one to transfer, mobilize life forces, bringing attention to the manner in which a fluid occupies a smooth space. Achieving inner power and attuning rasa can augment the possibility of making and preparing the right jamus for the right problem at the right moment. It is in this way that jamu beverages can be understood as tailored vegetal flows that can enable, restore, or clarify fluid bodies.

This movement and open-endedness came from thinking through the ocean, fluidities, winds, lines, and water. While my work in Java, Indonesia, and in Cape Town, South Africa, was mainly to follow plants, thinking through water showed to be a fruitful path to merge sociocultural and ecological issues into what Ingold (*The Life* 12) calls a study of the life of lines in a world without objects. Upon looking back to my earlier research in the Amazon with these thoughts, it brings entirely new sense to my understandings of what was going on at the time.

If, as anthropologists, we can find ways to attend ethnographically to those processes of form amplification and harnessing as they play out in the Amazon, we might be able to become better attuned to the strange ways in which form moves through us (Kohn 160). The Amazon is soaked with water, both in the air and earth, even the forests being places to travel by canoe when the tide is up. Upon describing how forests think in the Amazon, Kohn cannot help but bring water up and, perhaps more importantly, how the logics and properties of form have largely escaped the ethnographic object. The lack of tangibility, the ephemerality, and elusive nature of water, as of sounds alluded to above, generally escape science as a whole. In a place where there is so much water, it becomes crucial to grasp how it moves (through) us. Kohn's attention was taken by whirlpools as emergent phenomena that appear under particular conditions whose form, should we block the water, would disappear. He continues to argue that whirlpools are something other than the continuous flow, "freer, more turbulent, and hence less patterned flow of water in the rest of the river" (166). The whirlpools would have novel properties, detaching themselves from the river, and exhibit "a coordinated circular pattern of moving water" (166). He further suggests that the whirlpool is other yet also less, as it would flow in a less free way "when compared to all the various less coordinated ways in which the water otherwise moves through a river" (166). While I do not agree with the idea that the whirlpool is more or less than the river it forms (which would place the striated as primary to the smooth, in deleuzoguattarian terms), nor that this kind of emergent phenomena can also explain symbolic reference as the author suggests, I do think the idea of harnessing form, in the sense of joining with water's movements, is an interesting one. The whirlpool in my view, however, would only be one of the possible motions taken by water and which, upon an encounter with humans, can be joined and create affects (or not). In other words, the whirlpool can be a plus value should it become meaningful to other forms of life that encounter it (or not). Hence the whirlpool would not have its own agency as an actor, nor would it be a lower order process of water, yet it is a form taken by water that one can harness to produce energy (or not). We can thus harness its form as suggested by Kohn, yet Bachelard suggests we also need to foster the intimate imagination of vegetative and material forces, which is how it can affect in more or less meaningful ways. I did not encounter any meaningful whirlpools during my many years of fieldwork in the Brazilian Amazon. Water, however, moved through me in subtle yet powerful ways as I was both carried by water as well as carrying new life in waters.

Chandler and Neimanis offer a discussion on water and gestationality that I will take partly literally here as my journey in the Amazon was immensely intensified with my first pregnancy. Arguing a similar point that I brought above with the issue of giving agency to actors, Chandler and Neimanis criticize Latour's project as "retaining one of Western philosophy's central ontological tenets—that is the active, rather than the facilitative, capacity of the entity that renders it worthy of political voice" (64). Following Kohn's suggestion that form or harnessing form can be effortless, these authors suggest that we need to attend to what flows beneath or carefully attune to water's material capacities which are gestional, yet also more than that, as gestation is joined by communication, contamination, dissolution, and destruction (65). Here again, I would suggest this is not flowing beneath, yet very much at the surfaces and contact zones. The authors nevertheless offer a fascinating discussion towards a new kind of ethics by taking from Levinas, also turning towards new materialism with Deleuze. In line with what I am arguing in this chapter, these authors also propose a break from Western ontological schemata. The idea which they bring is that "all bodies—human, other animal, vegetable, meteorological, geophysical, or otherwise—necessarily 'water' one another in key co-constitutive ways" (65). Contrary to Latour's actor-network, which suggests that entities have agency, it is proposed that we need to undo the prerequisite for a bounded entity. This is what I discussed with jamu in Java, and also what I found in the Amazon where water permeates people and place with great intensities given its abundance. My own body undergoing foetal becoming only increased these intensities and it is again in dealings with plants that this came to my attention. As in Java and in Xhosa practices in the Cape, plants are prepared in fresh liquid form with the most potent drink prepared into a beverage called rami. It is through water that the wisdom of this plant can be passed to humans, usually shamans. The drink is also used to treat different ailments such as stomach flu. While I was experiencing flu-like symptoms and in my state of early pregnancy, a missionary nurse visiting the village suggested I take the milk from a green papaya, another watered up fresh plant juice. Indigenous women, however, explained this would potentially provoke an abortion. A shaman rather suggested we undergo a rami ritual. As watered up rami was offered to me following a tobacco fumigation, the shaman carefully made sure it reached a careful threshold by sensing my pulse, or the speeds and rhythms taken up by waters in their passage through my body. While the swampy waters of the Amazon carry multiple forms of life, so do we, making water a flow that we might prefer joining in its formlessness rather than in form. The gestational ethics proposed by Chandler and Neimanis is one of becoming milieu, of responding "to the needs of habitats, the ecological dwellling places and sources of nourishment that give rise to and support life as plural" (79). This is what seems to be done in healing with plants in the Amazon, as well as at two edges of the Indian Ocean where waterways move into and across lives, enabling to go on with ways of caring and carrying on with the more-than-human.

Conclusion

One of the main arguments I made in this chapter is that to know water, we need not take it apart, nor stop its flow by turning it into an object (whether a compound or bioresource) or form, yet we can learn to affect and be affected by its plasticity as a "capacity to both receive and give form" (Sanabria 40). I suggested that by placing ourselves in the middle of things, in this case within water's movements, we can find a line of flight away from stern imaginations of worlds split into nature on one side, and culture on the other, to get closer to what is going on. This implies letting go of the idea that humans and nonhumans are bounded subjects or objects. I showed how numerous anthropologists suggest we think with water and how water inspires ways of understanding worlds. Through my three fieldwork sites, I explored how bodies understood as fluid make medicine preparations with plants attend to bodies of winds and flows in worlds in flux. I also showed how thinking with water enables us to find commonalities in between these fieldsites, as well as how water impregnates them in different ways. Hopefully, I provided some insights into ways in which water's presence might also constitute inspiration and opening in an imagination that perdures, as it rests in correspondence to its vital motions and matter passing through both human and nonhuman lives, rather than solely lead to commodification and closure in an imagination that rests in form. Human healing in the contexts I evoked passes through watered-up plant lives, honing abilities to create affects.

NOTES

1   For some it is the atomic bomb, for instance leaving traces across the globe, which would mark the beginning of the Anthropocene, while for others it takes us back to the beginning of agriculture some 12,000 years ago.

2   Agamben holds that the anthropological machine is manifested through culture in two forms, ancient and modern. The ancient anthropological machine works by humanising the animal, while the modern anthropological machine works by animalizing the human. (https://thrownintotheworld.wordpress.com/2013/08/04/the-anthropological-machine/#_ftn3). In both cases, he suggests we need to give it a rest since it causes separation, sorrow, conflict, and hierarchies of lives, which are harmful for both the human and the more-than-human.

3   www.dictionary.com/browse/water.

4   One variety of *ubulawu* is named more specifically *undlela ziimhlophe* in Xhosa (Hirst, "Roots"; "Dreams") and corresponds to the botanical taxon *Silene capensis* (syn. *S. undulata*).

5   http://www.britannica. com/EBchecked/topic/285876/Indian-Ocean.

6   http://api.sg/main/index.php?option=com_content&view=article&catid=57:special-articles&id=36:the-mystery-of-javas-spirit-queen. Accessed 28 June 2015.

REFERENCES

Abram, David. *The Spell of the Sensuous*. New York, NY: Vintage Books, 1996.

Agamben, Giorgio. *L'Ouvert. De l'homme et de l'animal*. Éditions Payot & Rivages, 2006.

Appadurai, Arjun. *Modernity at Large: Cultural Dimensions of Globalization*. University of Minnesota Press, 1996.

————, editor. *The Social Life of Things: Commodities in Cultural Perspective.* Cambridge University Press, 1986.

Arendt, Hannah. *The Human Condition.* University of Chicago Press, 1958.

Bachelard, Gaston. *L'Eau et les Rêves.* Corti, 1942.

Bateson, Gregory. *Steps to an Ecology of Mind.* Balantine Books, 1972.

Bergson, Henri. *Creative Evolution.* Translated by A. Mitchell. Macmillan, 1911.

Capra, Fritjof. *The Web of Life: A New Scientific Understanding of Living Systems.* Anchor Books, 1996.

Carse, Ashley. "Water. Editor's Introduction." *Cultural Anthropology,* 2010, https://culanth. org/curated_ collections/10-water.

Chandler, Mielle, and Astrida Neimanis. "Water and Gestationality: What Flows beneath Ethics." *Thinking with Water,* edited by C. Chen, J. MacLeod, and A. Neimanis, McGill-Queen's University Press, 2013, pp. 61–83.

Chang, Hasok. *Is Water H20? Evidence, Pluralism and Realism.* Springer, 2012.

Chaunu, Pierre. *L'expansion européenne du XVIe au XVe siècle.* PUF, 1969.

Deleuze, Gilles, and Félix Guattari. *A Thousand Plateaus: Capitalism and Schizophrenia.* Translated by Brian Massumi. University of Minnesota Press, 1987.

Descola, Philippe. *Par-delà nature et culture.* Éditions Gallimard, 2005.

Ferzacca, Steve. *Healing the Modern in a Central Javanese City.* Carolina Academic Press, 2001.

Foucault, Michel. *Sécurité, territoire, population. Cours au Collège de France (1977–78).* Gallimard/Seuil, 2004.

Haraway, Donna. "Anthropocene, Capitalocene, Plantationocene, Chthulucene: Making Kin." *Environmental Humanities,* 6, 2015, pp. 159–165.

Hastrup, Kirsten, and Frida Hastrup, editors. *Waterworlds. Anthropology in Fluid Environments.* Berghahn Books, 2016.

Helmreich, Stefan. "Human Nature at Sea." *Anthropology Now,* vol. 2, no. 3, 2010, pp. 49–60.

————. *Sounding the Limits of Live. Essays in the Anthropology of Biology and Beyond.* Princeton University Press, 2016.

Hirst, Manton. "Dreams and Medicines: The Perspective of Xhosa Diviners and Novices in the Eastern Cape, South Africa." *The Indo-Pacific Journal of Phenomenology,* vol. 5, no. 2, 2005, pp. 1–22.

————. "Root, dream & myth: The use of the oneirogenic plant Silene Capensis among the Xhosa of South Africa." *Eleusis. Journal of Psychoactive Plants & Compounds,* 4, 2000, pp. 121–149.

Illich, Ivan. *H₂O and the Waters of Forgetfulness: Reflections on the Historicity of "Stuff."* Dallas Institute of Humanities and Culture, 1985.

Ingold, Tim. *The Life of Lines.* Routledge, 2015.

————. "Materials against materiality." *Archaeological Dialogues,* 14, 2007, pp. 1–16.

Kohn, Eduardo. *How Forests Think: Toward an Anthropology Beyond the Human.* University of California Press, 2013.

Laplante, Julie. *Becoming-plant in Indian Ocean worlds: Lines, flows, winds, and water,* 2015, http://read.hipporeads.com/becoming-plant-in-indian-ocean-worlds-lines-flows-winds-and-water. Accessed 14 June, 2017.

——. "Becoming-Plant: Jamu in Java, Indonesia." *Plants & Health: New Perspectives on the Health-Environment-Plant Nexus,* edited by L. Olson and J.R. Stepp, Springer International Publishing, 2016, 17–65.

——. "Devenir humain-plante aux abords volcaniques de l'océan Indien." *Cahiers d'anthropologie sociale,* vol. 14, 2017, pp. 153–170.

——. *Healing roots. Anthropology in life and medicine.* Berghahn Books.

——. Jamu Stories–Anthropological Film 104 minutes, 2015 https://www.youtube.com/watch?v=CMRZRw1z2Fw.

——. *Pouvoir guérir: médecines autochtones et humanitaires.* Presses Université Laval, 2004.

Laplante Julie, et M. Sacrini. "Efficacité thérapeutique comme ligne de fuite. Le cas de la médecine jamu." *Anthropologie et sociétés,* vol. 40, no. 3, 2016, pp. 137–159.

Latour, Bruno. "Another Way to Compose the Common World." Lecture given at an Executive Session of the AAA Annual Meeting, Chicago, 23rd November, http://www.brunolatour.fr/sites/default/files/132-AAA-CHICAGO-PHIl-ANTH-2013.pdf, 2013. Accessed 18 June 2017.

——. "How to Talk About the Body? The Normative Dimension of Science Studies." *Body & Society,* vol. 10, no. 2–3, 2004, pp. 205–229.

Mauss, Marcel. "Essai sur le don: forme et raison de l'échange dans les sociétés archaïques." *L'Année sociologique* (nouvelle série), vol. 1, 1923–1924, pp. 30–186. Alcan.

Samuels, David W., Louise Meintjes, Ana Maria Ochoa, and Thomas Porcello. "Soundscapes: Toward a Sounded Anthropology." *Annual Review of Anthropology,* 39, 2010, pp. 329–45.

Sanabria, Emilia. *Plastic Bodies. Sex Hormones and Menstrual Suppression in Brazil.* Duke University Press, 2016.

Steinberg, Philip E. "Of Other Seas: Metaphors and Materialities in Maritime Regions." *Atlantic Studies,* vol. 10, no. 2, 2013, pp. 156–169.

Strang, Veronica. *Water: Nature and Culture.* Reaktion Books, 2015.

Wagner, John R., editor. *The Social Life of Water.* Berghahn Books, 2015.

Waters, C., et al. "The Anthropocene is functionally and stratigraphically distinct from the Holocene." *Science,* vol. 351, no. 6269, 2016, pp. 137–147.

Aquatic Insights from Roger Deakin's *Waterlog*

Michaela Keck

Roger Deakin and British "New Nature Writing"

Roger Deakin (1943–2006) was a British nature writer and environmental activist who published books, articles, and pamphlets; he also wrote, produced, and directed films and TV programs. His interest in nature focused on the intimate as well as intricate interconnections between humans and their nonhuman environment in an increasingly socially regulated and technologically mediated world. Deakin himself not only insisted on the simple pleasures and joys derived from the direct involvement with and experience of nature, he also possessed a wealth of knowledge of ecological processes and their interrelations with human lives, and in particular, of the biodiversity of his local environment. Deakin's witty, poetical literary voice and his profound knowledge of the ecology and regional environment still speak to us in his published writings: *Waterlog* (1999), *Wildwood* (2007), and *Notes from Walnut Tree Farm* (2008).[1] The book titles already underscore Deakin's intimacy with elemental nature—especially water and wood—and his use of the longstanding tradition of Anglo-American nature writing.

Deakin belongs to the older generation of the British new nature writers, a group of authors who rose to prominence in the 2000s, among them

Robert Macfarlane, Mark Cocker, Kathleen Jamie, Richard Mabey, and more recently John Lewis-Stempel, William Atkins, and Helen Macdonald. Despite their greatly varied thematic foci and writing styles, these writers share a concern for the everyday connection with local and regional nature rather than the exotic and faraway and, in so doing, continue "the rich history of British nature writing and environmental thought" (Moran, 2014, p. 50). At the same time, they critically engage with the poetics and politics of earlier nature writers and their often nostalgia-inflected, didactic, at times gloomy appeals for the conservation of a disappearing countryside. Scholars have praised the new nature writers for their "commitment to both scientific, scholarly observation of nature" (Moran, 2014, p. 59) and their awareness of the "now familiar phenomenological predicament" (Hunt, 2009, p. 72) of the constructedness of their nature experiences. As Hunt further notes, these authors manage to convey "the uniqueness of particular encounters in the environment while bringing to bear the full force of cultural context upon a subject" (pp. 72–73). Acutely attuned to the complex interrelations of the ecological-material and ideological-representational realities of nature and culture, these new nature writers shun such currently popular modes of expression as apocalypse, dystopia, and the hyperreal. Indeed, the fact that these British writers eschew the dominant fictional disaster modes of literary representations of the Anthropocene may account for the comparatively little scholarly attention they have received outside of the UK. As I want to suggest, however, there are important lessons to be gleaned from these more soft-spoken writers and their "green flânerie" (Hunt, 2009, p. 71) at a time of ecological crisis and the rise of nationalist and narcissist voices, not least Deakin's emphasis on the psychoecological well-being and regenerative powers derived from what he calls "wild swimming." Furthermore, the immersion in the watery element has, for Deakin, a decidedly communal and socially vital character.

In *Waterlog*, Deakin points out the importance of water for human as well as nonhuman life in a globalized world where escalation of commodification, digitalization, and regulation impacts as much on local environments as it alters the general human relationship with nature. He understands water neither as a technologically purified resource nor as a marketable product, but he does not mythicize water as a spiritual force either. Rather, and as I argue, he considers the element of water to be an active force which is intricately interconnected to other life forces, both human and nonhuman. *Waterlog* is based on Deakin's aquatic journey through all kinds of British waterholes, rivers, coastal areas as well as human-made indoor and outdoor pools from 1996 to 1997. Structured according to the seasonal cycle of a single year, the book testifies to water as a living and life-giving element.

The Art of "Wild Swimming"

Roger Deakin's swimming journey has been instrumental in the current renaissance of "wild swimming" in the UK. Indeed, some call Deakin the "godfather" (Jarvis, 2015, p. 23) or "high priest" (Lowe, 2011, p. 108) of the modern wild swimming movement in Britain. The ecopsychological preoccupation with and passion for water, as Robin Jarvis (2015) reminds us, harks back to the Romantic era when the outdoors became central to the intellectual as well as bodily exploration of the self and the relationship between human and nonhuman nature (pp. 3–4). For poets such as Coleridge, Keats, and Byron, the bodily immersion in the numerous water surface areas of Britain offered them as much sensual pleasure and recreational enjoyment as it provided them with poetic and metaphysical inspiration. Others, such as Shelley and Swinburne, were fascinated by the seductive powers of water and cultivated an erotic, even compulsive relationship with it (Sprawson, 1992/1993, p. 99). As both Jarvis and Sprawson demonstrate, in the British literary tradition swimming is a predominantly masculinist and elitist tradition, although women and the working class were prominent participants in the swimming culture that emerged in the nineteenth century, be it as leisure activity, athletic competition, or popular mass entertainment.[2] Deakin's swimming experiences, however, distinguish themselves in various ways from those of his predecessors.

In Deakin's swimming feats it is generally the water that possesses the muscle, propelling him onto the beach "like a turtle" (1999, p. 131) and leaving him stranded and vulnerable. His self-deprecatory and humourous comments regarding his preference for the rather "unmanly" breaststroke, combined with his occasional wearing of wetsuit and booties, undermine any virile swimmer's heroics and remain true to his introductory claim: "I am no champion, just a competent swimmer with a fair amount of stamina. Part of my intention in setting out on the journey was not to perform any spectacular feats ..." (p. 5). Indeed, Deakin's *Waterlog* is no story of phallocentric power and instead acknowledges awkwardness, interruptions, irrational fears, and vulnerability. During his first attempt to cross the Fowey River, he is intercepted by the coastguard. After wallowing in the muddy bottom of the Helford River, he is beset by a nasty, feverish cold. Moreover, he openly admits to his dread "about what could be lurking beneath the [water's] surface" (p. 191), and unashamedly enjoys bathing (as opposed to swimming) in various lidos and sea baths. And at his climactic swim at Hell Gill, he decides to turn back when he reaches "an overhang of rock" which "stretche[s] off into a gloomy void beyond" (p. 230). Even so, the lack of testosterone-driven competitiveness in Deakin's swimming activities must not deceive us into underrating Deakin's physical achievements.[3]

Notably, Deakin's swimmer's journey draws on a feminine language and imagery that suggest water's receptive, nurturing, and regenerative qualities at the same time as they reveal his interest in understanding how water acts on and relates to him as he immerses himself in the element. While ecofeminists (King, Merchant, Plumwood, Warren) warn that feminine projections onto the environment potentially perpetuate the domination of nature and women (alongside other oppressed groups), Deakin links femininity with the environment in order to show the self always as a self-in-relation (see his chapter 3). In this way, he challenges not only current ways of knowing water and how it relates to human and other life forces, but also underlines the value of water as a life substance rather than as what we have come to know as the—admittedly precious—resource called H_2O.

Part of the motivation for his swimming journey, as Deakin states in the introductory chapter in *Waterlog*, is to explore what D. H. Lawrence in one of his poems has called the mysterious "third thing, that makes water" in addition to its chemical composition: "H_2O, hydrogen two parts, oxygen one" (Deakin, 1999, p. 5). This does not mean that Deakin is searching for some mythical substance beyond any specific material and cultural qualities. Rather, he attempts to experience and thus comprehend the element of water as material-biological as well as immaterial-psychological, and in a secular sense, a spiritual element. Or, as he would put it in *Wildwood*, his immersion in water relates to the element as it "exists in nature, in our souls, in our culture and in our lives" (2007, p. x).

When introducing his notion of "wild swimming" in *Waterlog*, Deakin (1999) specifically places it in opposition to a "virtual reality" where "more and more places and things are signposted, labelled, and officially 'interpreted'" (p. 4). He therefore deliberately and hyperbolically opposes the bodily activity of swimming in "natural" water to an increasingly dematerialized and transcorporeal experience of the environment in contemporary computer culture, on the one hand, and western societies constrained by an ever-increasing regulatory frenzy, on the other. As he demonstrates in *Waterlog*, paradoxically—and unless driven by corporate or class interests—the regulatory social intervention in the outdoors is often triggered by environmental and health concerns. However, even though some of the waterscapes into which Deakin immerses himself are also threatened by pollution, toxicity, and overfertilization, demonstrating the characteristically "compromised condition" (Clark, 2014, p. 80) of nature in the Anthropocene, this does not prevent him from stressing the "natural" and "wild" (Deakin, 1999, p. 4) aspects of water. To underscore his point, Deakin consistently links his introductory reflections about swimming to the Thoreauvian notion of the "wild" and "wildness," as it can be found in Thoreau's seminal essay "Walking."[4] Here, the nineteenth-century American environmentalist likewise plays off a bodily activity, namely that of walking, against an increasing individual and communal detachment from (non)human nature in the context of the far-reaching socioeconomic and ecological changes brought about by the nineteenth-century industrial and technological revolutions. Structurally, *Waterlog* also echoes Thoreau's peripatetic essay in that Deakin (1999) departs from and returns to his doorstep—i.e., the moat of Walnut Tree Farm—and in that he frames his "amphibious ramble[s]" (p. 170) with preliminary remarks about his motivation and a final perambulatory coda— here an autumnal swim in the sea.

Deakin (2008/2009) knows, of course, that the British outdoors is "not a wilderness in the American sense" (p. 11). Still, Deakin (1999) defines his "wild swimming"—as Thoreau does his "art of Walking"—as a transgressive and subversive activity that involves "getting off the beaten track and breaking free of the official version of things" (p. 4) in order to explore exterior nonhuman and inner human nature, a quest that otherwise threatens to be buried under the habitual routines of daily life. Thoreau (1862), for whom walking remained a central daily exercise throughout his life, proclaims his "art of Walking" to be a profoundly sensuous and bodily activity through which humans can still become "part and parcel of nature" and attain "a feeling of absolute freedom and wildness" (p. 71). Similarly, Deakin (1999) declares to leave "behind the land" and "enter the water" in order to be "*in* nature, [become] part and parcel of it" and "regain a sense of what is old and wild in these islands" (pp. 3–4; emphasis in original).

Among scholars, the significance of Thoreau's nineteenth-century essay has sparked some controversy. While Richard Schneider, for instance, claims that the essay's rhetoric ought to be rigorously contextualized within the ideology of Manifest Destiny and westward expansion, ecocritics and deep ecologists such as Max Oelschlaeger, Lawrence Buell, or William Cronon insist on the essay's ecocentric concerns and have linked it to Thoreau's other writings, in particular his forty-seven volumes of journals. Indeed, and as I have argued elsewhere, when approached from a sociological perspective, Thoreau's perambulatory exercises in "Walking" highlight the persisting interdependence of human and nonhuman relationships in the face of socio-cultural transformations which foster an ever-growing detachment between humans and their environment (Keck, 2006, pp. 54–60). To quote Norbert Elias (1956), even though the human relationship with the environment in western industrial societies demonstrates "a relatively high degree of detachment" which, in turn, is related to a greater "control of emotions in experiencing nature," by no means does this "require the extinction of other more involved and emotive forms of approach" (p. 228). Hence, when Deakin draws on Thoreau's (1862) famous peripatetic dictums that "life consists in wildness" (p. 97) and that "in Wildness is the preservation of the World" (p. 95), he likewise stresses the continued human involvement with nonhuman nature despite the ongoing transformations of social (and biological) processes. However, where Thoreau's essay "Walking" responds to the changes of the industrial and technological revolutions in the nineteenth century, Deakin's *Waterlog* reacts to the changes of the digital revolution, the regulatory interventions of neoliberalism, and the anthropogenic hazards of the twenty-first century, meeting these challenges head-on with wit and a notable portion of pugnacity.

Water's Regenerative Powers

From the outset, Deakin (1999) introduces water as an active, dynamic, and powerful entity that significantly contributes to, molds, and even creates human life. When swimming, he states, humans surrender to "amniotic waters," which means that they inhabit a prenatal and prelinguistic evolutionary stage that is "both utterly safe and yet terrifying" (p. 3). As Deakin explains, water represents an autonomous yet ambivalent force, which may either lovingly embrace and nurture human life like a maternal "womb" (p. 3), or violently change and destroy it. Deakin here points to the dual meaning that diverse cultures generally attribute to water—as life-giving and life-taking (Strang, 2015, p. 69)—and in so doing, underlines the active powers that water exerts upon human life and culture. "Following water, flowing with it," as he puts it, promises new perspectives and insights, and brings about a "metamorphosis" (Deakin, p. 1999, p. 3). Although Deakin does not lose sight of the ambiguity of water and its destructive forces throughout the book, he generally emphasizes the regenerative and procreative powers of water that animate matter, life processes, as well as the human imagination.

Western phenomenologists have likewise underscored water's procreative aspects and ascribed feminine properties to the element.[5] In his study *H₂O and the Waters of Forgetfulness*, philosopher Ivan Illich (1986) begins his critical historical study of the "stuff" (p. 3) that we call water by also linking it to the womb. As a Platonic motherly dwelling space, Illich explains, the womb signifies space as receptacle rather than space as expanse, and therefore as "'space-as-substance'" (p. 16). Space-as-substance, he elaborates further, can still be smelt and felt based on "the personal experience of living and dwelling in precategorical 'founded' space" (p. 17), that is, space before it is socially constructed and utilized. By now, however, western societies have come to know water mostly in reductive and highly abstract terms. No longer an element that is experienced by the senses or as an element that is itself an autonomous, living force (pp. 75–76), it has become the commodity referred to as H_2O, which is loathed as a potential health risk and, hence, managed and monitored according to its degree of purity.

Illich's linking of water with the womb as receptive space-as-substance based on a precategorical, personal, and felt experience, is useful for examining Deakin's representations of "wild swimming" and the immersion into water as well. When Deakin interlinks the cultural history of swimming and the changing meanings of water in British culture with his own swimming journey, he also associates his personal experiences with birth and becoming, thus underscoring an immediate, sensory relationship with the watery element so that it indeed becomes space-as-substance experienced with the body and the senses. As he swims through a Welsh river, for instance, the water turns into the womb that delivers him: "I slid, scrambled, waded, swam, plunged and surfed through [the river] until I was delivered into a deep, circling pool" (Deakin, 1999, p. 95). Deakin experiences another birthing process when, "[b]orne down [the] magical uterus" of Hell Gill gorge, "the slippery blue-green wetness and smoothness of everything and [his] near-nakedness, only [make him] more helpless, more like a baby. It was like a dream of being born" (p. 229). In addition, he scents, hears, and feels water: there is, for example, the smell of wet grass and of the bleach of the indoor pools. There are also the sounds of gurgling, gushing, or percolating water. At times water's cold tears painfully through him; at others it provides a pleasant coolness, while the power of the tide and the underwater currents contribute to the felt experience of water. Deakin also observes water's changing colours and movement, from crystal river currents to opaque green stagnant surfaces to the snowy white of the ocean breakers, all of which underline the visual experience.

Admittedly, at times the experience of "wild swimming" is in itself mediated by a black rubber wetsuit. This wetsuit, which "travel[s] about with [him] like [his] shadow," makes "a long swim in cold water bearable, even comfortable" (p. 8). He admits that it deprives him of "experiencing the full force of [the] physical encounter with cold water" (p. 9). However, by comparing his wetsuit to an otter's fur, Deakin also rationalizes that this extra, protective layer allows him to swim in all kinds of waters, temperatures, and seasons. Wetsuit or no wetsuit, what emerges in *Waterlog* is an intensely physical and felt relationship with water, which—like the womb—is at once receptive and regenerative. At a time when, as new nature writer Robert Macfarlane (2007) notes in *The Wild Places*, there is an unprecedented "disembodiment and dematerialization" in the "felt relationship with the natural world" (p. 203), *Waterlog* relates a deeply sensory and physical encounter with water as Deakin gives substance—body, life, and feeling—to the element. At the same time, "wild swimming" not only brings the swimmer into contact with an element that is substantial and alive, it also shows that the human self in water is always a self-in-relation—to water and a larger web of life. This relational aspect of Deakin's swimming activities stresses processes of becoming and coming-into-being. Furthermore, it offers illuminating insights into unorthodox ways of thinking about the human self as being in water and/or becoming part of a larger interconnected, dynamic, and living world.

The Relational Aspects of "Wild Swimming"

Deakin's (2008/2009) sensory relation with and experience of water intimately connects him with the fascinatingly diverse "web of activity" (p. 264) of manifold regional microcosms which, in turn, connect him to the larger macrocosm. As he puts it more radically in one of his journal entries: "The swimmer, dissolving himself in water, immerses himself in the natural world and takes part in its existence" (p. 283). In *Waterlog*, this dissolution and immersion manifests itself twofold. On the one hand, there is the profound connectivity with water as substance as Deakin swims, floats, and is himself swept along by the element. On the other hand, when engulfed in water, he joins a flow of materials, substances, and organisms, be they water, sand, air, algae, fish, or other human beings, alongside which and by which he himself transforms. The significance of the dynamic, relational connectivity inherent in Deakin's "wild swimming" can be better understood and explored with the work of anthropologist Tim Ingold, who conceptualizes human involvement in the world as a continuous, open-ended process of coming-into-being in a field of interwoven lines and ever-evolving relations, or what he calls the "meshwork."

The meshwork—a term Ingold (2011) borrows from spatial theorist Henri Lefebvre—is, as he explains, "a tangle of interlaced trails," not unlike "the vines and creepers of a dense patch of tropical forest, or the tangled root systems" (p. 71), which may be familiar to anyone with experience digging in the garden. Importantly, in the meshwork "beings grow or 'issue forth' along the lines of their relationships" (p. 71). As in a network, each element of the meshwork plays an active part. In contrast to network theory, however, the notion of the meshwork does not distinguish between the elements and their relations. "Things *are* their relations" (p. 70), according to Ingold, meaning that humans—among other things—participate in the currents and flows of the world they inhabit. Although aware of the dramatic impact of anthropogenic activities, Ingold nevertheless emphasizes a particular condition of inhabiting the world, namely of "living *in* the world" (p. 47; emphasis in original) and being "alive to the world" (p. 67), which means being in a continually unfolding relationality with and dynamically responsive to the multiple processes and formations in the environment.

With his considerations of the meshwork, Ingold critically engages with Martin Heidegger's philosophy of dwelling, James Gibson's ecological approach to visual perception, Bruno Latour's actor-network theory, and Gilles Deleuze and Felix Guattari's rhizomatic connections (amongst other philosophers and scientists), aiming to reanimate "the western tradition of thought" (p. 64). In so doing, he muses that those who are alive to the world "seek not to stamp their will upon the earth but to take flight with the birds, soar with the wind, and converse with the stars" (p. 17)—and, one is tempted to add, as Deakin (1999) writes in *Waterlog*, "flow *with* water" (p. 250; emphasis in original). In fact, Ingold's notions of the meshwork and being alive to the world illuminate the multiple relations with the environment in Deakin's experience of "wild swimming," relations which are at once constitutive and transformative. In Deakin's swim of Hell Gill, for instance, he joins in a dynamic meshwork of the life forces of water, rocks, and the sky:

> with the sheer rock and just a crack of sky above me, I felt at once apprehensive and exhilarated. Water was cupped, jugged, saucered, spooned, decanted, stirred and boiled. It was thrown up in a fine spray so you breathed it in, it splashed in your face, it got in your ears, it stung you with its force, it bounced back off every curving surface, it worked unremittingly to sculpt the yielding limestone into

the forms of its own well-ordered movement. Beneath the apparent chaos, all this sound and fury conformed to the strict laws of fluid dynamics. (p. 229)

Here, swimmer and environment are interrelated in a tangle of flux and movement whose motion and noise are expressed by the accumulated verbs. Gyrating down the gorge, the "fine spray" of the water and Deakin's face, his ears, and breath intertwine with each other and the sky, the air, and the limestone. As a result, he emerges from this experience transformed into a being that is intimately related and highly responsive to the "wetness and smoothness of everything" (p. 229) and, hence, more vulnerable.

Notably, Ingold (2011) also associates vulnerability with those who respond to the flux of their environment "with care, judgement and sensitivity," a disposition which, as he claims, is a "source of strength, resilience and wisdom" (p. 75). I want to suggest that it is the responsiveness and relationality of Deakin's immersion in water that constitute one of the lessons to be learned from *Waterlog*. But to take Hell Gill as the cathartic experience of his "wild swimming" would be to overlook the many other moments of connectedness with fellow swimmers and non-swimmers— plants, animals, people, and their artefacts. There is, for example, Deakin's swim in the Rhee:

> I drifted downriver all through the meadows, by pollard willows in a row down the far bank, overtaken by the occasional punt. Tractors worked the flat fields and lovers walked in the meadows or lay together on the bank. Here and there I met friendly anglers in muddy bays between the rushes. I glided on in the still green water, brushed by the rubbery stems and pads of lilies … . Moorhens jerked along the mudbanks on luminous green legs, their red bills and jet-black feathers vivid in the evening light. (p. 43)

Moving along with the river's currents, Deakin participates in, becomes part of, and responds to a field of material, organic, and social relations, in which the processes of plant life relate to human activities and vice versa, interweaving further with the forces of water, animal life, the light, and even a variety of sounds along his way. Indeed, his swimming makes visible his own movement along the Rhee, his immersion in and connectedness with the currents, the evening light, and the sounds of the water and the tractors.

Ingold (2011) notes that the weather in particular is conspicuously absent in the conceptualizing and theorizing of who or what is alive, while mediating the relationship between humans and their environment. He argues that the meshwork must include not only things, persons, animals, and organisms, but also the substances, media, and phenomena (e.g., the weather, light, and sound) in which humans are immersed and which they perceive. As he asserts, when being in and moving through light and sound (p. 138), humans inhabit what Ingold calls an "open world" (p. 117), that is, a world in which its inhabitants as well as the phenomena they perceive and experience—the sky and the earth, the weather, light, sound, and feeling (p. 129)—are immersed in a tangle of generative relations. It is this immersion in a dynamic, relational meshwork that constitutes Deakin's (1999) "wild swimming," whether he joins the flows of the lilies, the rushes, and the seaweed, or whether he "mingle[s] with mullet" (p. 170), salmons, frogs, and eels; whether he communes with gravelly river bottoms, the fine sands of the beaches, or the mud of the Helford River, or whether he swims on misty spring mornings, hazy summer afternoons, or in the rainy dusk of late summer days. In short, as he submerges himself in the flow of water, Deakin always immerses himself in the life processes of a world-in-formation as well.

Made of Water

While Deakin's emphasis is on water as a force that can be sensed and felt, and as a substance where the self is always experienced in relation to the meshwork, i.e., the manifold forces of a dynamic world-in-formation, his immersion into water also involves his mind, imagination, and subconscious. Thus, the experience of "wild swimming" becomes, to once more borrow an expression by Tim Ingold (2011), "the engagement of a mindful body" (p. 133). As Ingold explains, to be human means to be at once a creature of and beyond the earth: only by rising beyond their human nature, by placing themselves outside the earth, as it were, can humans also know themselves as beings made of the materials the earth is composed of (pp. 113–114). In *Waterlog*, Deakin replaces the earthy part of being human with the element of water, so that to be human comes to mean being at once a creature of and beyond water. Indeed, I want to propose that it is this very idea of transcending one's own aquatic nature in order to know that one's nature consists of water, which is expressed in Deakin's (1999) perhaps most enigmatic and oxymoronic statement of "dreaming and drowning" (p. 171) in water.

Observing that the human body consists mostly of water and that it moves "with the water around it" (p. 3) when swimming, Deakin first establishes that being human means consisting of water. The material nature of being human, therefore, always points to the aquatic rather than the terrestrial realm, the underwater world rather than dry land. Accordingly, Deakin defines this aquatic human nature through downward movement brought about actively, as well as by the force of water: he feels himself sinking, subsiding, and drowning; he is submerged in, dives, drops, and descends into water. Conversely, he rises beyond his aquatic human nature by daydreaming, thus leaving the "unconscious world of the sea" (p. 14) to enter the subconscious world of the human mind. By switching from an exterior to an inward focus on his thoughts and imagination, he attains an altered state of consciousness, which is defined by an upward movement into a transcendent sphere that invites thought, reverie, and imagination. Like the downward motion into the aquatic terrain, this upward motion is also the result of his agency as well as other forces: he hangs suspended, floats, and drifts; he is borne up by the water and feels himself flying. As he ponders human nature in his daydreams, his thoughts revolve around the evolutionary relatedness of humans to the amphibian species and, not least, to water itself. He finds support for his musings about the aquagenesis of human life in the writings of scientists and anthropologists (Alister Hardy and Elaine Morgan) who argue that humans actually "spent ten million years … as semi-aquatic waders and swimmers," whereas human "life on dry land is a relatively recent, short-lived affair" (Deakin, 1999, p. 147).[6] Alternately "dreaming and drowning" in the sense of rising beyond his own amphibious nature to know himself as a creature of water, Deakin re-connects with his own aquatic nature as well as his imagination and, thus, with the evolutionary amphibious history of the human species. In his actual "wild swimming," Deakin also connects with people—amphibious and terrestrial.

The Social and Communal Aspects of "Wild Swimming"

There is a decidedly social and communal dimension to Deakin's *Waterlog*. Rather than seeking out remote water holes, lakes, or rivers, Deakin sets out for places cherished and well known in the history of British swimming. Furthermore, while he enjoys the occasional solitary swim, he also embarks on his "wild swimming" with friends and other amphibiophiles. Even on those occasions when his fellow swimmers do not join in the relational immersion in water, their presence—including their memories and stories—still contributes to a greater understanding of water. To follow the water therefore means to follow people, their stories, and histories as well. This idea, in turn, expands his "wild swimming" to include delving into the Fens with an eel trapper by boat, exploring the Malvern springs and the history of hydrotherapy, and taking dips in various swimming clubs, even in London's urban outdoor lidos. In this way, water becomes a site of social and communal experience and connectivity as well.

A perhaps characteristic moment of water as a site of social and communal experience and connectivity is when Deakin (1999) meets with "a whole family tribe of river bathers" (p. 110) at Fladbury on the River Avon. Here, he is shown around the mill by the water, is initiated into the art of maneuvering a coracle, swims alongside the family, and converses with them about their "mutual concern for the right to native swimming" (p. 111). Indeed, water here is a veritable "swimmer's dream" (p. 110), where kindred spirits can come together for their shared passion of "wild swimming." In moments such as these, Deakin foregrounds the social and communal pleasures of water as well as other people's stories about it. But he never distinguishes between water as a social and communal site, on the one hand, and the immersion into water as substance and the experience of the meshwork, on the other. As he swims with his fellow "amphibians" in the Avon, he feels the river's gentle current and the different temperatures of the water layers, and he enjoys sitting "amongst the rippling minnows" (p. 114).

However, the communal water site is threatened not only by the increasingly fluctuating water levels resulting from drainage systems and the common straightening of the river's natural course, but also by the health and security concerns of the Environmental Agency. In a letter, the Agency warns the family of river swimmers against leptospirosis and Weil's disease, both of which, as it states, result from industrial and agricultural pollution. By the same token, the family is advised not to let its children swim close to the weir unattended or, even better, to go swimming in the local pool rather than the River Avon. Yet as Deakin counters, evidence suggests that these supposed risks are minimal and that, on the contrary, the Agency is actually annihilating the joys, pleasures, and general benefits for health and well-being derived from swimming by grossly exaggerating and distorting scientific data. According to his own findings, the risk of contracting Weil's disease is very small, and it is even smaller for active swimmers than for the average British population.[7] To him, the official clamor against the supposed health risks that lurk in British rivers and waterholes is part of a larger politics according to which Britain's water surface areas—and by implication society—are under an increasingly regulated regime that feeds public anxieties as well as misinformation, and thus effectively enhances the detachment between society and nature even further.

With this argument, Deakin also comments on social transformations in the relationship between humans and their non-human environment. Citing social policy analyst Ken Worpole, he suggests that since the 1990s society has undergone a "return to the private, the indoor and [a] retreat from collective provision" as can be seen by the "decline of the lidos" (p. 144). While other people are glued to their TV and computer screens, Deakin immerses himself in water as substance and communal site, opposing the increasing online connectivity of British society to his connectivity with water and the meshwork of life.[8] Likewise, sociologist and psychologist Sherry Turkle (2011), who studies the effects of robotics and connectivity culture on present American society, articulates concerns about people's transforming "sense of being human" (p. 2). She claims that under the new regime of mobile communication technology, people lose their "sense of physical connection" (p. 157) to communal spaces. Turkle also observes a growing other-directedness to "validate" (p. 177) the self, which, as she argues, gives rise to "narcissistic ways of relating to the world" (p. 179) rather than experiencing it directly.[9]

With his observations about increasingly regulated lives, whether through digital screen culture or institutional signposting, Deakin anticipates what the American writer Richard Louv (2005) would call "nature deficit disorder" in his bestselling book *Last Child in the Woods*. Louv uses the term to describe the unprecedented disconnection of contemporary American individuals and society from the environment, brought about by such recent developments as digitalization and biogenetic engineering, as well as the ever-growing administrative and legal apparatus that generates and spreads a culture of fear about natural dangers, which—ironically —derive from anthropogenic impact.[10] Indeed, Deakin finds himself confronted with warning signs throughout *Waterlog*. There are signs that warn of health risks, those that caution against trespass onto private property, and others that alert him to stay on designated paths or prohibit jumping into rivers from bridges for safety reasons. With his "wild swimming," Deakin takes a stance against this increasingly regulated and regimented state of Britain's rivers and furthermore insists on his right to access and swim in them. Frequently, upper-class owners and owners with vested corporate interests (often in fishery) deliberately fence in riparian land to keep the public out. Deakin, however, who seems attracted rather than deterred by their warning signs, fiercely protests against such claims to exclusive rights, as the argument at the water meadows of Winchester College demonstrates:

> "Excuse me," came a voice, "does that fence mean anything to you?"

> This was unmistakably school talk, and I turned round to confront two figures straight out of Dickens; a short and portly porter with a beard and Alsatian, and a gangling figure on a bike with binoculars, strawberry-pink with ire, the College River Keeper. I introduced myself and enquired the cause of their disquiet. They said the river was the property of the college, and full of trout for the pleasure of the Old Wykehamists who sometimes fish there. It was definitely not for swimming in by *hoi polloi*. (p. 31)

As self-proclaimed "wild swimmer," Deakin of course sympathizes with the *hoi polloi* and opposes the exclusive rights of members of the British upper class, insisting on the right to swim as analogous to the cherished British right to roam through the country so enthusiastically declared by then Secretary of State for National Heritage, Chris Smith. Although a river belongs to the landowner whenever it runs through private property, there is a grey area regarding the right of access to it, since riversides belong to what has been legally defined as "open country" and, hence, as accessible. Furthermore, Deakin points out that according to the 1949 National Parks and Access to the Countryside Act, riverside "includes the river as well as the banks" (p. 33), which means that in any area that is "open country" there is also the right to swim. Or, as he suggests to the two river keepers: "But surely, … we should all have access to swim in our rivers just as we should be free to walk in our own countryside" (p. 31).

With his notion of "wild swimming," which includes the right to access British water surface areas, Deakin remains rooted in the countercultural mindset of a left-of centre politics that believes in the anarchic powers of the individual and the community. In fact, his own environmental activism dates back to the 1970s. At first "an influential member" (Hunt, 2009, p. 75) of the Friends of the Earth, in the late 1970s and early 1980s, he became one of the co-founders and the "media-strategist" (Moran, 2014, p. 52) of Common Ground, a nonprofit organization for the arts and the environment located in Dorset. *Waterlog* contains the key messages of Deakin's environmental activism, which is directed above all at the local biosphere and community, an idea that has proven successful until today and which I consider another important lesson to be learned from the book.

Wherever he swims, Deakin carries out the central idea of Common Ground to speak up in creative ways for the distinctiveness, particularity, and heterogeneity of local, commonplace spaces as cultural and natural landscapes. In the organization's 1993 manifesto entitled "Losing Space," Sue Clifford and Angela King underline the connectedness between these local, cultural landscapes and the lives and identities of their inhabitants. While acknowledging that "discontinuities" in today's landscapes no longer allow for a deep relationship with the land, Clifford and King (1983) nevertheless speak of "an invisible web" (p. 8) that connects the local community with their environment. They therefore promote local distinctiveness based on a responsive, dynamic, detailed yet fractioned way of taking action.[11]

In the same spirit, Deakin deliberately avoids such spectacular areas as the Lake District, or the most popular tourist places in Wales and Cornwall, instead turning his attention to nearby swimming places, many of which are now forgotten and out of use. In his descriptions, these water places are special, even magical, an example of which is his own moat at Walnut Farm. Entering the moat for a swim in May, for instance, he carefully steps into the water so as not to "disturb the insect, mollusc and amphibian city, already far into the rhythms of its day":

> The submerged jungle of Canadian pond weed was beginning to thicken … At the end of my first two chilly lengths, a frog leapt off the bank almost straight into my face, and others watched me from the water. That they are far outnumbered now by the toads is due, I think, to predation of their tadpoles by the newts, … . There is no native creature quite so exotic or splendid as the male great chested newt, … . They are the jesters of the moat, with their bright orange, spotted bellies and outrageous zigzag crests, … . I hung submerged, in the mask and snorkel, and watched these pond-dragons coming up for air, then slowly sinking back into the deep water, crests waving like seaweed. (p. 71)

Waterlog abounds with such descriptions of fascinatingly diverse, beautiful, and precious yet always peculiarly local environments. Still, at no point does Deakin trivialize the tremendous powers of water that shape these natural-cultural surroundings and, by implication, the communities residing there, in manifold ways.

Conclusion

There are, then, several lessons to be learned from Deakin's *Waterlog* with its poetic celebration of "wild swimming." First, while living in the Anthropocene certainly poses unprecedented challenges for humans regarding their direct involvement with their environment, Deakin reminds us that there still is a connection to and connectivity with nature, which can be equally enjoyed by serious "wild swimmers" and, less ambitiously, by those who prefer sea bathing or public pools. No matter how, the pleasures derived from the connectivity with water invite us to join the meshwork and to always experience ourselves in relation to other life forces, including substances and media such as water, light, and weather, as well as organisms and plants, animals and humans. As *Waterlog* demonstrates, water is part of the meshwork of life and, hence, a substance that is exhilaratingly alive and far removed from the commodity commonly known as H_2O, or worse, bottled water. Water as part of the meshwork is also a substance that animates life in general, and the human body and imagination in particular. After all, Deakin's swimming journey suggests that humans are of water at the same time as they transcend it.

From a less philosophical point of view, *Waterlog* teaches us with wit and an appropriate dose of self-deprecatory humour that we do have access to manifold local waterscapes around us, and that in order to experience and appreciate them in their diversity and distinctiveness, we need neither develop a parochial mindset nor resign in the face of the many rules and regulations imposed on us by our safety-conscious and anxiety-ridden societies. Instead, Deakin advocates responsiveness and optimism. On the one hand, he derives his optimism from his "wild swimming" as a deliberate, self-willed, and therefore subversive socio-political activity; on the other hand, his optimism stems from the sensual pleasures generated by his swimming *with* water. Indeed, this very optimism is perhaps the most important lesson to be gleaned from Deakin's *Waterlog*. Truly contagious, it sustains his transgressive yet receptive way of joining in and—in moments of serendipity—connecting with life on land and in water.

NOTES

1   *Wildwood* and *Notes from Walnut Tree Farm* were published posthumously. Like *Waterlog*, *Notes from Walnut Tree Farm* follows the cycle of one year. It consists of selections from the entries of over 130 notebooks and diaries Deakin left behind and which today are archived in the literary collections of the University of East Anglia.

2   Jenny Landreth focuses on women in the British history of swimming. She notes that before the emergence of the early twentieth-century "swimming suffragettes" (2017, p. 64) and before women were properly taught how to swim, there still were women who were competent, athletic swimmers throughout the nineteenth century. However, their activities were called sea bathing rather than swimming (p. 36). Jane Austen, herself a passionate sea-bather, is perhaps the best-known British female writer whose late eighteenth-century and early nineteenth-century novels include sea bathing (Sprawson, 1992/1993, p. 27).

3   Deakin's ecofeminist language and thought are also central to his other writings and even turn up in Robert Macfarlane's *The Wild Places*. Here, they are an important addition to Macfarlane's (2007/2008) poetically rendered excursions to places where nature and culture are intricately intertwined. While Macfarlane at times seems to be driven by the desire to prove himself against natural forces in faraway places, Deakin's fictional presence introduces the appreciation of nearby, often overlooked "wild places," be they the life-thronged crevices of the grykes at their feet (p. 168) or the holloway network of southern England in which they become enveloped (pp. 213–238). The holloway is a former network of old pathways that, long-forgotten and fallen out of use, has been reconquered by wildlife of all sorts.

4   The essay was published posthumously the year of Thoreau's death in 1862 in the *Atlantic Monthly*. While this final printed version has its origins in lectures from 1850s, Thoreau continued working on it until his death (Knott, 2002, p. 70).

5   In *Water and Dreams: An Essay on the Imagination of Matter*, French philosopher of science Gaston Bachelard (1999; his original work was published in 1942) notes that water is "profoundly *maternal*" as it is a substance "that we see everywhere springing up and increasing" like "a *continuous* birth" (p. 14; emphasis in original).

6   While Deakin refers to the works of Hardy (1960) and Morgan (1972), marine biologist Richard Ellis's *Aquagenesis* (2003) has since further explored the theory and history of the human species evolving from life in the sea.

7   Investigating the matter, Deakin (1999) comes to a very different conclusion than the overcautious Environmental Agency: "Dr Robin Philip, an epidemiologist at the University of Bristol, … found that the risks of contracting Weil's disease, and of dying from it, were actually lower among [recreational water-users] (including swimmers) than for the total British population. He states: ' … the chance of dying from Weil's disease associated with bathing and water sports is about 1:20 million exposed persons (i.e., one case in the UK every four years)'" (p. 113).

8   Deakin's frequent references to the mediation of the outdoors through television in *Notes from Walnut Tree Farm* seem almost quaint by today's standards of permanent online connectivity. However, his actual concern relates to a larger general social

detachment from the environment, which he equates with isolation and loneliness. While he sees himself connected "to the trees, the house, the meadows, the birds, the insects," he observes that "so many people are so cut off from all the other things, the trees, etc., … " (2008/2009, p. 157).

9 Like Louv and Deakin, Turkle also draws on ideas by Henry David Thoreau. Contrary to scholars who "believe that the new connectivity culture provides a digital Walden" (2011, p. 275), Turkle is concerned with the costs of networked lives, among them loneliness, a simplification of what it means to be human, or the growing investment in performing multiple selves.

10 As Louv (2005) states, he does not use the term "nature deficit disorder" in a "scientific or clinical sense" (p. 99). Rather he finds it a useful term to explain what he considers an unprecedented disconnection between America's children today and the environment. This disconnect is one "factor that may aggravate attentional difficulties for many children" (p. 99).

11 As Clifford and King (1983) put it metaphorically: "There never has been any need to bulldoze the whole building site or to demand the pronunciation of your 'h's" (p. 21).

REFERENCES

Bachelard, G. (1999). *Water and dreams: An essay on the imagination of matter* (E. R. Farrell, Trans.). Pegasus. (Original work published 1942).

Clark, T. (2014). Nature, post nature. In L. Westling (Ed.), *The Cambridge companion to literature and the environment* (pp. 75–89). Cambridge University Press.

Clifford, S., & and King, A. (1993). Losing your place. In S. Clifford & A. King (Eds.), *Local distinctiveness: Place, particularity and identity* (pp. 7–21). Common Ground.

Common Ground. (1983). History. Last modified 2017. https://www.commonground. uk/history/

Deakin, R. (1999). *Waterlog: A swimmer's journey through Britain*. Vintage.

Deakin, R. (2007). *Wildwood: A journey through trees*. Penguin.

Deakin, R. (2008/2009). *Notes from Walnut Tree Farm*. Penguin.

Elias, N. (1956). Problems of involvement and detachment. *British Journal of Sociology, 7*, 226–252.

Hunt, S. E. (2009). The emergence of psychoecology: The new nature writings of Roger Deakin, Mark Cocker, Robert Macfarlane and Richard Mabey. *Green Letters: Studies in Ecocriticism, 10*(1), 70–77.

Illich, I. (1986). *H_2O and the waters of forgetfulness*. Marion Boyars.

Ingold, T. (2011). *Being alive: Essays on movement, knowledge and description*. Routledge.

Jarvis, R. (2015). Hydromania: Perspectives on romantic swimming. *Romanticism, 23*(1), 250–264.

Keck, M. (2006). *Walking in the wilderness: The peripatetic tradition in nineteenth-century American literature and painting*. Winter.

Knott, J. R. (2002). *Imagining wild America*. The University of Michigan Press.

Landreth, J. (2017). *Swell: A waterbiography*. Bloomsbury.

Louv, R. (2006). *Last child in the woods: Saving our children from nature-deficit disorder.* Algonquin.

Lowe, G. (2007). Wild swimming. In K. Czarnecki and C. Rohmann (Eds.), *Virginia Woolf and the natural world: Selected papers from the Twentieth Annual International Conference on Virginia Woolf* (pp. 108–15). Clemson University Digital Press.

Macfarlane, R. (2007). *The wild places*. Granta Books.

Moran, J. (2014). A cultural history of the new nature writing. *Literature & History, 23*(1), 49–63.

Sprawson, C. (1992/1993). *Haunts of the black masseur: The swimmer as hero*. Vintage.

Strang, V. (2015). *Water: Nature and culture*. Reaktion Books.

Thoreau, H. D. (1991). Walking. In *Nature and walking* (J. Elder, Ed. & Intr.), pp. 71–122. Beacon Press. (Original work published 1862)

Turkle, S. (2011). *Alone together. Why we expect more from technology and less from each other*. Basic Books.

II. FORMATIONS:
Water as LifeBlood

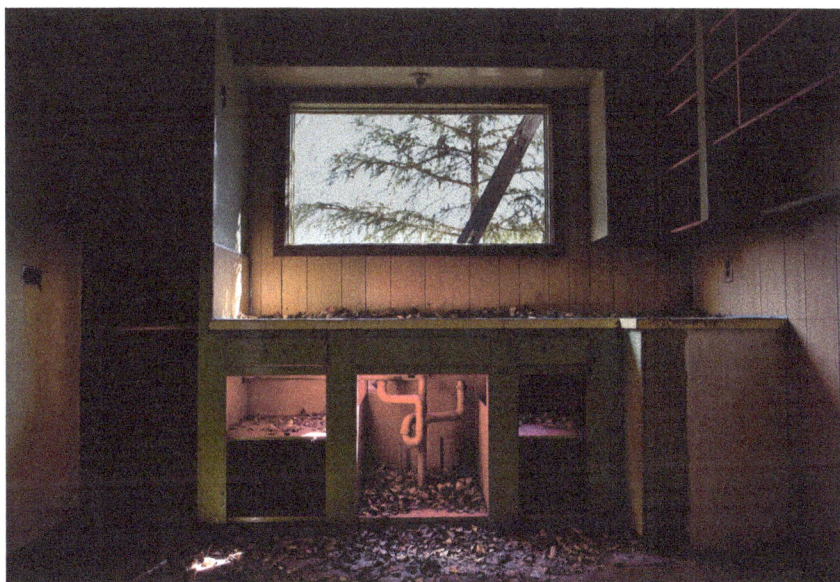

Photo courtesy Robert Boschman

Introduction

The water being shut off happens in the present moment, but addressing the shutoff means addressing a longer history that has been silenced in the process of re-vitalizing the city: Detroit's trauma is rooted in the past.

—C.R. Grimmer, Chapter 3

There is a long history of cultural disruption here. Problems seen today stem from imposed societal structures that replaced fundamental ways of being and knowing. Taking land from the people and taking people from the land are a pervasive theme and reality.

—Denise L. Di Santo, Chapter 4

When the fish cease to exist, the people also cease to exist.

—Marcella LaFever, Shirley Hardman, and Pearl Penner, Chapter 5

In the preceding chapter, Michaela Keck writes, "Wherever he swims, [Roger] Deakin carries out the central idea of Common Ground to speak up in creative ways for the distinctiveness, particularity, and heterogeneity of local, commonplace spaces as cultural and natural landscapes." As Deakin's political activism is one with his swimming in practice, and as Keck's chapter itself transitions from theory to physical action, C.R. Grimmer's analysis of the water shutoffs in Detroit, Michigan deals with the very real political complexities of water in the urbanized commons. Grimmer takes up water as a common right through not only recent histories in Detroit and Flint, but also a disparate pair of works that appeared at roughly the same time: Jim Jarmusch's *Only Lovers Left Alive* and Beyoncé's *Lemonade*. In the context of these two widely acclaimed works of art, Grimmer juxtaposes the formative experiences of Flint and Detroit residents in relation to water and access to water—this in the additional historical frame in which 17,000 residents had lost access to water in their homes for delinquent water bills (p. 65). As is found in the preceding chapters, Grimmer argues against the convenient corporate lie that water can be "coded as a neutral life source" (p. 64).

Denise L. Di Santo also pushes against this misrepresentation of water as neutral and pure and a matter of choice, not of necessity, arguing instead that water is lifeblood. She too focuses on drinking water and access to water within the context of cultural and historical continuities, especially in the Tucson Basin and the Athabasca River Basin. Across Canada and the U.S., with specific attention paid to northern Alberta and Arizona as well as the Pacific northwest, Di Santo outlines how "Indigenous communities have found themselves on the frontlines to protect water and land, their very means of existence, since the arrival of early settlers. Despite regulation and protective guidelines to manage water, decisions that benefit the economy fail to account for how they adversely affect the environment—the very foundation of all human economies. There is a lack of accounting and accountability for the costs ultimately borne by local communities. It is time to change our relationship with water" (p. 86).

This call for change in the relationship between human community and water is powerfully echoed in the third and final chapter in this section. Here Marcella LaFever, Shirley Hardman, and Pearl Penner contribute important and original work as scholars and curators. In carefully documenting the voices of the Stó:lō peoples and other First Nations along the Fraser River who appeared before the 2012 Cohen Commission of Inquiry into the Decline of Sockeye Salmon in the Fraser River, these writers perform an invaluable service. They use the term "lifeblood" twice in their chapter: once to describe the Fraser River from the perspective of the Indigenous peoples who have lived in relation to it since time immemorial; and once to call on non-Indigenous Canadians to engage in a different kind of listening "to stories that express the values that are the lifeblood for Indigenous communities when engaging in business" (p. 140).

—Robert Boschman and Sonya Jakubec, editors

3

Water Formations, Water Neutrality, and Water Shutoffs: Posthumanism in the Wake of Racial Slavery

C.R. Grimmer

In 2013–2014, three accounts of water and urbanization arose in the Metro-Detroit area. One, *Only Lovers Left Alive* (*OLLA*), a feature film directed by Jim Jarmusch, arrived in theaters, telling the story of vampires who temporarily live in Detroit to enjoy its cultural vestiges after white flight and prior to gentrification. In the same year, Detroit water shutoffs and Flint water poisoning entered the media, as residents of actual cities began protracted battles with their respective administrations over access to clean, affordable water. In this essay, I focus on these concomitant accounts of how water is currently linked to urbanization—through gentrification, water shutoffs in Detroit, and water poisoning in Flint—as they emerge in popular media productions about post-industrial urban spaces. In 2016, with *OLLA* out on DVD and both the Detroit water shutoffs and Flint water poisoning unresolved, *Lemonade*, Beyoncé's visual album, which she directed with Kahlil Joseph on the history of racialization and post-industrial urbanization, also came out. Unlike the two previous accounts, as I will argue, *Lemonade* offers a perspective that centralizes, rather than submerges, the significant role racialization plays in linking water and urbanization.

Detroit's water shutoffs bear relevance to my readings of *OLLA* and *Lemonade*. Taken together, these three accounts reveal that a relationship between water, urbanization, and racialization corresponds to alternately neoliberal and anti-neoliberal accounts of post-industrial urban life. I define neoliberalism here as the championing of the free market as a space for organic, proliferative growth and opportunity that naturalizes differential economic status through rhetorics of choice and individualism. To provide context for the film analysis, I will first turn to the backdrop for both films in Detroit. Then, I read a scene in *OLLA* that I argue epitomizes its neoliberal portrayal of inhuman, apathetic vitalities through water, which is coded as a neutral life source evacuated of racist histories and thus usable to mythologize post-industrial urban spaces as prelapsarian Edens ripe for gentrification. This neutrality works in tandem with what I am terming apathetic vitalities, or an apathetic affect toward sustaining life through resources such as water that depends upon the perception of those resources as uniformly available and abundant. This, I argue in the final section, operates in contrast to *Lemonade*'s use of "water formations" in tandem with hyper vitalities. *Lemonade*, through water formations, indicts the violent histories of water with relations that have variously racialized populations, even as water itself becomes a conduit for anti-racist and posthuman resistance to the violence of water privatization and regulation. Water formations work in tandem with what I am terming hyper vitalities. While not in binary opposition to apathetic vitalities, the term describes affects and representations of vitality that contrast apathy by elucidating the necessary, urgent relationship between cultural and natural resources necessary for creating and sustaining life.

As I will argue, both *OLLA* and *Lemonade* explore variously racialized inhumanisms and modes of apathetic and hyper vitalities through water. In both films, water acts as a key conduit to the historical, racialized constitution of "the human," directly or indirectly gesturing toward the historical role of water politics, privatization, regulation, and traversal in enacting racial violence or creating alternatives to that violence. *OLLA* presents a neoliberal narrative of gentrification in watery, urban landscapes through atemporal historical trajectories. These inhuman trajectories disavow the material presence of racialized subjects in urban areas by attempting to portray water as an abundant, neutral, life-giving resource. To do this, the film enacts what Denise Ferreira da Silva (2007) terms "engulfment," an apt, watery metaphor for the neoliberal filmic process of incorporating its own critique into itself to appear progressively posthuman in its relationship to nonlinear time and apathetic vitality. This is enacted through what I call water neutrality, which is a way of submerging historical time and violences by naming water as a natural, neutral resource seemingly available to whoever chooses to avail themselves of it—a form of ecological colourblindness. However, the visual and historical erasing of racialized violence through water politics in the city, in fact, inadvertently points toward the material formations of that violence and resistance. This is figured through Jim Jarmusch's inhuman vampires and their neutral relationship to water, as the capitalistic specter of water is disproportionately distributed to Detroit businesses. In these arrangements, residents are blamed for wrong "choices" that give rise to denying people the status of rights-bearing human. I then argue that water formations, in contrast to water neutrality, are taken up in Beyoncé's visual album and film, *Lemonade,* to resist this mode of violence via rhetorics of the human and nonhuman. In creating a different articulation of posthumanist relations to water and performing a hyper vitality, Beyoncé's film offers a critique of neoliberal colourblindness and water neutrality, while also engaging with what Habiba Ibrahim (2016) terms "oceanic lifespans" and what Christina Sharpe (2016) terms "the wake" of racial slavery and its afterlives. In other words, water across these narratives demands an examination of the violence of racialization as well as the resistance to this violence, as media accounts of Detroit water shutoffs resort to the language of "human rights," and both filmic responses challenge the historically situated category of the "human" in relation to water as property.

Only Lovers Left Alive: Water Neutrality and Apathetic Vitalities

In April 2013, the Detroit Water and Sewage Department (DWSD) entered a "contract with Homrich, a demolition company, to carry out 70,000 shutoffs in 730 days [in Detroit, MI] … sponsored by Rodney Johnson of Grosse Pointe" (Bellant et al., 2014). The DWSD reported that the goal was to do damage control over the debt incurred by the DWSD by delinquent water bills. A year later in Detroit, residents began a protracted battle over the shutoffs in their homes. Seventeen-thousand residents in Detroit had by now had their water shut off (Ley, 2014), and many of them attended a "Water Affordability Fair" to learn about payment options. Yet, those who attended claimed that they were unfairly billed or had not received adequate billing and notifications of a potential shutoff. Throughout the protests, an undercurrent of the value of industrial and post-industrial buildings,[1] businesses, and manufactured objects compared to actual residents came to the forefront: in June 2014, the Detroit City Council approved an 8.7% rate increase, even as those who called themselves the "Defenders" spotted thousands of delinquent bills (Bartkowiak, 2014), and private companies were hired to regulate water access. This happened despite three United Nations representatives who visited Detroit and declared the shutoffs a violation of human rights (Abbey-Lambertz, 2015). In response to rising tensions over who and what were still receiving clean water in Detroit, the state gave one million dollars to DWSD in what was called the Detroit Residential Assistance Program. In the program, residents could apply for up to $1,500 toward delinquent bills. This was only a fraction of debt relief for some residents who were contesting balances as high as $5,700 (Winchester, 2016) or the third of the DWSD debt that was due to "high dollar commercial and municipal accounts" (Bellant et al., 2014). Similarly, while Detroit proposed in August 2014 to restructure and sell off $5.2 billion of the water debt, declaring bankruptcy and potentially lower water rates, more shutoffs to residential water were already in place by August 25, 2014.

In 2016, when *Lemonade* came out, Detroit residents were remarking on how commercial and municipal properties owed $41 million of the debt compared to $26 million from homes, and while residents had their water shut off when they disputed their bills, the businesses and government-owned properties did not (Kurth, 2016). In the historical context of the 2013–2016 water shutoffs, *OLLA* and *Lemonade* represent two different media responses to water, post-industrial urbanization, and the battle over what is considered a rights-bearing "human"—a battle also and contemporaneously taken up by the Black Lives Matter movement. Detroit's water shutoffs create a current of cultural responses to the regulation of and access to literal water through representations of water and racialization. These popular culture (*OLLA* and *Lemonade*) and protest (Black

Lives Matter) responses wield the metaphorical and historical use of water to comment on the status of a rights-bearing "human," each variously critiquing or re-constituting the category as necessary to provide access to water as a life source.

While *OLLA* is a film that situates itself in various parts of Detroit, in my analysis, I focus on a scene where the two protagonists of the film, vampire lovers Adam and Eve, do a self-guided car tour of the city at night. This scene encapsulates the film's white liberal critique of the city's politics that attempts to empty its contemporary history and articulate it instead as prelapsarian Eden ripe for gentrification. Eve says to Adam, "So this is your wilderness. Detroit." Adam responds immediately with, "Everybody left."

They here survey the seemingly empty landscape as uninhabited and wild, evacuating the city of its history and inhabitants to re-narrate it as nature. They go on to survey selective, historic sites: Adam describes the Packard Plant, a famously abandoned car factory in Detroit, as a space where "they once made the most beautiful cars." He calls it "finished," and the statement as a metaphor for the city becomes apparent when Eve responds, "But this place will rise again." When he questions her on that probability, she responds, "Yea. There's water here. And when the cities in the south are burning, this place will bloom." This prediction builds on the naturalization of the city's seeming emptiness by portraying it as ripe for a process of re-inhabiting due to nearby abundant, "natural" water sources.

Blended with silence and string instruments are visuals of empty streets and graffitied buildings, all from the perspective of the "touring" car, where Adam offers to take Eve to Motown Museum. Since it is late at night, they would only view it from the outside; Eve declines the tour, calling herself "more of a Stax girl," referencing a Tennessee based record label for soul and blues music that is known for "uniting" people from various racial and ethnic backgrounds. Adam does not immediately respond, but then has the idea to instead drive by Jack White's house. As they pass, she exclaims, "Oh, I love Jack White!" which corresponds to the one concert they attend by an indie rock band aptly labeled, "The White Hills." They converse about Jack White being his mother's seventh son, and then end their tour at the Michigan Theater, which has also been abandoned. Here they reminisce about how beautiful the space must have been—"Can you imagine?"—for concerts and movies, describing it now as "just a car park."

The opening of the scene's dialogue around wilderness frames water as a natural and neutral resource for gentrifying urban spaces, likening such a gentrification process to a naturalized (re)production or "blooming." The scene attempts to cast actual Detroit residents as having already left, and this re-narration of white flight is crucial to the dialogue of wilderness naturalizing otherwise disproportionate access to resources such as water. In other words, as the Detroit water shutoffs effectively make the city uninhabitable, even unlivable, for its inhabitants in a present, material manifestation of a longer atemporal project of racialization across watery topographies, the film in kind culturally erases the residents by saying they have left. Especially since Detroit protests around the water shutoffs happened contemporaneously to the film, this declaration submerges the city's history of white flight, implying that those who exist in the city do not matter enough to count. This dialogue of erasure alongside empty city visuals creates a mythic, idealized Detroit landscape that uses nearby water to "bloom" while eclipsing the social relations of the water shutoffs. Water becomes a crucial conduit here for naturalizing a neoliberal racialization that assuages white colonial attempts to gentrify the city, that is, naturalizing the process by likening it to the life-sustaining possibility of water and portraying that resource as uninhibited and neutrally available to whoever might "choose" it. This rhetoric of choice belies material manifestations of water regulation and privatization in the city, where residents are in the choiceless predicament of being unable to pay the water bills while the city attends to the companies that, through lawyers, negotiate lower payment rates and loan forgiveness.

Adam and Eve thus critique the category of the human as apathetically alive vampires that siphon the residents' remaining resources, including access to life through water. However, the vampires become the "new" Adam and Eve as their capitulation to a posthuman subjectivity reinscribes the ideals of the white, neoliberal, heteroreproductive, property-owning, and resource-distributing human. I explore this heteroreproductive component in the *Lemonade* analysis, but it is useful here to index how the rhetoric of blooming corresponds to the potentially heteroreproductive Adam and Eve who now inhabit the city. This selective historicization of urban areas seems to initially hold forth an atemporal logical promise to un-do the violence of neoliberal linear progress through time and location.

Yet this very promise of the atemporal exists in tension with the city's actual water shutoffs. Thus the film's romanticization of neutral, natural resources and implicit rhetoric of choice for accessing those resources belies the neoliberal violence of rights-bearing humanity through accounts of choice-bearing agency. As a result, those who wield control over water are given the status of patriarchal subjecthood as ideal humans deserving clean water (those who "left" and those who will return to make the city "bloom"), whereas those subject to the water shutoffs outside of the film's gaze are implicitly seen as less than human, while also not permitted the status of vampiric posthuman via a new Adam and Eve. Through *OLLA*'s rhetoric of naturalized neoliberalism, then, the racialized subject is made to bear the risk of water neutrality and valued precisely in their capacity to do so. The vampires' use of the atemporal implies that if a Detroit resident still lives there, then their complaints that access to water, or a life-source, has been severed can be portrayed as an unwillingness to do as the vampires can do: simply leave and participate in the more productive global market or access the abundant, nearby water. Water as a clear, odorless fluid and naturally occurring resource becomes a metaphor for what is not only atemporal but a dehistoricized logic of neoliberalism that would submerge the city's racial, historical violence as it plays out in the present tense of the Detroit water shutoffs.

The film attempts to eliminate the racialized lives of the city to justify the project of naturalized gentrification by harnessing abundant local water sources, but in that very process inadvertently points toward real-world protests around water shutoffs and the historical, material reality of the urban space. Thus the neoliberal account of atemporal history in Detroit through vampiric lifespans opens to a critique of neoliberal justifications for violent gentrification. That gentrification process hinges on a free market portrayal of water as a neutral life source, posthumanist apathetic relations to vitality, and a selective focus in framing the post-industrial urban landscape's historical materials. When Detroit residents protested water shutoffs in 2014, they insisted on visibility, but not for fantasy narratives emptying and articulating the city as "wild" through nearby resources. Through this visibility, they demanded that viewers recognize their organization around ongoing violence enacted through exposure to seemingly invisible precarity (loss of a life-sustaining resource that runs underground and, while mentioned in the film, remains unseen). The implication of precarity that brings Detroit's past vulnerability into a present, ongoing vulnerability pushes against the film's vampiric narrative of the ideal neoliberal human who can transcend geography as a rights-bearing (post)human in the global market, apathetically apprehending vital resources such as water. The vampires' apathetic vitality becomes inextricably linked to vampiric capital while the vampires themselves do not even have to think about or fight for these basic components to life.

The film, in using apathetic dialogue around water as abundant and neutrally available, inadvertently highlights its real-world counterpart: the vocalized protests over precarity that demand access to that same resource, highlighting water's history and necessity. The water being shut off happens in the present moment, but addressing the shutoff means addressing a longer history that has been silenced in the process of re-vitalizing the city: Detroit's trauma is rooted in the past.[2] Meanwhile, neoliberal popular media, such as *OLLA*, portray residents as absent, anticipating the water withholding's genocidal implications for a racialized landscape, even as the resource itself is represented as neutral and "colourblind" to that history. The violent logic of utility bills—"earning" the right to "pay" for clean water and electricity—is naturalized as a matter of financial and livable choice.

In their selective framing of the city and its history, Adam and Eve demonstrate Denise Ferreira da Silva's concept of neoliberal "engulfment." Their characters portray an idealized posthuman subject de-materialized from and evacuated of its all-too material, racial relation to privatizing and regulating life-sustaining resources. Da Silva uses the term *engulfment* for the "watery" material and metaphorical modes of governance that create otherized subjects only to overwhelm their modes of resistance into a narrative of neoliberalism's promise. They consistently put the "other's" own world-making at bay in favour of neoliberal opportunity (2007, chap. 4). Their world view encompasses the very material deaths that result from this taking up of otherized identities, in addition to their lands and resources, including water. Engulfment requires an exteriorization of the subject's internal conflict onto an otherized body to make possible the conception of an essential "self" that can achieve "transcendental poesis" (Da Silva 2007, chap 4). Engulfment is a theorization, then, of the subject/other rooted in recognizing the other *as other* precisely to defend the premises of neoliberal transcendence. This becomes apparent when Adam and Eve drive through Detroit and describe the city as a wilderness, selectively memorializing predominantly Black cultural movements—Motown—and replacing them with colourblind or predominantly white musical productions—Jack White and The White Hills. The historical presence of Motown is relegated to the past through a museum, then co-opted by indie rock to supplement neoliberalism's promise of "arts" through gentrification.

Even this past, then, is made other in favour of neoliberal colourblind promises of alternative histories and futures, such as the reference to preferring the South's Stax and its explicit multi-ethnic, colourblind tradition of funk, soul, and the blues. The film promises a musical era's atemporal possibility through a contemporary record company, but simultaneously makes "other" and "past" a social, political, and racial movement local to Detroit. *OLLA* thus both engulfs Motown by the alternative narrative about Stax and memorializes it. Additionally, the vampires then bring into the present Jack White's childhood home, which appears inhabited, unlike the passing scenery of empty post-industrialism. This exteriorizes Adam and Eve's inner conflict over musical production—they are also musical artists—onto Motown as an "other" to produce a markedly "white" and colourblind transcendence of Detroit's musical history, or the production and circulation of musical arts for profit. Water becomes the conduit for Adam and Eve, whose names reference the Biblical genesis of reproduction, to foreclose the "other's" potentially non-heteroreproductive modes of world-making, such as Motown, and resistance, such as protests around water shutoffs, in favour of the neoliberal promise of a colourblind aesthetic that naturalizes a form of reproductive world-making in a free market's neutralized access to water and music. The seeming promise of an atemporal narration of Jack White's childhood into the present engulfs the actual, historical experience of Motown continuing in Detroit from past into the present. The inclusion of historical matter with water otherizes racialized bodies and their musical production while also co-opting them to construct neoliberal narratives of whiteness, property relations, and categories of "humanness" in the arts and posthumanism, a racializing process further examined in the *Lemonade* analysis.

OLLA here writes off a foundational component of life, water, as inherently neutral through a rhetoric of personhood and human-making that creates populations excluded from the protections of human status. It is not simply that the engulfment of "others" is created through a disavowal of the simultaneous harnessing and foreclosure of life possibilities through water regulation; it is also articulated as a cultural process at the abstract level rooted in a rhetoric of "choices" made by those who are externally criminalized: "[Racism] ensures that certain people will live an 'abstract existence' where 'living' [is] something to be achieved and not experienced" (Cacho, 2012, p. 7). That is, while Adam and Eve experience life because it is an achievement they can take for granted (vampiric immortality), apathetically apprehending its necessary resources, they abstract Detroit's actual racialized bodies that fight for access to life via water. The privileged human as posthuman here depends upon the potential "bloom" of vitality promised by neoliberal personhood and capitalist business obtaining, or owning, resources such as water. The construct of a rights-bearing, legally protected human is naturalized in an attempt to erase historical and cultural formations through actions such as the Detroit water shutoffs. *OLLA* "literally [establishes] watery grounds that [make] land and its resources extremely valuable to developers precisely because the land [is now] worthless to everyone except the poor of colour whose lives were not deemed worthy of rebuilding" (Cacho, 2012, pp. 13–14). In a cruel logic, then, the film holds forth the promise of moving beyond the foreclosures of humanness as they have been constructed by linear accounts of past, present, and future in relation to "natural" resources that make life livable, such as water. The film simultaneously grounds its posthumanist critique in the racialized bodies' removal from the protected status of "posthuman" enough to wield rights over those same, life-giving resources.

Part of the cruel irony stems from the film's merging of the cultural and natural, especially in musical performance and urban space histories. The irony here also opens to modes of cultural resistance that wield the relationship between cultural representation and natural necessity for resistance against making human and posthuman through violent racialization. In their "tour" of Detroit, Adam and Eve re-visit the sites of musical production. In addition to this, though, and central to the plot of the film, Adam is a musician himself, collecting various famous guitars, producing records, and in the most "human" laden night scene, attending a White Hills concert. The humans in the scene are primarily young, white gentrifiers enjoying a show at a small music venue. The Michigan Theater, an abandoned homage to prior concert halls and movies, is featured as well. Evoking the auto industry's formative role in creating and destroying the city, the theater stands where the first Ford model was produced. The theme of using cars to tour the city, indicting cars in creating and devastating the city, and bemoaning the central, continued presence of cars over against the arts undermines how the vampires themselves constitute idealized global neoliberal citizens who can enter or leave the city by car or plane. This fact corresponds to their subject positions as individual creative musical geniuses who are present as a bi-product of the globalization that caused car factories to outsource labour, divesting Detroit inhabitants of employment and hence the ability to pay their water bills.[3] The water narratives for blooming, then, are naturalized through ties to cultural blooming, which is opportunistically and racially selective regarding cultural memory.

Lemonade: Water "Formations" and Anti-Racist Hyper Vitalities

In April 2016, three years after *OLLA* and the initial media attention directed towards the Detroit water shutoffs, Beyoncé released her sixth studio album, *Lemonade*. While the more famous image from Beyoncé's album, which informs my use of the term "water formations," occurs in the film's final single, "Formation"—where she slowly sinks into the water on top of a police car in an area supposed to symbolize Katrina's devastation in the Bayou—I turn here to the use of water, spoken word, and both liquidly and technologically mediated breathing and speaking to draw out *Lemonade*'s Black feminist critique of water and racial capital.

The film opens with a watery, indeterminate sound while the camera pans around Beyoncé leaning against a car so that her yellow fur coat and yellow braided hair are the primary visuals. Before the viewer can disentangle the technological and ecological posthuman elements involving both desire and immersion, the scene cuts to the sound of birds and wind with images of abandoned houses and landscapes. This dramatic shift is followed by wordless, harmonizing female vocals, with a single electronic instrument joining in the background, followed by another dramatic cut to Beyoncé on her knees in front of a closed theater curtain, where she begins singing about her lover's betrayal. There is an additional cut to Beyoncé alone in a field as the opening song's refrain, "pray to catch you whispering/pray you catch me listening," begins. The explicit juxtaposition of technological cultural production and "nature" contrasts starkly with *OLLA's* attempts to portray the post-industrial urban spaces as simply natural and Edenic, and this contrast becomes explicitly historicized even as atemporal logics are centered in Beyoncé's lyrics, music, and visuals.

This first song is interrupted by spoken word throughout the first section of the film, "Intuition." In this spoken word section, Beyoncé speaks to her unfaithful lover, layering anti-humanist sentiments on the passage of time, living, and subjectivity. As the scenes cut between cameos of famous women of colour in plantation-era clothing and make-up, Beyoncé describes the lover as like her "father, a magician" for being able to "exist in two places at once," and as she explains that this is part of a larger tradition of the "men in [her] blood," she also states how "the past and future emerge to meet us here." In the final scene of this spoken word portion, she is alone in a bathtub, and the line, initially romantic, turns to a sarcastic "What luck. What a fucking curse." The collapse of time and space implicates the historical violence against racialized populations. The "past" of racial slavery is depicted as continuing into the present: as the "curse" of how past and present emerge together in what Sharpe calls "the [precarity] of the ongoing disaster of the ruptures of chattel slavery" (2016, p. 5). I would add that such precarity has been perpetuated across and from the trans-Atlantic slave trade as it corresponds to the water shutoffs in racialized urban spaces.

The folding of time so that Beyoncé cannot proceed linearly as a subject from past to present to future through the water in her bathtub is also evident in the juxtaposition of scenes where she and other women are garbed in plantation attire or where she is alone in a field wearing a black hoodie that zips from the back. The revised narration of plantation-era slavery with Black women in formal dresses (rather than as slaves) simultaneously re-capitulates the past as liberatory while bringing that past's violence into the present, reflected by the sarcastic "what luck" in tandem with "what a fucking curse" and amplified further by cameo facial expressions. Here Beyoncé narrates the ongoing wound of U.S. racism alongside and through the wound of a lover's and father's betrayal. This narration is what Sharpe articulates as the "wake [producing] Black death and trauma" by "meeting here" to simultaneously "insist on Black being into the wake" (2016, p. 11). That is, the cameos and Beyoncé's opening to the visual album's story insist on the literal and cultural Black life that continues in the larger historical project of racializing populations. The ability to exist in the wake through these scenes articulates both the violence of and resistance to normative aging and linear, historical temporal progression as part of neoliberal life management and violent racialization. In these opening scenes, Beyoncé harnesses the atemporal as accusation, exposing historical violence. She does so in blatant contrast to Jarmusch's Adam and Eve and their focus on submerging it. Further, however, she also creates a utopic opening, gesturing to possibilities that include "being" in contradiction to Adam and Eve's prelapsarian Eden with its heteroreproduction.

Beyoncé roots such possibilities in posthumanist vitalities that refuse apathetic, neutral relations to life management via water privatization and regulation, in turn implicating Detroit's water shutoffs. Thus, these opening scenes—with Beyoncé leaning against the car, which cuts to a tub and plantation-era life—take up "oceanic lifespans" to index "the presumed normativity of Black subjects who could exceed the normal lifespan of a (white) human" (Ibrahim, 2016, p. 314). While, as I have argued, *OLLA* engulfs this anti-racist posthumanist critique within its neoliberal portrayal of vampiric subjectivity, *Lemonade* uses water to create a historical analysis of water politics through oceanic lifespans: the somber music, facial expressions, and plantation-era set in these opening scenes, juxtaposed with urban landscapes and a closed theater curtain, speaks to the violence of the "making ageless" that undergirds normative human progression through time. While Jarmusch's vampires inhabit apathetic vitality to siphon the landscape's supposedly neutral and natural resources, such as water and memorialized cultural production, the murky grounds that make this apathy possible are re-materialized through Beyoncé's collection of cameos, faces, and bodies of women of colour in plantation-era clothing while simultaneously representing contemporary cultural formations. These scenes call attention to what Ibrahim historicizes through her analysis of "the contemporary vampire narrative [as] an outcome of New World colonialism and enslavement" (2016, p. 316). Ibrahim's delineation of oceanic lifespans brings to the surface anti-racist vampire narratives that offer alternatives to a colourblind posthumanism that would otherwise disavow neoliberal accounts of age and time. As Ibrahim argues, normative narratives of time and aging depend upon monstrosizing the alternatively aged or childlike Black subject. As I have argued here, colourblind posthumanist vampire narratives reconstruct these normative moorings. In turn, *Lemonade,* through its opening scenes of relations to the technological, ecological, historical, and propertied formations of time and "human," attends to the "oceanic" element of such lifespans.

This introductory section's oceanic posthumanist vitality is produced in part through open collaborative and historicized cultural media. Within the first song on *Lemonade,* the women dressed in atemporal attire are also famous women of colour activists, producers, athletes, and artists. The film has over twelve cameo appearances, ranging from model Winnie Harlow, tennis player Serena Williams, actresses Amanda Stenberg and Quvenzhané Wallis, ballerina Michaela DePrince, and family members and activists such as Beyoncé's daughter Blue Ivy and mother Tina Knowles, and finally mothers who lost their sons to police brutality, including Sybrina Fulton, Gwen Carr, and Lesley McSpadden. These cameos are central to the album, reflecting the larger collaborative nature of *Lemonade*'s production through an homage to networked subjectivity and insurgent modes of kinship. Through repeated emphasis on collaboration, cultural production becomes the explicit, non-heteroreproductive co-constitution of artists. They are not defined by the conditions of historical violence, but emerge from them to elucidate continued violence and Black cultural theft into the present, simultaneously resisting by "being" in this cultural moment, which is, as Sharpe notes, in the "wake" of racial slavery—as in a funeral wake and the trans-Atlantic slave trade ships' wake. This co-constitutive agency contrasts sharply with *OLLA*'s neoliberal project of a singular, boundaried body working individually or in heteroreproductive concert, such as Adam and Eve alone while creating music. Again, at the end of my analysis of these scenes, I examine this kinship through Beyoncé's musings on paternity. Here, though, the cameos in atemporal attire create a relation to vitality and time that, instead of memorializing like *OLLA*, makes undeniably present the violence of either disrupting or submerging such networked relations. The album offers less a story of heteroreproductive gentrification "blooming" in urban desolation than a repeated "[turning] away from the lead singer as the exclusive artist," centering multiple modes of insurgent life and cultural production.

Co-constitutive subjectivity happens through "more producer-driven and collaborative musical productions" (Weheliye, 2002, p. 30), than memorializing Motown's past and celebrating an individual musician. Beyoncé builds on Weheliye's analysis of R & B posthumanisms by also calling out the co-option of Black cultural production in white-dominated musical genres. These genres include rock and country, with rock co-opted in *OLLA* by predominantly white artists and vampires, as the predominantly Black artists of Motown are mourned and memorialized. As Beyoncé's scenes and attire shift from urban, to rural, to mythical, so too do the musical genres shift. Participants tell the story in bath tubs, buses, underwater bedrooms, rivers, post-industrial urban streets, country fields, and so on with each genre change, signalling how Black cultural musical production gets co-opted by other musical genres while that cultural theft is merged with land, bodies, and elements for life, such as, most notably, water. Beyoncé's critique builds on Weheliye's historicized posthumanism in R & B, examining musical production itself as elucidating the "curse" of historically violent formulations of "human" and "posthuman" in culture, while simultaneously attending more historically to Black cultural production. Such an attention calls out *OLLA's* own posthuman as property-owning to be rights-bearing, with property-owning dependent upon the material, geographic, and cultural theft of Black bodies and cultural production.

Clarifying this theft includes indicting Adam and Eve for memorializing Motown in favour of colourblind Southern record labels or white male rock performers. Engulfing and colourblind, these submersions of musical history build into *OLLA's* self-possessed posthuman and global subjectivities; *Lemonade's* contrasting re-materialization of that musical history surfaces the racial violence and theft for creating such subjectivities in the first place. In other words, *OLLA* and neoliberal posthumanism's cultural theft belies the material theft of racialized bodies that undergirds human and posthuman subjectivities "possessing" any body that can, in turn, privatize and regulate water. This possessive logic happens through a colourblind neutrality that naturalizes cultural relations to resources necessary for life itself. Thus, the networked subjectivity and production of *Lemonade* critiques whiteness as continuing to take subjectivities produced within Black arts traditions, such as country and rock coming out of soul, funk, and other genres that, in turn, came out of gospel and freedom songs (Young, 2012, p. 303). These attestations to anti-racist posthumanist options as well as historical violence are enacted through the wake work of water formations.

Water formations, then, work by historicizing cultural production to de-naturalize the property logic inherent in accessing water, surfacing colourblindness's non-neutral terms and the mythology of an individual, self-contained human or posthuman subjectivity. In other words, while in *OLLA* water is a neutral, invisible, natural resource readily accessed through a cultural production evacuated of violent, historical, racialized moorings, in *Lemonade* water is a formation made hyper-visible and hyper-necessary in its relation to vitality. The hyper-visible water itself, as well as its historicity and necessity for both living and cultural life in *Lemonade*, produces various hyper-vitalities refusing to apathetically apprehend water and, by proxy, vitality itself. These scenes act as both accusation and launching point for an insurgent mode of vitality that contrasts any rights-bearing human or posthuman logic dependent upon possessing water. The opening scene ends, for instance, by returning to the song's refrain, "Pray you catch me." It then shifts wordless, harmonized vocals as Beyoncé, with outstretched arms, falls off an urban building's side. The expected death cuts instead to her plunging into water. Her voice describes a series of religious modes of cleansing and starting over, invoking Yoruba religions alongside Christian ones, alternately merging with background electronic music to sound like speaking underwater. When Beyoncé falls into and is submersed in water, seeming to have drowned, she gazes underwater at what appears to be her dead self, but then proceeds variously to speed up or slow down as she comes back to life without surfacing. This coming back to life happens through paradoxically inhaling the water as she describes her attempt to be feminized by dominant cultural standards. Yet, the spoken word concludes the impossibility of receiving love through such an engendering as she comes back to life, inverting the historical submersion and death of Black bodies via the trans-Atlantic slave trade and continued water violence, such as the shutoffs, as she also creates a vitality in contradiction to binary gender norms.

The scene juxtaposes human matter's slowed response within water with a technological "fast forward" effect, attesting to both oceanic lifespans' violence and its proliferative possibilities for living. Such possibilities deploy an insurgent relationship to atemporal passages of neoliberalism's otherwise linear, normatively aging time. When Beyoncé breathes bubbles out, for instance, they do not always float to the top, and when she breathes the bubbles back in, she de-naturalizes the body's boundaried, linear relationship to life via water and a slowed or accelerated aging process. This scene attends to the history of creating and violating Black subjectivity through the trans-Atlantic slave trade, access to bathing pools, and water regulation in spaces such as Detroit, even as it creates an alternative vitality. Beyoncé's subject redeploys water's relationship to life sustenance without "mastering" it, regulating it, possessing it, distributing it through capitalistic means, and so on. Her work constitutes the site of a hieroglyphics of the flesh that contradicts *OLLA*'s transcendence of bodily necessity through apathetic vitality and water neutrality. According to Hortense Spillers (1987), the violated flesh of the captive, Black female slave body becomes the site integral to the property relations built into possessing a legible, discrete body of patrilineal kinship. Spillers marks in this site a hieroglyphics of the flesh which bears the narrative and grammar of the otherwise disavowed violence and suffering integral to the make-up of a present tense's narrative and grammar for White, heteropatriarchal history (pp. 75–76). It is thus the hieroglyphics' grammar that also promises deviations from the norms that commit racializing violences against the flesh.

These hieroglyphics open to proliferative possibilities through water's atemporal, but deeply historical articulation of oceanic lifespans in *Lemonade*. Beyoncé variously speeding up or slowing down visuals and spoken word creates an alternative grammar for articulating life, culture, and water politics in contrast to the normative passage through that same time. Beyoncé's death as a birth opens to a watery site of hyper vitality that merges the technological and the ecological, casting a posthuman hieroglyphics of the flesh that responds to and resists privatization and regulation of life sources, like water. As Ibrahim has articulated, oceanic lifespans and reckoning with normative aging and time can be added to a hieroglyphics of the flesh, and it is here that I return to Beyoncé's opening scene, where, in a bathtub, she reflects on the patrilineal line carried within her blood. The spoken word on her father and lover continuing the "tradition of men in [her] blood," existing in two places at once through merged past and present, builds on Spillers' analysis of the Black female slave body's violation as integral to building and maintaining normative "human" status through property rights. Those rights are transferred in culturally sanctioned heteroreproduction. Spillers notes that the U.S. racial slavery's female body loses essentialized femininity and "'motherhood' as female blood-rite/right" so that "the captive female body locates precisely a moment of converging political and social vectors that mark the flesh as a prime commodity of exchange" (p. 75). That is, gender, heteroreproduction, and property rights become inextricably linked through the violation of Black female bodies lacking legal recourse to claiming their children. As this "gendered female unravels" under property logics, the "customary lexis of sexuality, including 'reproduction,' 'motherhood,' 'pleasure,' and 'desire' are [sic] thrown into unrelieved crisis" (p. 76). Spillers highlights how the female body's dispossession is linked to "father-lacking." Father-lacking becomes "property lacking" in racial slavery, denying patrilineal kinship to evade property transference, marking this non-heteronormative law as "monstrous" and nonhuman. As *Lemonade* takes this up with Spillers, the film examines the "prevailing social fiction of the Father's name, the Father's law" as one that grants humanness based on property logics. Rather than create a restorative grammar of gender and property, though, which like *OLLA* would engulf racialized subjectivity in its own violence, Spillers and *Lemonade* turn to alternative grammars through "insurgent ground" (p. 80), a ground I read here as necessarily, productively watery.

    Lemonade puts a hieroglyphics of the flesh into a post-racial slavery context so that rhetorics of capitalist and biological life management through life sources, such as water, inadvertently create the insurgent grounds for their own violence. Beyoncé's musings on male betrayal, for instance, instead of describing ungendering to demonize Black men, turn toward restoring the relationship to her lover and father without recuperating patrilineal relations. They exist in her own blood and without her engendering normative femininity. These deviations from patrilineal relations elucidate the historical violence dating back to the trans-Atlantic slave trade perpetuated in that violence's wake: neoliberal rhetorics of choice for buying water and colourblind neutrality for accessing water as property logics dependent upon violent racialization. Water centers the "oceanic" in lifespans within (the bathtub and her spoken word in water), alongside (processions along water and taking a baseball bat to fire hydrants) referencing (Yoruba religious references to renewal) water. Since normative grammar proceeds as legible through lineated time and space, Beyoncé's technological and ecological speeding up and slowing down of linguistic cultural production re-centers that grammar's dependence on the body for its temporal meaning. Her critique also builds on Ibrahim's addition to Spillers' analytic by framing normative aging and ableness as dependent upon monstrosizing Black bodies and non-heteronormative or heteroreproductive kinship relations. Ibrahim opens to a potential, posthuman insurgent ground that refuses normative temporal grammars, particularly through aging, as Ibrahim sees it, in science fiction narratives about vampires. Here, *Lemonade* centres the literal and cultural "oceanic" in Ibrahim's oceanic lifespans to create a posthuman subjectivity historicizing and politicizing the property logics inherent in water access.

At the end of the spoken word section underwater, Beyoncé emerges out of a courthouse and begins to dance, sing, and smile to the song "Hold Up," releasing water from the courthouse and urban landscape in her wake. As she navigates urban, post-industrial streets, she takes a baseball bat to different cars, panopticon-like surveillance cameras, and notably a fire hydrant that subsequently releases its water. In these scenes, she nods to, laughs with, and interacts with others on the set, who join in her celebratory release of anger. This includes children dancing in the water that she releases from the urban landscape via the fire hydrant. This scene contrasts with Adam and Eve's tour through Detroit, which portrays colourful street art as monotone from the car's spectator position, containing the soft music and dialogue. Adam and Eve act as apathetic voyeurs to the otherwise inherent vitality of Detroit and its inhabitants. *Lemonade*, on the other hand, contains the angry lyrics of "Hold Up," itself juxtaposed with Beyoncé's bright yellow dress, arrays of urban colour, and sun-glinting water in an urban space. The contrast between her lyrics and visuals offers a hyper vital, affective entry point for historicizing the anger toward policing (courthouse, surveillance cameras, and cars) and the neoliberal regulation of life within (privatized and withheld water) urban spaces. Water for Beyoncé is not a neutral, invisible, readily available resource, here, but rather implicated and made hyper visible through the fire hydrant and courthouse. Beyoncé's hyper vitality through ecological water and cultural urban life comes from the watery death as a birth, enacting what Sharpe (2016) terms "wake work": "to encounter myriad silences and ruptures in time, space, history, ethics, research, and method" for those "who teach, write, and think about slavery and its afterlives" (p. 12). Wake work happens in *Lemonade* partially by releasing water as a counter-violence to its privatization and regulation, making hyper vital and hyper visible water's relation to life's proliferative possibilities.

Conclusion

Lemonade acts as a powerful relief to the heteroreproductive normativity of Adam and Eve in its scenes of birth out of water, as well as to the neoliberal, rights-bearing human rhetoric that sets life and death up as a binary that brackets normative, linear progression. Beyoncé takes "back" water both figuratively and literally without recourse to humanist property rhetorics or dominant posthumanist capitulations of apathetic, colourblind, neutral relationships to life and its necessary resources. This historical and political indictment applies also to a site of race and water: Detroit and its water shutoffs. Although in *Lemonade* the urban space is unspecified, another contrast to *OLLA*'s distinct naming of Detroit, the history itself is re-materialized, made actual to its audience, while *OLLA* places Detroit within a vague, global narrative of capital possessing nebulous historical formations and promising gentrifiable futures. Beyoncé's more ambiguous urban spaces, such as the city portrayed in "Hold Up," expand an analysis of the Detroit water shutoffs that would, otherwise, attempt to isolate the violence as exception to the general rule. Detroit is no exception. It is instead, as *Lemonade* insists, water's history in various urban and rural settings expanding to a national and globalized history of racial slavery and colonialism. Thus, while *OLLA* romanticizes post-industrial and urban landscapes as a colourblind opportunity for Edenic gentrification and posthumanist individuals, it de-historicizes and de-materializes the violation and theft of racialized bodies, a violence that produces the neoliberal vampiric vitality that Jim Jarmusch apparently overlooks.

Whereas *OLLA* engulfs a critique of the rights-bearing human in its re-constitution of the category through water neutrality and apathetic vitality, *Lemonade* historicizes the violent, racialized exclusions inherent to the category of "rights-bearing human" through water formations and hyper vitalities. Both *OLLA* and *Lemonade* thus engage with atemporal responses to neoliberal, racialized violence in variously urbanized spaces, harkening to the all-too material reality and its history in the trans-Atlantic slave trade. This history connects to the reality of water being systemically shut off to increasing numbers of urban, oftentimes racialized residents of Detroit. However, the two films produce vastly different accounts of posthumanist possibility through their opposite relations— water neutrality as against water formations—to water's historical role in producing the conditions for those possibilities. What water offers in such narratives, as highlighted in *Lemonade* and its relationship to Black Lives Matter and protests around the Detroit water shutoffs, is an undeniably material conduit for re-materializing and historicizing these simultaneous emergenc(i)es.

NOTES

1   In July 2014, water was reported to be "gushing" from an abandoned building in Detroit, signaling poor use of water to many residents.

2   "Detroit has lost more than a million residents since 1950, but the city limits and water infrastructure haven't similarly shrunk. That's part of why Detroiters pay some of the highest water rates in the country—despite a poverty rate more than double the national average" (Abbey-Lambertz, 2014). In other words, Detroit residents literally pay for the white flight of urban centres, while their corresponding poverty is used to blame them for not being able to pay their bills.

3   This stop at the theater also frames the abandonment of the city and its arts in a past tense, ripe for rock and hip, liberal aesthetics to gentrify it; yet, in Detroit, as residents know, there are still historic theaters that produce and attract many concerts, including Motown-inspired popular music, such as at The Fox Theater and The Fillmore. Even in

other scenes of the film, the two lovers slow dance together to Denise LaSalle, known as the "Queen of the Blues" and a musician out of Tennessee, again belying the blues history local to where they dance. Further, the scene spotlights reaping the benefits of Black arts cultures without avowing any historical roots in the violent dependency on racial capital-slavery and its afterlives.

REFERENCES

Abbey-Lambertz, K. (2015, March 20). Here's how Detroit is trying to make sure massive water shutoffs don't happen again. *The Huffington Post*. http://www.huffingtonpost.com/2015/03/20/detroit-water-shutoffs-department-_n_6909730.html

Bartkowiak, D. Jr. (2014, June 17). Detroit city council approves 8.7% water rate increase. *Click on Detroit*. http://www.clickondetroit.com/news/local/detroit/detroit-city-council-approves-8-7-water-rate-increase

Bellant, R., Lila C., Coffey, S., Damaschke, M., Howell, S., Levy, K., & and Orduno, S. (2014, October 14). Timeline: The story of Detroit's water. *Detroiters resisting emergency management*. http://www.d-rem.org/timeline-the-story-of-detroits-water/

Cacho, L. M. (2012). *Social death: Racialized rightlessness and the criminalization of the unprotected*. New York University Press.

Da Silva, D. F. (2007). *Toward a global idea of race*. University of Minnesota Press.

Ibrahim, H. (2016). Any other age: Vampires and oceanic lifespans. *African American Review, 49*(4), 313–327. https://doi:10.1353/afa.2016.0049

Jarmusch, J. (Director). (2013). *Only lovers left alive* [Film]. Recorded Picture Company.

Knowles, B., and Kahlil J. (Directors). (2016). *Lemonade* [Film]. Good Company and Parkwood Entertainment.

Kurth, J. (2016, April 1). Detroit hits residents on water shut-offs as businesses slide. *The Detroit News*. http://www.detroitnews.com/story/news/local/detroit-city/2016/03/31/detroit-water-shutoffs/82497496/

Ley, S. (2014, August 2). Detroit water: Affordability fair flooded with customers, Mayor Duggan constructing plan for water turn-offs. *Click on Detroit*. http://www.clickondetroit.com/news/detroit-water-affordability-fair-flooded-with-customers

Sharpe, C. (2016). *In the wake: On blackness and being*. Duke University Press.

Spillers, H. (1987). Mama's baby, papa's maybe: An American grammar book. *Diacritics, 17*(2), 64–81. https://doi:10.2307/464747

Weheliye, A. G. (2002). "Feenin": Posthuman voices in contemporary Black popular Music. *Social Text, 20*(2), 21–47. doi:10.1215/01642472-20-2_71-21

Winchester, H. (2016, July 7). Water shutoffs bring concern over welfare of children. *Click on Detroit*. http://www.clickondetroit.com/consumer/water-shutoffs-bring-concern-over-welfare-of-children

Young, K. (2012). *The Grey Album: On the blackness of blackness*. Graywolf Press.

4

When Water Isn't Life: Environmental Justice Denied

Denise L. Di Santo

Water and Cultural Continuity are Linked

I looked around the hamlet of Fort Chipewyan, nestled on the vast and beautiful shores of Lake Athabasca in northern Alberta. Commonly referred to as Fort Chip, it is also known by some to be the oldest settled community in Alberta, established in 1788. For those who know the real history, this place was occupied much earlier in time, named in recognition of its inhabitants, here long before European fur traders arrived. In the midst of thought, and seeing for the first time the area as it is, dominated by water, the words of my new friend, local to the area, resonated oddly. He said very directly to me, "don't drink the water." But what struck me most was that this wasn't the first time I had heard of this advice being given.

As the conversations continued during my visit to Fort Chip, it became very apparent that illness affecting the community was being linked to the local drinking water. Driving past the graveyard in town, I noticed most spaces within the confines of the white picket fence were taken. When I asked if the rare bile duct cancer mentioned was occurring in one segment of the population, I was told that it was showing up in all ages in the members of the community. There seemed to be no question in my friend's mind and in the minds of others with whom I spoke: this full graveyard reflected the health of the local residents and the health of the water.

The perception that the illnesses presenting in the community were connected to local waters mirrored another community's observations I had come to know in another place and time. The residents of South Tucson had contended with a similar situation, where many believed that the aquifer that served as their water supply was tainted and was bringing illness and death. These perceptions were questioned and negated by government officials and others in the region for decades, but the community was eventually proven correct. Indeed, there was much to be concerned about, and it was in the water.

A common theme observed in the field of environmental studies is one in which Native American and minority communities are disproportionately affected by environmental contamination. All too often, untenable situations unfold where irresponsible and unaccountable development and industrial practices persist over time, resulting in degraded watersheds and water resources. In other words, local surface and groundwaters become a source of concern rather than a source of reliable drinking water. For Indigenous communities, this often translates more broadly and more profoundly. The connection with water, land, and the natural world forms the critical, supportive structures of culture and spiritual belief systems.

Across Canada and the United States, Indigenous and underserved communities continue to find themselves in local battles to conserve their way of life and livelihoods. For the community of South Tucson, accepted industrial practices that led to the contamination of the sole water supply resulted in widespread impacts on community health. Expansive oil and gas development and other extractive industries in northern Alberta have led to the disconnection of First Nations communities with traditional lands and practices, and subsequently, threatened cultural continuity. In other places, such as the Pacific Northwest, ecosystems that once supported salmon have been degraded to such an extreme that millions of restoration dollars and over a decade of efforts by dedicated experts have not restored watersheds or recovered species to the extent that local tribes can harvest their "crop." Indigenous communities have found themselves on the frontlines to protect water and land, their very means of existence, since the arrival of early settlers. Despite regulation and protective guidelines to manage water, decisions that benefit the economy fail to account for how they adversely affect the environment—the very foundation of all human economies. There is a lack of accounting and accountability for the costs ultimately borne by local communities. It is time to change our relationship with water.

This chapter provides environmental justice context for the characterization of impacts that stem from decisions made without regard for ecosystem or human health. What follows are watershed-based examples highlighting the lack of consideration for local expertise and values, and failure to integrate key perspectives into decisions affecting local waters. Also included is an exploration of community response to impacts and approaches taken—and not taken—to address the effects of pervasive and flawed decision-making approaches to managing natural resources.

Environmental Justice and the Evolving Frontline

Involving people in decisions that affect their community is needed along the path toward achieving the goals of environmental justice. Traditionally, environmental organizations and groups typically did not address the concerns of minority and Indigenous communities. This is changing. Those citizens and groups historically concerned with *environmental equity*—community leaders and associations, labour groups, and some religious organizations—are pushing for meaningful involvement in decisions that affect underserved communities. Recently, Canadian First Nations as well as Native Americans have been pushing for the opportunity to set environmental policies and direction by leading the dialogue to make decisions that affect water in their communities. Here lies the opportunity to shift to a trajectory of sustained watershed health.

Environmental racism is a term coined by Robert Bullard (1993). *Environmental justice* has evolved and expanded out of this term. Environmental racism refers to a state in which some racial or visible minority groups are environmentally worse off than other groups within the broader society. The term focuses on unequal protection from environmental hazards and identifies the conditions that lead to environmental racism. According to Bullard: "Ecological inequities in the United States result from a number of factors, including the distribution of wealth, housing, and real estate practices, and land use planning ... . Taken together, these factors give rise to what can be called 'environmental racism': practices that place African Americans, Latinos, and Native Americans at greater health and environmental risk than the rest of society" (1993, p. 319). While problem identification is associated with Bullard's definition of environmental racism, solutions and ideal states are associated with the term *environmental justice*. For the purposes of this discussion, environmental justice is defined as the achievement of equal protection from environmental and health hazards for all people, regardless of race, income, culture, or social class.

Moreover, another related term employed above, *environmental equity*, asserts that no person, group, or community should hold greater privilege or right to environmental resources over others, and refers to the "equal protection of environmental laws" (Bryant, 1995). Defining environmental equity merely in terms of risk becomes problematic, as the location of environmental hazards does not simply correlate with risk to health. Therefore, epidemiological evidence must also be weighed in order to determine risk to communities and individuals. This is part of the solution to achieving environmental justice. Environmental racism and inequity are sometimes used interchangeably with environmental justice, but it is important to note that they have different meanings, that there are differences in what constitutes "discrimination" and "inequity" so that practical policies and decisions can be made to address the problem of environmental inequity.

In a discussion of government-based remedies for "environmental injustice" by Ringquist (1997), the point is made that it is necessary to look at discrimination either in terms of intent or in terms of outcomes. When the decision-making process produces discriminatory outcomes, a question arises: Are these decisions always legally actionable or only if there is actual discriminatory intent behind the decision? As Bullard (1995) points out, not only is the burden of proof on affected individuals or communities to prove harm and discrimination, but proving intentional or purposeful discrimination in a court of law is next to impossible.

While the environmental movement began in the late 1960s and 1970s, the environmental justice movement came to the fore in the 1980s. During this time, residents of the predominantly African-American Warren County, North Carolina, fought the disposal of polychlorinated biphenyl contaminated soils in a local landfill (Bullard, 1990). This is considered a watershed event in the movement in the United States, as it called national attention to the association between toxics and poverty.

The environmental justice movement is fundamentally different from the environmental movement. Participants in the environmental justice movement generally claim working-class roots, focus on local environmental problems, are concerned with human health, employ a grassroots style, and attempt to democratize science and politics (Gottlieb, 1993). The environmental justice movement has its roots in minority and low-income community participation. This is in contrast to the environmental movement in which middle- and upper-middle class individuals are typically involved with issues affecting natural environments in general. Furthermore, the environmental justice movement may be credited with redefining "environment" since environmental justice concerns include all aspects of an individual's living environment, natural or urban, including in a recreational or occupational setting. The environmental justice movement is a response to environmental and social issues at a local level, with the potential to expand globally to national and international levels as natural resources and the natural capital base, in general, are depleted.

As early as 1971 federal regulators in the United States recognized that exposure to environmental pollutants was not distributed equally: minority communities experienced disproportionally high levels of environmental risk (Ringquist 1997, citing U.S. Council on Environmental Quality, 1971). Yet it was not until 1990 that the first national gathering on environmental justice occurred. This event, a conference held by the University School of Natural Resources, resulted in the formation of the Michigan Coalition. This coalition then drafted a letter to the United States Environmental Protection Agency (USEPA) demanding action on environmental risks in minority and low-income communities as well as on tribal lands. William Reilly, then administrator of USEPA, set up a working group, which resulted in a two-volume report, *Environmental Equity: Reducing Risk in all Communities*, one of the first steps taken by the agency to formally recognize a link between minority, low-income, and underserved populations and potential exposure to environmental toxins. The 1992 report recommended that USEPA and other government agencies expand their outreach programs to ensure that minority and low-income communities are included in the policy process. In order to achieve such an outcome, the report recognized the need to work with local and regional grassroots organizations. In addition, the report made clear that "the language, format and distribution of written materials, media relations, and efforts in two-way communication could all be improved." The National Environmental Justice Advisory Council (NEJAC), a federal advisory group to the USEPA, thus developed a Model Plan for Public Participation.

The Model Plan for Public Participation, as outlined by NEJAC, contained two guiding principles and four critical elements. According to the NEJAC Model, the two guiding principles of public participation are to (a) encourage public participation in all aspects of environmental decision-making; and (b) maintain honesty and integrity in the process and articulate goals, expectations, and limitations. The guiding principles of the model stress equal partnerships among stakeholders and agencies. How does this model regard Indigenous communities and recognize the unique position they hold as rights holders? There was also a stated recognition that building successful partnerships is important, and that "interactions must encourage active community participation, institutionalize public participation, recognize community knowledge, and use cross-cultural formats and exchanges" (National Environmental Justice Advisory Council, 1994).

During the same year, in 1990, the Indigenous Environmental Network (IEN) was established. This organization is an example of grassroots response to environmental degradation in the context of cultural-environmental injustice. The IEN is currently based in Bemidji, Minnesota, but works across the United States and Canada, and more recently has operated more globally. According to their website, the mission of the Indigenous Environmental Network "is to protect the sacredness of Earth Mother from contamination & exploitation by respecting and adhering to Indigenous Knowledge and Natural Law."

In 1994, U.S. President Bill Clinton issued executive order 12898, "Federal Actions to Address Environmental Justice and in Minority Populations and Low-Income Populations." It called on federal agencies to make environmental justice part of their mission. Twenty years later, under the Obama Administration, the USEPA launched Plan EJ 2014, a set of strategies to recommit and reinvigorate the environmental justice efforts of that agency. Fast forward to 2017 and contrast this history of presidential action on environmental justice to the newly formed U.S. administration's expressed intent and actions to roll back those efforts initiated under the Obama Administration. Citing concerns of the impacts of the proposed policy shift, and the anticipated failure to address environmental justice, the USEPA Environmental Justice Director resigned.

In Canada, attention has turned in recent years to the plight of First Nations relative to water supply and other natural resource issues. Of all the drinking water advisories in Canada, almost 10% were in First Nations communities, yet Indigenous populations make up just four percent of the total population (Jeffrey, 2016). Many First Nations have been on boil water advisories for decades; more than a significant percentage of communities have been forced to boil water for their daily use on a continuous or repeated basis. This lack of access to water can be attributed to many factors and often under different scenarios. However, in many instances, these communities are not equipped with adequate treatment facilities, or lack trained operators to maintain existing facilities so that they can safely treat and serve water to their communities. Further, many communities draw drinking water from wells and from a questionable or, in some cases, a clearly contaminated water source. The Safe Drinking Water for First Nations Act of 2013 is an example of federal legislation not delivering on its name, in part because it was developed and enacted without collaboration or consultation with First Nations.

In late 2015 through early 2017, the Standing Rock Sioux Nation drew support from both Canada and the United States when they were faced with a potential threat to the local river and waters they rely on. "Water is life" became the battle cry of the water protectors. The Dakota Access Pipeline (DAPL) was proposed for hazardous hydrocarbon conveyance through traditional lands. This route was chosen after the citizens of Bismarck, North Dakota protested the pipeline that would cut through lands about ten miles away from the town. These conflicts continue to play out, as decision-making approaches and regulatory frameworks do not provide for inclusive and meaningful dialogue that reflects community interests and the realities of critical connections with water.

Tucson Basin, American Southwest

Tucson Tide
Blue darkening skies
Monsoon's precious water falls
Desert dust swirls

Water as Currency in the Lifeblood Exchange Economy

The Tucson basin stretches approximately 1,000 square miles within the Sonoran Desert in the American Southwest. A land of intrinsic beauty, it is also home to a diverse human population, including the Tohono O'odham Nation that comprises the second largest Native American land holding in the United States (their lands are now fragmented through artificial divisions that have come under further threat with a proposed border wall between the United States and Mexico). This division of Tohono O'odham lands has resulted in an artificial division of the society. Adjacent to the designated reservation lands of the Nation is South Tucson, a small, racially diverse city, with over 80% of the population identifying as Hispanic or Latino.

Expanding on my research and study of the extent of groundwater contamination in Tucson, I had reached out to a long-time resident and community leader of South Tucson. She looked across the table at me. I listened to her account of the community's experience that had begun years earlier and was continuing to unfold. When she said the words "economic extortion" I understood, with a new appreciation, the level of complexity and impact that contaminated groundwater can have on an affected population. The observation and connection being made was stated very clearly to me that day in 1997 in the dry desert lands of Arizona.

Health problems among south-side Tucson residents are connected to the indiscriminate and unregulated dumping of industrial wastes that occurred over a period of 30 years beginning in the 1950s. It has been estimated that more than 4,000 gallons of the volatile organic compound, trichlorethylene, drained into the aquifer near the Tucson International Airport during that time. At the time of discovery, the toxic plume had migrated to reach a length of over six miles underground. The areas in greater Tucson most affected by hazardous wastes are where low-income households are located, and where the vast majority of residents are visible minorities, namely in South Tucson.

Prior to 1981, groundwater wells drawing from the federally designated sole source aquifer (SSA) within the area provided drinking water for over 47,000 people. An SSA is the only water available and therefore critical to supply a local population. It would be decades before the connection between groundwater contamination and health of the South Tucson community was officially recognized. This public unveiling of the impacts of standard industrial practices was the result of water monitoring required under new legislation in 1980. It was then that the federally designated sole source aquifer became part of the ten-square mile federally designated "Superfund" site.

The legislation that governs these officially designated contaminated sites is known as the Comprehensive Environmental Response, Compensation, and Liability Act (CERCLA). It is more commonly known as Superfund, referring to the federal trust fund from which moneys are allocated yearly to sites under the federal cleanup program. CERCLA, and its amendments, established prohibitions and requirements concerning closed and abandoned hazardous waste sites and provides for liability of persons responsible for releases at these sites.

In the case of the Tucson International Airport Area (TIAA) Superfund site, listed in 1983, the contaminated water and soil were the result of aircraft refitting and manufacturing operations by several aircraft companies—primarily contractors of the U.S. Department of Defense. These contractors provided a very significant portion of jobs in the area, ultimately at the expense of public health. Thus, the phrase "economic extortion" resonates. In other words, the externalized costs to the local environment—or costs of doing business—were borne by local residents over time through contact with the toxins in the water and living environment.

Stages of Community Response to Contaminated Water

Public participation at the TIAA site began long before CERCLA legislation was enacted or TCE was officially recognized to be in Tucson's municipal water supply, and so it was, in a sense, unscripted for many years prior to the Act. Brown's Model of Popular Epidemiology (Brown, 1993) is useful to put the community response and history of community involvement into perspective. The model explains how laypeople or communities detect and act on environmental hazards and diseases. It is based on a similar case of water contamination in Woburn, Massachusetts, which is strikingly similar to the South Tucson situation.

In the 1970s, local Tucson residents like Melinda Gonzales noticed that several of her neighbours were being diagnosed with lupus and cancers, including leukemia (Kay, 1985). She began to identify clusters in the neighborhood where the affected people lived. By this time, residents had noticed, separately, both pollutants and the illnesses. This is identified as the first stage in "popular epidemiology," the phenomenon in which non-experts detect and act on environmental hazards (Brown, 1993).

Residents then began to hypothesize that there was a connection between their illnesses and their environment. In popular epidemiology, this is identified as the second stage of community response (Brown, 1993). Some local people thought that they may have been exposed to radiation in the area. Speculation that health problems may be linked to the water supply began with one resident suggesting that a high salt content was causing his plants to do poorly. A more dramatic statement was made by an eighteen-year old, days before he died from cancer; his words to his sister were "don't drink the water" (Kay, 1985).

In the third stage, community residents share information and gain a common perspective. This third stage is also evident in the Tucson situation. People with access to information and links in the neighborhood, such as public health nurses, teachers, and the clergy, showed others their findings. After her husband died of lymphoma, a volunteer nurse at a church school who lived in the affected area made a list of local people afflicted with serious illnesses (Kay, 1985). Other residents found that the health of their neighbours became a common topic of discussion during local gatherings.

The next stage that is apparent as a community response is the pursuit of knowledge from health officials and scientific experts (Brown, 1993). Doctors were contacts as a matter of course when people became ill. Aside from this, *The Arizona Daily Star* newspaper enlisted the help of experts to pursue health surveys and to interpret the results of their findings.

Dr. Michael Gallo, Chairman of the Department of Environmental and Community Medicine at Rutgers Medical School in New Jersey, noted in 1985 that the clusters of illnesses were significant. However, he also stated that he could not cite any scientific or experimental evidence linking TCE to the diseases. A researcher at the National Cancer Institute and a local brain surgeon suggested that there might be some links, but that the population size was not large enough to make the findings statistically significant (Kay, 1985).

Angry residents eventually organized into groups to pursue their investigation; this occurred in Tucson after the 1981 detection and public announcement of TCE in some private and public wells. Organizing in this way is seen by Brown (1993) to be the next stage in popular epidemiology practice. News articles in *The Arizona Daily Star* published as a reprint series in May 1985 led to heightened awareness and anger among the affected residents of Tucson's south side. At this time, a primary interest group called Tucsonans for a Clean Environment organized in response to the contamination problem and health concerns of the community. The group sent a petition to the USEPA in July 1987 pressing for government support for health services and medical monitoring of south side residents who had been exposed to trichloroethylene. By 1992, this group had a mailing list of over 600 citizens (U.S. Environmental Protection Agency).

Other groups eventually contributed their support to the community residents. Included were the Toxic Waster Investigative Group/Arizona Environmental Coalition, the Human Ecology Action League, the Sierra Club, and the Southern Arizona Environmental Council. In response to community interviews conducted by the EPA in June of 1989, the community listed several concerns, which had not changed significantly since the community relations plans were completed for the Superfund process in 1982 and 1986 (U.S. Environmental Protection Agency, 1992). Among these concerns were health effects, total cleanup of groundwater contamination, air quality, property values, the credibility of government agencies, and the potentially responsible parties.

The sixth stage of community response develops when government agencies get involved as a result of citizen group pressure. As studies are conducted, there is often inconclusive evidence linking the contaminant to health problems (Brown, 1993). This is certainly true in the case of

Tucson. In 1985, Pima County's Health Director dismissed the community's concerns during a public meeting, blaming their ills on lifestyle practices. Residents were offended and outraged at the flagrant response. Lloyd Novick, Director of ADHS from 1984 to 1986, responded to concerns by forming a committee made up of ADHS and County Health officials, outside scientists, and interested parties to review available health data. The Committee on Suspected Illness in Southwest Tucson completed the review in 1986. As recommended, a two-part study on the health effects and past TCE exposure was carried out by the ADHS.

The research indicated that there were "no adverse health problems or unusually high number of deaths that would have received exposure to TCE." But there was one exception to this first phase of study: there was a statistically significant increase in leukemia for males aged five to nine (U.S. Environmental Protection Agency, 1992) during the period between 1969 and 1985. However, a second study for the period of 1970 to 1986 concluded that there was no significant increase in rates of various cancer types in the community. Enraged residents chose not to accept this finding. This led to the next stage, in which residents enlisted the help of experts to conduct their own study.

Community residents insisted on "more accurate" future studies and monitoring of their community health. The residents brought in nationally known scientists as part of the legal process of the lawsuit that was to follow. In response to community concerns, the state and county funded the TCE Program at the El Pueblo Clinic in a south Tucson neighbourhood. As described in a clinic information pamphlet, the program "provides outpatient primary care services for individuals who have lived, worked, or attended school in the contamination area between 1945 and 1981." The public funding is limited to aid those who do not have other health insurance coverage, and not all services are funded.

The lawsuit brought in federal court represents the eighth stage of litigation and confrontation as identified under Brown's model. In 1991, after six years of litigation, the residents of the affected south Tucson neighborhood were successful in their pursuit of problem recognition and compensation. Hughes Aircraft Company agreed in an out of court settlement to pay 84.5 million dollars. After legal fees and court costs, approximately

1,600 litigants were awarded 49.2 million dollars (Coile, 1991). Other lawsuits followed.

In this stage of the popular epidemiology model, the community pressed for corroboration of their findings by officials and government agencies. For its part, USEPA officially identified trichloroethylene as a "B2 Carcinogen" which means "probable" based on animal studies. The agency approved a Maximum Contaminant Level (MCL) of 5 parts per billion (ppb) in drinking water in 1989.

In 1991 it was announced that four new studies tied south side illnesses to the tainted water supply (Bagwell, 1991). The Dallas law firm that handled the lawsuit paid for the studies to be conducted by three researchers. One study found that the contaminated water "caused or substantially contributed to" illnesses in the local residents including cancer, lupus, multiple sclerosis, and scleroderma (Bagwell, 1991). The other studies reported similar findings and added that the presence of fourteen other chemicals in the water may have had a synergistic effect. Since the Tucson community is the largest to be affected by widespread contamination of a primary water supply in the United States, it continues to be under study by medical researchers and the Agency for Toxic Substances and Disease Registry (ATSDR).

The controversy over the health effects of TCE continued with two reports issued by the ATSDR in 1996 in which no conclusive evidence of TCE effects in the Tucson community is reported (ATSDR, 1996). This was received with skepticism and anger among the community. Local doctors disagreed on the hazards of TCE and human health (Nash, 1997; Abrams, 1998; Orient, 1998). To many residents of the South Tucson community, the effects of TCE on their community are very real and most report knowing someone whose health has been compromised or has lost family members due to illnesses connected to TCE exposure.

Several years later, the south Tucson community became a model for EPA's public participation process at Superfund sites. On the heels of a long history of calls for answers from local leaders and health practitioners regarding the effects of the hazards placed in their community, it became a positive part of the story, at least in terms of increased involvement of the community in remediation decisions. Although progress has been made at great expense to residents, corporations, taxpayers, and local ecosystems, the aquifer will never be recovered to its pre-contaminated state. More recent news reports that the community of South Tucson is embroiled in a new struggle, again linking illnesses in the community to another industrial contaminant found in the water (Davis, 2017).

Athabasca Watershed, Northwestern Canada

This place, Chipewyan
Pain, love, and beauty
In the sands and water shine
To be reconciled

Cultural Discontinuity as an Outcome of Watershed Degradation

The Athabasca glacier is part of the family of glaciers that make up the Columbia Icefield in the Rocky Mountains and serves as the headwaters of the river that carries its name to the Peace-Athabasca Delta and into Lake Athabasca. The Athabasca River, unhindered by dams, flows for over 1,200 kilometres. It is the largest river set entirely in Alberta, although a small portion of its approximately 100,000 square kilometre watershed crosses into Saskatchewan. A water basin rich and diverse with pristine mountains, plains, wetlands, and boreal forest connecting the landscape, it is juxtaposed with one of the most intensive and extensive industrial developments on the planet. The same could be said for the basin's polarized and conflicting socio-cultural make up of rich traditional cultures existing alongside wealth traded for the health of land and waters. The importance of natural hydrologic connectivity to ecosystems and culture in this landscape cannot be overstated.

On the eastern shore of Lake Athabasca is Fort Chipewyan, a community primarily shared by First Nations and Métis people who have settled over time along the water. Transportation into and out of the community is limited to air travel and winter roads, but accessibility by land may change as the climate warms. The rich ecological setting of this lower basin area is protected to a limited extent through the protected areas of Wood Buffalo National Park and the Athabasca Dunes Ecological Reserve. Although this watershed begins and ends with artificially delineated and reserved areas of special interest with "protected" status, including Jasper National Park in the headwaters, landscape alterations made outside of those areas are in sharp contrast to the relatively intact, but vulnerable ecosystems of these reserve and park lands. The effects of intensive mineral extractive operations permeate the land and water beyond developed project areas, and the fallout includes the uprooting of Indigenous people and culture.

There is a long history of cultural disruption here. Problems seen today stem from imposed societal structures that replaced fundamental ways of being and knowing. Taking land from the people and taking people from the land are a pervasive theme and reality. Changes in ecosystem health within this watershed have been observed and documented by people that are most connected to the land—fishers, trappers, hunters, and gatherers of food and medicines. Perhaps the most politicized situation came in 2009 with the reporting of fish caught in Lake Athabasca with physical deformities. The official closure of the fishery followed in more recent years. One resident of Fort Chipewyan described the loss of species noted more recently in his thirty years of working his traplines; birds, beetles, and fish seem to be nearly non-existent and water levels are not predictable as they once were. A local Dene hunter also explained that government officials have advised that the organ meats of ungulates, significant for traditional use and food source, are no longer safe to eat (Jerry Adam, Personal communication, June 2017). To make the matter worse, rare bile duct cancers rates within the community are perceived to be connected to the water, and many residents no longer trust their water supply. The impacts on culture and community health are in lock step with the degradation of ecosystems.

The irony of these situations brings into question the criteria for decisions that are made, and to what and at whose expense. Consider the loss of the commercial fishery: the much anticipated and newly constructed fish processing plant in Fort Chipewyan stands mothballed and is never used. Consider the seventy-year-old elder and former fisher who, with little choice in means to support himself and his family, asks the land for forgiveness while he operates heavy machinery in the oil sands industrial development in the lower Athabasca. Meanwhile, large blue plastic containers of water are carried into the Athabasca Chipewyan First Nation elders lodge, adjacent to the sandy shores of Lake Athabasca, this lake once the provider of water and food security. This is "cultural genocide"— people are disconnected from land and water that make up their very essence and way of life. What happens to the relationship between land and spirit when access to traditional lands is removed and spiritual practice is hampered?

Environmental and ecosystem changes in the Athabasca basin have been widely studied and documented. Evidence of anthropogenic landscape change is contained in historic and contemporary maps, volumes of scientific and personal journals, satellite imagery, monitoring and observational data collected by scientists and local people over time, and perhaps most revealing, in the stories told by First Nations and Métis people of the area. These sources are all key pieces that exist to inform and guide decisions that are needed today, and are, in fact, necessary to improve watershed and community health going forward.

Indigenous peoples have established protocols and practices under which they manage themselves and coexist with other species in the landscape. But unlike others, who make decisions that run counter to nature, Indigenous knowledge and experience span thousands of years, wherein they belong to the land, not the other way around. Spiritual, physical, and mental well-being are at the heart of decisions made by Indigenous leaders and communities, with actions held to a long-term multigenerational standard of care. As such, respect is given to the relationship with other species and effects on others long into the future. A Dene elder with roots in the Fort Chipewyan area describes the sacred connection and dialogue with nature and all its beings as creating a "spiritual symbiotic relationship with the land" (Patrick Deranger, Personal communication, October 2017). This relationship and regard for nature aligns with true sustainability, in ways necessary for maintaining life across landscapes and temporal scales. However, under pressure that comes with increasingly scarce resources, and specifically with reduced access to land, water, and food, a sustainable way of life is in critical disarray in the Athabasca basin. It follows that disconnection from land results in a loss of "sense of place" and may then translate into a profound loss of "sense of self."

Adding to the burden of lack of access to resources, large swaths of the lower Athabasca basin have been taken into production, with developed sites left in a degraded state over long periods of time. New hydrocarbon extraction projects come on line and developed oilsands project areas remain non-functional. Pipelines built to carry the extracted hydrocarbons from the area create additional, linear disturbances at the physical sites they occupy, along with the access roads that interfere with habitat. Taken together, these features impose disruption to hydrology and access to land. Developed oil project areas no longer provide ecosystem goods and services; where habitat has not been taken, unhealthy habitat for a multitude of species has been created. The cumulative impacts to the watershed known as "death by a thousand cuts" are mostly unabated and continue to mount under obliteration that compounds on a massive scale.

There seems to be no hard deadlines to decommission projects and rehabilitate lands and water that have been extensively degraded. In spite of a requirement for land reclamation plans, there is little movement by industry toward large-scale reclamation due to assigned activity status, let alone toward rehabilitation, remediation, and the ultimate state of restoration. A very small percentage of affected land and water has been reclaimed. Restoring ecosystem and watershed health and, more specifically, hydrologic function and processes is not realistic under current technological and financial capability, or corporate willingness. This landscape, with its reduced capacity for supporting life, has deep scars that may never be healed in current lifetimes. The enabling conditions and incentives for restoring water and land to the previous state that would support healthy, sustained ecosystems and communities in these areas of the basin do not currently exist.

Water is a treaty right, also enshrined in the Canadian *Charter of Rights and Freedoms* but this right seems largely unsupported in regulatory systems, which have been implemented with little Indigenous input. The federal *Safe Drinking Water for First Nations Act*, a Canadian legislation developed under the Harper tenure in 2013, has been met with criticism by First Nations leaders for its lack of consultation (Jeffrey, 2016). This is indicative of the disconnect between policy and practice, particularly when it comes to water. The Act also allows for the transfer of liability of broken water treatment systems to First Nations. Ironically, broken natural systems are what led to the necessity of the Act in the first place; ecosystem services that once assured clean water for over a millennium were decommissioned by way of industrial development and land-based practices that have been taking place over a few decades.

Under the United Nations Declaration of the Rights of Indigenous Peoples (UNDRIP), of which Canada is a signatory, there is hope that there will be processes and actions that transcend the current system. A transformed system is needed where there is meaningful dialogue, voices are heard, and perspectives are reflected in water-related decisions and outcomes going forward. Shared natural resource decision-making is called out in UNDRIP and this serves as a mandate for all government levels to intentionally engage and share space at the table. Traditional Ecological Knowledge (TEK) gained and passed on for generations, representing another way of knowing, has been nearly entirely ignored in policy and decision-making at all levels. To continue along this path is our peril.

Salish Sea, Pacific Northwest

Unto the Salish Sea
Rain running on rock
Seeps into sweet cool earth
Dark glistening sea

It is Cheaper to Protect Than Restore

The watersheds of the Georgia Strait, the Strait of Juan de Fuca, and Puget Sound have supported a rich ecosystem that sustained Indigenous communities of the Salish Sea for a long period of time. To many who know the Pacific Northwest, salmon is an iconic species of the region. The infrastructure necessary to support competing land uses such as agricultural, urban, and forest industry development has disrupted the journey of this anadromous fish species. Alterations to watersheds have also resulted in degraded water quality to the point of being toxic in many areas. This loss in habitat and watershed health was a highly significant factor in the listing of Puget Sound salmon species under the U.S. Endangered Species Act in the late 1990s.

Efforts to restore habitat and recover listed salmon species have been taking place across watersheds on both sides of the border between Canada and the United States. Watershed-based, multi-stakeholder groups focus on recovering salmon under fifty-year plans include targets for restoring and protecting environments critical to the species, such as riparian, wetland, estuary, and nearshore marine environments. Multiple millions of dollars and hours of dedicated experts, government officials, stewardship groups and citizens have been invested in the implementation of these watershed-based salmon recovery plans. It is indeed cheaper to protect watersheds than it is to restore them. Hydroclimatic change is bringing another layer of challenge to restoration efforts. There is still a long way to go to increase salmon species abundance and ensure the continuance of Pacific Northwest culture.

The dialogue and relationship that have formed under the effort to restore and protect watersheds and recover salmon species have resulted from a nearly twenty-year commitment of many organizations and individuals. Although not always in perfect alignment in terms of policy, timelines, and approach, the goal to recover salmon through various actions, including protection and watershed function-based restoration, is shared. Efforts are limited by inadequate funding, opportunistic-reliant projects, voluntary-based implementation, and politics. The *Treaty Rights at Risk* white paper came out as a shot across the bow from tribes in the Puget Sound region in 2011. The message communicated to Washington state and local governments was clear: habitat restoration is not on pace with what is needed or reflective of supportive court decisions for the recovery of salmon. The collaborative effort and long-term commitment to recover salmon is to be lauded; however, a shift in focus toward protection of water, along with the integration of other ways of knowing and practices, is necessary now.

A New Relationship With Water as the Way Forward

Watershed health and community resilience are inextricably linked. As we move into the future, it will be evermore critical to protect and restore water. Watershed function is critical in the provisioning of water, yet restoring lost landscapes is a very costly endeavour. There is no economy in the misuse of water going forward. The idea that water is an unlimited resource is a concept only suited to a past in which natural resources were regarded as solely ours for the taking. The current trajectory that we are on is a result of policy not keeping pace with the realities of the carrying capacity of ecosystems, and of decisions not founded in inclusivity. Watershed health is a key determining factor of how resilient a community will be under a changing climate.

Climate change is bringing a decrease in weather predictability and an increase in extreme events, such as flood, drought, and temperature shifts, creating an urgency to make decisions that provide net environmental benefits over the long run. Natural resource management decisions must account for long-term impacts—perhaps adopting the "seven generations rule" to guide us toward equilibrium in our natural and economic systems would be wise. A longer term, sighted approach is what climate adaptation and resiliency planning demand. This is not a new concept.

In our every deliberation,
we must consider the impact of our decisions
on the next seven generations.
(Iroquois Confederacy Maxim)

Indigenous communities and leaders of Native American tribes have long held that a multi-generational view provides a necessary basis for sound decision-making. Beyond that, we cannot ignore nature. As an elder of the Tsuut'ina Nation has stated, "natural laws supersede man-made laws" (Bruce Starlight, Personal Communication, January 2018). We can make all the laws we want and manage ourselves how we wish based on those rules, but ultimately the outcomes of our actions show up in the form of balanced or degraded ecosystems. As long as environmental and economic policies and regulations are disconnected from the realities of the carrying capacity of the Earth, we will see inequitable and unsustainable actions and impacts on water and land and ecosystems of which we are a part.

Watershed resilience and environmental justice are linked. Policies and practices that promote the externalization of costs to our environment are not sustainable. Decisions that result in degraded environments cannot continue to be borne by those who happen upon the mess—now or in future—or by those who call these places "home." It is members of underserved communities who are disproportionally impacted. This is playing out as we witness more dislocation of people from marginalized lands and degraded watersheds. Adding to the vulnerability of communities is the recognition that coastal and low-lying areas are more prone to storms, flooding, and sea level rise. It is time to choose a different path guided by principles of equity, justice, and sustainability rooted in wisdom and experience, and set a trajectory leading to a more resilient future.

There is a need to employ alternative approaches in natural resources decision-making processes that consider long-term impacts on water and communities. The goal of ensuring that watersheds retain the capacity to provide clean water must be shared. Indigenous knowledge, as rooted in adaptive tendencies and in basic principles of sustaining life in complex systems, are a key to unlocking enduring solutions. Redistribution of power is needed, and this is best begun in a process where there is space and time for meaningful and inclusive dialogue. Local perspectives are integral to water-related decisions and management actions, and must be taken into account under ever more challenging, environmental conditions. Just as tributaries come together as part of a dynamic system to form a vibrant river, what is needed is to identify a confluence of ideas where cross-cultural knowledge provides a way forward, toward enduring solutions for water—the shared resource necessary for life, yet not assured for all.

REFERENCES

Abrams, H. K., McDonald, M., & Rosales, C. (1998, February). About that TCE. *Sombrero*. Pima County Medical Society Publication.

Agency for Toxic Substances and Disease Registry (ASTDR). (1996). Public Health Assessment for TIAA [Draft]. Department of Health and Human Services.

Bagwell, K. (1991, July 7). Four new studies tie south side ills to tainted water. *The Arizona Daily Star*.

Brown, P. (1993, October). Popular epidemiology challenges the system. *Environment, 35*(8), 16–41.

Bryant, B. (1995). *Environmental justice: Issues, policies, and solutions*. Island Press.

Bullard, R. D. (1990). *Dumping In Dixie: Race, class and environmental quality*. Westview Press.

Bullard, R. D. (1993). Race and environmental justice in the United States. *Yale Journal of International Law, 18*, 370–380.

Bullard, R. D. (1995). Government should work to ensure environmental justice. In J.S. Petrikin (Ed.), *Environmental justice* (pp. 70-84). Greenhaven Press.

Coile, N. (1991, March 21). Legal fees deplored in Tucson TCE case. *The Arizona Daily Star.*

Davis, T. (2017, April 16). South-side Tucsonans mobilize for another water-pollution struggle. *Arizona Daily Star.* Retrieved October 11, 2017, from http://tucson.com/news/local/south-side-tucsonans-mobilize-for-another-water-pollution-struggle/article_25aafd92-3a5a-5550-bbd6-9fc0d02cd0dd.html

Gottlieb, R. (1993). *Forcing the spring: The transformation of the American environmental movement.* Island Press.

Jeffrey, R. (2016, March). The end of the line. *Alberta Venture,* 62–68.

Kay, J. (1985, May). *The Arizona Daily Star.* (Reprint series)

Nash, S. (1997, December). TCE's scary; so is poor journalism. *Sombrero.* Pima County Medical Society Publication.

Orient, J. M. (1998, April). That big bad TCE scare. *Sombrero.* Pima County Medical Society Publication.

Ringquist, E. J. (1997). Environmental justice: Normative concerns and empirical evidence. In N. J. Vig & M. E. Kraft (Eds.), *Environmental policy in the 1990s: Reform or reaction?* (pp. 231–254). Congressional Quarterly Inc.

U.S. Environmental Protection Agency. (1992). *Tucson International Airport Area (TIAA) Superfund Site, Community Relations Plan, Region 9.*

Indigenous Stories and the Fraser River: Intercultural Dialogue for Public Decision-Making

Marcella LaFever, Shirley Hardman, and Pearl Penner

Isabel: How in the name of George and the dragon can someone come along, bend over, pick up a river, and carry it off into the distance away over yonder as if it were a sack of potatoes? Hmm? Can you tell me that Annabelle Okanagan of Kamloops, B.C.?

Annabelle: We are not allowed to fish the waters of that river anymore, are we now Isabel Thompson of Kamloops, B.C.? Not as of yesterday, Wednesday, the twenty-fourth of August, 1910 at ten past eleven. And if that's not taking the river away from us, then tell me Isabel Thompson of Kamloops, B.C., please tell me what is?

—Thomson Highway, *Ernestine Shuswap Gets Her Trout*

On December 15, 2015, the Truth and Reconciliation Commission of Canada (TRC) released its final report (Honouring the Truth) and calls to action related to Canada's responsibility to engage in measures for reconciliation related to the oppressive legacy of colonization (Calls to Action). The calls to action are addressed to all sectors of Canadian institutions, governing bodies, and citizens in the areas of child welfare, health, language and culture, the justice system, business, public service, and education. These calls include actions related to a public intercultural dialogue such as a commitment to "promote public dialogue, public/private partnerships, and public initiatives for reconciliation" (p. 10) and "meaningful consultation, building respectful relationships, and obtaining the free, prior, and informed consent of Indigenous peoples before proceeding with economic development projects" (p. 14).

Colonization of the Americas and the accompanying attitudes that viewed Indigenous peoples as sub-human is a legacy that continues to divide and oppress peoples through practices of racism and prejudice (Miller, 2011). The negative effects of Indian Residential Schools, where Indigenous children were taken from their families and sent to institutions that were meant to rid them of their culture and where they often suffered abuse and even death, are a part of history that Canada is only starting to acknowledge and come to terms with (Canada's residential schools, 2015). The truth and reconciliation process in Canada is meant to begin a wholistic healing between communities and lead to the breaking down of barriers to relationship building. A sustained public dialogue that is built to include participatory practices of Indigenous peoples is essential to truly engage in this process.

Previously, in 2010, the government of Canada initiated an inquiry into the declines of Sockeye salmon stocks in the Fraser River (Cohen Commission Inquiry) and called for those who had a stake in Sockeye salmon population management to give evidence (Terms of Reference, 2010). Eight of the twenty-one groups granted standing represented twenty-eight-plus First Nation councils, bands, and Indigenous organizations (Clarkson, 2012; Participants, 2010). The purpose of our research is to investigate the use of storytelling as a culturally distinct communicative act (Mendoza & Kinefuchi, 2016), particularly as a communicative act for Indigenous communities in Canada and specifically in British Columbia (Harvey, 2009). Tuhiwai-Smith (1999) states that "The acts of reclaiming, reformulating and reconstructing Indigenous cultures and languages have required the mounting of an ambitious research programme, one that is very strategic in its purpose and activities and relentless in its pursuit of social justice" (p. 142). The use of Indigenous methodologies in investigations of intercultural public dialogue and decision-making is not new (LaFever, 2008). However, Indigenous storytelling has not been explored as a way of changing participatory expectations.

The intent of this project is to contribute to the body of research on ways that dominant culture members can change their conceptions of what participation for Indigenous communities in public dialogue and decision-making means. When peoples do not feel that they are heard on issues of public interest, especially when the method of public consultation does not fit with cultural practices for participation, society misses out on important contributions to the public discourse (LaFever, 2011). Building on these understandings, this project seeks to determine how Indigenous storytelling was used, to what extent, in what forms, and to what purpose as part of the submissions by Indigenous[1] groups to the Cohen Commission hearings. Answering these questions was vital for answering the ultimate question: Were Indigenous stories heard and understood in ways that demonstrated a direct impact on the recommendations contained in the final Cohen Commission Inquiry report?

The researchers in this project see the telling of stories as particular types of communicative acts that both create and are born from particular cultural world views (Bourdieu, 1991). When cultural groups and individuals interact (e.g., in the context of public dialogue), world views often clash as expectations and practices of communication differ. The following section explores the concepts of intercultural communication and storytelling, with particular focus on North American experiences of Indigenous peoples.

Intercultural Public Dialogue

Indigenous communities around the world face historically negative conditions in their pursuit of economic and community development activities. A major challenge, therefore, is to facilitate increased representation of marginalized community members in public dialogue about community development. Public dialogue in North American society is seen as a way for all citizens to engage in democratic processes (LaFever, 2011). When citizens engage with each other in making decisions about their communities, they are participating in and creating the meaning of democracy.

For the purposes of describing intercultural dialogue, Buber's (1972) definition is the most appropriate because it emphasizes dialogue as embedded in social context. Buber argued that "meaning" constructs not only the interpersonal relationship but also the societal institutions that govern human action. Dialogue, as Buber defined it, is a genuine attempt to create something new. Community development is a process of making decisions about social structures, and community requires the development of long-term relationships. It is for these reasons that the Buberian definition of dialogue underpins the present study and its exploration of intercultural dialogue in public participatory processes.

Based in the knowledge that narratives have an impact on public policy development (Crow & Janes, 2018) and despite some history of the Canadian government asking for Indigenous peoples to tell their stories as part of government consultation, such as in the Mackenzie Valley Pipeline Inquiry (Scott, 2012), little research has focused on adapting public dialogue routines to accommodate practices that vary from those of the dominant culture and, in particular, research on the dynamics of using Indigenous storytelling as a communicative practice in contexts of public dialogue and decision-making.

Story and Storytelling as a Communicative Act

Story and storytelling have long been studied and theorized in many academic disciplines, e.g., anthropology, sociology, and psychology. In the field of communication, this research comes by way of the study of rhetoric (the art of persuasive language) and the concept of narrative scholarship. Burke (1966) defined humans as symbol-making animals where symbols are the tools that allow us to create stories that give order to human experience. Bormann's (1972) concept of symbolic convergence explains how communication creates groups connected by emotions, motives, and meanings through the sharing of narratives. Building on the work of these two scholars, Fischer (1986) describes humans as *homo narrans*, indicating that all forms of human expression and communication are ultimately created in stories. A communicative definition of story sees stories as a way of ordering and presenting a view of the world through a sequential description of a situation involving characters, actions, and settings. Further, Sunwolf and Frey (2001) list five functions for stories used in communication: ways of connecting people, ways of knowing, ways of creating reality, ways of remembering, and ways of visioning the future. These theories help to inform how stories, storytelling, and contexts of public dialogue are connected.

In thinking about contexts of public dialogue, there is an interesting relationship between the topics people focus on in contemporary communities and the topics communities considered important to discuss about their historical past. Stories told in a community are cultural constructions and provide a richer understanding of fundamental cultural issues (Clarkson, 2012). This understanding may be intuitive for the participants in a particular culture, but is not necessarily obvious for an outsider. Our interpretations of these issues are also culturally constructed (King, 2005). As Cruikshank (1987) states, the concern for interpreting stories is not with determining "truth value" or with "getting the facts straight," than with asking how our ideas about "truth" and "facts" are constructed in the first place.

An example of community and cultural constructions is captured in Jo-Ann Archibald's (2008) telling of "Searching for the Bone Needle." She states that Eber Hampton's story took on integral meaning for her and that she sought and was granted permission and encouraged to adapt the original story to suit her own cultural context. Archibald the trickster was renamed Coyote (old man coyote). Others close to Archibald, or those with shared cultural experiences, will recognize the significance of Archibald's choice: that coyote is not only as he appears in the current story—but is the collection of all of the antics described in the multitudes of stories in which coyote makes appearances. To know about coyote and understand coyote's role in particular stories, the listener necessarily connects coyote to his history and in many instances to his reputation. For Archibald, she tells her reader that she chose coyote "because Coyote in all his/he/its forms has become my trickster of learning" (p. 35).

Colonizers have long considered storytelling as a part of Indigenous oral history to be mere myth, superstition, and perhaps entertainment (Smith, 1995; Thompson, 1929). However, stories are a powerful means of expression and fortunately Indigenous scholars have themselves emphasized and explained their cultural significance (Abel, 1993; Archibald, 2008, Basso, 1996; Cajete, 1994; King, 2016). Linda Tuhiwai-Smith (1999) reiterates that Indigenous stories "are ways of passing down the beliefs and values of a culture in the hope that the new generation will treasure them and pass the story down further" (p. 144), and explains further that "familiar characters can be invested with the qualities of an individual or can be used to invoke a set of shared understanding and histories" (p. 145). Stories are used to reinforce socially beneficial behaviours and remind us of, or teach us who we are. Stories are used as tools to educate and to heal individuals and social relationships (Hardman, 2015/2016). Stories connect individuals to the land.

The Fraser River, the geographic focus of the Cohen Commission Inquiry, is the heart and lifeblood of the Stó:lō (people of the river). The unsatisfying relationship between First Nations peoples and the Canadian government on many issues is every day presented in abundantly clear reporting in the newspapers, on the radio, and on television (Gleeson, 2019; Moore, 2019). Recognition of Aboriginal rights and title to land and resources are major concerns for the Stó:lō who have never signed treaties with past or present governments. Successful Stó:lō leaders today spend much of their time negotiating these rights on many different levels. In the face of being able to achieve such independence through self-determination, Stó:lō leaders are also deeply engaged in trying to gain economic independence for their communities.

Stories are used to illustrate the history of places/territories and culture. Stories from the peoples of what is now called the Fraser River are such "living voices of its Peoples and their cultural, spiritual, and contemporary relationships" (Armstrong & William, 2015, p. 1). As might be expected, the significance placed by Stó:lō peoples on the Salmon is captured in their storytelling. The Stó:lō, and other First Nations along the Fraser River, have origin stories (Sxwôxwiyám) that explain the beginnings of the Salmon and how they came to populate the Fraser River and its tributaries. Recently the Fraser River Discovery Centre (2014) recorded two versions of the Fraser River Salmon origin stories. Dr. Sonny Naxaxalhts'i McHalsie shares this up-river Stó:lō origin story alongside Larry Grant who reveals the Musqueam origin story about the Salmon people.

Stories within communities are revered as Indigenous ways of knowing, an integral part of finding out and passing on knowledge about how the world works (Cardinal, 2004; Cruikshank, 1987; Deloria, 1999; Goulet,

1998; Tuhiwai-Smith, 1999). When looking at stories as a way of knowing, it is important to recognize how stories function as ways to illustrate history, to describe lives and the places where people lived, and to acknowledge the many ways that humans create linkages. To this end we not only sought to identify stories told at the Cohen Commission Inquiry, we wanted to know why these particular stories were told, and if these purposes for storytelling were acknowledged.

Methodology

Materials from the Cohen Commission Inquiry hearings (2012) include evidentiary documents and transcripts. We extracted each record/presentation submitted by an Aboriginal group or individual. In total we identified 125 Indigenous submissions over the course of the commission proceedings. There were nine during the opening hearings (June 2010), ten in public forums (August–October 2010), ninety-five during the evidentiary hearings (October 2010–September 2011), and eleven during the closing hearings (November 2011). Once files were prepared (i.e., relabelled and saved in pdf format), we used NVivo qualitative research analysis software for coding.

All files were renamed using a label for the type of hearing (Opening=OH, Public=PH, Evidentiary=EH, Closing=CH), the date of the submission, and the name of the presenter. Occasionally the presenter was a lawyer who was speaking or tabling a document on behalf of an Aboriginal group, or reading a written submission from a First Nation member.

The future of the Stó:lō is intimately tied to the future of the salmon and we, as researchers, felt Stó:lō story forms were an important place to start in this project. The initial scheme for (de)coding[2] was based on Sqwelqwel, oral narratives relating to personal history, and Sxwôxwiyám, oral histories that describe the distant past. These are the two types of traditional Stó:lō stories (Stó:lō Heritage, 2003).

Secondly, we (de)coded the two types of stories by looking for themes that identified how and why a particular story was told. We noted commonalities and differences between stories, ways that stories were used within the larger context, citation of the origin/keeper of the story, and prefaces or prologues to using a story.[3]

After completing the second step of (de)coding, we recognized that while the themes we identified were relevant, this categorization did not do an adequate job of answering the question regarding their purposes of use. Subsequently we re-(de)coded all stories using Tuhiwai-Smith's (1999) *Twenty-Five Indigenous Projects* (Appendix A). We recognized in using her work that participating in public dialogue to preserve a way of life is a social justice issue for the Indigenous people who have depended on the gift of the salmon for thousands of years.

Lastly, we conducted an analysis of the final recommendations contained in the Cohen Commission Inquiry report to see whether the purposes of the stories we identified were reflected in the recommendations.

Findings

Out of all the Indigenous submissions, eighty-eight of them included at least one story told by approximately forty speakers.[4] Within the submissions, seven Sxwôxwiyám were told, although recording the number of Sqwelqwel became unwieldy and we concentrated rather on identifying examples from our two forms of secondary (de)coding (thematic and the use of Tuhiwai-Smith's work).

Sxwôxwiyám

Sxwôxwiyám (stories of long ago) were used only occasionally during formalities of introduction at the beginning of the hearings (the gift of salmon from the creator) and to place stories of the salmon within various territories represented at the hearings. These included stories from the Haida, Laich-Kwil-Rach, Secwepemc, Stó:lō, Nlaka'pamux, and Tl'azt'en. For example from the 13 December 2010 transcript, Chief Charlie from Sts'ailes (Chehalis; Stó:lō territory) relates:

> in the beginning of time when the world was first created, between the sun and the moon, when those feelings and emotions came together, we were all equal and the same and through evolution from that time, some took different shape and different form. Some became the winged, some became the four-legged, some became the plant people and the root people, some became the ones that swim in

the rivers and the ocean and some became human. There was an agreement in time that all our relations, all living things, they would give themselves to us as humans because we were the weakest. They would give themselves for food, shelter, clothing, utensils and for medicine. And all they asked for in return was to be respected and to be remembered; so when the salmon return in the beginning of the year, we have a ceremony to give thanks and gratitude to the salmon people for returning and giving themselves to us again. It's a part of that agreement of paying respect and giving gratitude.

For the Sts'ailes people and the Stó:lō peoples the story that Chief Charlie shares is referred to as a Snoweyelh or "our laws." The teachings contained in the story provide a road map of how Stó:lō must live as Stó:lō peoples. When the fish cease to exist, the people also cease to exist.

As a Stó:lō one knows that when we fail to follow the teachings there are consequences. It is not a quaint superstition but rather an intrinsic part of who we are as Stó:lō peoples. (Swelchalot personal correspondence)

Additional origin stories also conveyed such things as territorial description and fishing agreements. For example, the story of Lhílheqey (Mt. Cheam) is that she is the only one of the Stone People who volunteered herself to be transformed to stone. She is called Mother Mountain, she is sacred, and she vowed to look after the Stó:lō people and their greatest resource, the salmon. Towering over the upper Fraser River, whatever she looks upon is part of Stó:lō territory. These themes and many more are also reinforced through the personal, family, and community stories, the Sqwelqwel.

Sqwelqwel

Sqwelqwel was the main form of Indigenous storytelling used in the Cohen Commission hearings, and a majority of Indigenous submissions (81/125) included a form of Sqwelqwel. These stories might be a personal experience, a story about family experiences from the past, or a story passed down across generations about a particular community. The following example contains all three of these themes, moving the narrative from the past, to the present, to questions about the future (statement read on behalf of Harvey Humchitt, Sr.):

> Sockeye salmon, like many of our natural sea resources, is very important to the Heiltsuk. We are known as the ocean-going people or the salmon people. I have seen the abundance of the sockeye in the 1960s where there were millions and millions of returning spawners reduced to just a handful of salmon. I have witnessed the flourishing salmon industry going from thriving communities to ghost towns. We are concerned that the loss of the sockeye salmon will change the way of life for the Heiltsuk. When I was a little boy growing up in Namu, I would go fishing with my dad and never thought there would be a day when we would have to worry about the salmon. Today, you look at the mighty Fraser and wonder whatever happened. How did we get to the state we are in and how much more can we do to the sockeye. What about our grandchildren and what will they have if we lose our salmon? We have always been taught that we need to take care of our natural resource and by doing that nature will provide for you. (10 November 2011, Ming Song, Heiltsuk Tribal Council)

This piece touches on several themes: how environmental change that turns thriving communities into ghost towns has an impact on the use and importance of salmon culturally for future generations and the value of the responsibility to take care of the environment. Based on our first type of secondary (de)coding, we explore these themes and others in the next section.

(De)coding by Theme

In this section, we highlight six themes most closely related to the salmon, fishing, and the river: (a) the use and importance of salmon culturally, socially, and as sustenance; (b) values; (c) territorial description; (d) environmental change; (e) oral histories proven by science; and (f) fishing/harvesting methods. The stories told always covered several of these themes. Subsequently we felt it is not appropriate or useful to pull items out of context. In offering examples here, we provide a full story and then highlight the themes demonstrated within that story, eventually capturing several examples of all the themes.

Use and Importance of Salmon Culturally, Socially, and as Sustenance

While all of the stories we include tell of the importance of salmon culturally, the story below gives very specific examples regarding how native fish relate to daily life:

> There are ceremonies for many, many different things: for death, for life, for change of life, for weddings, for namings. There's all kinds of ceremonies that go on where we would have salmon that is served to the people because salmon is such a vital part of who we are as a people and we were supposed to share the wealth of our land … what we're supposed to share. It's really difficult to explain but there's one example I have of how it becomes medicine, becomes soul food … . My grandmother was very, very ill and she was not able to keep things down and it was going on three weeks, four weeks, and she was getting very fragile and frail … but she kept saying that she was wishing for sturgeon soup. So finally I was able to find a chunk of sturgeon and I brought it to my grandfather, on my dad's side. And my grandfather cooked some soup for her. I picked it up later and brought it to my grandmother and she ate the soup. Had about three or four feeds of it. And then she got better. She started eating again and started carrying on again and she was quite well again for some time. (13 December 2010, Chief Charlie, Chehalis)

Essential to ceremony throughout all aspects of community life, the needs and wellness of a single person become an expression for the whole. This story is also an excellent one to highlight the value of sharing, not only between individuals, but as a governance system that sustains everyone. Salmon is equated to medicine as sustenance of the soul; not as a drug that cures us, but as healing for the spirit.

Values

Sharing is clearly a value expressed in the previous story, but here is an example of this next theme that is perhaps more subtle:

> One night when my grandfather and I were fishing, he lost his trunk key. I think he locked it in the trunk, and we were supposed to cut the nose and fin off the fish, and the knife was in the trunk. And so we just put the fish in the sack and put them in the back seat and we were going to do it when we got home. But Dave Teskey was at the entrance to the bay when we were pulling out. And he stopped us to ask us how many we got, and he looked at them and said, why are they in the back seat? And we said, well, we locked the key in the trunk and the knife's in the trunk. And he said, oh, so they're not marked. And we said the knife's in the trunk and there's nobody else down here, eh. So he pulled them all out, and he marked them himself with his own knife and put them back in the sack and then sent us on our way. We had a pretty good relationship with him. (12 May 2011, Grand Chief Ken Malloway, Stó:lō)

So many stories are about generations of families fishing together and we cannot skip over the importance of hearing about the value of relationships within families, in communities, and with contacts outside the community, as in this encounter with a Department of Fisheries official. The meaning of this story, however, goes much deeper than valuing relationships between people; it evokes the disconnection between systems of governance where the colonialist government structure requires the fins of fish to be cut to prove that they are legally caught. Circumstances here depend on individual integrity and the character of people involved to see beyond the rule book. Implied in the story is that the result could have gone in a very different and negative direction as they all too often have.

Territorial descriptions

As in the story above, family relationships are touched on in this next story, but it goes further to describe in detail the waterways as geographic features of Pilalt territory, and how fishing is governed by family histories of fishing in particular places as the knowledge of those places is passed along from generation to generation.

> For our history, our tribe, in particular, the Pilalt Tribe, I think we believe a lot in kinship ties [and the relationship to] … the waterways that we used, prior to contact. We had a territory that sustained our lifestyle and so we go right from Hunter Creek, which is just in between Popkum and Hope, down just west of Chilliwack, which is the Halal Tribe and all through that area along the Fraser River. We have several fishing areas. Number one, we do our main fishing in Cheam, around the Cheam Beach and in that area from Jesperson Road to Hunter Creek … . We have family sites in Yale, as do other families from the Stó:lō territory. I also am fortunate that myself and my direct descendants have fishing areas up in Union Bar, which is just above the Hope Bridge. My husband is from the Union Bar Reserve. And other members of our family ever since I can remember have fished up there and I think Kat described it as the Alexandra Bridge. I call it Spuzzum. (13 December 2010, Councillor Quipp, Cheam)[5]

Values and waterways as territorial description were themes that we identified in this story. This next story uses these themes as well and speaks more specifically to the theme of environmental change.

Environmental change

Environmental changes prompted the enactment of the Cohen Commission Inquiry and came at a critical juncture, although Indigenous peoples had been pointing out environmental change for a long time already:

> As one of our elders up in Canim Lake said, "Salmon is our firstborn child." ... We're related to all living beings. And the problem is that we ought not to focus just on a particular species, but what we ought to be focusing on is the interconnectedness between the species, between us and the species, between the environment and the species that we're concerned with. That is traditional ecological knowledge. It's a life-lived experience through observation as well. We worked hard, for example, in trying to maintain the Deadman River where the farmers went in and cut down all the trees right up to the edge of the river ... .[What] that led to was the warming of the water, which harmed the fish. So we had to negotiate with the farmers, say, "Look, we want to try to—20 feet back we'll fence off the riverbank on each side and we'll re-vegetate it so that the vegetation could grow over and cool down, keep the water streams cool." And also, bears go in and eat the salmon and take it out and help fertilize the riverbanks and help maintain the vegetation over the stream banks, particularly the spawning grounds—a lot of places now have cabins and houses and the bears can't go over there and help re-vegetate and maintain a healthy habitat, ecosystems ... the clear-cut logging in the mountains has led to siltation of the spawning beds, which has caused serious harm. (14 December 2010; Dr. Ignace; Skeetchestn)

It was difficult to pick a single story to represent the environmental change theme such as the one from Mr. Alexis (Tl'azt'en) who tells how people used to talk about walking across the backs of the salmon to cross the river. We chose this one because in addition to describing change, it also relates those changes to the science of the water temperature and the ecosystem that includes the important role of the bears. This story also describes efforts that were made to work with neighbours, and to communicate to build relationships with neighbours for everyone's benefit.

Oral Histories Proven by Science

Science as a tool of confirmation is something that also became a theme of these stories, not only because science is what government decision-makers value but, as we demonstrate later in the third coding, because it is a way of celebrating Indigenous knowledge.

Archaeology plays a big part in supporting oral histories and the following two examples provide evidence about fishing sites, ecosystems, types of fish as food sources, use of an ocean economy, and habitation of the land:

> Our history goes back millennia. Couple of years ago, in one of our fishing sites on Stuart Lake, a historical fishing site that our people used to gather and to do the salmon fisheries, there was an archaeological dig there [at that time]. And they dated the artefacts there to be back to 12,000 years. So that's one of the areas that our people used to converge onto to do their traditional winter fisheries for salmon. The pictographs on the rock bluffs of Stuart Lake date back about 30,000 years. And the pictographs themselves depict the animals and the fish that we utilize throughout the systems in the Carrier—Carrier Nation territories. (14 December 2010, Mr. Alexis, Tl'azt'en Nation)

Within this story are also expressions of value in gathering to work together as community to harvest fish and record pictographs for communication.

Fishing/Harvesting Methods

Gathering to fish as a community is an important part of a method of harvesting, but many stories provided much greater detail about particular methods, how they related to particular sites, and how and why methods changed over the years to conform to colonial governance. In this story we also see how the value of sharing, respect, the importance of communication are all a part of the process of fishing:

> In my community, we have 150 community members that live on the reserve, and about that much off the reserve, because the size of the reserve is very small … . In the immediate area just below the reserve, you can throw a rock across the river. It's incredibly narrow. This gave excellent [place] to hold our salmon when we fished. [One time] we're having too much fun … . We had 250 salmon. You can only pack 15 to 20 up the hill at a time, and it is well over an hour to get up top. It is steep. It is a hard, hard climb. At that time, we were still using baskets with a head strap. So at nine years old, I was able to pack 20 salmon up that hill and do it five times a day … . My grandmother used to always tell me that there are certain times that we'd go fishing … she would wait until the mock orange blossoms came out on the trees, on the bushes, then she would say, "Now we're going to go fish spring salmon." I asked her, "How come? There's fish in the river right now. I see them when I walk down there. I can see them swimming by." She said it's because those fish belong to those people up there, respecting the northern tribes and those people that actually owned that fish. That was part of a universal sharing formula that was communicated between nations, respecting each other and the fish resource. (14 December 2010, Chief Sampson, Siska)

While this section has not provided an exhaustive explanation of every story or theme that we noted, we feel that the examples give a good snapshot of themes contained in the whole body of the stories. These themes provide a good grounding in what the Cohen Commission Inquiry wanted to learn about: communities, environmental changes, and fishing practices. However, we also felt that we did not have an adequate description of the purposes that Indigenous groups and individuals wanted to achieve by conveying these particular stories. Subsequently we reviewed all the stories with an emphasis on why groups and individuals chose particular stories and ways of telling those stories.

(De)coding for Purpose

To do a better job for looking at purpose through an Indigenous world view lens, we re-coded all the stories using Dr. Linda Tuhiwai-Smith's (1999) work on Indigenous methodologies (Appendix A). We found that five of Tuhiwai-Smith's projects (testimonies, storytelling, representing, protecting, and negotiating) encompassed all the stories within the broad context of the hearings themselves. Participation by Indigenous groups and individuals in presenting to the Cohen Commission embodied these processes. Presentations were *testimonies* that used forms of *storytelling*. All submissions were *representing* the voice of Indigenous communities to a decision-making body. Participating in the hearings also involved *negotiating* in that storytelling in testimonies acted strategically towards long-term survival. These stories can also be seen as acts of *protecting* because the overall goal of telling these stories was not only to protect the salmon, but life itself. The central teaching of the Stó:lō snowoyelh (laws), "S'ólh Téméxw te íkw'élò. Xólhmet te mekw'stám ít kwelát. This is our land. We have to look after everything that belongs to us" (Stó:lō Heritage, 2013, p. 1) reinforces that salmon are not just a natural resource, but integral to sustaining communities, customs and beliefs, art and ideals, and sacred sites.

In addition to the five contextual purposes, we identified eleven more of the projects (Indigenous community objectives for participating) that were directly represented through the stories: claiming, celebrating, remembering, Indigenist processes, intervening, connecting, envisioning, reframing, Indigenist governance, naming, and discovering the beauty of Indigenous knowledge. Again, while we only provide one example of a story related to each project here, the stories often encompass several projects.

We did not locate Tuhiwai-Smith's remaining nine projects in the overall context or in the particular stories told; these projects were not within the scope of these particular hearings (revitalizing/regenerating, reading, writing/theory making, gendering, restoring, returning, networking, sharing, and creating). For example, the purpose of stories was passing on knowledge outside of Indigenous communities, not within their own networks; and while Indigenous language was used in the stories, the purpose for including language was not primarily to increase language survival.

Following are each of the purposes we identified and a story that demonstrates that purpose.

Claiming: histories making assertions about rights and dues (to tribunals, courts, and governments about territories and resources, or about past injustices). In this example Larry Grant asserts a right to maintain a thriving, long-established culture based on the generosity, wealth, and economic relationship that his Musqueam ancestors enjoyed and shared at the time they welcomed Europeans to their shores.

> [The Musqueam people] were here to greet the Spanish Captain Narvaez and the English Captain Vancouver to be greeted to this territory when they first came. As my ancestors did, I also want to raise my hands in welcome to everyone here today at this Commission hearing. They greeted the strangers on those ships and many of them brought fish forward, fish to give, fish to trade. It was a major, major part of our culture. And we are the people that have lived on this delta, which is now called Metro Vancouver, for 9,000 years and have lived in Musqueam continuously for 4,000 years; … for the 9,000 years up until colonization it sustained us, it sustained our culture. And with the introduction of colonization and industrial fisheries it's been depleted in a short century. Industrial issues, it's not really what it's about for us because 85 percent of our diet prior to colonization was salmon or other fish product and today we are lucky if we can get one salmon for the whole year per capita. If the salmon disappear our culture disappears in that—a big portion of our culture disappears. (15 June 2010, Larry Grant, Musqueam)

Celebrating: accentuates the degree to which Indigenous peoples and communities have retained cultural and spiritual values and authentically resisted colonialism. Here Rod Naknakim reminds the Commission of Inquiry that despite the injustice of having cultural practices outlawed by an invading government, the culture is still strong and sustaining practices are intact.

> We, despite the potlatch being prohibited and outlawed, until '72 we still potlatched right through, my grandfather on my father's side particularly. He used to have—he used to have big speakers outside his house. He had a big house, and he'd have hymns playing, but inside he'd be potlatching with the elders. And we've been able to keep this alive amongst our people. But there always is salmon part of the potlatch, you know, to feed. But more than that, there's songs. My brother's wife is a twin, and she—she owns a salmon dance with her twin sister. Because that's what we do is, you know, give that to the twins. (15 December 2010, Rod Naknakim, Laich-Kwil-Tach Treaty Society)

Remembering: connecting bodies with place and experience of a painful past and people's responses to that pain. This story from Chief Sampson lays out in detail the devastating and continuing impact of colonial practices on communities.

> Sitting down at the river with my grandfather before he passed away and he talked about Nlha7apmx people and he talked about what he remembers and what he was told by his grandparents of the past. For example, even right in my area, there's the Siska Indian Band, there's the Skuppah Indian Band, and there's the Kanaka Indian Band, but prior to that, it was just the Skuppah. But because they—at least this is the way he understood it … because they were a powerful group and they controlled such a productive piece of the river, that it was then easier for the department to split that community into three and create three communities with three sub-chiefs that would then play a part in the divide and conquer, where they would segregate the communities

into numbers, this band being bigger than this other band, and they getting more resources through the Department of Indian Affairs, further to fragment the nation. (14 December 2010, Chief Sampson, Siska)

Indigenist processes: privileging of Indigenous voices that counters negative connotations such as primitive, backward, and superstitious. As did Larry Grant, President Guujaw confirms and emphasizes that a well-organized system of commerce has always been a way in which communities thrived from the salmon.

> Commerce is an ancient thing on the coast. It isn't something that started up with fishing licenses. Our people fished and traded and did all those things for thousands of thousands of years amongst the different nations and amongst ourselves. There's people who specialize in different kind of fishing and people who provided for other people with other—that had other things to trade, and it's just normal course of events that commercial fishing would be a way that our people would make a livelihood. (15 December 2010, President Guujaw, Haida Nation)

Intervening: the process of being proactive and of becoming involved as an interested worker for change. In addition to reiterating intimate knowledge of the patterns of the salmon, Rod Naknakim tells how Indigenous communities and individuals have not been complacent in working to manage fishing practices, but have been highly involved in wanting commercial management to be done right.

> [My grandfather] tells me the story when him and Tommy Hunt went to see B.C. Packers and to shut down the herring industry, and it did get shut down for 20 years, because they were fishing it out. And with the help of the company, they were able to persuade DFO to do that. Then in I think it was '80s, when we put the ribbon boundary in, in Johnstone Strait. They wanted to close us down, but we convinced DFO

we can stay open and still fish if we marked off certain areas in Johnstone Strait that we wouldn't fish in. We still don't fish there today, and we're the ones that initiated that effort … it's not the easiest place to fish because of the strength of the tide … you could lose your net, if you fish in the wrong place or the wrong stage of the tide. And the timing of the set is all the difference in the world on whether you're going to get any fish at all. My grandfather always amazed me on how well he knew the water, and when the fish were coming and how many … . And our guys, they got to know which run was which just by looking at the fish, the size generally, and sometimes the spots. But what my grandfather was famous for was predicting the size of the run coming in. And he'd often get into fights with DFO. He'd be in their office telling them to open it, there's a big run coming, and quite often he was right. That amazed me. (15 December 2010, RodNaknakim, Laich-Kwil-Tach Treaty Society)

Connecting: linking people to each other, to lands and their place in the universe as related to issues of identity and place, to spiritual relationships and community well-being. The story told here by Dr. Ignace is rich in all the purposes expressed in this project. The relationships of individuals are not given merely as protocol, but as a way of connecting responsibilities to community; to having been asked to witness; to knowing where you come from; and acknowledging those who are keepers of the history.

My mother's mother was Meléni Paul and she's from Kamloops. And her husband is the son of Chief Edward Eneas. And Chief Edward Eneas' wife was Sulyen, who was also a medicine woman. She was a medicine woman—the daughter of a medicine woman, Miliminetka (phonetic), meaning medicine water. As well as that, she had a brother and an uncle, Jimmy Antoine (phonetic), who was chief, and Joe Tomah, who was also a chief. And Joe Tomah was one of the chiefs among our Nations here that met with Sir Wilfred Laurier in 1910 … and we made an offer to Canada back then, back then in 1910. They told it and we still abide by that Sir Wilfred Laurier memorial. They entered into our homeland and became guests, although uninvited guests in our house, that they wished to be brothers with us. And as such, that we were prepared to offer up to Canada half of our homeland, land, water, timber, everything. What is ours will be yours and what's yours will be ours. But there was a provision in it—a relational provision in it that we must help each other to be great and good. (14 December 2010, Dr. Ignace, Skeetchestn)

Envisioning: using strategies that ask Indigenous peoples to imagine a future where they rise above present-day oppression and recognize the power that Indigenous peoples have to change their own lives and set new directions. In telling this story, B. Gaertner demonstrates that Indigenous peoples do imagine a better future for the generations to come and one that includes a return of the salmon. They also know what it will take.

Another story that I hear often at the meetings on the Fraser River of the Indigenous women who are representing the upper reaches of the Fraser River who have for centuries relied on what are called the early Stuarts salmon and they come to the meetings now and want to make sure that we all know that there aren't fish for their families, there aren't fish to can, there aren't fish to dry, and there aren't fish to freeze. It's a difficult picture to imagine those differences and it's difficult to imagine Elders who are not having salmon to get through the winters and what that means when they contemplate their children and their grandchildren in this watershed. Finally, I want to end with the teaching from an Elder and I think that this should inspire our work also, and that is that the salmon will not return in abundance, she told me. Remember, the salmon will not return in abundance until human beings stop fighting and arguing about them. (16 June 2010, B. Gaertner, First Nations Coalition)

Reframing: taking greater control over the ways in which Indigenous issues and social problems are discussed and handled and what it means to be Indigenous (e.g., asset rather than deficit). Chief Charlie reframes the activities of seasonal economies and accompanying ways of life from something not good enough, to one that is healthy, uplifting, a contribution to community, and a necessity.

> I'm a fisherman. I've been fishing most of my life, since I can remember. I go out on the water and it—the actual practice of fishing—is a medicine. So for me to go out on the water it's medicine. If anyone—if anyone—if you have different gifts or different hobbies or different things that you're good at, and when you do —the reason why you have that hobby, whatever you're good at, you do that because it's peace of mind. It's medicine for you. It's a way to clear your mind, clear your spirit. And you do that and you make things with your hands. For fishermen, it's the same thing. Hunters, they describe it in a similar way. People that play sports do all these different things the same way. That's the same thing for fishermen. (13 December 2010, Chief Charlie, Chehalis)

Indigenist governance: process of extending participation outwards through reinstating Indigenous principles of collectivity, public debate, and value systems geared to meet contemporary social challenges without imposing particular types of governmental systems based in colonialist practices. Chief Charlie's story, here, continues in reinforcing the reframing above and extends to explaining orally and culturally transmitted laws that direct how the people should live without the devastating effects of imposing a system from outside.

> Going back to the kind of traditional laws of our peoples, what we call snowoyelh, everyone is born with a different gift … . My Uncle Buster said, "You're born with a gift. Everybody's born with a gift. That gift becomes your job. That gift becomes your place in your community." And so if you

were the hunter and you went out hunting and you provided meat for those in your village and your community, and maybe you weren't the fisherman. So when it was the fisherman's turn to go out and catch fish, he brought you fish. Maybe he was gifted at working with his hands and working the cedar, working with wood. In exchange, they would share with each other their different gifts for survival. Same with spiritual people. A spiritual person might not have the time, energy, or whatever, to go out and to hunt or to fish or to work with their hands. And so if I go and look for help from a shxwlem, a way of thanking that person for carrying their gift in a good way, I'll bring them something that I do. So I'm a fisherman. I'm going to bring them canned fish, I'm going to bring them smoked fish. I'm going to bring them whatever I have as a way of thanking them for the gift that I've been blessed with, thanking them for their gift in looking after me. And so, yeah, those traditional laws, our social laws, need to be our social laws. (13 December 2010, Chief Charlie, Chehalis)

Naming: restoring the world by using the original Indigenous names for the landscape, as well as in the naming of individuals so that the histories are carried in the names. Place names are certainly not a mandate of the Cohen Inquiry, but the details and naming given here by Grand Chief Terry relay not only an expectation that places will be known by the names used in Indigenous communities, but explain that communities know their territory, the landscapes that are their responsibilities to look after.

The Bridge River is in the northern sector of the St'at'imc country, and above us would be the Pavilion people. That would be the northernmost reaches of the St'at'imc or up in and through into the northern territory then of the Secwepemc ... . There are seven communities that are directly located in and around the area of our community, and I think that the Xaxli'p or the Fountain people are across the river from us on the Fraser. Just south of us would be the people we call the Tit'q'et or the Lillooet, and also Sekw'el'wás or Cayoose. Over the—over the mountain is Lake—Seton Lake, and there is the Seton people that live in that area. (14 December 2010, Grand Chief Terry, St'at'imx)

Discovering the beauty of Indigenous knowledge: uncovering Indigenous knowledge systems alongside Western science and technology to work for Indigenous development that recognizes values related to ethics, relationships, wellness, and leading a good life. The detail of this story explains very clearly how a particular fishing practice, based in a particular Indigenous knowledge system, has worked for a very long time to manage the fishery throughout numerous communities.

> Our people had the special person with a special gift that knew the dialects of the people along the river and communicated. They call this person the messenger or the natanayani (phonetic) in our language. And these people communicate to see the conditions of the runs and to see if there's abundance or not. And once a decision is made to fish based on the abundance, the hereditary system kicks in. Our hereditary chiefs from the different clans; in our territory we have four different clans: the Lusilyoo, the Lhts'umusyoo, the Granton, and the Lohjeboo. They call all our head chiefs and these are the people that decide whether there's going to be fisheries or not. (14 December 2010, Chief Thomas Alexis, Tl'azt'en Nation)

Looking for themes was an important step in mentally sorting through these stories, but the eleven projects we identified from Tuhiwai-Smith's work helped us to look and listen more closely from an Indigenous world view, and led us to a place where we could start to answer our third research question about the impact of Indigenous storytelling on the final recommendations of the Commission.

Stories and the Final Recommendations

Chapter 2 of Volume 3 of the final Cohen Commission Inquiry report (Recommendations, 2012) contains 75 recommendations for changes to protect and revive the health of the river and the Sockeye salmon fishery. We firstly sorted the recommendations by inclusion of the terms First Nation(s) and Aboriginal. These are the terms that Judge Cohen used to distinguish these stakeholders from other parties giving testimony. Twelve out of the 75 recommendations include the term First Nations or include extensive discussion referring to the terms First Nations/Aboriginal. The term First Nations is used distinctively in the report from "stakeholders," i.e., as First Nations and stakeholders.

In the next section, we focus on the twelve recommendations that contain lengthy discussions of First Nation fisheries and connect them to five overall aspects of the report:

- authority for oversight (Recommendations 1, 39, and 63)[6]

- salmon farming vs. wild salmon (Recommendations 7 and 16)

- fish data and economic impact (Recommendations 25, 31, and 35)

- economic and socio-economic impacts (Recommendations 36, 37, and 38)

- conservation and fishing practices (Recommendations 39 and 40)

Drawing from the report, we define these aspects in the following ways. *Authority for oversight* speaks to who has the responsibility to protect Canada's fisheries resource. Second, while *salmon farming* refers to the commercial enterprise of growing salmon outside of their natural environment, *wild salmon* is about the natural cyclical process of salmon returning from the ocean to rivers and streams where they were spawned. *Fish data* involves statistics and counting of salmon for tracking and predictive planning. *Economic and socio-economic impact* is about the integral effect of salmon on culture, communities, and livelihoods and, lastly, *conservation and fishing practice* looks to the past, the present, and the future of sustaining and improving salmon populations with the capacity to harvest for a variety of purposes.

Authority for Oversight

In his discussion of the recommendation, Judge Cohen refers to already-established policies and related reports. In relation to authority for oversight of the salmon fishery, he does not diverge from seeing the Canadian government and specifically the Minister of Fisheries and Oceans as having ultimate decision-making power. However, regarding conservation of Fraser River Sockeye specifically, he states that the British Columbia government must be involved. Judge Cohen acknowledges that "aboriginal fisheries organizations expressed a desire to participate in the management of the fishery at the highest levels" (p. 8) but wanted/needed to build more technical capacity.

Judge Cohen emphasizes that despite ultimate authority being with the federal ministry, First Nations communities must continue to play a "pivotal role" (p. 8) because of important contributions and perspectives they bring. He specifically recognizes that there are "constitutionally protected Aboriginal and treaty rights" (p. 9) with unique priorities, but also highlights that conservation is the responsibility of the government and not that of Aboriginal or non-Aboriginal users. The discussion also notes that many existing policies and practices have created an expectation for shared management authority and many Aboriginal groups assert a right to manage the fishery. In light of his reassertion of the government's right as the ultimate decision-making body, Judge Cohen ends the discussion by "strongly encourag[ing] consultation, co-operation, and collaboration" (p. 10) with First Nations.

Farmed Salmon vs. Wild Salmon

As in the authority for oversight section, Judge Cohen refers to existing policies regarding both salmon farms and oversight of wild salmon issues. Most of the discussion regarding fish farms and the connection to First Nations is prefaced by recommendation #3 that fish farms should not be part of the mandate of DFO but rather regulated as an industry and as a product. However, Judge Cohen then discusses more extensively the implementation of the Wild Salmon Policy and affirms that First Nations should have input into siting of those farms in recommendation #16, because current policy did not take into account conflicts with wild salmon migration routes.

Further, in the Wild Salmon Policy, Cohen expresses no confidence that implementation will be successful unless the funding model changes and is directed towards an "integrated strategic planning process" (p. 14) that provides for input from, and funding for First Nations in regards to involvement in management processes. The collaboration within this integrated planning process, Cohen notes, is in addition to the constitutionally mandated duty to consult First Nations. Also, essential to the planning process, as Cohen describes it, is decision-making transparency through "annual public implementation progress reports" (p. 15). He emphasizes that this transparency is particularly important for providing a basis for the decision when input from stakeholders and First Nations is not incorporated into final decisions.

Fish Data and Economic Impact

First Nations' involvement in numerical counts of fish is primarily discussed by Cohen in relation to selective fishing (avoiding non-targeted fish and releasing those that are caught unharmed), fishery monitoring (including catch reporting), and stock assessment (population dynamics and forecasting). Cohen received qualitative catch assessments from DFO testimony that indicated reports from First Nations fisheries as being good and fairly reliable with 90% of the catch accounted for, while commercial and recreational catch estimates were fair and reliability medium to good.

Cohen's recommendations regarding both selective fishing and catch assessments were that count systems should be enhanced for accuracy with more specific statistical measures and, in addition, that commercial and Aboriginal economic opportunity fishers should contribute equally to the "cost of catch monitoring, subject to any accommodation required in support of an exercise of an Aboriginal right" (p. 36). The recommendations also included language about enforcing penalties for non-compliance and for reporting illegal harvest counts that, from the discussion, were aimed primarily at the commercial fishery.

In regards to stock assessment, Cohen notes in the final paragraph of the discussion portion that "because escapement enumeration and other stock assessment activities require hands-on participation and occur in the traditional territories of many First Nations that have a historical connection to the Fraser River sockeye salmon fishery, I support the suggestion that DFO encourage the involvement of members of such First Nations in these activities" (p. 37), in particular with counting adult salmon that make it past the fishery to their spawning grounds. Both access to fish quantity as well as the time labour of count involvement have economic as well as socio-economic impacts.

Socio-Economic Impacts

In addition to Recommendation #35 regarding monitoring, as noted above, three recommendations, numbered 36–38, are even more specific to the connection between economic and socio-economic impacts. These areas of impact are related to not only food but also sustaining/reclaiming culture.

According to Cohen's summary, "Food, Social, Ceremonial" (FSC) fishing had historically been operationalized by DFO, in light of no specific legal or operational definition, as priority access allocation to Fraser River sockeye salmon (after conservation). At the time of the report, Cohen notes from testimony heard that DFO considered "group's population, recent FSC harvests, harvest preferences, and availability of fish species in the area," while First Nation testimony stated the considerations as being "preference in fish species, the breadth of species available, access of other First Nations to the species, and the status of fish resources" (p. 38).

Cohen summarizes that when no agreement on the quantity and conditions could be reached, "the FSC allocation was determined by DFO." He closes the discussion with a statement that in his view, it is "important that First Nations actively assist DFO in reaching appropriate FSC allocations by providing DFO with information on the unique aspects of their culture that are relevant in deterring their FSC needs." Recommendations in relation to FSC include DFO coming to a better definition of FSC and negotiating agreements with specific First Nations by encouraging them to provide information on practices, customs, and tradition relevant to sockeye salmon use.

The third recommendation related to socio-economic impacts looked at the move away from the catch as much as you can to the assigned catch share system and the desire of DFO to further this "share-based management" for the commercial fishery. The assigned shares could be either individual quotas (IQ) or individual transferable quotas (ITQ), but the testimony from First Nation submissions that Cohen cites indicates

> expressed concern about moving to an ITQ system for salmon fisheries because they say the move to ITQ in other fisheries had led to permanent change without adequate consultation or consideration of First Nations' rights and interests. They want to discuss overall allocation policy before DFO makes decisions on share-based management. (p. 39)

The recommendation on this point sets a timeline (approx. one year) for DFO to complete its analysis of socio-economic implications for implementing various models, to decide which was preferable, and to implement that model.

Conservation and Fishing Practices

Conservation of both salmon and salmon habitat, and sustainability of the fishery, were the major impetus for the formation of the Commission. The final two recommendations we highlight here that include discussion of First Nations testimony are numbers 39 and 40. The first asks DFO "to conduct the research and analysis necessary to determine whether in-river demonstration fisheries are, or are capable of, achieving tangible conservation benefits or providing economic benefits to First Nations in an economically viable or sustainable way" (p. 41). The second determines that DFO should "should develop its future policies and practices on the reallocation of the commercial Fraser River sockeye salmon fishery (including allocations for marine and in-river fisheries) in an inclusive and transparent manner, following a strategic and integrated planning process" (p. 43).

These two recommendations are tied together in that testimony given by First Nations regarding in-river demonstration fisheries (allocating fish for economic/commercial purposes to First Nations farther upstream), since they provide "employment, training, and economic opportunities that may not otherwise be available ... opportunities to those who are often the poorest of the poor" (p. 41). At the same time Cohen notes that he has doubts that these fisheries meet the objective of DFO "to address conservation concerns associated with marine mixed-stock fisheries and to provide economic benefits to First Nations" (p. 40).

In this section, we have been able to provide only a snapshot of the recommendations in which First Nations interests are specifically named or where First Nations were a large part of the discussion leading to the recommendation. This information underpins, in the following section, the discussion of our third research question regarding whether the stories told by Indigenous participants are evident in the final recommendations.

Discussion

Answering the first of our research questions was a relatively simple task as we began to read the Cohen Commission transcripts. Yes, stories were used and by many participants. Forty presenters representing Indigenous groups used stories in a total of 88 out of 125 oral submissions.

The next question about type of story was also relatively easy to answer by using Stó:lō story types as the framework. The dominant type of story used related to personal, family, and community histories. However, stories from long ago were evoked in special circumstances during formalities of introduction at the beginning of the hearings (the gift of salmon from the creator), and to place stories of the salmon within various territories represented at the hearings. These tellings reinforced the extent to which First Nations in the entire Fraser Valley eco-system honoured the role of the salmon in their world views.

To answer our question as to why particular stories were told, we (de) coded all the stories twice. First, we looked at the six themes we discussed in this paper: the importance of salmon, cultural values, territorial descriptions, environmental change, oral histories confirmed by science, and fishing practices. Second, we found eleven of Tuhiwai-Smith's projects reflected in the stories the presenters chose to convey: claiming, celebrating, remembering, Indigenist processes, intervening, connecting, envisioning, reframing, Indigenist governance, naming, and discovering the beauty of Indigenous knowledge.

As to whether or how the told stories connected to the final recommendations of the report, we first note that underlying the use of the term First Nation(s) throughout the final recommendations is a recognition by the Commission that First Nations are distinct from any other type of contributor to the hearings. This certainly reflects the stories told as they are distinctive in their content and from their defining of place that is particular to the territories of the First Nations presenters. In this way, Judge Cohen also recognizes the importance placed on salmon.

However, one information-conveying practice throughout the recommendations is that the term *First Nations* is almost always paired with those who are referred to as stakeholders (26/38 times in the first 30 recommendation discussions), which ultimately detracts from recognizing the distinct and cultural importance of First Nations. This pairing negates story purposes such as claiming, celebrating, connecting, and naming.

To better illustrate how the importance of the distinction is lost when First Nations is always paired with the term stakeholders, we can look to the Salmon origin stories that were shared. For example, when Chief Charlie from Sts'ailes starts the story with the words "in the beginning of time when the world was first created" this is not a mere storytelling device, but the statement that when the fish cease to exist, the people also cease to exist. Commissioner Cohen, however, in persistently pairing First Nations and stakeholders in the recommendations has not identified the salmon as anything other than an economic tool, as it is with any other stakeholder. Chief Charlie conveys from the story that "There was an agreement in time that all our relations, all living things, they would give themselves to us as humans because we were the weakest. They would give themselves for food, shelter, clothing, utensils and for medicine." These are not economic tools but rather life itself.

Additionally, the recommendations do not generally distinguish between individual First Nations and how their interests may be different in different territories. For example, recommendation #36 states, "Following consultation with First Nations, the Department of Fisheries and Oceans should articulate a [singular] clear working definition for food, social, and ceremonial (FSC) fishing," but then does ask in recommendation #37 to "encourage the [individual] First Nation to provide DFO with information on its practices, customs, and traditions that is relevant in determining its food, social, and ceremonial needs." There is a tension between these two recommendations that does not get away from seeing economic gain and cultural reliance as the same thing. When we look to the example from Siska Chief Sampson, who told the Commissioner how "My grandmother used to always tell me that there are certain times that we'd go fishing … she would wait until the mock orange blossoms came out on the trees, on the bushes … I asked her, 'How come? There's fish in the river right now … ' She said those fish were for other people upriver," we recognize that this was part of a sharing formula that respected both humans and fish. There are relationships and responsibilities that are hard to contain in a single definition or a fish count.

The importance of relationships among First Nations, within communities, in families, and even with DFO officers or the B.C. Packers is evident in the stories, as for example the stories of Rod Naknakim and Ken Malloway that tell about sharing salmon runs and consulting together about when to fish. These stories of relationship are reinforced in Cohen's discussion of the fish count accuracy being better from First Nations fishers, but subsequently ignored in Recommendation #31, which states that both commercial and Aboriginal economic opportunity fishers should contribute equally to the "cost of catch monitoring." The stories were consistent with other evidence that demonstrated a differing cultural world view, including value placed on responsibility to care for the salmon, but this was not reflected in the recommendation.

Finally, we add here comments about the language Commissioner Cohen used in describing First Nations' involvement in future directions of the fishery as not fully recognizing the possible purposes of the stories told. For example, in the discussion of Recommendation #1, he uses the words "expressed a desire to participate in the management of the fishery," when story after story told of centuries of Indigenous peoples paying attention to management of the fishery, and goes on to say they "ought" to, rather than must, play a pivotal role (p. 8). He also states that it is not within the Commission's mandate to "assess the merits of such claims" (p. 10), but that he "encourages" consultation, co-operation, and collaboration by DFO, without suggesting whose mandate it might be to determine a right to management. All of these instances show a consistent use of grammatical qualifiers: words or phrases that, in these cases, decrease the impact of what is being expressed. Other examples of qualifying language were found in repeated calls for creating process that provide for "input" (p. 14, p. 22), "inviting response" (p. 15), "may have … an obligation to consult" (p. 16), and "encourage the involvement" (p. 37) of, from, and with First Nations. This language reflects making opportunities for consultation, but not for cooperation, a future that was envisioned in the story offered by an Elder and conveyed by B. Gaertner.

Conclusion and Implications

In attempting to connect the findings here to the task of responding to the calls to action of the Truth and Reconciliation Commission, we reflect on what Senator Murray Sinclair (the chair of that Commission) said in noting that reconciliation will only happen if Canadians, as a country, agree to and are committed to the project in all sectors of society. The calls to action ask Canadians to promote public dialogue, public/private partnerships, and public initiatives for reconciliation and engage in mean-ingful consultation, building respectful relationships, and obtaining the free, prior, and informed consent of Indigenous peoples before proceeding with projects. This means being fully engaged in a respectful communi-cation relationship.

Meeting the Commission's calls to action will only be possible if the people of Canada are communicating in ways that are understandable for each other. For non-Indigenous Canadians, this means listening more and listening in different ways than in the past. Listening in different ways to stories of Indigenous peoples' experiences with the systems of child welfare, education, health, justice, and other public services. Listening in different ways to stories about the importance of First Nation languages and culture. And listening differently to stories that express the values that are the lifeblood for Indigenous communities when engaging in business.

Stories form a vital part of public dialogue; they are used to both pro-vide information and accomplish specific purposes on behalf of Indigenous communities that reclaim culture and reframe negative views that contrib-ute to the oppression that Indigenous peoples experience. Such purposes demonstrate the strength, values, and knowledge that will contribute to the revival and resurgence of the salmon. One immediate implication that ties the stories to the Cohen Commission Inquiry recommendations is that those who testified have already given the requested "information on [First Nation] practices, customs, and traditions that [are] relevant in determining ... food, social, and ceremonial needs" and have provided the basis for "a [singular] clear working definition for food, social, and ceremonial (FSC) fishing." The stories are here. How many times do they need to be told? It is the hearing that needs to change.

This project has potential for application across a broad spectrum of contexts. Knowledge about public participation and social inclusion among dominant and co-culture groups (i.e., First Nations in the Fraser Valley) can be used to have a positive impact on communities where Indigenous groups have not been heard or consulted by the newcomers in their territories. Tuhiwai-Smith's projects are just one way to start thinking about a new way of listening.

The five recommendation themes we chose to explore in this chapter were those most directly related to the spirit of the People of the River, the salmon. These themes about the use and importance of salmon, values that guide interaction, the prominence of waterways in territorial description, stark stories demonstrating environmental change, the pride of telling how oral histories have been confirmed by science, and the array of and changes to fishing methods start to provide a wholistic picture of lives and communities. The stories that talk about fishing methods, and the resulting changes and impacts on practices, could be a future project itself. The stories that we included in this work only introduce the possibilities for learning how to listen to stories in a public dialogue context.

Linda Tuhiwai-Smith did not develop her list of twenty-five projects as an analysis tool, but we are grateful for her list because of its contribution to helping us understand something about the purposes of using particular stories at the Cohen Commission Inquiry. Presenters had relatively little time to convey thoughts and feelings about something so vital to the survival of their cultures, and they chose to tell these particular stories. We can hear these stories as demanding social justice rather than conveying historical and cultural information.

To echo the words of Thomson Highway's fictional character Isabel Thompson, yes, it is possible to "come along, bend over, pick up a river, and carry it off into the distance away over yonder as if it were a sack of potatoes." Listen to the stories of cultures different from your own with a different ear.

NOTES

1   In this paper we primarily use the term Indigenous when referring to individuals and communities who inhabited the land before colonizers invaded it. Other terms such as First Nation, Métis, Aboriginal, Native, and Indian are used when found in source materials or when government documents refer to them as legal designations.

2   As we engaged in our analysis of stories, we came to recognize that the use of the academic and methodological term "coding" forced us into a non-Indigenous world view of creating non-fluid/binary categories within which to place our understanding of stories. We explored other ways of being able to talk about the process from a more Indigenous world view and decided to work from a definition of communication that highlights all communication as already "coding" cultural meaning. Therefore, this spurred us to think about what we were attempting was rather a "decoding" of the meaning of oral histories within an Indigenous context.

3   When using stories from the transcripts in this paper, our goal was to keep the words true to the way they had been originally transcribed. We did, however, correct spelling of names and words from Indigenous languages that were recorded phonetically in the transcript whenever we could.

4   The researchers acknowledge that we may have missed some speakers/stories due to the extensive number of transcripts we analyzed.

5   While this is a beautiful description of colonial place names that define the territory, Councillor Quipp takes time to *name* her fishing place—something that comes up in the coding of the 25 projects.

6   Numbers associated with particular recommendations (Appendix B)

REFERENCES

Abel, K. M. (1993). *Drum songs: glimpses of Dene history*. McGill-Queen's University Press.

Archibald, J. (2008). *Indigenous storywork: educating the heart, mind, body, and spirit.* UBC Press.

Armstrong, J. C., & William, G. (2015). *River of salmon peoples*. Theytus.

Basso, K. (1996). *Wisdom sits in places: Landscape and language among the Western Apache*. University of New Mexico Press.

Bormann, E. G. (1972). Fantasy and rhetorical vision: The rhetorical criticism of social reality. *Quarterly Journal of Speech, 58*, 396–407.

Bourdieu, P. (1991). *Language and symbolic power* (J.B. Thompson, Intro/ed.; G. Raymond & M. Adamson, Transl.). Harvard University Press. (Original published in 1982).

Buber, M. (1972). Between man and man. Macmillan.

Burke, K. (1966). *Language as symbolic action: Essays on life, literature, and method.* University of California Press.

Cajete, G. (1994). *Look to the mountain: An ecology of Indigenous education.* Kivaki Press.

Calls to Action. (2015). *Truth and Reconciliation Commission of Canada.* Retrieved June 27, 2017, from http://www.trc.ca/websites/trcinstitution/File/2015/Findings/Calls_to_Action_English2.pdf

Canada's residential schools: The history, Part 1, Origins to 1939. (2015). McGill-Queen's University Press. Retrieved June 27, 2017, from http://www.myrobust.com/websites/trcinstitution/File/Reports/Volume_1_History_Part_1_English_Web.pdf

Cardinal, T. (2004). *Our story: Aboriginal voices on Canada's past.* Doubleday Canada.

Clarkson, M. (2012). Speaking for sockeye, speaking for themselves: First Nations engagement in the Cohen Commission (2009–2012) [Unpublished master's thesis]. University of British Columbia.

Cohen Commission of Inquiry Final Report. (2012). Public Works and Government Services Canada. Retrieved June 27, 2017, from http://epe.lac-bac.gc.ca/100/206/301/pco-bcp/commissions/cohen/cohen_commission/LOCALHOS/EN/FINALREPORT/INDEX.HTM

Crow, D., & Jones, M. (2018). Narratives as tools for influencing policy change. *Policy & Politics, 46*(2), 217–234.

Cruikshank, J. (1987). Myth and tradition as narrative framework: Oral histories from Northern Canada. *International Journal of Oral History, 9*(3), 198–214.

Deloria, V. (1999). *Spirit & reason: The Vine Deloria, Jr., reader.* Fulcrum Publishers.

Fischer, W. R. (1985). *Homo narrans* the narrative paradigm: In the beginning. *Journal of Communication, 35*(4), 74–89.

Fraser River Discovery Centre. (2014, September 19). Hiqw Stó:lō - The Big River [video recording]. Retrieved June 26, 2017, from https://vimeo.com/106639607

Gleeson, R. (2019, August 6). *N.W.T. fisher says government is too controlling.* Retrieved August 6, 2019, from https://www.cbc.ca/news/canada/north/nwt-fishers-say-government-too-controlling-1.5233952

Goulet, J.-G. (1998). *Ways of knowing: experience, knowledge, and power among the Dene Tha.* University of Nebraska Press.

Hardman, S. S. S. (2015). From the other side: A mother's story. In L. E. Eastman & L. Ellis (Eds.), *First lady nation: Stories by Aboriginal women*: Vol. III (pp. 179–190). Professional Woman Publishing.

Hardman, S. S. S. (2016). Who told you I was bleep bleep Indian? In L. E. Eastman & L. Ellis (Eds.), *First lady nation: Stories by Aboriginal women*: Vol. IV (pp. 145–153). Professional Woman Publishing.

Harvey, M. (2009). *Speaking in S'ólh Téméxw: Language dynamics in Stó:lō approaches to the BC treaty process.* University of Victoria Ethnohistory Field School.

Honouring the truth, reconciling for the future: Summary of the final report of the Truth and Reconciliation Commission of Canada. (2015). Truth and Reconciliation

Commission of Canada. Retrieved June 27, 2017, from http://www.trc.ca/websites/ trcinstitution/File/2015/Honouring_the_Truth_Reconciling_for_the_Future_ July_23_2015.pdf

King, T. (2003). *The truth about stories.* University of Minnesota Press.

LaFever, M. (2008). Communication for public decision-making in a negative historical context: Building intercultural relationships in the British Columbia treaty process. *Journal of International & Intercultural Communication, 1*(2), 158–180.

LaFever, M. (2011). Empowering Native Americans: Communication, planning, and dialogue for eco-tourism in Gallup, New Mexico. *Journal of International and Intercultural Communication, 4*(2), 127–145.

Mackenzie Valley Pipeline Inquiry (Canada). (1977). *Northern frontier, northern homeland: The report of the Mackenzie Valley Pipeline Inquiry/Mr. Justice Thomas R. Berger* (Vol. 2). Printing and Publishing Supply and Services Canada.

Mendoza, S. L., & Kinefuchi, E. (2016). Two stories, one vision: A plea for an ecological turn in intercultural communication. *Journal of International and Intercultural Communication 9*(4), 275–294.

Miller, R. J. (2011). The International law of colonialism: A comparative analysis. *Lewis & Clark Law Review, 15*(4), 847–922.

Moore, Angel. (2019, August 5). *Muskrat Falls land protectors take one last shot to stop flooding of reservoir.* Retrieved August 6, 2019, from https://aptnnews. ca/2019/08/05/muskrat-falls-land-protectors-take-one-last-shot-to-stop-flooding-of-reservoir/

Participants granted standing, Cohen Commission. (2010). Interim report. Retrieved June 9, 2021 from http://www.watershedwatch.ca/wp-content/uploads/2012/07/ CohenCommissionInterimReportFull-Oct2010.pdf

Scott, P. (2012). *Talking tools: Faces of aboriginal oral tradition in contemporary society.* CCI Press.

Smith, P. (Ed.). (1995). *Favorite North American Indian legends.* Dover.

Stó:lō Heritage Policy Manual. (2003). Stó:lō Nation Lalems ye Stó:lō Si:ya:m (LYSS). Retrieved June 27, 2017, from https://labrc.com/wp-content/uploads/2015/10/Stolo-Heritage-Policy-Manual.pdf

SunWolf, & Frey, L. R. (2001). Storytelling: The power of narrative communication and interpretation. In W. P. Robinson, & H. Giles (Eds.), *The new handbook of language and social psychology* (pp. 119–135). Wiley.

Terms of Reference, Cohen Commission. (2010). Retrieved June 27, 2017, from http://epe. lac-bac.gc.ca/100/206/301/pco-bcp/commissions/cohen/cohen_commission/ LOCALHOS/EN/TERMSOFREFERENCE.HTM

Thompson, S. (Ed.). (1929). *Tales of the North American Indians.* Indiana University Press.

Tuhiwai-Smith, L. (1999). *Decolonization methodologies, research and Indigenous peoples.* University of Otago Press.

Appendix A

"Twenty-Five Indigenous Projects" (from Tuhiwai-Smith, 1999, Chapter 8)

Claiming = histories making assertions about rights and dues (to tribunals, courts, and governments about territories and resources or about past injustices)

Testimonies = a formal way of giving oral evidence of collective memory

Storytelling = individual oral histories that contribute to a collective story of place, beliefs, and values connecting the past to the future

Celebrating survival/survivance (survival and resistance) = accentuates the degree to which Indigenous peoples and communities have retained cultural and spiritual values and authentically resisted colonialism

Remembering = connecting bodies with place and experience of a painful past and people's responses to that pain

Indigenist processes = privileging of Indigenous voices that counters negative connotations such as primitive, backward, and superstitious

Intervening = the process of being proactive and becoming involved as an interested worker for change

Revitalizing and regenerating = actively engaging in increasing language survival through widespread use (education, broadcasting, publishing, and community-based programs)

Connecting = linking people to each other, to lands and their place in the universe as related to issues of identity and place, to spiritual relationships and community well-being

Reading = critical review of "history" and the Indigenous presence in the making of that history

Writing & theory making = employing writing in a variety of imaginative, critical, and functional ways

Representing = being able as a minimum right to voice the views and opinions of Indigenous communities in various decision-making bodies through the politics of sovereignty and self-determination

Gendering = challenging gender role expectations that were put into place from the patriarchal perspectives of colonizers to include full participation of women in political decision-making

Envisioning = using strategies that ask Indigenous peoples to imagine a future where they rise above present day oppression and recognize the power that Indigenous peoples have to change their own lives and set new directions

Reframing = taking greater control over the ways in which Indigenous issues and social problems are discussed and handled and what it means to be Indigenous (e.g., asset rather than deficit)

Restoring = a wholistic approach to problem solving that restores well-being spiritually, emotionally, physically, and materially through healing rather than punishing, and through community appropriate policies and programs

Returning = returning lands, rivers and mountains, artifacts, and resource gathering places to their Indigenous owners; connecting individuals with their communities and birth families

Democratizing and indigenist governance = process of extending participation outwards through reinstating Indigenous principles of collectivity, public debate, and value systems geared to meet contemporary social challenges without imposing particular types of governmental systems based on colonialist practices

Networking = building knowledge and data bases on the principles of relationships and connections so that information is passed quickly throughout Indigenous communities, including the ability to establish trust with participants by clearly stating their positioning and their purposes

Naming = restoring the world by using the original Indigenous names for the landscape as well as in the naming of individuals so that the histories are carried in the names

Protecting = defending and preserving people, communities, languages, customs and beliefs, arts and ideals, natural resources, sacred sites, and more through a variety of means including alliances, charters, and conventions, etc.

Creating = transcending the basic survival mode by using resources and capabilities to create and be creative in order to rise above circumstances, to dream new visions, to preserve old ones, and to foster invention, discovery, and simple improvements to peoples' lives

Negotiating = thinking and acting strategically to recognize and work towards long-term goals for survival

Discovering the beauty of our knowledge = uncovering Indigenous knowledge systems alongside Western science and technology to work for Indigenous development that recognizes values related to ethics, relationships, wellness and leading a good life

Sharing = collect and share knowledge among Indigenous peoples, communities, and across the world; demystifying knowledge and information and speaking in plain terms to the community.

Appendix B

List of recommendations specifying First Nations (from Cohen Commission of Inquiry Final Report, 2012)

1) In relation to Fraser River sockeye, the Department of Fisheries and Oceans should follow the principle that the minister is the ultimate authority in decisions about conservation, fisheries management (subject to the Pacific Salmon Treaty), and, within areas of federal jurisdiction, fish habitat. DFO should consistently reflect this principle in all its agreements and processes with First Nations and stakeholders.

7) The new associate regional director general responsible for implementation of the Wild Salmon Policy should, by March 31, 2014, and each anniversary thereafter during implementation, report in writing on progress in implementation of the policy, and the Department of Fisheries and Oceans should publish that report on its website. Each annual report should invite responses from First Nations and stakeholders, and all responses should be promptly published on the DFO website.

16) After seeking comment from First Nations and stakeholders, and after responding to challenge by scientific peer review, the Department of Fisheries and Oceans should, by March 31, 2013, and every five years thereafter, revise salmon farm siting criteria to reflect new scientific information about salmon farms situated on or near Fraser River sockeye salmon migration routes as well as the cumulative effects of these farms on these sockeye.

25) Within 30 days of the minister of fisheries and oceans approving the Integrated Fisheries Management Plan (IFMP), the Department of Fisheries and Oceans should make public the rationale for the harvest rules set out in the Fraser River Sockeye Decision Guidelines section of the IFMP.

31) The Department of Fisheries and Oceans should ensure that all Fraser River sockeye salmon fisheries are monitored at an enhanced level (achieving catch estimates within 5 percent of actual harvest, with greater than 20 percent independent validation). To meet this objective, DFO should

- enforce penalties for non-compliance with catch-reporting requirements,

- confirm the role of fishery officers in reporting illegal harvest numbers to fisheries managers and establish a system to incorporate such numbers into official catch estimates,

- establish a program for independent catch validation,

- provide sufficient and stable funding to support enhanced catch-monitoring programs, and

- treat commercial and Aboriginal economic opportunity fishers equally regarding any requirement of fishers to contribute toward the cost of catch monitoring, subject to any accommodation required in support of an exercise of an Aboriginal right.

35) The Department of Fisheries and Oceans should support the involvement of members of First Nations in escapement enumeration and other stock assessment activities in their traditional territories.

36) Following consultation with First Nations, the Department of Fisheries and Oceans should

- articulate a clear working definition for food, social, and ceremonial (FSC) fishing, and

- assess, and adjust if necessary, all existing FSC allocations in accordance with that definition.

37) In the context of negotiating an agreement with a specific First Nation, the Department of Fisheries and Oceans should encourage the First Nation to provide DFO with information on its practices, customs, and traditions that is relevant in determining its food, social, and ceremonial needs.

38) The Department of Fisheries and Oceans should, by September 30, 2013, complete its analysis of the socio-economic implications of implementing the various share-based management models for the Fraser River sockeye fishery, decide which model is preferable, and, promptly thereafter, implement that model.

39) The Department of Fisheries and Oceans should conduct the research and analysis necessary to determine whether in-river demonstration fisheries are, or are capable of, achieving tangible conservation benefits or providing economic benefits to First Nations in an economically viable or sustainable way before it takes further action in expanding in-river demonstration fisheries.

40) The Department of Fisheries and Oceans should develop its future policies and practices on the reallocation of the commercial Fraser River sockeye salmon fishery (including allocations for marine and in-river fisheries) in an inclusive and transparent manner, following a strategic and integrated planning process such as Action Step 4.2 of the Wild Salmon Policy.

63) The Department of Fisheries and Oceans should not include in fishing licences a clause that allows for retention of "mortally wounded" Fraser River sockeye salmon.

III. HISTORIES:
On Four Continents

Introduction

As in the rest of the Legal Amazon, the Upper Xingu region faces severe problems related to deforestation, loss of biodiversity, and changes in rainfall patterns (among other ecological issues), closely interlinked with social, cultural, and economic diversity.

> —Fernanda Viegas Reichardt, Andrea Garcia,
> and Maria Elisa de Paula Eduardo Garavello, Chapter 6

Clearly defining the roles of all interest-driven stakeholders is a necessary condition to realise sustainable water supply and management in Northwest Cameroon.

> —Henry Bikiwibili Tantoh, Chapter 7

The colonial [Indian] government's intention was not only to expand agriculture to generate revenue, but also to use the river system as a tool to take control of the forests from Indigenous peoples.

> —Arivalagan Murugeshapandian, Chapter 8

When comparing northern British Columbia to the Yukon in terms of land-use planning and watershed management, some notable differences in planning practice emerge.

> —Reg Whiten, Chapter 9

Just as water connects language and culture, as we have just seen, the movements of water across time and place leave connections that can be examined as histories. Formations and signs of life, exquisitely given cultural examination in the preceding chapters, can also be traced in geological histories—such as the Burgess Shale fossil beds in the Canadian

Rockies. Sea floor animals, likely killed by changes in their environment and fossilized over 500 million years ago, moved in the power of water and land to get deposited in an area that is just a few hours away from where we live in the eastern foothills of the Canadian Rockies. Histories of human management of water over time and place offer similarly graphic accounts of power.

Our first disciplines and professions in the health sciences (the editors were both practising nurses) rest on histories of water, health, and hygiene traced to the continental land masses, extending to the pursuits of empire and to simply sustain life. Ancient Greek and Roman philosophers and physicians alike knew that health was linked to water hygiene; indeed, politics of water technologies, management, and infrastructure originated in the Antiquities.

In the four chapters that follow here, historical examinations from Brazil, Cameroon, India, and Canada highlight the powerful connection of colonizing practices across time and place. Working in South America, Reichardt, Garcia, and de Paula Eduardo Garavello point to the power of resistance and disruption in knowing social and legal water connections, while Tantoh invites readers to reflect on the role of water in community and collective governance in Cameroon, Africa. Continents apart, the power of colonial practices severing Indigenous people from their water histories, uses, and hydroscapes are common connections in both Arivalagan Murugeshapandian's South India case study and Whiten's Mackenzie River Basin account.

—Robert Boschman and Sonya Jakubec, editors

6

Unexpected Connections? Water Security, Law, Social Inequality, Disrespect for Cultural Diversity, and Environmental Degradation in the Upper Xingu Basin

Fernanda Viegas Reichardt, Andrea Garcia, and Maria Elisa de Paula Eduardo Garavello

The study presented in this chapter integrates the so-called "XINGU Project: Integrating land use planning and water governance in Amazonia: towards improved freshwater security in the agricultural frontier of Mato Grosso." Founded by the Belmont Forum, it consists of a group formed by some of the leading funding agencies for research projects on environmental change in the world, including the São Paulo Research Foundation (FAPESP), Brazil. The XINGU Project, initiated in 2013, proposes to address the interlinked main natural and human issues on water security at the agricultural frontier of the Mato Grosso State, Brazil.

Thus, this chapter looks to the Environmental Law and Sociology sub-area of research of the XINGU Project. We explore the linkages between water security, social conflicts, and fragilities, and the challenges of responding in legal terms to water security risks in ways that avoid more social violence in the Upper Xingu Basin, especially for the socio-environmental vulnerable communities.

The Upper Xingu Basin and the Environmental Law and Sociology Subarea of Research

The Xingu River Basin is among the main basins of the Amazon River Basin and the most extensive water network of the planet. In order to better plan the social and economic development of the Amazon region, the Brazilian government instituted the political concept of "Legal Amazon." With an area that corresponds to about 59% of the entire Brazilian territory, the "Legal Amazon" encompasses the states of Brazil that belong to the Amazon Basin, and among them the Mato Grosso State. According to the federal government, the nine states that are part of the "Legal Amazon" have similar economic, political, and social problems, and are inhabited by nearly 60% of the Brazilian Indigenous population (Ministry of National Integration [MI], n.d.).

According to the data of the Socio-Environmental Institute (ISA), the Xingu River Basin has a land area of about 51 million hectares, equivalent to approximately five-and-a-half times the size of Portugal. The headwaters region—the Upper Xingu Basin—is located in the northeast of the Mato Grosso State, Brazil, corresponding to 34% of the entire Xingu Basin. It is in a transition area between two different biomes: the Amazonian Biome, which represents 79.7%, and the "Cerrado Biome" (Brazilian savanna), which represents 20.3% (ISA, 2012). For a visual example of the Cerrado Biome in the Pimentel Barbosa Indigenous Reserve, one may refer to Figure 6.1.

The Evergreen Seasonal Forest, with peculiar physical and floristic characteristics and a high degree of endemism, is predominant in the Upper Xingu Region. Red and Yellow Latosols, flat topography, and a stable rainfall regime are attributes that stimulated the expansion of pastures and mainly soybean cultivation. The conversion of the pioneer economic activities (e.g., livestock) to soybeans transformed the Mato Grosso State into Brazil's largest soy producer, with 9.323 million hectares of planted area. According to the economic data of the Brazilian Agricultural Research Corporation (EMBRAPA), the production of 30.514 million tons of soybeans (2016–2017 crop) is considered fundamental for the

FIGURE 6.1. Cerrado [Brazilian Savannah], Pimentel Barbosa Indigenous Land. Photo by Fernanda Viegas Reichardt.

Brazilian agribusiness-based economy (Brazilian Agricultural Research Corporation [EMBRAPA], 2017).

The regional land profile is characterized by a high concentration of medium and large farms, which account for 70% of the Upper Xingu Basin. Around 24% of the territory corresponds to 16 Indigenous Lands that are inhabited by approximately 19 different ethnic groups. The Conservation Units are unrepresentative, accounting for 1% of the Upper Xingu territory. There are still 46 rural settlements arising from agrarian reform, which represents no more than 4% of the area of the Basin (ISA, 2012).

The region still faces severe problems related to deforestation, loss of biodiversity, changes in rainfall patterns (among other ecological issues) closely interlinked with social, cultural, and economic diversity. Different socio-cultural factors and their impacts played a leading role in the environmental degradation of the Basin (ISA, 2012). For example, most people who immigrated to the Upper Xingu coming from mid-west and northeast Brazil are cattle ranchers. Those people traditionally raise cattle based on low-input management such as building dams along the rivers

FIGURE 6.2. Amazon Basin, "Rio das Mortes." Photo by Fernanda Viegas Reichardt.

for the cattle and keeping livestock partially free by not fencing natural fragments.

In the field of social and legal research, we argue that the local water resources conservation must exceed the regulatory technical aspects, as the Brazilian Forest Code does. According to the premises of Democracy and Human Rights (as guarantees of cultural diversity), an equitable water management requires the inclusion of a range of socio-environmental diversity. Thus, a whole complex of dynamic rules—encompassing issues of the hydrological cycle, ecological aspects, and the respect of social diversity—is urgently required in legal interpretation to ensure the legal water protection of the of the rivers located in the Legal Amazon (see Figure 6.2 for a visual example of the of the "Das Mortes" River located in the Legal Amazon).

According to Heckenberger's (1996) archaeological research, the prehistory of the Upper Xingu begins around a thousand years ago. Radiocarbon dating indicates first occupations between 950 and 1050 A.D. At that time, the cultural pattern of the Upper Xingu tradition was established, recognizable archaeologically by a distinctive ceramics industry, settlement pattern, and circular villages with central squares. This pattern remains intact to date. The Upper Xingu is the only area in the Brazilian Amazon where the continuity of Indigenous occupation can clearly be demonstrated from prehistoric times to the present. By 1400 A.D., the villages reached impressive proportions (20–50 hectares). These villages are among the largest villages in any area of lowland South America in prehistoric times. It is estimated that these villages sheltered about a thousand people and that in the western Culuene (or Kuluene) River lived probably more than ten thousand Indigenous people (Heckenberger, 1996).

It is important to highlight that archaeological records are notoriously difficult to obtain in the Amazon region due to the hot and humid climate and the considerable logistical difficulties that arise in the fieldwork. With respect to written documents, the first ethnographer who visited the Upper Xingu was Karl Von den Steinen (1855-1929). Through Von den Steinen's studies ("Unter den Naturvölkern Zentral-Brasiliens" or "Among the Aboriginals of Central Brazil"), we know that in the late nineteenth century more than 3,000 people lived in the Upper Xingu in 31 different villages. After Von den Steinen, other scientific and military expeditions entered the region and recorded the presence of its inhabitants. From the 1940s on, a new chapter in the history of the Xingu peoples began, blending with the history of the creation of the Xingu Indigenous National Park (ISA, 2002).

In the Upper Xingu, the non-Indigenous occupation process dates back to the 1940s, with the "Roncador Xingu Expedition." This expedition was an initiative of President Vargas' government to acquire and integrate the region into the country. In the formation of the "Aragarças" and "Xavantina" urban centres, the facilities of the Brazilian Aeronautic bases, with local Indigenous people's subsequent domination, have created the first conditions of the colonization process. However, the non-Indigenous occupation of the Upper Xingu was only intensified from the 1970s, 1980s, and 1990s onwards. Among the causes for this delay are the bad navigation conditions in the Xingu region. The colonization of the Upper Xingu was only possible after the construction of the BR-158 and BR-163 federal roads, which developed later into a network.

Indigenous peoples currently living in the southern portion of the Xingu Indigenous National Park are the Aweti, Kalapalo, Kamaiurá, Kuikuro, Matipu, Mehinako, Nahukuá, Naruvotu, Trumai, Wauja,

FIGURE 6.3. Etenhiritipá Village, Pimentel Barbosa Indigenous Land. Photo by Fernanda Viegas Reichardt.

Yawalapiti, Ikpeng, Kaiabi, Kisêdjê, Tapayuna, and Yudja peoples. The Xavante people currently live in nine different Indigenous lands, outside the Xingu Indigenous Park (ISA, 2002) (Figure 6.3).

In addition to the Indigenous peoples, fishermen and riparian communities also inhabit the Upper Xingu. Traditional populations, including fishermen and riparian peoples, were recognized by the Decree 6,040/2007. The Brazilian Federal Prosecution Service (*Ministério Público Federal Brasileiro - Procuradoria da República de Altamira*) recognized the Xingu Basin as a "Traditional Peoples Basin." In this sense, for data interpretation the Environmental Law and Sociology subarea of research must respect the regulatory framework below:

Universal Declaration on Cultural Diversity: The Universal Declaration on Cultural Diversity is a declaration adopted by the General Conference of the United Nations Educational, Scientific and Cultural Organization (UNESCO) at its thirty-first session on November 2, 2001. This Declaration is comprised of twelve articles; Article 1, entitled "Cultural diversity, the common heritage of humanity," states that "As a source of exchange, innovation and creativity, cultural diversity is as necessary for human-kind as biodiversity is for the nature. In this sense, it is a common herit-age of humanity and should be recognized and affirmed for the benefit of present and future generations" (United Nations Educational, Scientific and Cultural Organization [UNESCO], 2001).

Convention 169 of Indigenous and Tribal Peoples Convention: The Indigenous and Tribal Peoples Convention, 1989 is the major binding international convention concerning Indigenous peoples, and a forerunner of the Declaration on the Rights of Indigenous Peoples. This Convention can be understood as a recalling of the terms of the Universal Declaration of Human Rights, the International Convention on Economic, Social and Cultural Rights, the International Covenant on Civil and Political Rights, and the many international instruments on the prevention of discrimination.

Pluralism Principle, as Fundament of the Federative Republic of Brazil: According to the Preamble of the Brazilian Federal Constitution, the democratic state must be "destined to ensure the exercise of social and individual rights, liberty, security, well-being, development, equality and justice as supreme values of a fraternal, pluralist and unprejudiced society, founded on social harmony and committed, in the domestic and inter-national orders, to the peaceful solution of disputes ..." (Brazil, Brazilian Federal Constitution, 1988).

Article 215 of the Brazilian Federal Constitution: The National Government shall guarantee to all full exercise of cultural rights and ac-cess to sources of national culture, and shall support and grant incentives for appreciation and diffusion of cultural expression (Brazil, Brazilian Federal Constitution, 1988).

Article 216, I and II of the Brazilian Federal Constitution: Brazilian cultural heritage includes material and immaterial goods, taken either individually or as a whole, that refer to the identity, action, and memory of the various groups that form Brazilian society, including: I. forms of expression; II. modes of creating, making, and living (Brazil, Brazilian Federal Constitution, 1988).

Federal Law 9.985/2000: From this constitutional prerogative defined in article 225 of the Federal Constitution, Brazil has created the National System of Units of Conservation (*Sistema Nacional de Unidades de Conservação* [SNUC]), through the Federal Law No. 9.985/2000, to devise a plan for sustainable development and land conservation. Basically, SNUC divides protected areas into two groups: full protection and sustainable use areas, and full protection areas in order to have flexibility on land use policies. Brazil has created a dynamic system of regulations that promote and require sustainability practices to be implemented. These are innovative frameworks as they offer the community the possibility to participate in decision-making and to apply financial mechanisms that make the system viable, as well as encouraging the conservation of natural environments (Brazil, Federal Law 9.985/2000 2000).

Federal Decree 6.040/2007: Defines Traditional Peoples and Communities as "groups differentiated culturally that recognize themselves as such, who have their own forms of social organization, occupy and use territories and natural resources as a condition for their cultural, social, religious, ancestral and economic continuity, using knowledge, innovations and practices generated and transmitted by tradition." Two characteristics are strongly evident in these groups. The first concerns territory, which is considered as a necessary space for the cultural, social, and economic reproduction of these communities, whether used permanently or temporarily. It is in these areas that the memory and the material basis of cultural meanings that make up the identity of the group are symbolically printed. Another important factor is sustainable development: it is common to use natural resources in a balanced way, with concern in preserving the resources for future generations. Communities are marked by subsistence economies. Decree 6,040/2007 also established the National Policy for the Sustainable Development of Traditional Peoples and Communities (PNPCT). The main objective of this policy is to promote the sustainable development of traditional people and communities, with emphasis on the recognition, strengthening, and guarantee of their territorial, social, environmental, economic, and cultural rights, with respect towards and appreciation of their identity, their organization, and their institutions (Brazil, Federal Decree 6.040/2007 2007).

Research Data

Our fieldwork started in 2016 with more than 24,000 kilometers of travelling in the Upper Xingu Basin and also in the municipalities of São Paulo and Cuiabá. In total, around 360 in-depth interviews through open-ended questioning with different social actors were made. Through these interviews, at least five different social groups were clearly identified for this research: (a) large and medium farmers[1]; (b) small farmers and agrarian reform settlers[2]; (c) fishermen and traditional riparian peoples; (d) rural workers; (e) and the Xavante people (traditional people of the Cerrado).

In addition to Cuiabá, the capital of the Mato Grosso state, the focus areas for the research include five municipalities of the south and east of the Xingu's headboard covering Campinápolis, Água Boa, Canarana, Ribeirão Cascalheira, and Querência, which are highly vulnerable to social-environmental conflicts. The municipalities of Água Boa and Campinápolis were selected for this study because they cover the Coluene River sub-basin. Along the river we can find a variety of human activity, use, and land occupation establishing the Coluene River sub-basin as having a cultural, social, and traditional importance for this study. Canarana, Querência, and Ribeirão Cascalheira are located in the headwaters of two major rivers, the Tanguro and the Suiá-Miçu, that also form the Xingu River. The municipalities still have a different social significance for this research owing to the colonization processes, which began in the 1970s but were actually intensified in the late 1990s. See Table 6.1-6.5 for information about the municipalities in the northeast of Mato Gosso state that are under more intense research processes.

Cuiabá, the capital of Mato Grosso, is a trading centre for an extensive cattle-raising and agricultural area. Cuiabá is among some of the fastest-growing cities in Brazil, followed by the growth of agribusiness in Mato Grosso, despite the economic recession that has in recent years affected Brazil as a whole. Two field trips to Cuiaba were made, respectively in March and April 2016. The interviews also focused on the agribusiness stakeholders and public agents.

TABLE 6.1: Characterization of the Municipality of Campinápolis/Mato Grosso state

Human Development Index - 2010 (IDHM 2010)	0.538
Territorial Area in km² - 2015	5,967,355
Resident Population - 2015	14,305
Indigenous Population - 2010	7,621
Literate Population	8,335
Health Facility Establishments - (SUS)	19
Total Employed Persons	879
Per Capita GDP R$ (Reais) - 2013	10,525.18

* Human Development Index (HDI) is a composite statistic of life expectancy, education, and per capita income indicators, which are used to rank countries into four tiers of human development.
** Unified Health System (SUS) is an administrative body responsible for the stewardship of both the public and private health systems, established in 1988 by the Brazilian federal government.
*** Per capita GDP is a measure of the total output of a region that takes gross domestic product (GDP) and divides it by the number of people in the region. Brazilian reais is the official currency of Brazil. Currently [06/2020], 1 real equals 0.24 Canadian dollars.

TABLE 6.2: Characterization of the Municipality of Água Boa/Mato Grosso state

Human Development Index - 2010 (IDHM 2010)	0.729
Territorial Area in km² - 2015	7,510,612
Resident Population - 2015	20,856
Indigenous Population - 2010	266
Literate Population	17,432
Health Facility Establishments – (SUS)	13
Total Employed Persons	5,085
Per Capita GDP R$ (Reais) - 2013	28,029.16

* Human Development Index (HDI) is a composite statistic of life expectancy, education, and per capita income indicators, which are used to rank countries into four tiers of human development.
** Unified Health System (SUS) is an administrative body responsible for the stewardship of both the public and private health systems, established in 1988 by the Brazilian federal government.
*** Per capita GDP is a measure of the total output of a region that takes gross domestic product (GDP) and divides it by the number of people in the region. Brazilian reais is the official currency of Brazil. Currently [06/2020], 1 real equals 0.24 Canadian dollars.

TABLE 6.3: Characterization of the Municipality of Canarana/Mato Grosso state

Human Development Index - 2010 (IDHM 2010)	0.693
Territorial Area in km² - 2015	10,882,402
Resident Population - 2015	18,784
Indigenous Population - 2010	1,349
Literate Population	14,851
Health Facility Establishments - SUS	16
Total Employed Persons	3,940
GDP per Capita R$ (Reais) - 2013	36,416.91

* Human Development Index (HDI) is a composite statistic of life expectancy, education, and per capita income indicators, which are used to rank countries into four tiers of human development.
** Unified Health System (SUS) is an administrative body responsible for the stewardship of both the public and private health systems, established in 1988 by the Brazilian federal government.
*** Per capita GDP is a measure of the total output of a region that takes gross domestic product (GDP) and divides it by the number of people in the region. Brazilian reais is the official currency of Brazil. Currently [06/2020], 1 real equals 0.24 Canadian dollars.

TABLE 6.4: Characterization of the municipality of Ribeirão Cascalheira/ Mato Grosso state

Human Development Index - 2010 (IDHM 2010)	0.670
Territorial Area in km² - 2015	11,354,805
Resident Population - 2015	8,881
Indigenous Population - 2010	794
Literate Population	7,097
Health Facility Establishments - SUS	6
Total Employed Persons	897
Per Capita GDP in R$ (Reais) - 2013	21,968.82

* Human Development Index (HDI) is a composite statistic of life expectancy, education, and per capita income indicators, which are used to rank countries into four tiers of human development.
** Unified Health System (SUS) is an administrative body responsible for the stewardship of both the public and private health systems, established in 1988 by the Brazilian federal government.
*** Per capita GDP is a measure of the total output of a region that takes gross domestic product (GDP) and divides it by the number of people in the region. Brazilian reais is the official currency of Brazil. Currently [06/2020], 1 real equals 0.24 Canadian dollars.

TABLE 6.5: Characterization of the municipality of Querência/Mato Grosso state

Human Development Index - 2010 (IDHM 2010)	0.692
Territorial Area in km² - 2015	17,786,195
Resident Population - 2015	13,033
Indigenous Population - 2010	1,349
Literate Population	10,544
Health Facility Establishments - SUS	14
Total Employed Persons	3,730
Per capita GDP R$ (Reais) - 2013	58,393.31

* Human Development Index (HDI) is a composite statistic of life expectancy, education, and per capita income indicators, which are used to rank countries into four tiers of human development.
** Unified Health System (SUS) is an administrative body responsible for the stewardship of both the public and private health systems, established in 1988 by the Brazilian federal government.
*** Per capita GDP is a measure of the total output of a region that takes gross domestic product (GDP) and divides it by the number of people in the region. Brazilian reais is the official currency of Brazil. Currently [06/2020], 1 real equals 0.24 Canadian dollars.

São Paulo State and São Paulo city also encompass our fieldwork owing to their importance for the Brazilian economy and agribusiness trade. From early January 2016, we interviewed some stakeholders of the agribusiness sector, corporate executives of trading commodity companies operating in Brazil, public agents, academics from different areas of research, and social actors from the third sector. All interviewed persons are directly or indirectly related to the Upper Xingu's agricultural frontier.

From late February and early March 2016, we covered the municipalities of Água Boa, Campinápolis, Canarana, Querência, and Ribeirão Cascalheira. All these municipalities are located in a transition zone between the Cerrado biome, characteristic of the Brazilian Central Highlands, and the Amazon rainforest. The landscape is flat—with the exception of Campinápolis—with a predominance of forests interspersed by savannas and farmland. Disturbed landscapes composed of pastures and farmland were observed throughout most visited areas.

The five municipalities face problems related to deforestation and social, cultural, and economic diversity. In some of these, the social-environmental problems are more intense than in others. However, from a socio-cultural point of view, the covered municipalities have some socio-environmental differences: biomes, soil types, vegetation, and relief; agricultural production models and technological support; colonization processes and socio-cultural and socio-economic issues. We emphasize that these differences could also be observed with high frequency within the same municipality. According to the Institute Brazilian Geography and Statistics data, among the visited municipalities the lowest human development index of the Mato Grosso State was registered in the municipality of Campinápolis, one of the communities with the highest concentration of Indigenous population in Brazil (Table 6.1). Among the 5,565 Brazilian municipalities, Campinápolis was ranked in the 5,339[th] place with human development indices comparable to the ones from Sub-Saharan Africa.

Social Groups Interviewed and the Main Results Obtained in the Upper Xingu

Large and Medium Farmers

- **visited municipalities**: Água Boa, Canarana, and Querência

- **origin of migration of this social group:** Brazilian South, Southeast, and Midwest

Intensive crop farming is a modern form of farming that refers to the industrialized production of crops. Intensive crop farming methods include innovation in agricultural machinery, farming methods, genetic engineering technology, techniques for achieving production in high scale, the creation of new markets for consumption, patent protection of genetic information, and global trade. These widespread methods in developed nations are also adopted in the Xingu region by large and medium farmers[3]. Soybean and corn producers of the municipalities of Água Boa, Canarana, and Querência have preference for medium and short-cycle crops, and the vast majority of the soybean and corn producers rely on trading companies to store the grain. The financing of the harvest is mostly done with owned resources or through partnerships with banks and trading companies. The crops are planted in owned and leased properties. According to data released by the National Supply Company (CONAB), for five consecutive years the Mato Grosso State was considered the largest producer of grain and fiber of Brazil. The main crops of the Xingu region are soybeans and corn. The largest drop in the 2016 harvest was attributed to corn (second crop), with a reduction of almost 23% in the annual comparison. The reduction in the 2016 harvest was the result of bad weather, with no rain in the decisive moments for the development of the crops. The main problems reported by soybean and corn producers were poor infrastructure for transporting soybean harvests; energy supply; unequal relationship and dependence on trading companies; and changes in rain cycles (irrigation is starting to be considered an alternative).

Regarding Brazilian environmental legislation, in 1965 Brazil created and passed its first forest code. Laws such as the Forest Code do not exist in many places across the world. The Forest Code should be a stringent law that should ensure that our world's largest rainforest is protected. Unfortunately, the effectiveness of the Forest Code was not perceived and enforcing it has proved to be quite difficult over the years. Given federal and local governments with few resources, the Forest Code has been nearly impossible to implement and monitor. Brazil has a total area of approximately 8,516,000 km^2 and at least five different biomes, excluding the transitional areas of Biomes. The Amazon rainforest alone covers 6,900,000 km^2, the size of Mexico, Mongolia, Peru, and Egypt combined. Covering two million km^2, or 21% of the country's territory, the Cerrado is the second largest ecoregion in Brazil after the Amazon. The area is equivalent to the size of England, France, Germany, Italy, and Spain combined. According to the WWF recent data, only 20% of the Cerrado's original vegetation remains intact; less than 3% of the area is currently protected by law (see Figure 6.4 for a visual example of the frontier between the Cerrado and Amazon Forest biomes).

In 2012, a new Brazilian forest code was put into effect. The development of the new code was marked by social conflicts. On one hand, farmers pushed for an update which would allow them to harvest their land with less restriction from environmental laws. On the other, during the elaboration of the new code, environmentalists and civil society groups strongly reacted trying to reduce the proposed changes without success.

FIGURE 6.4. Canarana and Querência Border. According to the Brazilian forest legislation, the political border between the municipalities of Canarana and Querência is also the frontier between the Cerrado and Forest biomes. The Forest Code does not specifically protect biome transition areas. Photo by Fernanda Viegas Reichardt.

The code, published in May 2012 (Law 12.651/2012), mainly served agribusiness interests with measures such as extending amnesties to illegal deforestation carried out prior to 2008, and reducing areas that should be permanently maintained as forest (legal reserves) or where clearing vegetation was prohibited (area of permanent protection), such as on steep slopes and the margins of rivers and streams. In fact, deforestation in the Upper Xingu Region continues. According to the Research Institute

"Instituto do Homem e Meio Ambiente da Amazônia – Imazon" data, by February-March 2016 deforestation in Mato Grosso State had increased by 190%.

Through the in-depth interviews using open-ended questioning with large and medium farmers, there were absolutely no references to the soy moratorium, an agreement that ensures that companies do not trade, acquire, or finance soybean crops linked to deforestation in the Amazon. There were no significant reports of other kinds of public or private environmental conservation actions. The major health-related problem reported by this social group concerns pesticide contamination. All the producers interviewed complained about the increase in pesticide use. One hundred percent of the interviewees reported that they frequently smell agrochemicals everywhere during the application.

The interviewed farmers frequently insisted that the Xingu Basin does not belong to the Amazon region and this denial justifies the imbalanced relationship with the Indigenous people. These farmers believe that the area in question needs "development" and Indigenous people represent "socio-cultural backwardness." The total absence of the State (federal, state, and municipal governments) as a regulatory institution is one of the strongest data points obtained in this research. It was absolutely not uncommon to listen to the questioning about the Indigenous people's rights and territory demarcation and registration. In some interviews, the questioning about the human condition of Indigenous peoples appears, especially regarding the Xavante. From a sociological (and not legal) point of view, it is possible to make a clear parallel between the local reality and South Africa's apartheid. Some of these human rights violations are seen in the data within the previous tables and the discussion to follow.

In relation to the local non-Indigenous population, agricultural production does not seem to bring the expected development. For example, the only hospital in the region is located in Água Boa, with only a few medical specialties, and is in poor sanitary condition. Recently, a new hospital was built in the Querência municipality. Hospital intensive care units in the region exist only in Cuiaba, Goiânia, and Brasília, located about 1,000 km from the Upper Xingu. For these social groups, access to healthcare is normally obtained out of the Mato Grosso State. Water supply and sanitation are still less than adequate, while some existing regulations are outdated (Tables 6.1-6.5).

Small Farmers: Agrarian Reform Settlers

- **visited municipalities:** Água Boa, Canarana, Querência
- **origin of migration of this social group:** Brazilian South and Southeast

In relation to Brazilian legislation, agrarian reform was initially conceptualized by the Federal Law 4504/64 called *Estatuto da Terra* or Land Statute. It is a set of measures that aim to promote the distribution of land in Brazil, through changes in ownership and use of rural properties, in order to address social justice and increase productivity. The possibility of implementing an agrarian reform in Brazil only occurred with the 1964 Constitutional Amendment No. 10 that inserted modifications in the Federal Constitution of 1946. Subsequently, the Brazilian Federal Constitution of 1988 presented the matter of agrarian reform in a progressive way, but still with conservative traits due to the country's private cultural heritage. The basic institutes of Brazilian agrarian law are currently oriented towards a fundamental right in the Federal Constitution. The law seeks to reconcile property with a social function of the land in order to better promote community justice.

However, the Brazilian agrarian reform has been severely criticized. The lack of infrastructure, limited policies geared to family farming, the financial difficulties of farmers, and low education are all factors that contribute to the limited success in the implementation of this law. Indeed, the law was beneficial to big producers and detrimental for small producers. The visited agrarian reform settlements highlighted the additional rural partnership agreements that supported soybean production, conforming with the family farming objectives, but demanding new layers of policy and work for smaller producers (see Figure 6.5 for a visual example of an interview carried out in a Rural Settlement in the municipality of Água Boa).

According to the interviews conducted in the rural settlements in the Xingu Region, one of the choices of soybean cultivation (instead of

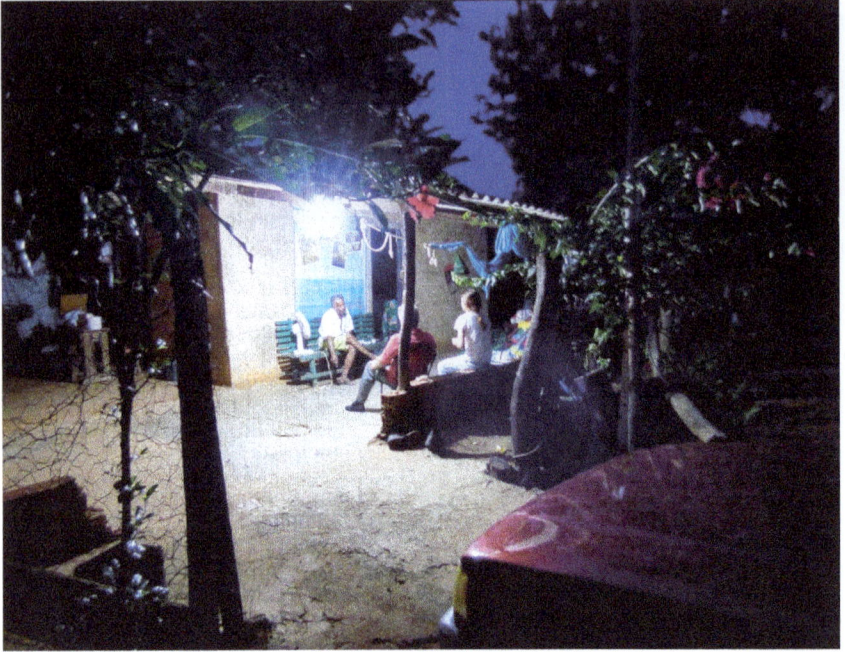

FIGURE 6.5. Fieldwork, P.A. Jaraguá Settlement, Agua Boa municipality. Photo by Fernanda Viegas Reichardt.

producing food relating to family farming) in the settlements stems from the Sanitary Vigilance of Mato Grosso. The Sanitary Vigilance prohibits the marketing of any goods of animal origin produced in the settlements like milk, butter, cheese, lard, eggs, or meat. The prohibition complies with the law and with the health and hygiene standards adopted by the Mato Grosso State, which should ensure good health for its residents. However, these measures negatively impact the tradition and history of family farmers.

This decision was taken without any support and financial incentives for the small producers. As a consequence, milk and milk-derived products are declining. In the rural settlement, some handmade agriculture products for local subsistence are still available locally. The technical assistance provided in the settlements has not been enough to overcome the serious cultivation problems the inhabitants face. All small producers interviewed complained about the increase in pesticide use, which even hinders the production of basic food (such as lettuce and cassava) for the community that lives in these rural settlements.

The State's efficiency in social and environmental conflicts resolution is very low, almost non-existent, leading to a very high rate of vulnerability for this population. Fundamental human rights such as basic sanitation, health, and education are absolutely precarious in the rural settlements visited. There are also not enough private or non-governmental organizations initiatives for local development. Access to drinking water is possible only by artesian wells, which represent a high cost for the poor local population. There are several reports of contamination of the wells by septic tanks. As a consequence, different health problems related to sanitary conditions were reported by the population. Among them was the growing number of cases of dengue fever in 2016.

Due to environmental legislation, the Federal Public Prosecutor's Office in Mato Grosso State initiated a public civil inquiry with the objective of investigating illegal deforestation in the Querência municipality. According to the Secretary of State for the Environment (Sema), around 60,000 hectares of native vegetation were burned in the rural settlement called "Brasil Novo." Unfortunately, this illegal deforestation has not been an isolated case in the region over the last decade. In the federal political discussions between the Brazilian Ministry of the Environment and the Brazilian Ministry of Agrarian Development regarding illegal deforestation, the consensus of the unsustainability of rural settlements in the state of Mato Grosso prevailed. There are also several reports of land abandonment caused by water issues in the region.

Fishermen and Riparian Peoples

- **visited municipalities:** Campinápolis, Canarana, and Querência
- **origin of migration of this social group:** unidentified

The main fishing arrangements observed along the Upper Xingu River basin were of artisanal and recreational fishing (fishing tourism). In the

São José do Couto District (Campinápolis municipality), the fishermen live near the rivers and practice artisanal fishing as their main activity. They also have, as complementary activities, subsistence farming and extractive activities.

The arrival of agriculture has promoted major changes to the natural environment, many of them related to water sources. All interviewed fishermen and riparian peoples complained about the increase in pesticides use. According to the statements of residents living in the São José do Couto District for at least twenty years, human occupation and deforestation growth have negatively affected fish stocks. These fishermen clearly perceive the decrease of some local fish species (especially large fish such as Pirarara and Jaú)[4] and report a great ecological imbalance in the Coluene (or Kuluene) River, which is one of the Xingu's main tributaries. However, predatory fishing and hunting tourism in the region are reported as a major problem for this social group. The high rate of homicides, child prostitution, and other forms of human rights violations also directly affect this population.

Regarding the Indigenous peoples, the Xingu Indigenous Park[5] lies across the agriculture frontiers in the historically highest-deforestation regions of the Amazon, as already reported in this chapter. In the 280,000 km² of the Park, most of the twenty-four Indigenous groups who inhabit the area depend on subsistence agriculture (cassava), hunting, and fishing. Indigenous peoples' historical management and use of these landscapes have enabled their long-term occupation and ultimately their protection. The different Indigenous peoples that inhabit the Park have a close interdependence relation with the natural resources, especially water: it is for this reason that they have a cosmological relationship with natural resources. Forest, water, and spirituality seem to go hand in hand. In fact, many of these peoples do not separate the concepts of environment, water, cosmology, and society.

However, according to the Indigenous groups' reports, dams, predatory fishing, road paving, logging, and mining have caused a large decrease in fish stocks. Added to these problems is the contamination of water resources by agrochemicals, untreated sewage, plastics, and other synthetic waste together with an increasing demand for agricultural commodities and the continued degradation of the upper headwaters outside the Xingu

Indigenous Park borders. Indigenous groups' reports on changing fire and rainfall regimes indicate that these facts may themselves also evidence climate change impacts, a new and serious threat. For example, in the year 2016–2017 the drought that hit the region drastically reduced cassava production. This root is the main source of food and raw material for the production of various products. During this period, there were numerous reports of famine in the Xingu Indigenous Park and, consequently, an increase in dependence on industrialized products.

It is important to highlight that Xingu headwaters are located outside the Xingu Indigenous Park, so that local Indigenous populations perceive the environmental impacts that occur in the surrounding area of the Park mainly through changes in water resources and climate. According to the testimony of the Cacique Yacuma Kamayurá (Indigenous chief of the Kamayurá people), "the stars are no longer telling us the right time to plant, nor do they announce the rainy season"; and "the water is becoming increasingly blurred, today the Xingu waters have a beer-like colour and is no longer crystal clear like before."

The high rate of human rights violations is also reported by this population. One of the most shocking examples of human rights violations reported by the Kuikuro Indigenous population of the Curumim Village relates to an accident suffered by a fifteen-year-old girl in 2002. Without going into the details of this accident, it is worth considering its consequences. Since 2002, the Indigenous woman suffers from paralysis in almost all her body, without any medical or legal assistance. We clarify that the term *paralysis* is not being applied in a technical way, because the family did not have access either to police or medical records reporting how the accident happened in addition to the girl's health condition. Lack of access to police or medical records formally prevented her family from securing justice or any kind of public legal support.

Human dignity is inviolable and it must be respected and protected by the Brazilian government. The dignity of the human person is not only a fundamental right in itself, but constitutes the basis of fundamental rights in the national and international law. Despite the law, the different kinds of human rights violations suffered by the local Indigenous population are usual and recurrent. Unfortunately, the above example, which clearly demonstrates the Brazilian State's (at the federal, state, and municipal levels) inefficiency in conflict resolution, is only one case among many of the most basic rights violation reported by these peoples.

Rural Workers

- **visited region:** Canarana, Querência, and Ribeirão Cascalheira
- **origin of migration of this social group:** Brazilian North and Northeast

Poverty is historically considered the major cause of the migratory flow in Brazil. In consonance with the criteria adopted by the federal government, populations in poverty conditions receive up to 70.00 reais per month. Populations in extreme poverty conditions receive up to 140.00 reais. This respectively corresponds to approximately 28.00 and 56.00 Canadian dollars in September 2017.

A study carried out by the United Nations in partnership with the Brazilian federal government through the International Policy Center for Inclusive Growth, published in April 2016, concluded that between 2004 and 2013, poverty rates in Brazil have decreased from 20% to 9%. Extreme poverty rates have also been reduced from 7% to 4%. However, the main aspects or profiles of poverty remain the same: they are more present in the Brazilian North and Northeast rural areas.

Western Amazon and Maranhão State have very high levels of agricultural poverty verging on catastrophic dimension. Hunger, thirst, diseases, unemployment, illiteracy, low rural incomes, limited landownership, and variable climatic conditions historically drive migration from this region to the rest of Brazil in search of jobs and better living conditions. In the last decades, the migratory flow has intensified to the Amazon agricultural frontiers, including the Upper Xingu Basin.

Several of the rural workers interviewed in this survey (men under thirty-five years of age) are formally employed by the agribusiness sector that operates under very high technology. The labour relationship gives them legal benefits and protections in compliance with Brazilian legislation. However, the previous results of interviews still reveal a situation of socio-environmental vulnerability with negative repercussions on production, health, and lifestyle. They also demonstrate human health issues, such as pesticide toxicity.

Informal work in the Upper Xingu was also reported, which is not covered by labour law provisions. Debilitating workdays, degrading working conditions, or restricting worker freedom were frequently reported. In some cases, interviewees cited child/underage labour and the use or threat of violence against workers. Some of the interviews describe true squalid working conditions, comparable to contemporary slavery. "Slave workers" are mainly used in the cleaning of the woods for the planting of seeds.

Other kinds of human rights violations were reported by this social group, including police violence, homicides, and child prostitution. In relation to public health, all the rural workers interviewed complained mostly about the increase in pesticide use. They reported problems such as headaches, eye and body itching, and an increase in cancer cases. Frequent use of pesticides of illegal origin, and clearly prohibited in Brazil, were also reported.

Xavante Indigenous People

- **visited region:** Água Boa, Campinápolis, Canarana, and Ribeirão Cascalheira

- **origin of migration of this social group:** Brazilian Midwest

According to data from the Demographic Census conducted by the Brazilian Institute of Geography and Statistics in 2010, the current Xavante Indigenous population of 19,259 individuals is distributed in twelve different territories.

Cacique Jurandir Siridiwe Xavante[6] (Figure 6.6) is the leader of the Etenhiritipá village, which is located in the Pimentel Barbosa Indigenous Territory between the municipalities of Canarana and Ribeirão Cascalheira, in the Brazilian central plateau between the Rio das Mortes and the Xingu River headwaters, where this research step was more deeply carried out. Cacique Jurandir reported that the first historical reference to the Xavante date from the eighteenth century, when they inhabited the northern and central regions of the state of Goiás. Mobility is a hallmark

FIGURE 6.6. Fieldwork, Cacique Jurandir Siridiwe Xavante, Etenhiritipá Village, Pimentel Barbosa Indigenous Land. Photo courtesy of Cacique Jurandir Siridiwe Xavante.

of this people, considered as nomadic or semi-nomadic, with long periods of dispersion in their territory. In the eighteenth century the discovery of gold began the expansion of the so-called Capitania de Goiás (later called Goiás State), which led to the policy of settlements, with reduction and pacification of the Indigenous peoples. During this period the Xavante became the target of military campaigns. Invasions of their lands, slavery, armed attacks, diseases, and resettlement projects were some of the factors that motivated them to move to the east, establishing themselves in the east of the River Xingu Basin and west of the Araguaia River. In the twentieth century, the contact of the Xavante groups with non-Indigenous society took place in different ways and at different times. Until the mid-1950s, some groups remained relatively isolated and independent. This isolation was interrupted by the occupation of their lands by the non-Indigenous population. At the end of the 1940s, the impossibility of other retreats and their very reduced territory forced the groups that currently inhabit the Indigenous lands of Pimentel Barbosa to establish permanent contact with the surrounding society.

The strategy developed by the Xavante people in an attempt to preserve their territory and maintain their tradition with autonomy is called the "Xavante Strategy." Eight young Xavantes participated in a student exchange program. They were able to live with "white men" families of different social classes for several years and study in the Brazilian metropolitan regions. Some of them have graduated and have some knowledge of the English language, such as Cacique Paulo Cipassé Xavante. They acquired knowledge of the Portuguese language and non-Indigenous culture and became interlocutors of their people and nowadays are politically active, social agents of their people.

Regarding socio-environmental issues related to the Xavantes, human community and physical space are integrated concepts for them, which can never be separated. Places where people inhabit gain a symbolic meaning through social and cosmological experiences. This is the concept of "Ró," which is a literal translation of the Akwén language to English and means "place" or "territory." Since the meaning of place/territory can be offered in distinct contexts and employed in the service of different goals, it is useful to distinguish the definition in the context used by the Xavantes. Thus, "Ró" can be interpreted as a unifying concept that encompasses different terms as "Cerrado" (tropical savanna ecoregion), territoriality (with social and cosmological meanings), and "A'uwe" (Xavante people). According to Cacique Jurandir Siridiwe Xavante,

> Ró is not only the place from which we take our food. It is also the source of our spiritual strength. It is where we teach each new generation how to become great warriors, how to become great hunters. Our relationship with Ró is very deep; we have strong physical and spiritual bonds with it. We perform many ceremonies in Ró, like the 'Wai'a' spiritual initiation. In Ró we prepare the wapté, pre-initiate boys, for the ear-piercing ceremony that transforms them into adults, and then we take them for hunting (May 27, 2015).

In other words, Ró is the existence condition of the Xavantes as A'uwe (or people).

As the Xavantes are traditionally hunter-gatherer (gathering wild plants and hunting wild animals), game meat is a central component of their diet and social life. The cultivation of maize is the most outstanding crop for the Xavante people and plays a key role in the Xanantes' socio-cosmology. Squash, cassava, and beans are also cultivated by them.

However, wild animals are becoming scarce in their territory. In different interviews, the Xavantes pointed out, as main causes of wild animal scarcity, deforestation, reduction of biological diversity due to soybean cultivation, and intensive use of pesticides. The lack of animal protein (game meat) and the contamination of fish and "tracajás"[7] by pesticides are severe issues, especially for the children. According to UNICEF's widely publicized report in September 2014, one of the most serious problems faced by the Xavante people is the infant mortality rate, the second highest in Brazil, surpassing the indices of countries such as Kenya, Ghana, Namibia, and Zimbabwe. Malnutrition is among the leading causes of infant mortality.

Despite the Xavante people's effort to maintain their culture, they cannot sustain their traditional livelihoods anymore. They are becoming increasingly dependent on goods and industrialized products. In this scenario, alcoholism appears as a serious factor (or consequence) of negative socio-cultural impacts. Diseases, especially dengue fever, tuberculosis, and influenza are major public health problems.

The state's absence in the conflict resolution causes several violations in human rights and cultural diversity rights. The relations established between the surrounding community and the Xavante people can be compared to the South African apartheid, although not legally formalized. Apartheid was a segregationist regime that denied Black people their social, economic, and political rights. In a similar way, informal rules, social control systems, and "racial" segregation are imposed on the Xavante people. The informal ban on attending certain public places, police violence, and the prejudice suffered by Indigenous students in schools are some of the reported examples. The factors presented in this section of the chapter lead, among others, to a critical social and environmental state of vulnerability that can be comparable to a veiled ethnocide.

Concluding Remarks

Despite the fact that the Brazilian Federal Public Ministry recognized the Xingu Basin as a "Traditional Peoples Basin," the regulatory framework, which includes, among other laws, the Universal Declaration on Cultural Diversity, is only formally observed and with very low local effectiveness. As in the rest of the Legal Amazon, the Upper Xingu region faces severe problems related to deforestation, loss of biodiversity, and changes in rainfall patterns (among other ecological issues) closely interlinked with social, cultural, and economic diversity. Thus, the expansion of an agricultural frontier in the Amazon Basin represents an unresolved tension between the allocation of water for agriculture and for different sociocultural and ecological demands.

The revised Forest Code was approved in 2012 after more than a decade of efforts by Brazil's powerful agricultural lobby. The changes weakened restrictions for landowners, allowing them to clear land closer to riverbanks, and allowed those who had illegally felled land not to face penalties if they signed an agreement to replant trees, which is unlikely to be enforced.

As a result of the retrogression of environmental law, deforestation takes on unimaginable proportions. Data from the Monitoring System for Deforestation in the Legal Amazon of the Brazilian federal government of the Amazon show that the rate of forest destruction increased by about 30% from August 2015 to July 2016. There were almost 8,000 square kilometers deforested in one year—a destruction equivalent to 128 forest football fields per hour. Currently, different infrastructure projects in the Amazon region are also a cause of serious social-environmental damage.

Social rights are violated in even greater proportions. Brazil is experiencing severe restrictions with respect to different social rights. For example, Brazil's Lower House discussed the rural labour reform proposed to allow producers to replace workers' wages with crops or land. The proposed measure is seen as the legalization of "modern slavery" by various national and international human rights bodies.

All these are serious and urgent problems that directly affect the most vulnerable local populations, and which can also be considered as crimes against humanity.

NOTES

1   A medium rural property has an area of 320 to 1,200 hectares, while a large rural property has an area greater than 1,200 hectares.

2   A *minifundio* is a rural property of less than 80 hectares, and a small property is an area between 80 and 320 hectares.

3   See above, note 1.

4   The redtail catfish, *phractocephalus hemioliopterus*, is known in Brazil as *pirarara*. It is the only extant species of the genus *phractocephalus*. The pirarara can reach about 1.8 m in length and about 80 kg in weight. The gilded catfish, *zungaro zungaro*, or *jaú*, as it is known in Brazil, is a South American catfish (order *siluriformes*) of the family *pimelodidae*. It is the only species of the monotypic genus *zungaro*. The jaú can reach 140 cm in total length, weighing around 50 kg.

5   The Xingu Indigenous Park (in Portuguese, *Parque Indígena do Xingu*) is an Indigenous territory of Brazil, first created in 1961 as a national park. Its purposes are to protect the environment and the several Xingu Indigenous peoples in the area.

6   "Cacique" is the title given to the leader of an Indigenous group.

7   *Podocnemis unifilis* is a species of bluish-black turtle with yellow spots. Popularly called *tracajá*, it lives in many watersheds in northern South America.

REFERENCES

BRAZIL (Brazilian Federal Constitution). (1988). Official Press. Retrieved June 13, 2017, from https://www.imprensaoficial.com.br/downloads/pdf/Constituicoes_declaracao.pdf

BRAZIL (Federal Law 9.985/2000). (2000). Official Press. Retrieved June 13, 2017, from http://www.planalto.gov.br/ccivil_03/leis/L9985.htm

BRAZIL (Federal Decree 6.040/2007). (2007). Official Press. Retrieved June 13, 2017, from http://www.planalto.gov.br/ccivil_03/_ato2007-2010/2007/decreto/d6040.htm

EMBRAPA (Brazilian Agricultural Research Corporation). (2017). *Embrapa Soy.* Retrieved June 8, 2017, from https://www.embrapa.br/soja/cultivos/soja1/dados-economicos

HECKENBERGER, M. (1996). *War and peace in the shadow of empire: sociopolitical change in the upper Xingu of Southeastern Amazonia, A.D. 1400-2000* [Doctoral dissertation, University of Pittsburgh]. Retrieved May 14, 2017, from http://booksali.net/diryy/war-and-peace-in-the-shadow-of-empire-by-michael-j-heckenberger.pdf

ILO (International Labour Organization). (1989). *Indigenous and Tribal Peoples Convention n. 169.* Retrieved June 13, 2017, from http://www.ilo.org/global/topics/Indigenous-tribal/lang--en/index.htm

ISA (Socioenvironmental Institute). (2002). " From the first expedition to the creation of the Park". Retrieved May 13, 2017, from https://pib.socioambiental.org/pt/povo/xingu/1541

ISA (Socioenvironmental Institute). (2012). "De Olho na Bacia do Xingu". Retrieved June 8, 2017, from https://www.socioambiental.org/pt-br/o-isa/publicacoes/de-olho-na-bacia-do-xingu

MI (Ministry of National Integration / Superintendence of the Amazonian Economic Valuation Plan). (n.d.). "Legislation of the Amazon Region". Retrieved June 8, 2017, from http://www.sudam.gov.br/index.php/plano-de-acao/58-acesso-a-informacao/86-legislacao-da-amazonia

UNESCO (United Nations Educational, Scientific and Cultural Organization). 2001. Universal Declaration on Cultural Diversity. Paris: UNESCO. Retrieved June 13, 2017, from http://portal.unesco.org/en/ev.php-URL_ID=13179&URL_DO=DO_TOPIC&URL_SECTION=201.html

Community-Based Natural Resources Management in Sub-Saharan Africa: Barriers to Sustainable Community Water Supply Management in Northwest Cameroon

Henry Bikiwibili Tantoh

Natural resources (NRs) remain essential to rural livelihoods and well-being across Sub-Saharan Africa (SSA) (Prager et al., 2005; Roe et al., 2009). However, these local communities face a number of dynamic processes, including increasing population, climate variations, and change. Drought and environmental degradation, for instance, have combined to result in increasing demand for NRs (Khanal, Santini & Merrey, 2014). These processes largely threaten the NR base, on which communities depend for their growth, livelihoods, and sustenance (Borrini-Feyerabend, Kothari & Oviedo, 2004). Writing in the context of Natural Resources Management (NRM)[1] and poverty alleviations, Prager et al. (2005) argue that the decline of natural systems through soil depletion, deforestation, overexploitation, and pollution represents a direct threat to nature-based income and contributes to increasing poverty. Thus, understanding and managing the dynamics of, and changes in NR use and availability at the community level is considered a challenge to sustainable development. This has been further supported by Cash et al. (2006), emphasising that sustainable development and resource management "at all levels" is a fundamental problem for commons management. A major concern, however, as observed by Cheru (2002), is that African countries have for too long lacked good governance, which is a fundamental condition in any form of NRM and Community Development (CD).

Centralised and top-down approaches to NRM have been a common feature in most SSA countries (Ivory Coast, Cameroon, Ethiopia, Madagascar, Sudan, Niger, Mali, and Guinea Conakry), placing very little attention on the importance of private agents and rural communities (Roe et al., 2009). These centralised management systems were thought to manage effectively NRs and promote industrialised development (Ribot, Agrawal & Larson, 2006). Ako, Eyong & Nkeng (2010), for example, observed that water resources in Cameroon have been managed from centralised systems with the Ministry of Water Resource and Energy (MINEE) and other related ministries and public agencies, and this has resulted in the marginalisation and disenfranchisement of rural communities where the majority of the poor reside (Njoh, 2012). This exclusion of rural communities in resources management, as argued by Amungwa (2011), has resulted in illegal access and destruction. However, there has been a shift in policy interventions towards adopting pro-community approaches in resource management (Tantoh & Simatele, 2017). This shift from the predominantly centralised NRM towards more decentralised approaches is known very broadly as Community-Based Natural Resource Management (CBNRM) (Stone & Nyaupane, 2014). CBNRM has, thus, been promoted by national and foreign governments as a promising approach to facilitate linkages between biodiversity conservation and community livelihood improvement (Borrini-Feyerabend et al., 2004). This approach to NRM has also developed in response to significant inefficiencies of centralised management systems and pressures from international institutions, as well as to the marked inertia of developing countries and rural communities to have a say in the management of their NRs (Jérôme Ballet, Kouamékan & Koffi, 2009).

It is within this context that CBNRM has been promoted and encouraged as being a promising alternative to neoliberal philosophy and a liberating model with emancipatory potential for comprehensive sustainable

NRM (Dörre, 2015). This is because CBNRM is one of the reasonable and workable strategies for pursuing biological conservation, socio-economic objectives, and rural development, particularly in developing countries (Roe et al., 2009). This is also due to the realisation that rural resource users must be responsibly involved in the management of their NRs, combined with the fact that Community Based Institutions (CBIs) have better knowledge of local needs and, when endowed with powers, are more likely to respond to local aspirations and be more easily held accountable by local populations (Barrow, Gichohi & Infield 2000; Tantoh & Simatele, 2017).

Chadwick (1949) notes that community involvement in CD initiatives in the Northwest and Southwest of Cameroon has a long history, which, dating back to the late 1940s and early 1950s, was the main form of rural development in the 1960s in this part of the country (see also Njoh, 2003). Recent trends in community participation have led to the re-emergence of Village Development Associations (VDAs) and Community Based Organisations (CBOs) in rural development projects owing to the economic downturn which Cameroon and many other SSA countries experienced in the late 1980s (Njoh, 2012). As a result, community members are increasingly assuming the adverse effects of the economic recession that plagued the country and the growing inability of the state to provide economic and social development by initiating and organising self-help organisations in the quest for improving their standard of living (Fonchingong & Fonjong, 2003). A major concern that often arises is how to encourage grassroots communities and strengthen CBOs to manage effectively their NRs to meet the needs of the increasing population and those of other sectors in the economy.

Musingafi & Chadamoyo (2013) have, for example, argued that the awareness of effectively managing Common Pool Resources (CPRs) has risen in prominence in recent years and resonates strongly in low-income countries, where conventional approaches for water resource management have been inappropriate, while many countries and communities are looking for ways to improve on current governance strategies. Recent research has suggested that SSA countries face a wide range of NR development and management challenges, such as conceiving the laws, regulations, and institutions required to manage NRs in a more economically productive, socially acceptable, and environmentally suitable manner, while implementing and enforcing the laws (World Bank, 2006; Sun, Asante & Birner, 2010). Many scholars hold the view that the crucial challenge in effective NRM in many parts of rural areas in SSA is how to dismantle the fortress of centralised management institutions and replace it with an all-inclusive system that is not the only protector and supporter, but also an enabler and liberator (Matarrita-Cascante & Brennan, 2012). It can, therefore, be argued from this standpoint that for any NRM system to succeed, new power-sharing relationships between communities, the state, and other actors must be worked out and established.

Despite the role and importance of rural communities in NRM, increasing debates over local communities' ability to manage sustainably their lands and NRs are a part and parcel of broader struggles over political and economic power in SSA countries (Njoh, 2002). Barrow et al. (2000) observe that grassroots communities involved in resource management are mostly regarded as passive beneficiaries of benefits generated in areas not under their control and collaborative management efforts, where power shared between state agencies and local people is largely inadequate. Roe et al. (2009) argue that the limited capability among CBOs to perform varied management is because of the predominance of a highly centralised approach to development planning, conditioned by government policies of the colonial and post-colonial eras. In the same light, establishing institutional arrangements that will ensure that facilities are provided and maintained in an efficient, equitable, and sustainable way is another challenge to sustainable water supply (Sun et al., 2010). The central question in this broad field is how to manage efficiently Water Resources in a way that meets the increasing needs of the rural population (for domestic uses and sanitation), while still conserving the local environment.

The more specific question this chapter addresses is how to achieve this balance in a context where a series of issues (top-down management, inadequate finance, and environmental factors) have multiplied both the range and uncertainties affecting the livelihoods and wellbeing of grassroots communities.

Solving all these issues simultaneously is unlikely, so this chapter argues that (a) grassroots communities must be consulted and fully involved in decision-making processes and given the opportunity to determine their own modes of management; and (b) defining clearly the roles of all interest-driven stakeholders is a necessary condition to realise sustainable water supply management in Northwest Cameroon.

Methodological Approach

This chapter uses empirical evidence collected in Northwest Cameroon between November 2015 and January 2016 through the use of methods inspired by the tradition of participatory research. The research was conducted in three rural districts: Mbengwi, Njinikom, and Ndu (Figure 7.1) in Northwest Cameroon. These rural districts were selected based on the availability of a community water supply project, the presence of a Water Management Committees[2] (WMC), socio-economic and geographic information such as age, gender, employment, and distances to water sources. These communities are also noted for initiating and realising CD projects through VDAs and CBIs. The Northwestern part of Cameroon is typified by common cultural and traditional attributes such as language and cultural norms and structures of community leadership as well as social NR use and management. The system of community governance and administration is through local chiefs, known as "Fons" in the Bamenda Grassfields.[3] Water supply management is community-based by WMCs and is administered through a gravity-led technique (a system where water is channelled from a watershed through springs and piped down to villages).

It was purposely decided to draw two communities from each rural district using a technique of allocation concealment, and this resulted in the selection of Tugi, Zang-Tabi, Baicham, Muloin, Njimkang, and Ngarum (Figure 7.1). A confidence level of 40% was further employed to draw a sample population and this resulted in a total of twelve households from each of the six villages. This gave a total of 72 households that were considered before being included in the study. A systematic random sampling procedure was then applied to the six study locations.

The first households in all locations were purposely selected and then specific intervals were applied to select the actual households based on their concentration. Where houses were very close to each other, the tenth household was selected; where they were moderately spaced, the sixth household was selected; and where the houses were widely spaced

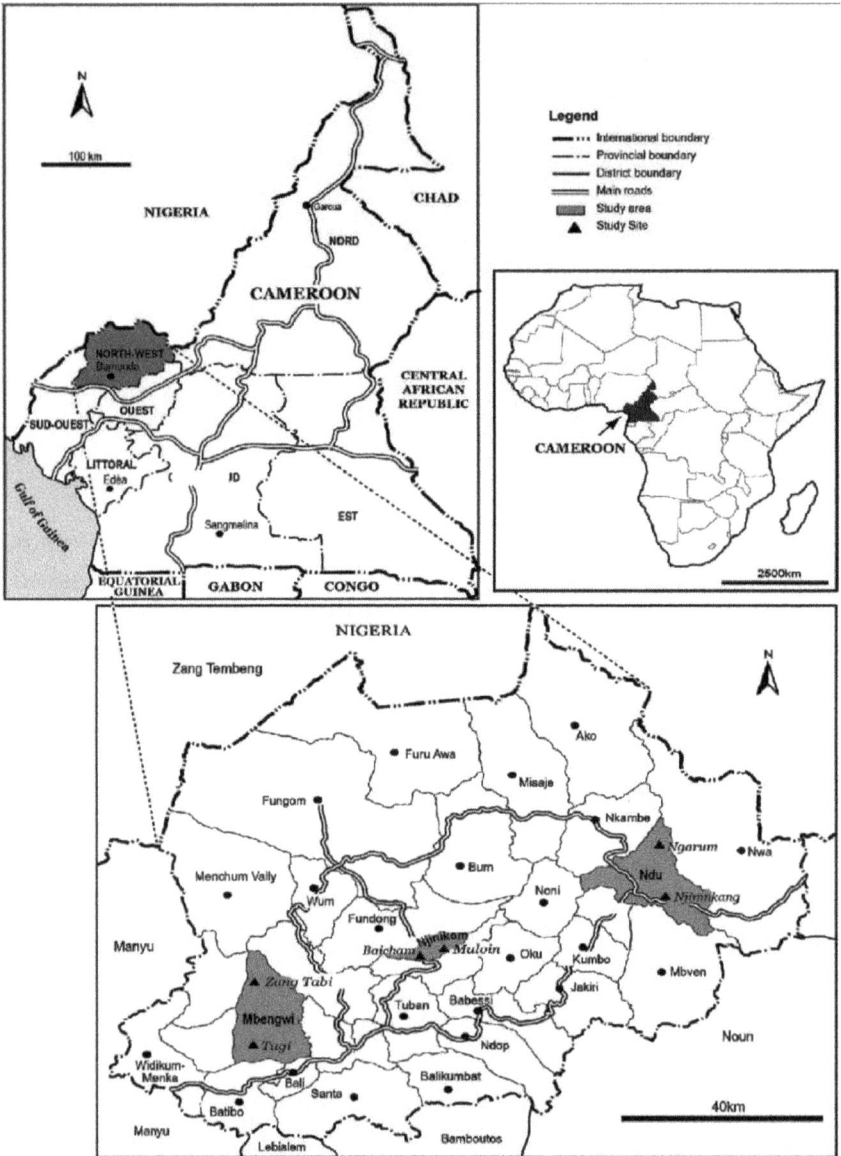

FIGURE 7.1. The Map of Cameroon and the Study Sites in Northwest Cameroon. From Cartography Unit, 2016, School of Geography and Environmental Studies, University of Witwatersrand, South Africa.

from each other, the third household was selected. In addition to this, the snowball technique was applied to identify and engage with key players involved in water resources management within the rural district.

In-depth interviews and discussions using semi-structured and open-ended questions were administered with focus groups and informed water specialists, WMCs, and other stakeholders. These include the officials from the MINEE, the Ministry of Agriculture and Rural Development (MINADER) as well as regional departments operating under these ministries in Northwest Cameroon. Furthermore, council officials, traditional leaders, and other Non-Governmental Organisations (NGOs) operating within the study sites were equally interviewed. In addition to this, 18 questionnaires (three for each of the six villages) were designed and administered to the WMCs to assess the management practices, financing aspects, decision-making processes, and the management of watersheds. To determine the level of community financial contributions towards the Operation and Maintenance (O&M) of the water system, a questionnaire was administered, and this process yielded information on household incomes and frequency of financial contribution to water supply management. In total, four officials from the different government ministries and three regional officials were included in the study. Interview conversations with the six members of CBOs were also conducted. Discussions with personnel from six WMCs were also carried out to understand the role and degree to which community leaders and community members participate in water supply and management issues. The aim of engaging with the various actors was to assess the institutional, policy, and management structures as well as management practices that exist in rural water supply in Northwest Cameroon. The empirical data were complemented by reviewing existing literature on the governance of NRs, CBNRM, and rural water systems.

Exploring CBNRM Discourses in SSA: A Literature Review

NRs are an essential component of communal livelihoods and they serve as a source of sustenance, especially in rural settings where they are obtained as CPRs (Nelson & Agrawal, 2008). Unfortunately, increasing population, rapid urbanisation, rising incomes, and changes in human behaviour as observed by Roe et al. (2009) have exerted pressure on the NRs, resulting in astonishing levels of environmental challenges and diverse management strategies. Although contemporary discussions would have us believe that the manner in which the natural environment is utilised and appreciated has significantly changed over the years, socio-economic and environmental processes have been the major drivers of these changes (Gruber, 2011). These developments have unfortunately occurred, particularly in the developing countries, where institutional and policy frameworks, as well as legislation, are ill-equipped to address the challenges that arise from these global processes (Ribot, 2002; Koppen et al. 2007). The resultant effects have been the continued downgrading and exclusion of grassroots communities from accessing their NRs and sharing in the benefits therein (Stone & Nyaupane, 2014).

Borrini-Feyerabend et al. (2004) contends that NRs have always been managed by grassroots communities through customary management practices with active community participation before colonisation. Fonchingong & Fonjong (2003), for example, argue that genuine community participation could be seen in the construction and maintenance of palaces, village to farm roads, inter-village roads, and shrines before European imperialism in Cameroon. With the advent of colonisation, Indigenous management systems were replaced with centralised, top-down management approaches (Rihoy & Maguranyanga, 2007). It has been argued that most central governments in SSA countries often view NR governance as a top-down affair with centralised approaches of environmental decision-making that place NRs under the control of state bureaucracies, and this marginalises local actors who are often dependent on the same resources for their livelihoods and wellbeing (Bartley et al., 2008). They further argue that a resilient central government was more competent in restricting community's demand, access, and use of NRs, which, if unrestrained by the central powers, would ultimately lead to its over-exploitation and destruction. This has been further supported by Cheru (2002), Simatele, Binns & Simatele (2012) who offer contradictory findings that most central government authorities are better placed than uneducated rural residents to make strategic decisions on environmental management and rural development. These observations, as argued by Nelson & Agrawal (2008), affirm the NRM strategy during the colonial era functioned to extend European administrative control into rural

African landscapes, which alienated the grassroots communities from participating in policymaking over the management of their resources.

Findings of centralised NRMs, for example (Amungwa, 2011; Ribot 2006), contradict that the best method for governing NRs to ensure its efficient use was transferring ownership and responsibility to national governments (Nuesiri, 2015). They argue that centralised management systems often have faulty designs, significant inadequacies, and sometimes favour corruption. A major challenge of the centralised management systems is the inability to devise rules that are effective in a variety of local circumstances, including different local peoples' needs, norms, problems, knowledge, and resource use characteristics (Rihoy & Maguranyanga, 2007). By the end of the last century, however, an increasing number of scientific studies have challenged the centralist view of NR governance advocating the managerial involvement of resource users (Prager et al., 2005; Tantoh & Simatele, 2017). Contemporary research suggests that a move from the top-down NRM system, which often had corrupt practices and significant inefficiencies, to a more devolved model known broadly as CBNRM (Community Based Natural Resource Management) will lead to sustainable outcomes (Roe et al., 2009).

According to Gruber (2011), CBNRM is one of the most talked about concepts in development literature in contemporary NRM chronicles, particularly in SSA. Hence, an increasingly theoretical and practical literature has developed, showing a plethora of different views for working with grassroots communities, together with the means and mechanisms by which NR users can be better involved in, and benefit from, NRM (Bartley et al., 2008; Rihoy & Maguranyanga, 2007; etc.). More recent arguments advocating CBNRM programmes have been elaborated by Stone & Nyaupane (2014) and Gruber (2001) on the basis that local populations are better positioned to: respond and adapt to specific socio-ecological conditions representing local interests and preferences; be well-informed about the intricacies of local ecological processes and management practices; be better able to mobilise local resources, both human and material, through locally adapted or traditional forms of access and management; be more accountable for their NRM decisions and actions, given the relative importance of the NR to their livelihoods and their proximity to the people they represent; and be more capable of adopting ways of managing their

NRs in a sustainable manner. Furthermore, local communities have greater knowledge of the intricacies of local ecological processes and practices, and are better positioned to manage effectively their NRs through local or traditional forms of access than distant managers (Ostrom, 1990).

The experiences of CBNRM over the past decades have, for example, demonstrated that community conservation approaches have been associated with various forms of decentralisation of power and authority (Ribot, 2002). Campbell & Shackleton (2001) make the same observations when they argue that the local people must have the power to decide over their NRs in order to encourage sustainability. Community-based Management (CBM) as used in water resources management, for example, is seen as a participatory approach to development whereby members of the community largely determine the ways and the means to control the O&M of their water system (Harvey & Reed, 2007).

It can, therefore, be argued that public participation is an essential attribute to all forms of CBM and CD initiatives supported by community members through subsidies either in cash or in-kind. The involvement of local populations gives rise to a great need for coordination between CBIs and the other related actors responsible for the governance of NRs (Jérôme Ballet et al., 2009). This process leads to the formulation and modification of the management rules within the framework of collective decision-making, which Njoh (2003; 2012) and Fonchingong & Fonjong (2003) describe as self-governance. They also note that community involvement and management have been considered by the international community as an important tool to enhance public engagement and ownership, a toll that evades the disarray of state bureaucracy in the management of NRs. The notion of CBNRM has, therefore, spread widely over the past few decades: it received extensive acceptance across most sectors in international development planning and management, including the management of rural water supplies in Africa (Harvey & Reed, 2007). A major question that arises is how to manage NRs effectively and efficiently in order to meet the needs of the rising population.

Despite the notable local and national achievements of rural community's involvement in NRM, fundamental challenges to CBNRM remain. Top-down control over NRs continues despite universal modification in the rhetoric over water, land, forest, and wildlife management. Nuesiri

(2015), for instance, argues that the decentralised community forest in Cameroon is still under the control of the government, as only managerial rights are transferred to the communities still closely supervised by the forestry department. In Zimbabwe's Communal Areas Management Program for Indigenous Resources (CAMPFIRE), moreover, powers were transferred to District Development Committees, but the committees were largely under the control of the central government (Mutandwa & Gadzirayi, 2007). Njoh (2002) holds the view that the problem of local tyrannies usually crop up since not all self-organised resource governance systems will be organised democratically or rely on the input of users. Some will be dominated by local leaders or elites who only change rules for their own advantage. Similar challenges, however, apply at the local level when local governance institutions are not downwardly accountable to the community and benefits are disproportionately captured by local elites (Tantoh & Simatele, 2017). Often, CBNRM interventions, as argued by Rondinelli (1991) and Ribot (2002), are not accompanied by the type of long-term investments in capacity-building required to ensure both broader participation and accountability of local community leaders.

However, McCord et al. (2016) point out that the polycentric[4] approach to NR governance could be a more practical, efficient, and effective method of NR governance. This is because successful institutional designs generate information that allows interest-driven actors operating at all levels to learn from other experiences. For instance, polycentric governance practices in the upper Ewaso Ng'iro River basin of Mount Kenya eventually encouraged active participation, capacity building, and decentralised powers among local actors, a process that led to allocating and coordinating water fairly while avoiding conflicts. Orchard & Stringer (2016) further observe that polycentric governance can foster the necessary relationships between and among actors who have a stake in the resource at multiple scales. This has been further supported by McCord et al. (2016) arguing that polycentric governance enhances inclusive decision-making from disparate groups, between and among multiple centres of authority and scales of governance. However, Orchard & Stringer (2016), on the contrary, note that no single level of governance can provide sustainable incentives for users to safeguard the long-term delivery of a variety of services, while imparting management of NRs to external experts. Supporting this assertion, McCord et al. (2016) emphasised that there is no blueprint governance or a one-size-fits-all model, as all human efforts to govern NRs face the problem of creating rules that make sense of the particular social, biophysical, and institutional context in which the resources exist.

The complexity of NRs at local, regional, national, and global levels requires nuanced governance systems involving input from local resource users in diverse fashions (Orchard & Stringer, 2016). Despite the pitfalls of polycentric NR governance, it is still a useful approach for encouraging flexibility, inter-linkages, adaptation, and resilience through the development of structures and processes to match the multi-scale nature of NRs.

Given these imperfections, it is crucial for policy analysts, decision makers, and CD practitioners to acknowledge that no single structure is more advanced relative to the other. The possibility of any given governance structure is likely to depend on a series of context-specific factors: the nature of the resource to be governed; the extent to which local resource users are organised to create, monitor, and enforce the rules for resource use and management; and the degree to which actors who are subject to these local organisational arrangements interact and collaborate with other actors who are external to the community (Bartley et al., 2008).

Institutional Framework of Water Governance in Cameroon

Cameroon is endowed with abundant water potentials; it is the second country in Africa after the Democratic Republic of Congo in terms of quantity of available water resources, estimated to be 322 billion cubic meters (Mafany & Fantong, 2006). This gives available water annually per inhabitant 21,000 cubic meters in Cameroon, three times the world's average (7,000 m^3); but potable water supply still remains a scarce resource because of inadequate management practices (Ntouda et al., 2013). The water resource is a public good in Cameroon and the institutional framework of Cameroon's water sector is characterised by the central role played by MINEE with conventional sectoral approaches in the hands of many other ministries and specialised institutions (Table 7.1).

Table 7.1 shows that Cameroon's water sector is also highly fragmented due to the centrality of the water resource in socio-economic development: many other ministerial departments and public institutions

TABLE 7.1. Ministries and Agencies Responsible for Water Management in Cameroon

Organisation	Ministries and Structure	Activities
Executing Agencies	Ministry of Energy and Water Resources (MINEE)	Central role in the management and protection of water resources at the institutional level.
	Ministry of Territorial Administration and Decentralisation (MINATD)	Intervenes in the field of water and sanitation through decentralised communities; develops disaster response strategies through the direction of civil protection.
	Ministry of Urban Development and Housing (MINDUH)	Intervenes in sanitation as part of the implementation of the national policy on urban development and housing.
	Ministry of Economy, Planning and Regional Development (MINEPAT)	Responsible for the preparation of general guidelines and development strategies, and coordinates the implementation of spatial planning studies.
	Ministry of Domains and Land Affairs	Manages the public and private domains of the State; prepares implements and evaluates the land and cadastral policy of the country.
	Ministry of Transport (MINTRANS)	Responsible for the politics of sea transport.
	Ministry of Industry, Mines and Technological Development	Intervenes in environmental problems related to pollution and sanitation inherent in industries.
	Ministry of Finance (MINFI)	Through the direction of the treasury, it intervenes as the Banker of the State for the financing of projects in the Public Investment Budget (BIP).
	Ministry of Agriculture and Rural Development (MINADER)	Responsible for agricultural hydraulics policy in relation to other organisations concerned; Responsible for rural community development projects.
	Ministry of Towns (MINVILLE)	Responsible for the politics of domestic water supply.
	Ministry of Livestock, Fisheries and Animal Industries (MINEPIA)	Intervenes in the management of water resources through its pastoral hydraulic service.
	Ministry of Environment and Nature Protection (MINENP)	Responsible for the development, planning the management of the environment, combating pollution and proposes measures for the sustainable management of natural resources.
	Ministry of Public Health (MINSANTE)	Health surveillance of communities, promotion of environmental health and hygiene, standardisation and regulation of spills in relation to the organisations concerned.
	Ministry of Commerce (MINCOMMERCE)	Responsible for the politics of commercialisation of water resources.

TABLE 7.1. *(continued)*

Organisation	Ministries and Structure	Activities
Technical and Advisory Bodies	National Water Commission (CNE)	It is the steering committee of the Project Management Team for the elaboration of the Integrated Water Resource Management (IWRM) plan. It is a consultative body of the government that helps to define and put in place water policy in Cameroon.
	National Environment Committee	Responsible for impact assessment of development actions on natural resources; raises public awareness for sound environmental management.
Water Management & Operations Organizations	Cameroon Water Utilities Corporation (CAMWATER) & Camerounaise des Eaux (CDE), Energy of Cameroon (ENEO)	CAMWATER/CDE is responsible for the production and commercialisation of the water resource. They operate only in urban areas and city centres. ENEO supplies hydroelectricity within the country.
Water Management & Operations Organizations	The Urban and Rural Land Development Mission (MAETUR)	Responsible for putting in place water supply and sanitation systems in low cost housing estates.
	Industrial Zones Development and Management Authority (MAGZI)	Responsible for the creation and management of industrial zones. It is also responsible for the design, construction, and management of secondary structures (water sanitation, etc.).
	Cameroon Real Estate Corporation (SIC)	Management of housing areas.
Funding Organizations	Ministry of Finance, International aid Organisations, Non-Governmental Organisations	Finance development projects in the domain of water resources.
Research Organizations	State Universities, Higher Education Institutions With Specialised Laboratories, Scientific Research Institutions	These organisations, which are generally under the supervision of the Ministry of Scientific Research and Innovation, carry out research in the water and sanitation sector.
Non-Institutional Actors	Non-Governmental Organizations (NGOs) Civil Society Organizations (CSOs), Community Organisations, Traditional Authorities	They work in the field of water and sanitation. They equally finance projects, provide technical assistance and advise rural communities in the management of rural community development initiatives.

From "Objectifs du millénaire pour le développement en Afrique," by K.K. Guy-Romain et al., 2006, *Cas du Cameroun, 7,* pp. 1–9; "Water resources management and integrated water resources management (IWRM) in Cameroon," by A.A. Ako, G.E.T. Eyong, and G.G. Nkeng, 2010, *Water Resources Management, 24*(5), pp. 871–888; and "Access to drinking water and health of populations in Sub-Sahara Africa," by J. Ntouda et al., 2013, *Comptes-Rendus – Biologies, 336*(5-6), pp. 305–309.

do interfere in the water sector. The Cameroon Water Utility Corporation (CAMWATER) and Camerounaise des Eaux (CDE) (which replaced the state-owned National Water Company of Cameroon [SNEC] after its privatisation in 2005) is the largest water-supply company in Cameroon and provides potable water only to urban centres where they are guaranteed higher returns, leaving rural communities to their fate (Njoh, 2012). Unfortunately these institutions, as Ntouda et al. (2013) point out, are unable to adequately supply drinkable water to the urban population despite the abundant water resources. This observation, as argued by Guy-Romain et al. (2006), is based on regulation and legislative lapses, as well as poor development and management of water resources, in addition to inadequate political will and commitment. The rural communities with increasing population and high levels of poverty are in the hands of CBOs, which seldom have financial capabilities and the technical know-how to adequately provide potable water to the inhabitants (Tantoh, 2011). It has been further argued by WHO & UNICEF (2014) that about 51% of the rural population do not have access to potable water supply; connection rates are also very low with only 14.5% of the rural population with individual access to drinking water in their premises. This has compelled rural communities to initiate and realise rural water systems to provide drinkable water to their inhabitants and improve their standards of living. The government further enhanced alternative cost-saving public service policies and strategies for supplying potable water, particularly in rural spaces (Njoh, 2003). This state of affairs has, therefore, mandated CBM initiatives to spearhead rural water supply in Northwest Cameroon.

Community Based Water Supply Management (CBWSM) in Northwest Cameroon

CBM and CD policies have a long history in Africa (Page, 2003). Fonchingong & Fonjong (2003) argue that genuine community participation in CD initiatives could be seen in rural spaces through communal work in Cameroon prior to colonisation. This approach to development was intensified by the British colonial masters in Anglophone Africa from the mid-1940s to 1960 and has become a common feature in CD in Northwest and Southwest (former British territories of) Cameroon (Chadwick, 1949; Page, 2003). A concerted effort towards CBM initiatives has, therefore, been under way in SSA since the early 1980s. The British introduced mass education and CD initiatives through compulsory unpaid labour and foreign subventions as a way to develop rural areas (Chadwick, 1949). This approach was not only intended to steer rural community's self-help projects, but also to be a piece of colonial propaganda (Page, 2014). It is no surprise that Village Development Projects (VDPs), realised through popular participation, are relatively common, well-managed, and successful in this part of Cameroon (Njoh, 2003). Although the post-independence period witnessed an increase in local participation, mostly in the execution of government initiated and sponsored projects, the 1990s saw an unprecedented increase of self-reliant projects through enthusiastic and committed local participation within the Grassfields (Fonchingong & Fonjong, 2003). Hence, CBM initiatives developed partly because of the inability of the government to provide basic amenities to rural communities, including potable water supply, but also because of the increased acceptance and recognition of the benefits of engaging the community in VDPs (Rondinelli, 1991). With the arrival of the colonial administrators, customary management strategies replaced the traditional management systems, cultural institutions, and practices with technocratic and centralised state management systems in the exploitation of NRs (Amungwa, 2011). This resulted in the degeneration of Indigenous knowledge systems, creating a disconnect between Indigenous and contemporary management methods (Roe et al., 2009).

Moreover, the changing context steered by the economic crisis that Cameroon experienced in the 1980s and the Structural Adjustment Plan (SAP) in the early 1990s created new challenges for the centralised management system (Fonchingong & Fonjong, 2003). Carmordy (2007), for example, further notes that the SAPs of the World Bank and the International Monetary Fund (IMF) have not enabled recovery, but rather speeded economic decline because of theoretical flaws in the underlying neo-classical economic model and a misreading of Africa's geographic and politico-economic context. As a result, many communities are being transformed by the eagerness and commitment of the local people led to action in organised village or farm communities. It is in this context that CBWSM has been recognised as a promising alternative to the top-down systems of management in Northwest Cameroon, coupled with the inability of the government to realise and sustain successfully water networks over extensive areas without involving grassroots communities (Njoh, 2003; Tantoh, 2011).

CBWSM has thus underscored the virtue of self-reliance, which emerged from the traditional method of NRM. This assertion was confirmed during interview discussions with community leaders in Northwest Cameroon on the importance of community participation in VDPs. The village chiefs from Njimkang and Ngarum, for example, stated:

> It is obligatory for all the sons and daughters in and out of the community to contribute to the realisation of any village development venture. This is usually coordinated by the Village Development Authority often mandated to visit major cities where members of the kindred reside to lobby for funds. (Interview, November 2015)

Interview discussions with focus groups in Baicham, Zang-Tabi, and Ngarum, comprised mostly of women, revealed that

> Potable water supply has been a major problem in the community considering the long distances covered to get water from streams which are of doubtful quality. The time spent by women and children in this exercise could have been channelled to other lucrative activities. So we have a duty to make all the necessary sacrifices to contribute both in-kind and in cash so that our community can be served with pipe-born water. (Interview, January 2016)

The above views underline and re-emphasise the importance of community participation in CBWSM. This observation, as argued by Tantoh and Simatele (2017), is premised on the basis that CBM has the potential and tendency to encourage the full participation of local people in any development venture. It has been argued by Njoh (2003) that community participation is crucial in the realisation of rural water supply systems through participatory modes such as enlistment, cooperation, and consultation. This is because residents feel a sense of ownership of the project through participation. This situation is evident in the Ndu, Njinikom, and Mbengwi rural districts in the Northwestern part of Cameroon where the contribution of community members in the realisation and management of the various community water systems in cash and in-kind have instilled a sense of proprietorship. The sense of ownership served, and continues to serve, to motivate residents to contribute in VDPs. Community participation was, however, possible with the help of CBOs in collaboration with VDAs to promote VDPs and foster development. In this regard, women were charged a minimum of 1500 FCFA (US$3) and men 2000 FCFA (US44). These contributions were complemented with compulsory manual labour such as supplying sand, cement, stones, and digging water distribution channels, which were conducted in turns by the different quarters and coordinated by village quarter heads. A promising strategy in the water sector, therefore, comprises communities mobilising and assuming control of their own water systems.

Community self-help has also been successful through the support and cooperation from public and private agencies in collaboration with CBIs. This partnership has become fundamental in the management of NRs, which involves sharing responsibilities between communities and supporting agencies subject to established norms. For example, national and international NGOs and other public institutions such as The Swiss Association for Technical Assistance/Swiss Association for International Development (SATA-HELVETAS), The Netherlands Development Corporation (SNV), Plan International Cameroon (PLAN Cam), Special Council Support Fund For Mutual Assistance (FEICOM), Water Supply and Sanitation Programme in Rural Areas (PAEPA-MRU), National Community Driven Development Program (PNDP), the Strategic Humanitarian Service (SHUMAS), and Grassfield Participatory and Decentralised Rural Development Project (GP-DERUDEP) have been involved in promoting CD projects in Northwest Cameroon. Their involvement is remarkable in the area of rural water supply and sanitation, protection of watersheds, and financial and technical assistance. These structures work in tandem with VDAs, CBOs, and WMCs in adopting and designing VDPs. Government agencies have sometimes served as catalysts for organising the community to participate in training local leaders. These functions are vital to initiating and sustaining community participation. Rondinelli (1991), for example, argues that even when services are provided entirely by public bureaucracies, some degree of community participation is crucial for informing public officials of the needs and desires of local residents and for improving the effectiveness of water delivery. Thus, public participation in CBWSM highlights the importance of the use of local experience as the inhabitants can easily offer vital ideas and suggestions that could lead to applicable and attainable solutions to water-related problems.

Effective CBM, therefore, depends on establishing operational processes for CBIs and WMCs regulating the water system, for effective O&M, and for evaluating performance. This is because engaging all the stakeholders correlates with community empowerment and sustainability outcomes and impressions. It has, therefore, become evident in policy platforms informed by the debate of sustainability whereby participation, responsibility, stewardship, and duty of care together constitute decisive factors in sustainable CBWSM initiatives. Despite the promising story of CBWSM approaches in Northwest Cameroon, results in practice have often been unsatisfactory, both in respect to organisations with executive authority and, in some instances, segments of the community.

Factors Affecting Effective CBWSM Initiatives in Northwest Cameroon

The water crisis that many communities face is progressively about how people, as individuals, and as part of a collective society, govern the availability, usage, and control of water resources and their benefits. The crisis that most communities and countries face has not only resulted from natural restrictions of water supply or the lack of financing and suitable technologies, though these are serious constraints; rather, the crisis comes from multifaceted failures in water management and governance structures (UNDP 2004). As water becomes an increasingly scarce resource—threatened both quantitatively and qualitatively—and as competing demands between different uses and users become steadily sharper, communities are devising coping strategies and adopting water resource regulations to address in detail the challenges facing the water sector. Results from the case study show that the roots of the water crisis in the Northwestern part of Cameroon can be traced to poverty, top-down

TABLE 7.2. Monthly Average Income, Contributions, and Water Collection Rates in Northwest Cameroon Fieldwork materials, 2016.

Occupation	Monthly Income			Monthly contributions for O&M		Collection Rate	
	Frequency	Monthly income (US$)	Percentage (%)	Private connection (US$)	Public stand taps (US$)	Frequency	Percentage (%)
Civil service	10	≥300	14	2	<1	8	80
Retired	6	100–150	8	2	<1	4	66.7
Business	5	100–150	7	2	<1	3	60
Carpentry/ Building	8	≤100	11	2	<1	4	50
Wine tapping/ Weaving/Hunting	13	≤100	18	2	<1	6	46.1
Farming	17	≤100	24	2	<1	5	29
Animal husbandry	7	≤100	10	2	<1	3	42.9
Others	6	≤100	8	2	<1	2	33
Total	**72**	**n/a**	**100%**	**n/a**	**n/a**	**35**	**n/a**

management, uncoordinated national development policies, as well as the lack of technical know-how and skills.

Table 7.2 shows that the prevalence of poverty is one of the major factors hampering effective CBWSM in Northwest Cameroon. This is because a greater proportion of villagers are engaged in seasonal agriculture (26%) with average monthly revenue of ≤ US$100. Considering the fact that these activities are periodic and unstable, it is difficult for those involved to have a steady source of income throughout the year.

Also, those involved in wine tapping, weaving, hunting, carpentry, building, animal husbandry, as well as persons with no stable occupation comprise 46% of the sampled population, generating an average income of ≤ US$100 a month. These unstable activities thwart the systematic contributions towards the O&M of the water systems. The remaining 18%, including government employees, pensioners, and small business owners, have steady incomes of US$100–300, but cannot solely handle the operating cost of the entire water system. Such low levels of income make it difficult for any inhabitant to promptly and regularly contribute <US$1 a month for the O&M of public stand taps and US$2 for private connections (Table 7.2). For example, only 35 of the 72 sampled populations, making 48.6%, could steadily pay the monthly O&M fee (Table 7.2). It becomes difficult for the WMCs to effectively manage the water systems and even to motivate the water caretakers. This situation, in turn, has led to the abandonment of some stand taps (Figure 7.2), with little or no rehabilitation of existing schemes. This observation has been supported by Harvey & Reed (2007), emphasising that one out of every four rural water facilities is poorly functioning in rural communities in the developing world due to poor O&M. It can, therefore, be argued that the poverty and the low levels of income of the population have an impact on the functioning and sustainability of rural schemes.

Another drawback to effective CBWSM initiatives in Northwest Cameroon is the disjointed water policies among many ministries and agencies (see Table 7.1) that do not communicate with each other (Guy-Romain et al., 2006). For example, the national water laws, policies, and regulations are defined by MINEE and other related ministries and applied throughout the national territory, with little consideration of the realities, especially in rural communities. Since many ministries are involved in

FIGURE 7.2. Dilapidated Water Catchment Tank and Abandoned Stand
Tap Due to Poor Management in Ngarum-Ndu Municipality, Rural North-
West Cameroon. Photo by Henry Bikiwibili Tantoh.

water management in Cameroon with each having its own management policy, effective implementation and enforcement become an issue. This is because information on interventions carried by one of the sectoral ministries in a region on a project is seldom disseminated and remains unknown to other ministries and users of the resource (Ako et al., 2010). Although the concept of CBM was often directed effectively in distinct projects, it has time and again been lost in the process of scaling up and, ironically, disrupted by centralised administrative approaches that failed. It would not be wrong to argue that water management reform has paid little attention to community-based water laws in rural areas within developing countries.[5]

In the same vein, uncoordinated water policies and legal frameworks have frustrated the application of the rules and regulations that govern CD initiatives, particularly water supply projects. Interview conversations with public officials in all the research sites revealed that CD initiatives are shaped by local norms and customs with support from the government departments. Based on discussions with the regional delegate of CD in Bamenda, in Northwest Cameroon, for example, the following was stated:

> The division of services within the department of community development has hampered collaboration between grassroots communities and public authorities. Most community development projects have been commissioned to private consultant companies, leaving the department of community development as animators [grassroots communicators and facilitators working for change]. Elected mayors do not also know how to make use of the resources and personnel at their disposal leading to unnecessary expenditure. (Interview, January 2016)

It is evident from the above discussion that the lack of collaboration between government departments (Departments of Community Development-DCD and Department of Rural Engineering-DRD) under MINADER and between the Council and the communities they are meant to serve is the main cause of unsustainable CBWSM initiatives. For instance, the division of the DRE from the DCD and the lack of co-operation between them have threatened the sustainability of rural water supply projects. The DCD is supposed to be responsible for project identification, feasibility studies, mobilisation of communities, and participatory diagnosis in preparing the communities for the execution of projects, while the DRE is charged with technical issues. However, the DRE singly executes VDPs when contacted by CBOs without consulting the DCD. This has resulted in the degeneration of collaboration between the communities and public authorities leading to flawed community projects. A classic example is the rehabilitation of the Zang-Tabi piped-water supply system that was contracted by the Mbengwi Council to Premier et Yoshim Entreprises (PEYE)[6] without consulting the VDAs and the WMC. Besides, this company has little or no understandings of the scenario of the community, their needs, challenges, or their preferences since the community was never consulted and a thorough feasibility study was never conducted. The community protested on several occasions, but their concerns were neglected as council encouraged the company to continue with the renovation. It is evident that some malpractices were involved in the award of the contract. The mayor and council officials who are supposed to enforce good governance principles are, on the contrary, perpetrating unorthodox management practices. This is a demonstration of power rivalries between public and local managers, with top-down management leading to lack of trust and corrupt practices. Several months after the handing over of the project to the community, leaks around the water tanks and ruptured pipes were common along the network.

Moreover, the notion of decentralisation, which is to facilitate the delegation of NRM to grassroots communities, has not been supplemented by the provision of adequate financial resources and the improvement of their capacities to empower them to take on these tasks. Top-down management, on the contrary, views communities as passive recipients to be led, not efficient actors whose dynamisms could be harnessed through empowerment. Such an approach sees central experts as knowledgeable, whereas only local people could know the exact nature of their problems and possible solutions. In light of recent events in community-based conservation, it is becoming extremely difficult to ignore the importance of watersheds in sustainable water supply. Interview discussions with the mayors of Ndu and Mbengwi municipalities, for example, revealed that

We face increasing problems conserving watersheds, particularly as the villagers depend on the environment and natural resources for subsistence. The watersheds are time and again encroached by cattle especially during the dry season because it is always flourishing with vegetation coupled with uncontrolled fires from agricultural practices. Also, the growth of eucalyptus at catchment perimeters, though an important economic activity within the municipality, has adverse effects on the water resource coupled with the effects of droughts. (Interview, December 2015)

The above sentiment speaks to the argument that, if community water supply in Northwest Cameroon is to be effective, there is the need for the water sources to be adequately protected by applying laws and regulations governing watersheds. This is because watersheds are the main sources of water that supply the community through the gravity-fed technique. Thus, it needs to be protected to assure sustained water supply. However, most of the watersheds within the study area are prone to environmental degradation. The watersheds are threatened by adjacent communities, which continue to affect the quality and quantity of the water resource. This has also been caused by increasing demands for food, leading to the encroachment and conversion of watersheds into farm and grazing lands. This generational occupation connected with high unemployment, low literacy, and high overall community poverty employs 26% of the economically active rural population. As a result, the predominantly poor rural population that depends almost entirely on land for livelihood and their economic activities have far-reaching effects on the water resource.

Conclusion

This chapter was designed to examine the barriers to effective and efficient CBWSM in rural Northwest Cameroon. The most obvious finding to emerge from this study is that inadequate finance, top-down management, uncoordinated policies, and environmental issues are some of the factors affecting the unsustainable supply of potable water. The findings of this study suggest that the different stakeholders are seen as a potential catalyst for addressing water supply problems within the communities, and a way of ensuring that various groups, including those traditionally marginalised from development, can contribute to effective management. CBWSM, therefore, provides an opportunity for communities and all the other interest-driven actors to engage in the management with roles and responsibilities clearly defined alongside those of the regulating authorities. A recurring lesson from experience is that problems of implementation and sustainability arise frequently when project designers either do not know about or simply ignore local conditions and consumers' preferences. Community participation and management are identified repeatedly in evaluations of water supply projects as primary factors affecting sustainability. The following conclusions can be drawn from the present study: for CBWSM to be effective, there must be increased motivation of local groups to (a) adopt water supply systems and to maintain them; (b) contribute regularly for O&M; (c) motivate WMCs to regularly monitor breakdowns and repair them; (d) improve the capacities of the WMCs for water systems maintenance and for implementing other types of community development activities; and (e) allow people to express their needs more effectively to central and local government officials, rather than telling them how to go about management.

NOTES

1   For all acronyms, see the Appendix at the end of the chapter.

2   Water management committee members are selected within the communities. They make major decisions concerning water management and are responsible for the implementation of certain tasks, such as the collection of maintenance fees and the organization of manual work in their communities.

3   The Bamenda Grassfields with Bamenda as the provincial capital represents most of the Northwest Province situated in the Western Highlands of Cameroon. It is called Grassfields because a greater proportion of the area is covered by grassland.

4   This is an approach to governance with multiple centres of decision-making and overlapping authority.

5   This is a set of mostly informal institutional, socio-economic, and cultural arrangements that shape community development, use, management, allocation, quality, control, and productivity of water resources.

6   This is a private construction company.

REFERENCES

Agrawal, A., & Gibson, C. C. (1999). Enchantment and disenchantment: The role of community in natural resource conservation. *World Development, 27*(4), 629–649.

Ako, A. A., Eyong, G. E. T., & Nkeng, G. E. (2010). Water resources management and integrated water resources management (IWRM) in Cameroon. *Water Resources Management, 24*(5), 871–888.

Amungwa, F. A. (2011). The evolution of conflicts related to natural resource management in Cameroon. *Journal of Human Ecology, 35*(1), 53–60.

Barrow, E., Gichohi, H., & Infield, M. (2000). Rhetoric or Reality? A review of community conservation policy and practice in East Africa. *Evaluating Eden Series no. 5.* International Institute for Environment and Development, London.

Bartley, T., Andersson, K., Jagger, P., & Van Laerhoven, F. (2008). The contribution of institutional theories to explaining decentralization of natural resource governance. *Society and Natural Resources, 21*, 160–174.

Borrini-Feyerabend, G., Kothari, A., & Oviedo, G. (2004). *Indigenous and local communities and protected areas: Towards equity and enhanced conservation.* http://doi.org/10.2305/IUCN.CH.2004.PAG.11.en

Campbell, B., & Shackleton, S. (2001). The Organizational structures for community-based natural resources management in Southern Africa. *African Studies Quarterly, 5*(3), 87–114.

Carmody, P. (2007). Constructing alternatives to structural adjustment in Africa. *Review of African Political Economy, 25*(75), 25–46.

Carmody, P. (2010). *Globalization in Africa: Recolonization or renaissance?* Lynne Rienner Publications.

Cash, D. W., Adger, W. N., Berkes, F., Garden, P., Lebel, L., Olsson, P., & Young, O. (2006). Scale and cross-scale dynamics: Governance and information in a multilevel world. *Ecology and Society, 11*(2), 12. http://doi.org/8

Chadwick, E. R. (1949). *Communal development in Udi Division of SE Nigeria.* UNESCO. (Unpublished).

Cheru, F. (2002). Debt, adjustment and the politics of effective response to HIV/AIDS in Africa. *Third World Quarterly, 23*(2), 299–312.

Dörre, A. (2015). Promises and realities of community-based pasture management approaches: Observations from Kyrgyzstan. *Pastoralism, 5*(1), 15.

Fonchingong, C. C., & Fonjong, L. N. (2003). The concept of self-reliance in community development initiatives in the Cameroon grassfields. *Nordic Journal of African Studies*, 12(2), 196–219. Retrieved from http://www.njas.helsinki.fi/pdf-files/vol12num2/charles.pdf

Gruber, J. (2011). Perspectives of effective and sustainable community-based natural resource management: An application of Q methodology to forest projects. *Conservation and Society, 9*(2), 159.

Guy-Romain, K. K., Mpakam, H. G., Ndonwy, S. A., Serges, L., Bopda, D., Géologie, L. De, & Ingénieur, D. (2006). Objectifs du millénaire pour le développement en Afrique. *Cas du Cameroun, 7,* 1–9.

Harvey, P. A., & Reed, R. A. (2007). Community-managed water supplies in Africa: Sustainable or dispensable? *Community Development Journal, 42*(3), 365–378.

Jérôme Ballet, Koffi, K. J., & Komena, B. (2009). Co-management of natural resources in developing countries: The importance of context. *Économie internationale, 4*(120), 53–76.

Khanal, P. R., Santini, G., & Merrey, D. (2014). *Water and the rural poor: Interventions for improving livelihoods in Asia.* http://www.fao.org/documents/card/en/c/9385d3f8-2282-4b41-ba80-0737aa37c520/

Koppen, B., van Giordano, M., Butterworth, J., & Mapedza, E. (2007). Community-based water law and water resource management reform in developing countries: Rationale, contents and key messages. In B. Koppem, M. van Giordana, & J. Butterworth (Eds.), *Community-based water law and water resource management reform in developing countries* (pp. 6-7). CABI Books.

Matarrita-Cascante, D., & Brennan, M. A. (2012). Conceptualizing community development in the twenty-first century. *Community Development, 43*(3), 293–305.

McCord, P., Dell'Angelo, J., Baldwin, E., & Evans, T. (2016, June). Polycentric transformation in Kenyan water governance: A dynamic analysis of institutional and social-ecological change. *Policy Studies Journal, 45*(4). https://doi:10.1111/psj.12168

Mafany G.T., & Fantong, W.Y. (2006). Groundwater quality in Cameroon and its vulnerability to pollution. In Y. Xu, & B. Usher (Eds.), *Groundwater pollution in Africa* (pp. 47-54). Taylor and Francis/Balkema.

Musingafi, M. C. C., & Chadamoyo, P. (2013). Challenges and prospects for potable water supply governance in Zimbabwe. *International Journal of Innovative Research in Management, 2*(1), 25–42.

Mutandwa, E., & Gadzirayi, C. T. (2007). Impact of community-based approaches to wildlife management: case study of the CAMPFIRE programme in Zimbabwe. *International Journal of Sustainable Development & World Ecology, 14*(4), 336–344.

Nelson, F., & Agrawal, A. (2008). Patronage or participation? Community-based natural resource management reform in Sub-Saharan Africa. *Development & Change, 39*(4), 557–585.

Njoh, A.J. (2002). Barriers to community participation: Lessons from the Mutengene (Cameroon) self-help water supply project. *Community Development Journal, 37,* 233–248.

Njoh, A.J. (2003). The Role of community participation in public works projects in LDCs: the case of the Bonadikombo, Limbe (Cameroon) self-help water supply project. *International Development Review, 25,* 85–103.

Njoh, A. J. (2012). Citizen-controlled water supply systems: Lessons from Bonadikombo, Limbe, Cameroon. In B. Balanyá, B. Brennan, O. Hoedeman, S. Kishimoto, & P. Terhorst (Eds.), *Reclaiming public water: Achievements, struggles and visions from around the world* (pp. 281). Transnational Institute (TNI) & Corporate Europe Observatory (CEO). https:// www.corporateeurope.org

Ntouda, J., Sikodf, F., Ibrahim, M., & Abba, I. (2013). Access to drinking water and health of populations in Sub-Saharan Africa. *Comptes Rendus - Biologies, 336*(5–6), 305–309.

Nuesiri, E. O. (2015). Monetary and non-monetary benefits from the Bimbia-Bonadikombo community forest, Cameroon: Policy implications relevant for carbon emissions reduction programmes. *Community Development Journal, 50*(4), 661–676.

Orchard, S. E., & Stringer, L. C. (2016). Challenges to polycentric governance of an international development project tackling land degradation in Swaziland. *Ambio, 45*(7), 796–807.

Ostrom, E. (1990). *Governing the Commons*. Cambridge University Press.

Page, B. (2003). Communities as the agents of commodification: The Kumbo Water Authority in Northwest Cameroon. *Geoforum, 34*(4), 483–498.

Page, B. (2014). And the Oscar goes to … Daybreak in Udi: Understanding late colonial community development and its legacy through film. *Development and Change, 45*(5), 838–868. http://doi.org/10.1111/dech.12119

Prager, D., Virdin, J., Hammond, A., Angell, P., Mcneill, C., & Evans, J. W. (2005). The wealth of the poor: Managing ecosystems to fight poverty. *World,* 268.

Ribot, J.C. (2002). African decentralization: Local Actors, powers and accountability. *UNRISD Democracy, Governance and Human Rights*, Paper no. 8, UNRISD.

Ribot, J. C., Agrawal, A., & Larson, A. M. (2006). Recentralizing while decentralizing: How national governments reappropriate forest resources. *World Development, 34*(11), 1864–1886. http://doi.org/10.1016/j.worlddev.2005.11.020

Rihoy, E., & Maguranyanga, B. (2007). Devolution and democratisation of natural resource management in Southern Africa: A comparative analysis of CBNRM policy processes in Botswana and Zimbabwe. *CASS-PLAAS CBNRM Occasional Paper, 18*, 1–62.

Roe D., Nelson, F., & Sandbrook, C. (2009). *Community management of natural resources in Africa: Impacts, experiences and future directions*, Natural Resource Issues No. 18, International Institute for Environment and Development, London, UK.

Rondinelli, D. (1991). Decentralizing water supply services in developing countries: factors affecting the success of community management. *Public Administration and Development, 11*(5), 415–430.

Simatele, D., Binns, T., & Simatele, M. (2012). Urban livelihoods under a changing climate: Perspectives on urban agriculture and planning in Lusaka, Zambia. *Journal of Human Development and Capabilities, 13*(2), 269–293.

Stone, M. T., & Nyaupane, G. (2014). Rethinking *community* in community-based natural resource management. *Community Development, 45*(1), 17–31.

Sun, Y., Asante, F., & Birner, R. (2010, September). *Opportunities and challenges of community-based rural drinking water supplies: An analysis of water and sanitation* committees in Ghana. IFPRI discussion papers 1026, International Food Policy Research Institute (IFPRI).

Tantoh, H. B. (2011). *Problematic of governance in the sustainable management of community projects: The case of potable water supply in Bambili Northwest Region of Cameroon.* [Unpublished master's thesis]. Université de Dschang-Cameroon.

Tantoh, H. B., & Simatele, D. (2017). Community-based water resource management in Northwest Cameroon: the role of potable water supply in community development. *South African Geographical Journal, 99(2),* 166–183.

United Nations Development Programme. (2004). *Water governance for poverty reduction*: Key issues and the UNDP response to Millennium Development Goals. Author: New York. WHO, & UNICEF. (2014). Progress on sanitation and drinking-water - 2014 update. In *The Joint Monitoring Programme for Water Supply and Sanitation, II,* 1–78. http://doi.org/978 92 4 50724 0

Appendix

List of Acronyms

Cameroon Water Utility Corporation	CAMWATER
Camerounaise des Eaux	CDE
Civil Society Organizations	CSOs
Common Pool Resources	CPRs
Communal Areas Management Program for Indigenous Resources	CAMPFIRE
Community-Based Institution	CBIs
Community-Based Organisations	CBOs
Community-Based Water Supply Management	CBWSM
Community-Based Management	CBM
Community-Based Natural Resource Management	CBNRM
Department of Rural Engineering	DRD
Departments of Community Development	DCD
Energy of Cameroon	ENEO
Central African Fanc	FCFA
Grassfield Participatory and Decentralised Rural Development Project	GP-DERUDEP
Industrial Zones Development and Management Authority	MAGZI
Ministry of Agriculture and Rural Development	MINADER
Ministry of Commerce	MINCOMMERCE
Ministry of Economy, Planning and Regional Development	MINEPAT
Ministry of Environment and Nature Protection	MINENP
Ministry of Finance	MINFI
Ministry of Industry, Mines and Technological Development	MINMIDT
Ministry of Livestock, Fisheries and Animal Industries	MINEPIA
Ministry of Public Health	MINSANTE
Ministry of Territorial Administration and Decentralisation	MINATD
Ministry of Towns	MINVILLE
Ministry of Urban Development and Housing	MINDUH
Ministry of Water Resource and Energy	MINEE
National Community Driven Development Program	PNDP
National Environment Committee	NEC
National Water Commission	CNE
Natural Resource	NR
Natural Resources Management	NRM
Non-Governmental Organisations	NGOs
Operation and Maintenance	O&M
Plan International Cameroon	PLAN Cam
Premier et Yoshim Entreprises	PEYE
Special Council Support Fund for Mutual Assistance	FEICOM
State-Owned National Water Company of Cameroon	SNEC
Strategic Humanitarian Service	SHUMAS

Structural Adjustment Plan	SAP
Sub-Saharan Africa	SSA
Swiss Association for Technical Assistance/	SATA
Swiss Association for International Development	HELVETAS
Netherlands Development Corporation	SNV
Urban and Rural Land Development Mission	MAETUR
United States Dollars	US$
United Nations International Children Emergency Fund	UNICEF
Village Development Associations	VDAs
Water Management Committees	WMC
Water Supply and Sanitation Programme in Rural Areas	PAEPA-MRU
World Health Organisation	WHO
World Bank and the International Monetary Fund	IMF

8

Taming the Tambraparni River: Reservoirs, Hydro-Electric Power Generation, and Raising Fish in South India

Arivalagan Murugeshapandian

Introduction

In South India in the second half of the nineteenth century, the colonial government transformed the environment significantly. In the Tambraparni River basin, it built reservoirs both in the plains and mountain forests to store river and rain waters and thus expand agricultural lands as well as generate electricity. In order to achieve this undertaking, the government produced alarmist discourse regarding flood potential in the guise of protecting local peoples and their property. Its engineered structures were used as instruments to take control of, and wrest water resources. During the post-colonial period that followed, the government gave priority to hydro-electric power generation over irrigation. The electricity department criticised local farmers as "unauthorised cultivators" and characterised their lands as "unauthorised lands" when farmers demanded the release of stored water from the reservoir. Electricity was sold to urban areas to power, among other things, a modern cotton mill, cinema halls, tube-well irrigation, and street lighting. All these activities were noted as modernisation of the district. Similarly, the volumetric space of the reservoir was utilised by the post-colonial fisheries department to raise commercially valuable fish stocks. This venture entailed dispossessing an Indigenous tribal community of their traditional rights; instead, Indigenous peoples were compelled to pay angling fees while catching fish for consumption.

This chapter engages and uncovers archival sources to explore the history of hydro-social relations governing the Tambraparni River system, and delineates the historical complexity of the system over a period of intense change, from the second half of the nineteenth century to the 1960s. I demonstrate how colonialism initially transformed surface waterscapes from irrigation to electricity regeneration in order to regulate and control water sources, and how, when India gained its independence, the new government transformed the region again by raising fish stocks in the reservoir created in the preceding period.

In the field of water history, there are two sorts of dominant historical river narratives: one concerning the dead river and a second regarding the conquered one. According to Tevdt and Jakobsson, the latter focused on "harnessed rivers" and "how control of rivers also meant social domination of some people over others."[1] This chapter adopts the second category of narratives, "The Conquered River," in order to analyse the Tambraparni River and its impact on socio-economic relations during and after the colonial period in this particular river basin in South India.

The Tambraparni River System

The river is seventy-five miles long, from its point of origin in Periya Pothigaimalai in the southern tip of Western Ghats to the Gulf of Manaar, Bay of Bengal. It travels through the Tirunelveli and Thoothukudi districts of Tamil Nadu State, South India. In 1879, A. J. Stuart described the river system as a "narrow green winding ribbon, with a silver thread in its centre, [which] represents the Tambraparni with its irrigated land—the wealth of *Tirunelvelly*."[2] The river contributes immensely to the anicut and supply channels constructed in the pre-colonial period for irrigation. In the 1920s, the Tambraparni drained an area of about 1,750 square miles both in the mountains and plains. In the *Tirunelveli District Gazetteer* in 1916, this river system was considered "first class" and "the chief river of the district."[3] Smaller rivers used to irrigate the upper basin paddy fields situated in the foothills, while in the plains the river has six major tributaries. Additionally, the Tambraparni has two sets of offshoots stemming from the mountains: the chief tributaries of Peyar, Ullar, Pambar, Kariyar, and Servalar; and the secondary tributaries of Sopar, Mylar, and Gowdalaiar. The river has a catchment area of 200 square miles in the forests and receives rainfall from both the southwest and northeast monsoons. Historically, rainfall has been heaviest during May to November with "rain in all months of the year at that elevation".[4] Hence, this massive river system is considered perennial.

Productivity of the Tambraparni

Pre-colonial Indigenous rulers channelised the flow of the Tambraparni River by constructing eight anicuts to irrigate paddy fields located near the basin. In the 1870s, the colonial authorities praised the masonry skill visible in these pre-colonial constructions. The river supplied water to 891 tanks to irrigate the fields; another 37,830 acres were irrigated through channel-fed tanks. The river and irrigation system were considered "the principal feature in the district"[5] in terms of their perennial supply of water to a total of 64,671 acres of fields, which produced two paddy crops every year without fail. A large number of tanks located in the plains were fed by rainfall drainage in addition to the river. A.J. Stuart, the nineteenth-century water collector of Tirunelveli, elaborately described it as follows:

> Even when tanks are connected by channels and anicuts with the rivers or streams which cross the district, the bulk of the supply beyond ten miles from the foot of the ghats, excepting only in the case of the Tamrapurni, is derived from the surface drainage of the country during heavy rain, by which the rivers are suddenly swollen into rapid torrents, whose waters are diverted by dam below dam, and led by channel after channel to multitudes of tanks with so much effect that it is rare that any water reaches the sea.[6]

Stuart admired the old irrigation system as "very ancient, … very complete with numerous anicuts cross the Tamrapurni and its affluents, and supply channels and tanks in a manner which reflects the highest credit upon the skill and energy of the ancient governments who constructed them."[7] The canal-fed irrigation system was classified into upper and lower systems. While the upper system fell into the Ambasamudram region, where paddy was cultivated as the prime crop, the lower system produced other crops such as turmeric, plantain, betel-leaves, and sugarcane. However, the colonial authorities criticised the old irrigation system when it started to build its own new anicut at Srivaikuntam situated in the lower system. It began to produce alarmist discourses on floods so as to justify the construction of a modern reservoir in both the plains and mountain forests.

Manufacturing Hydraulic Fears

From the outset of British colonization, the colonial government reviewed the old irrigation system and concluded that it was "not very efficient."[8] The government proposed to build new reservoirs at Srivaikuntam and the Papanasam lower hills in order to tame the floods. The colonial government's intention was not only to expand agriculture to generate revenue, but also to use the river system as a tool to take control of the forests from Indigenous peoples.

The authorities cited earlier floods to justify dam building. They argued that about twelve floods had occurred between 1810 and 1931. As mentioned earlier, the plains and the foothills have historically received rainfall from the northeast monsoon while the mountain forests received rainfall from the southwest monsoon. The district witnessed the "most serious"[9] floods in 1810, 1827, 1847, 1869, 1874, 1877 (twice), 1880, 1895, 1914, 1923, and 1931. According to the colonial authorities, these floods caused "a great deal of damage"[10] to irrigation networks, roads, and livestock. Frightening narratives about the floods were publicized. J.B. Pennington, then the water collector of Tirunelveli, estimated the damage at about 30,000 rupees during the floods of 1880. Further, the collector produced the following statement: "What would have been the result if there had been heavy rain on the Papanasam hills and six or seven feet more water in the Tambraparni proper, as might easily have happened, it is impossible to contemplate without very serious anxiety. Almost certainly the river would have topped the banks above Srivaikuntam and swept away everything right down to the sea more completely than even in 1877."[11]

The colonial government depicted the Tambraparni, flowing from the mountain forests above Papanasam down to the sea, as the "most dangerous river."[12] The sloped nature of the terrain, it was argued, made the flow more forceful. Hence, a reservoir was proposed to shield the existing irrigation networks, roads, and fields from flooding.

In 1881, the Tirunelveli irrigation department requested that the government appoint a public works officer "to specially investigate under the Tambraparni"[13] with the purpose of expanding the existing irrigation system. The district collector, Pennington, proposed increasing the capacity of the existing tanks and constructing new tanks for protecting the valley from drought. In the 1881 Proceedings of the Madras Government, he argued that "building infrastructure would make the land valuable and bring benefits to the government." Moreover, Pennington was quite confident of the project's success and its acceptance by the locals. He said that the district had "the extraordinary enterprise of the people: only provide water and the people will do all the rest. There is no fear of their declining it or failing to utilize every drop."[14] Ultimately, the Madras Board of Revenue deputized an officer to investigate the feasibility of the scheme.

The Srivaikuntam Anicut

Srivaikuntam is situated in the lower basin of the Tambraparni River system. Historically, the system supplied water to tanks located at Srivaikuntam through Marudur Kilakal and two other main channels from both sides of the river. Similarly, channels cut from the river system in Srivaikuntam six miles below on the north and south banks fed tanks situated in Korkai and Attur, from which stored water was distributed through chain tanks to far-off fields. The ancient system irrigated about 12,800 acres. This was the situation until the construction of Srivaikuntam anicut or dam in 1868. As mentioned earlier, the colonial authorities evaluated the existing irrigation system and concluded that it was "most defective" and "the head-sluice of the southern channel was … completely silted up." Under these circumstances, the district engineer made it clear in 1855 that the proposed Srivaikuntam dam project was meant "to enlarge and improve this decrepit and wasteful system."[15]

The final construction of the proposed anicut in the Tambraparni River was instrumental in the massive agricultural expansion on the

TABLE 8.1. Expansion of Agricultural Land

Faslis*	Increase of Revenue (Rs.)	Area Irrigated (Acres)
1870	- 2,750	18,712
1871	+ 16,321	21,222
1872	- 15,327	17,183
1873	+ 23,140	22,648
1874	+ 37,504	26,255
1875	+ 41,452	30,019
1876	+ 22,351	33,451
1877	+ 44,873	34,255
1878	+ 51,283	35,238

*Fasli means calendar of 12 months from July to June. In India, it was introduced for land revenue and record purposes. Faslis 1280 to 1288 correspond to 1870 to 1878. Source: Proceedings of the Board of Revenue, 1879, Board No. 3, 256.

south bank of the river during the last quarter of the nineteenth century. In 1875, the then water collector of Tirunelveli, R.K. Puckle,[16] reported on it elaborately. The Srivaikuntam dam construction brought 100% of uncultivable lands into the fold of cultivable fields and resulted in the doubling of agricultural revenue in the lower Tambraparni River system.[17] Table 8.1 illustrates the revenue increases of irrigated land in the region over time between 1870 and 1878.

The 100% increase in revenue highlighted not only the benefits of constructing the dam, but also local farmers' efforts and acceptance of the project. It was proposed that the revenue generated would subsequently be used to build a reservoir in the hills. The government also declared that it built the anicut in the plains to tame floods. Now, it would focus its attention and energies on constructing reservoirs in the mountains to store river water.

Measuring Rainfall and the Construction of the Reservoir

In the late nineteenth century, with the Srivaikuntam anicut completed, the colonial government proceeded to build two reservoirs on the lower slopes of the mountain forests. To implement the scheme, it started to measure water sources to establish the viability of setting up a rain-gauge in the catchment areas. Farmers belonging to the Tambraparni upper basin formally asked the government for the same in the Papanasam forests.

In 1885, the colonial government set up rain-gauges to measure rainfall in the elevated forests as well as the plains. It conducted precipitation measurement for two reasons: to find "the relation between the total rainfall … and the water-supply to the river during the same period" and to capture "the changes which may take place in the water-supply during the comparatively dry season."[18] The data assured that the rainfall on the hills accounted for "the greater part of the annual supply available for irrigation" in the district. In 1912–1913, the government again conducted[19] rain-gauge readings in connection with the mountain reservoir project. In 1922, the landed proprietors[20] of Kannadiyan Canal located in the river valley requested similar measurements. The proposed reservoir construction, in reality, took fifty years to reach fruition.

Regulating the Water

The colonial state explored the possibility of tapping revenue from other forest resources in the beginning of the twentieth century.[21] It regulated surface water utilisation to create revenue in addition to funds collected from irrigation usage. Temples accessed river water freely to fill temple tanks for common usage, but the government questioned this and asked the temple trustees to pay a water tax. Yet, at the same time, the government also allowed a modern mill to access river water without taxation. The contemporary landscape of the Papanasam Upper Dam is featured in Figure 8.1.

In 1883, the Messrs A. and F. Harvey & Co sought permission from the government to construct an anicut and channel half a mile above the head of Papanasam falls to provide sufficient water to operate 150 horse-power turbines. It planned to start a cotton spinning mill at the foothills, and needed "a quantity of water not exceeding 20 cubic feet per 1' [minute]

FIGURE 8.1. The Contemporary Landscape of the Papanasam Upper Dam. Photo by Arivalagan Murugesapandian.

throughout the year to operate a turbine of a cotton factory."[22] The company claimed that the project was "new to this Presidency [Madras] or even to India."[23] Further, it assured that it would neither pollute nor diminish the water supply. The collector of Tirunelveli enquired with the board of revenue "whether any charge will be made for the use of water, and if so, how the charge is to be calculated."[24] But the board reiterated that "no charge for the use of the water-power should be made."[25]

As far as the quantity of water was concerned, the superintending engineer, H.R. Meade, noted that the 20 cubic feet per 1" was sufficient to irrigate 1,330 acres. Further, the engineer observed that the government should allow 10 cubic feet per 1" only for this operation and should not give exclusive right over the river water. A clarification was issued that the quantity would depend on the availability of water. The company replied that "we trust the Government will not impose any unnecessary stipulations, as we find it not easy to induce English capital to embark in such industries in India, and, if heavy restrictions be imposed, it will become impossible."[26] However, the collector of Tirunelveli strongly recommended "the concession of an exclusive right to the water for a limited term of years, certainly not less than 15, … because the enterprise is of a novel description and its success can hardly be considered to be at all assured."[27]

In the end, the board of revenue supported[28] the application but without assurance on the exclusive right to use water. Still, it would not ask anything for accessing the water. In effect, then, the government permitted the company to commence the venture on the lower forest slopes without charging a water tax. It considered the opening of a spinning mill a modern enterprise, a progressive venture, and a march towards civilization.

Meanwhile, the local temple trustees had accessed river water to fill the temples' tanks for centuries, as this was considered an absolute traditional right. In the 1930s, the government tried to abolish this right and asked the temples to pay a water tax. The trustees opposed and sued[29] the government based on the following grounds: the worshippers used the temple tanks to wash before entering the temple; conducted a special worship in the tanks during festivals, and used the water to wash vessels and irrigate the temples' flower garden; and, significantly, the general public also accessed the tank for washing purposes. The trustees argued that the temple tank water was accessed for common usage and not as a commercial venture.

The Papanasam Scheme: Agricultural Production vs. Hydro-Electric Production

In 1938, the government instituted a hydro-electric power project on the lower forest slopes where it constructed two reservoirs from upper and lower dams. It used the reservoirs[30] to generate hydro-electric power with the intention to supply power to neighbouring districts in addition to irrigation. It built the lower dam at Pechiammankoil, where the estimated submerged area was about 260 acres.[31] The upper dam constituted a major project at Kariyar with an estimated submerged area of 360 acres. The hydro-electricity department contracted to provide a powerhouse with 4,000 KW capacity near the Papanasam lower dam. When in 1944 the hydro-electric powerhouse came into operation,[32] the post-independence government stated that it would be "self-remunerative in nature."[33]

Just over a decade later, Tambraparni farmers approached the government to release water from the Papanasam reservoir to save the kar season's paddy crop. The kar constitutes a double-crop cultivation season falling between June 15 and September 15, regulated by the southwest monsoon. According to the farmer's association,[34] farmers cultivated paddy in an area of 3,500 acres that required water for about a month. They petitioned the government to release water from the reservoir to save the crop. At the same time, the authorities received another petition[35] from the Kadamba tank farmers in Tiruchendhur taluk[36] concerning cultivators below the Kadamba tank. Farmers there had cultivated the third crop for the year after the failures of the first two crops. Indeed, this had been the pattern for the past seven years. They now asked the authorities to release water to reap a harvest.

The collector of Tirunelveli argued that the existing crop season of kar cultivation was raised after the harvesting of "advance kar crop" and therefore warned that farmers had planted "at their own risk"; they would "not be considered" for a "special supply of water."[37] The electricity department accused these farmers of making an "unauthorised cultivation" of "unauthorised crops."[38] Water was critical also for the paddy crop variety used, given its long maturity period—between 90 to 100 days—and which, according to the same department, required large quantities of it. However, the chief engineer for irrigation stated[39] that the water storage position in the reservoir was "satisfactory"; he requested the release of 1,400 cusecs (cubic meter per second) from the reservoir for one week. The electricity department agreed to release the water for four days; it was reluctant to discharge water for cultivation after considering the inflows in Papanasam reservoir, because it was "less than normal" and had "poor" inflow. Furthermore, the department complained that the water release would cause a power shortage and that it would be "difficult to allow further special releases for irrigation from the reservoir in the present circumstances."[40]

Farmers from Tirunelveli sub-division sent another petition[41] to increase the water supply because they received "a very poor supply" of water from the reservoir; cutting off the special supply of water for cultivation would adversely affect them. Tirunelveli farmers responded with profound worry. They argued that the electricity department's decision would "dangerously affect the crops" and bring "a serious catastrophe" to the cultivation system. They again requested a special release of water from the reservoir to "save thousands of acres of paddy crops … and save thousands of families from ruin." The government ordered the release of 1,400 cusecs for twelve days from the Papanasam reservoir and the electricity department discharged the water despite warning of power cuts.[42]

"Tail End" — "Poor Storage"

In 1956, tail-end farmers, particularly from the village of Iruvappapuram, Srivaikuntam taluk, sent a telegraph to the Minister of Public Works asking for the release of water to protect the advanced stage of their paddy crops.[43] These farmers cited instances from the colonial period when the government had released water for irrigation, even though the reservoir at that time was low. During that period, the reservoir had weak inflow contributing to poor storage in the two tail-end anicuts, while affecting 5,700 acres of paddy crop that required two spells of watering before harvest. Under these circumstances, farmers had demanded that the colonial government release water from the reservoir, which demand was accepted.

In response to this current crisis, the chief engineer for irrigation requested the release of 900 cusecs of water for five days to meet the situation, which was reported as "really bad."[44] He calculated the amount of water deemed necessary based on the inflow into the reservoir. Though the electricity department reported that the Papanasam reservoir had, what it called, "the poorest storage,"[45] it nonetheless released the required amount of water for saving the crop. But it underscored that any future special release of water would be "extremely difficult." Later, the villagers, land owners, members of legislative assembly, and cultivators telegraphed the Chief Minister, the Ministers of Public Works, and the Minister of Agriculture regarding this matter.[46] The electricity department cautioned that the special release would bring the water to draw-down level in the reservoir and that would affect power generation. Again, the irrigation department requested the discharge of 500 cusecs for about eight or 10 days to save 55,000 acres of paddy, though it would cause power cut.[47] Finally, the required amount of water was discharged for a week to save the standing crop after getting inflow from the catchment area.[48]

Conflict

In Tirunelveli district, Indigenous farmers had traditionally used the Tambraparni River to cultivate two seasonal crops (kar and pishanam).[49] This changed after the construction of Papanasam reservoir and powerhouse in the mountain forests. Both the electricity department and the irrigation department had never encountered problems distributing water to farmers when the flow was sufficient from the catchment areas to the reservoir. But the two departments inevitably encountered difficulties during poor inflows because each required water for its own purposes—power-generation and irrigation respectively.[50] Lack of water set the stage for conflict.

The electricity department gave preference to hydro-electric power generation over releasing water for irrigation. In 1948, the government formulated a regulation regarding the release of water from the reservoir to try to tackle the situation.[51] It revised the regulation in 1954,[52] when the post-independence government ordered the release of water from the reservoir with an increase in the quantity from 2,000 cusecs to 3,000 cusecs, from June 16 to March 31. Additionally, as an alternative for weather contingencies, it also ordered the retention of 2,000 cusecs for release at any time during the year. Finally, the government announced that "any balance [in the reservoir] not drawn within two fortnightly periods after that in which impounding was made or before November 1 whichever is earlier shall lapse and become part of the electricity department storage."[53]

In response, the district water collector requested that the two fortnight period for withdrawal of impounded water be cancelled, as it could not deploy the full quantity of water allocated for irrigation purposes during the rainy season. Against this background, the collector remarked that it was "impossible to operate on this credit within this short period. The rule should be amended to permit this extra quantity being drawn up to the end of March."[54] Further, "if the rule is not amended, what will happen is that the credit will accumulate during the rainy season and will lapse before the rainy season ends so that during January and February, when water is required for irrigation, we may not be able to take advantage of the additional storage that was received during the rainy season."[55] The electricity department argued with the collector saying that the timeframe of November 1 was fixed "with a view to have greater head and storage during the North-East monsoon period and subsequently to meet power requirements during the summer months." It was also noted that "the interests of power storage for which the dam was built will not be safeguarded."[56] In the end, the government made it clear that the Papanasam reservoir was "purely a power project and the power storage" had "to be safeguarded."[57]

"Written with Tears of Blood"

In 1957, lower basin farmers, particularly from the Srivaikuntam and Maruthur anicut regions, faced water shortages for their kar paddy crops comprising more than 25,000 acres. Farmers reported the situation as "very serious"[58] and that the crops were "sure to fail" without immediate assistance. They took their grievance[59] to the government through petitions and personal meetings, urgently requesting water from the Papanasam reservoir and complaining to the Minister of Public Works about the stubborn attitude of the executive engineer. In their petition, they used phrases like "the petition is written with tears of blood" to highlight their plight and begged the minister to take stern action against the engineer's inaction. "We swear in the name of Gandhi through submitting a remorseful letter that if this sort of executive engineer serves in each district there will be no choice left to farmers but to starve and beg after leaving agriculture."[60]

Farmers from the villages of Arumugamangalam, Maramangalam, and Kottarakurichi also urgently requested water from the reservoir connected to the Srivaikuntam dam. The tank there dispensed water to 2,500 acres of double crop wetland situated in the three villages. The villagers primarily depended on agriculture for their livelihood. This was highlighted in their petition as follows: "many poor families with their cattle who are mainly depending on agriculture income alone will have to meet untold sufferings and hardships and lead to chaos and death from starvation. In the last kar season also there was a partial failure."[61] The water problem was addressed not only by the cultivators belonging to the affected villages, but also by their farmers' association.

At the same time, the Tirunelveli farmers' association demanded the discharge of water by arguing for priority to agricultural production over power generation. Their petition underlined the importance of agriculture in the wake of the food crisis in the country during that period. The association cited recent instances in which water had been discharged from the reservoir. The year before, in 1956, the government had discharged water to the upper and tail-end areas when the reservoir water level was lower than twenty-seven feet. Now, one year later, when the water level was seventy-two feet, the government refused. Farmers represented by their association were distressed and perplexed. They admitted that the seventy-two-foot level would "not be sufficient to water the 80,000 acres of kar paddy crops and at the same time produce the normal quantity of electricity also,"[62] but the association nevertheless urged the government to discharge the water immediately to save the paddy crops. The members argued that small industries such as rice mills and cinema theatres could manage power cuts if water was released to irrigate the paddy fields. "Government will come to the correct conclusion of saving the kar crops and lakhs of kottahs of kar paddy, especially at this juncture when our whole country is undergoing a food crisis because of so many reasons."[63]

The Kalloor Melakkulam farmers tried another strategy to provoke the government to discharge water from the reservoir: they remembered how the former colonial authorities had "protected the cultivators by dispersing water from the Papanasam reservoir to save their crops at a critical situation, even when the reservoir hit the water at the lowest level of 40 feet." They criticized the post-independence government for failing to address the grievances of its own people: "We have realized that nothing is going to happen in this country when incompetent officials occupy office."[64] The Public Works Department[65] asked the Electricity Department to release 1,800 cusecs of water from the Papanasam reservoir for ten days, but the Electricity Department agreed to discharge only 1,200 cusecs. The discharge did not serve the purpose, so the Irrigation Department suggested the release of 800 cusecs and 300 cusecs again from the reservoirs of Papanasam and Manimuthar respectively. Still, conditions remained "very precarious" even after the Irrigation Department demanded[66] another 1,100 cusecs of water release from the Papanasam reservoir.

"A Purely Power Reservoir"

Time and again during the mid- to late-1950s, the Electricity Department encountered opposition from various quarters—from farmers, members of the legislative assembly, and a host of associations—for not releasing water to protect standing crops. Cultivators, especially from the tail-end lower and upper basin of the Tambraparni, sent repeated, urgent petitions. Yet the Electricity Department refused to budge, maintaining that the reservoir was what it called "a purely power reservoir"[67] not meant for irrigation. It explained that its department employed stored water solely for running hydro-electric turbines.

As demand for released water remained high during this period, there was not enough water for irrigation infrastructures to save many standing crops. According to the department's estimate, unauthorised cultivation varied between 1,900 to 10,000 acres during 1950 and 1955. Illegitimate cultivation was in and around 4,102 acres in 1950, 3,900 acres in 1951, 10,000 acres in 1952, 8,500 acres in 1954, and 1,900 acres in 1955. Given this situation, the department suggested the levy of "the maximum penalty" against the unauthorised cultivators to prevent illegitimate cultivation. Further, it remarked that the cultivators ignored the warning issued about the illegal extension of cultivation owing to "a wide margin of profit [from agriculture], despite the penal assessment." The department strongly recommended the elimination of unauthorised cultivation in order to run the power-house turbine without interruption. It said this of the functioning of the power house: "it is absolutely essential to work the Papanasam reservoir to the extent of rotating the generators at least, to maintain the voltage in the area. If the generators do not revolve, voltage regulation will be impossible and there will be failure of power supplies with the result that several industries in the southern areas will be badly hit." The electricity department established two arguments to dismiss the cultivators' requisition, namely that the dam was "a purely power reservoir," and that the cultivation was unauthorised. It considered power generation as indispensable for "the march of civilization."

Utilising Volumetric Space

The post-independence government later used the volumetric water space for aquaculture by introducing commercially valuable fish seeds. Conflict emerged between the forest and fisheries departments in terms of controlling the revenue generating from the fish rearing. Fish breeding intruded into Kanis' traditional rights of fishing in certain rivers.

The fisheries department approached the government to regulate inland fishing in the reserved forests after building reservoirs in the mountains. In 1949, the government issued a sanctioning order[68] to the fisheries department to take control over the water spread areas of upper dam, lower dam, and Tambraparni River up to Papanasam bridge located near the temple in the foot-hills for five years. By 1950 the aforementioned water spread areas were brought[69] under the India Fisheries Act, 1897 to exploit aquatic resources by issuing licenses. The fisheries department issued fishing licenses[70] and managed these resources under the supervision of one field man and three fishermen. They were involved in guarding the fishery, preventing illicit fishing, collecting fingerlings, and conducting systematic exploitation of the fish stocked in the reservoir. The department sought[71] three years extension from the government to continue its control over the water-stored areas.

In 1958, the lake was opened to professional fishermen to fish with nets, in addition to licensed anglers. The fisheries department issued licenses under the condition that "fishing of all kinds except with one line with not more than 25 hooks"[72] was banned in the water-stored areas. It also permitted the license holder to fish only after making prepayment of the prescribed fee. The department prohibited the catching of gourami and mirror carp and permitted fishing within 100 yards of any masonry work near the jetty, while banning the display of the catch for sale near the water-stored areas. It collected eight *annas*[73] per day, two rupees per month, and twenty rupees for a year for one angler with one line and not more than 25 hooks.

"Original" vs. "Introduced Fish"

The forest department raised the issue of "original" vs. "introduced fish" after settling the matter of who had the authority to issue fishing licenses. It objected to the fisheries department's crediting the revenue of fisheries into the forest department's account. The fisheries department paid a nominal rent to the forest department for having its water-spread areas in the reserved forests. Even so, the forest department demanded suitable compensation for the task of protecting the fish population within the waters in the reserved forests. The board of revenue defended the fisheries department saying that the department alone should conduct the cultural operations in the water-spread areas to increase fish population.

However, the forest department countered that "the product [fish population] is a product given by nature [that] has developed within Reserved Forest. As such, the Forest Department is entitled to it."[74] It also criticized the introduction of fresh water fish in the upper reaches because the fish found in the locality was the salt water variety, which came from the seas to spawn and breed in the creeks of the reserves. The fish population increased in the water stored areas "without the interference" of the fisheries department and not because of the cultural operations. The forest department claimed that it protected and conserved the fish population in the reserved forest. It also clarified that the river system already had its own fish population and that it should be entitled to that. The department also justified its claim by stating the following: "The areas of Papanasam Upper and Lower dams, though not dis-reserved, have been handed over to the Electricity Department collecting land value and the fishing right in these dams are not sold by this Department nor the revenue credited to the Forest Department."[75] In this context, it demanded that the fishery revenue "must be credited" to its account.

The board of revenue dismissed the claim of the forest department. Here, both departments competed for the volumetric aquatic space and the revenue obtained from it. Later, the fisheries department harassed the Kani tribal community for fishing in the Tambraparni River between the upper and lower dams where the community did angling or fishing for their own consumption. For a while, they were forced to pay the fee for fishing and were not allowed to practice their traditional rights.

Conclusion

This chapter outlines how fluvial potentialities were tamed to generate revenue at the expense of poor farmers and Indigenous peoples. First, the colonial Indian government churned out an alarmist discourse on floods to build reservoirs to store water for irrigation, with the long run aim of expanding agriculture for revenue purposes. Second, it tried to abolish the common rights of access to temple tanks while permitting modern industrial mills to access river water without any tax. Third, it utilized the reservoir to generate hydro-electric power to modernize the state. In the post-independence period, the same strategy was followed in the name of "the march of civilization." The post-independence government, however, gave preference to power generation and, in the process, marginalized cultivators while also using stored-water areas to breed fish.

NOTES

1   Terje Tvedt and Eva Jakobsson, "Introduction: Water History is World History," in *History of Water: Water Control and River Biographies, Volume 1*, ed. Terje Tvedt and Eva Jakobsson (New York: I.B. Tauris, 2006), xix.

2   A. J. Stuart, *Manual of the Tirunelvlly District in the Presidency of Madras* (Madras: The Government Press, 1879), 3.

3   H. R. Pate, *Tirunelveli District Gazetteer* (Madras: Government Press, 1916; repr., Tirunelveli: Manonmanium Sundaranar University, 1993).

4   Pate, *Tirunelveli District*, 16.

5   Stuart, *Manual Tirunelvelly*, 3.

6   Stuart, *Manual Tirunelvelly*, 5.

7   Stuart, *Manual Tirunelvelly*, 16.

8   F.H. Hebbert to J.B. Pennington, November 18, 1880, *Proceedings of the Board of Revenue*, Revenue Department, Board No. 88, January 20, 1881, Tamil Nadu Archives [TNA], Chennai, India.

9   T.A. Whitehead to the Court of Wards, August 27, 1937, *Proceedings of the Conservator of Forests*, No. 451, Mis., TNA.

10   J.B. Pennington to the Secretary of the Board of Revenue, August 5, 1881, No. 429, *Proceedings of the Board of Revenue*, Revenue Department, November 2, 1881, Board No. 2,589, TNA.

11   J.B. Pennington to the Secretary of the Board of Revenue, August 5, 1881, No. 429, *Proceedings of the Board of Revenue*, Revenue Department, November 2, 1881, Board No. 2,589, TNA.

12   *Proceedings of the Board of Revenue*, Revenue Department, December 1, 1879, Board No. 3, 256, TNA.

13   *Proceedings of the Madras Government*, Revenue Department, November 21, 1881, No. 1766, TNA.

14   *Proceedings of the Board of Revenue*, Revenue Department, November 2, 1881, Board No. 2,589, TNA.

15   Pate, *Tirunelveli District Gazetteer*, 173.

16   R.K. Puckle to the Board of Revenue, November 21, 1874, No. 623, *Proceedings of the Board of Revenue*, Revenue Department, January 4, 1875, Board No. 4, TNA.

17   *Proceedings of the Board of Revenue*, Revenue Department, December 1, 1879, Board No. 3, 256, TNA.

18   D. Brandis, *Suggestions Regarding Forest Administration in the Madras Presidency* (Madras: The Government Press, 1883), 77.

19   *Public Works Department Administration Report, 1912–1913*, part-II, Irrigation (Madras: The Government Press), TNA.

20   The Proprietors to the Prince of Wales, the King-Emperor, the Two Houses of London Parliament, the Indian Secretary of State, the Delhi Viceroy, the Madras Board of Revenue, the Collector of Tirunelveli, *Proceedings of the Conservator of Forests*, January 19, 1922, No. 14, Mis., TNA.

21   Arivalagan Murugeshapandian, "Forests, Environmental Change and Tribal Communities in Colonial Tamil Nadu" (PhD diss., University of Madras, 2014).

22   H.R. Meade to the Collector of Tirunelveli, February 23, 1883, No. 779, *Proceedings of the Board of Revenue*, Revenue Department, April 10, 1883, Board No. 997, TNA.

23   Messrs. A. and F. Harvey and Co to the Collector of Tirunelveli, February 7, 1883, *Proceedings of the Board of Revenue*, Revenue Department, April 10, 1883, Board No. 997, TNA.

24   J.B. Pennington to the Board of Revenue, February 2, 1883, No. 58, *Proceedings of the Board of Revenue*, Revenue Department, February 13, 1883, Board No. 411, TNA.

25   J.B. Pennington to the Board of Revenue, February 2, 1883, No. 58, *Proceedings of the Board of Revenue*, Revenue Department, February 13, 1883, Board No. 411, TNA .

26   Messrs. A. and F. Harvey and Co. to the Collector of Tirunelveli, March 8, 1883, *Proceedings of the Board of Revenue*, Revenue Department, April 10, 1883, Board No. 997, TNA.

27   J.B. Pennington to the Board of Revenue, March 11, 1883, No. 154, *Proceedings of the Board of Revenue*, Revenue Department, April 10, 1883, Board No. 997, TNA.

28   J.B. Pennington to the Board of Revenue, March 11, 1883, No. 154, *Proceedings of the Board of Revenue*, Revenue Department, April 10, 1883, Board No. 997, TNA .

29   Public Works and Labour Department, G.O., No. 2685 (I), Mis. Series, October 26, 1931, and G.O. No. 2861 (I), Mis. Series, November 16, 1931, TNA.

30   Public Works Department (Electricity), March 29, 1938, G. O., No. 653, Press., *Proceedings of the Conservator of Forests*, May 23, 1941, No. 216, Mis., TNA.

31   *Proceedings of the Conservator of Forests*, January 6, 1941, No. 9, Press., TNA.

32   The Chief Engineer for Electricity to the Secretary, July 28, 1956, Public Works Department, TNA,

33   Public Works Department, August 16, 1956, G.O., No. 3555, Mis.; The Chief Engineer for Electricity, Madras to the Secretary, August 15, 1954, TNA.

34   *Peikulam Pasana Vivasayigal Abiviruthi Sangam* (Peikulam Irrigation Cultivators' Developmental Association), Iruvappapuram Village, Srivaikuntam taluk, Tirunelveli district.

35   The members of Madras Legislative Assembly to the Chief Engineer for Irrigation, August 6, 1955, G.O. No. 4342, Ms., November 18, 1955, Public Works Department, TNA.

36   Sub-division of a district.

37   Tirunelveli Collector's Endorsement, No. L. Dis. 15005/55, August 5, 1955, Tirunelveli Division Letter No. 1039R, August 2, 1955, G.O. No. 4342, Ms., November 18, 1955, Public Works Department, TNA.

38   The Executive Engineer to the Superintending Engineer, August 10, 1955, No. 2898-SE, G.O. No. 4342, Ms., November 18, 1955, Public Works Department, TNA.

39   The Chief Engineer for Irrigation to the Secretary, August 5, 1955, G.O., No. 3555, Mis., August 16, 1956, Public Works Department, TNA.

40   The Chief Engineer for Electricity to the Secretary, August 18, 1955, Public Works Department, G.O., No. 3555, Mis., August 16, 1956, Public Works Department, TNA.

41   A petition was submitted to the Minister for Public Works, August 17, 1955, G.O., No. 3555, Mis., August 16, 1956, Public Works Department, TNA.

42   The Chief Engineer for Electricity to the Secretary, September 1, 1955, G.O., No. 3555, Mis., August 16, 1956, Public Works Department, TNA.

43   Telegraphic message to the Minister of Public Works Department (Irrigation), July 25, 1956, G.O., No. 4037, Mis., September 25, 1956., Public Works Department, TNA.

44   U. Ananda Rao to the Chief Engineer for Electricity, July 26, 1956, G.O., No. 4037, Mis., September 25, 1956, Public Works Department, TNA.

45   The Chief Engineer for Electricity to the Secretary, July 28, 1956, G.O., No. 4037, Mis., September 25, 1956, Public Works Department, TNA.

46   G.O., No. 4037, Mis., September 25, 1956, Public Works Department, TNA.

47   U. Ananda Rao to the Chief Engineer for Electricity, August 6, 1956, G.O., No. 4037, Mis., September 25, 1956, Public Works Department, TNA.

48   The Chief Engineer for Electricity to the Secretary, August 7, 1956, Public Works Department, TNA.

49   Season of cultivation produces single crop; the north-east monsoon regulates the season between October 15 to January 15.

50   The Special Chief Engineer (Public Works) to the Chief Engineer (Electricity), August 7, 1954, Public Works Department, TNA.

51   Public Works Department, G.O. No. 53, Mis., January 6, 1948, TNA.

52   The Special Chief Engineer (Public Works) to the Chief Engineer (Electricity), August 7, 1954, G.O., No. 4037, Mis., September 25, 1956, Public Works Department, TNA.

53   Rules for the Regulation of the Papanasam Reservoir on the Tambraparni River (as agreed to now between Chief Engineer for Irrigation and Chief Engineer for Electricity, for which Government-approval is sought). G.O., No. 4037, Mis., September 25, 1956, Public Works Department, TNA.

54   The Collector of Tirunelveli to the Board of Revenue, March 20, 1955, G.O., No. 4037, Mis., September 25, 1956, Public Works Department, TNA.

55   The Collector of Tirunelveli to the Board of Revenue Secretary (Land revenue), September 16, 1955. G.O., No. 4037, Mis., September 25, 1956, Public Works Department, TNA.

56   The Chief Engineer for Electricity to the Government Secretary, G.O., No. 4037, Mis., September 25, 1956, Public Works Department, TNA.

57   The Commissioner of Land Revenue, Commercial Taxes and Prohibition to the Government Secretary, October 19, 1955, Public Works Department, G.O., No. 4037, Mis., September 25, 1956, Public Works Department, TNA.

58   The Chief Engineer to the Government Secretary, August 7, 1957, G.O., No. 2967, Ms., August 31, 1957, Public Works Department, TNA.

59   Representation was made by cultivators, members of the legislative assembly, members of farmers' associations, and officer bearers of welfare committees to the Chief Minister, Ministers of Irrigation, and Electricity, the Collector, the Chief Engineer, and the Executive Engineer, G.O., No. 2967, Ms., August 31, 1957, Public Works Department, TNA.

60   G.O., No. 2967, Ms., August 31, 1957, Public Works Department, TNA.

61   The Secretary, Arumugamangalam Welfare Committee to the Minister of Electricity and Transport, G.O., No. 2967, Mis., August 31, 1957, Public Works Department, TNA.

62   R. Nallakannu, District Vivasayigal Sangam, Tirunelveli to the Minister for Electricity, G.O., No. 2967, Mis., August 31, 1957, Public Works Department, TNA.

63   The *lakh* is a unit of measurement in South Asia equal to 100,000. The *kottah* is a unit of grain equal to 140 kilograms.

64   Kalloor Melakkulam Farmers to M.S. Selvaraj, Thruchendur Constituency Member, G.O., No. 2967, Mis., August 31, 1957, Public Works Department, TNA.

65	The Chief Engineer to the Government Secretary, August 7, 1957, G.O., No. 2967, Mis., August 31, 1957, Public Works Department, TNA.

66	U. Ananda Rao, Chief Engineer (Irrigation), to the Government Secretary, August 22, 1957, G.O., No. 2967, Mis., August 31, 1957, Public Works Department, TNA.

67	This note was submitted with reference to the oral orders of M (E) on August 13, 1957, G.O., No. 2967, Mis., August 31, 1957, Public Works Department, TNA.

68	G.O., No. 177, Mis., January 10, 1949 (Development Department), *Proceedings of the Conservator of Forests*, No. 77/57, Mis., April 8, 1957, TNA.

69	G.O., No. 2322, Mis., June 9, 1950 (Development Department) cited in the letter of the Director of Industries and Commerce to the Government (Agriculture Department), March 31, 1954, *Proceedings of the Conservator of Forests*, No. 77/57, Mis., April 8, 1957, TNA.

70	G.O., Ms. No. 2272, May 14, 1953 (Development Department), *Proceedings of the Conservator of Forests*, No. 77/57, Mis., April 8, 1957, TNA.

71	The Director of Industries and Commerce to the Government (Agriculture Department), March 31, 1954, *Proceedings of the Conservator of Forests*, No. 77/57, Mis., April 8, 1957, TNA.

72	G.O., No. 4214, Mis., December 27, 1958 (Food and Agriculture Department), *Proceedings of the Board of Revenue* No. 68/59, Mis., February 26, 1959, TNA.

73	*Anna* is the basic unit of Indian currency during the colonial period; one anna is equal to 1/16 of rupee.

74	The Chief Conservator of Forests to the Board of Revenue, *Proceedings of the Board of Revenue*, No. 104/57, Mis., April 24, 1957, TNA.

75	K. Andiappan, "Conservator of Forests to the Chief Conservator of Forests," April 26, 1956, *Proceedings of the Board of Revenue*, No. 104/57, Mis., April 24, 1957, TNA.

REFERENCES

GOVERNMENT RECORDS

Proceedings of the Board of Revenue, Board No. 2,589, TNA, Chennai.

Proceedings of the Board of Revenue, Board No. 3, 256, TNA, Chennai.

Proceedings of the Board of Revenue, Board No. 3178, TNA, Chennai.

Proceedings of the Board of Revenue, Board No. 4, TNA, Chennai.

Proceedings of the Board of Revenue, Board No. 411, TNA, Chennai.

Proceedings of the Board of Revenue, Board No. 88, Tamil Nadu Archives [TNA], Chennai, India.

Proceedings of the Board of Revenue, Board No. 997, TNA, Chennai.

Proceedings of the Board of Revenue, Forest No. 10, TNA, Chennai.

Proceedings of the Board of Revenue, G.O. No. 947, TNA, Chennai.

Proceedings of the Board of Revenue, No. 104/57, Mis., TNA, Chennai.

Proceedings of the Board of Revenue, No. 68/59, Mis., TNA, Chennai.

Proceedings of the Conservator of Forests, No. 14, Mis., TNA, Chennai.

Proceedings of the Conservator of Forests, No. 216, Mis., TNA, Chennai.

Proceedings of the Conservator of Forests, No. 451, Mis., TNA, Chennai.

Proceedings of the Conservator of Forests, No. 77/57, Mis., TNA, Chennai.

Proceedings of the Conservator of Forests, No. 9, Press., TNA, Chennai.

Proceedings of the Madras Government, Board No. 1766, TNA, Chennai.

Public Works and Labour Department, G.O. No. 2685 (I), Mis., Chennai

Public Works and Labour Department, G.O. No. 2861 (I), Mis., TNA, Chennai.

Public Works and Labour Department, G.O. No. 4037, Mis., TNA, Chennai.

Public Works Department (Electricity), G. O., No. 653, Press., TNA, Chennai

Public Works Department, G.O. No. 2967, Mis., TNA, Chennai.

Public Works Department, G.O. No. 3555, Mis., TNA, Chennai.

Public Works Department, G.O. No. 4342, Mis., TNA, Chennai.

Public Works Department, G.O. No. 53, Mis., TNA, Chennai.

OFFICIAL PUBLICATIONS

Brandis, D. *Suggestions Regarding Forest Administration in the Madras Presidency.* Madras: The Government Press, 1883.

Pate, H. R. *Tinnevelly District Gazetteer.* Madras: Government Press, 1916. Reprint, Tirunelveli: Manonmanium Sundaranar University, 1993.

Public Works Department Administration Report, 1912-1913, part-II, Irrigation. Madras: The Government Press, 1914.

Stuart, A.J. *Manual of the Tirunelvelly District in the Presidency of Madras.* Madras: The Government Press, 1879.

SECONDARY SOURCES

Murugeshapandian, Arivalagan. "Forests, Environmental Change and Tribal Communities in Colonial Tamil Nadu." PhD diss., University of Madras, 2014.

Tvedt, Terje, and Eva Jakobsson. "Introduction: Water History is World History." In *History of Water. Volume 1: Water Control and River Biographies*, edited by Terje Tvedt and Eva Jakobsson, ix-xxiii. New York: I.B. Tauris, 2006.

A Tale of Two Watersheds in the Mackenzie River Basin: Linking Land Use Planning to the Hydroscape

Reg Whitten

The Mackenzie River Basin is the largest in Canada, covering 1.8 million square kilometres and has source waters in six basins found within three provinces and two territories.[1] The Mackenzie River itself is also the longest river in the country at 1,802 kilometres and has the 12th largest freshwater delta in the world. Its mean discharge of 9,700 m³/s is second only to that of the St Lawrence with a peak discharge that normally occurs in June. Upon completion of the Mackenzie River Basin Transboundary Waters Master Agreement in 1997, the Mackenzie Basin Management Board (MBMB) was established as an educational and advisory body to serve as "a cooperative forum to inform about and advocate for the maintenance of the ecological integrity of the entire Mackenzie watershed" (Mackenzie River Basin Board, 2015). The Peel River and Kiskatinaw River watershed are shown in Figure 9.1. Concerns over industrial development in its source water basins of British Columbia and Alberta were first raised in 1972, following completion of the WAC Bennett Dam, but continue to the present time resulting from cumulative land-use change. In this chapter, we contrast two basins with very different hydroscapes[2] in the Mackenzie Basin to illustrate the extent of research, planning, and

FIGURE 9.1. The Mackenzie River Basin. From Government of Alberta.

management efforts relating to the challenges of sustainable water stewardship (Mackenzie River Basin Board Secretariat, 2003; Mackenzie River Basin, 2017; Alberta Environment and Parks, 2017).

The Upper Kiskatinaw Watershed Story

When the City of Dawson Creek's water supply system was constructed by the U.S. Army Corps of Engineers during World War II, it would have been hard to imagine just how much the landscape within the upper Kiskatinaw River watershed (UKRW) of northeast BC would change in the decades to follow. The unstable silty drainage system that gave definition to its original Woodland Cree name "kîskatinâw sipi" as "steep hill or cutbank river" is known for its very erodible riparian terrain, with high natural spikes in turbidity after spring freshet and intense rainfall periods (seen in Figure 9.2). Very little land-use activity in those days would have added to this impact in the watershed. Other contemporary water

FIGURE 9.2. The Kiskatinaw River With Steep Erodible Slopes. Photo by Kit Fast.

management challenges relate to incidental surface water diversion and sediment loading to the Kiskatinaw River from expanding gas industry roads and pipeline infrastructure.

Traditional resource-use by the region's Aboriginal peoples of Treaty 8 (BC) and rural settlers recorded plentiful harvests of ungulates (moose, deer, and caribou) and fish (rainbow trout, Arctic grayling, whitefish, dolly varden, pike, and pickerel). Today, much of the Indigenous use has been curtailed in this watershed owing to increased cumulative land-use change that has degraded some sub-basins due to habitat loss, degradation, and wildlife displacement. Other Indigenous communities based at Kelly Lake (Cree Nation, First Nation, and Apetokosan Nation [Kelley Lake Métis Settlement Society]) have relied on the watershed as part of their traditional use territory for hunting, fishing, and trapping; however, there is no record of their interests having ever been assessed. One study suggests key indicators of northern Caribou winter habitat quality have deteriorated in the UKRW, but further work is needed to document direct effects of industry versus other factors for this provincially blue listed species (Forest Practices Board, 2011b). Given that hydro-ecological interactions are critical elements for maintaining healthy watersheds, such changes to riparian, wetland habitats, and aquatic species are all important

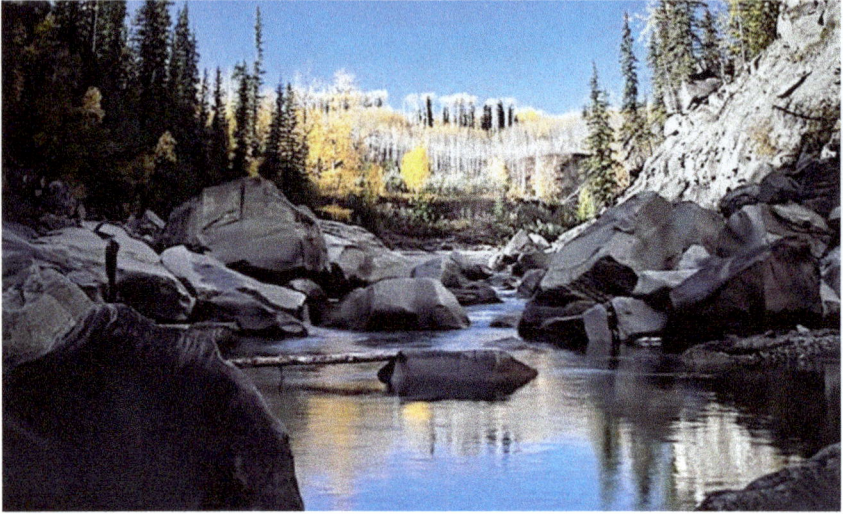

FIGURE 9.3. The Upper Kiskatinaw River. Photo by Kit Fast.

sustainability indicators for water quality and flows. The UKRW can be seen in Figure 9.3.

Dawson Creek's existing water system serves a population of 12,115 in the city, 689 in Pouce Coupe, plus an additional rural population of about 3,000 for bulk water supply (BC Stats 2016; City of Dawson Creek, 2013).[3] In 2014, the city daily water demand for *all* residential, commercial, industrial (gas fracking), and agricultural uses for Dawson Creek and Pouce Coupe was estimated to be 550 litres per person per day (City of Dawson Creek, 2014). This represents about 44% of the 18,000 m^3 per day the city is permitted to draw from the Kiskatinaw River. When the river is low—typically in late summer, fall, and winter—the city can extract only 9,000 m^3 per day, and a recent report stated that "if (shale gas industry) fracking water use was eliminated, daily per-person consumption would drop to about 435 litres; as a result, the current water source would be adequate until 2048 assuming current patterns of use" (City of Dawson Creek, 2014, p. 4). It is interesting to note that the city was successful in 2013 in obtaining permission from the BC Water Comptroller to divert up to half its licensed volume for private water transport sales to Alberta, as a means of generating local government revenues to support shale gas industry development. This was possible given that its water licence was in place prior to the passage of the 1996 Water Protection Act, which prohibits water removal except through exemption by existing tenure, as is the case with many large industrial water licences in northeast BC.

As development intensified over the past twenty years, so too have concerns about impacts to surface flows and quality with various forms of Crown and private land development by gas, agriculture, and forestry. These include rapid expansion of water course crossings and increased surface disturbance to wetlands and riparian areas. A 2011 Forest Practices Board study that examined the topic of cumulative effects management determined there were over 1,200 authorized tenures,[4] with over 37 crossings located on erodible soils resulting in a continuing source of sedimentation from human activities. Some sub-basins were therefore classified as a high risk to water quality (Forests Practices Board, 2011b).

Planning for Land-Use and Watershed Stewardship

Watershed management planning at the City of Dawson Creek goes back to the mid-1980s leading to an integrated watershed management plan (IWMP) in 1991, one of the first planning initiatives for a municipal water purveyor in the province (Government, 1991). The purpose of the IWMP was to detail a land and resource management plan for the watershed that would ensure that water quality, quantity, and timing of flows are given the highest priority in all resource management decisions affecting domestic drinking water supply, forestry, fish and wildlife habitat, recreation, oil and gas, mining, and other land use activities. Critical issues at that time centred around flow availability to support city water demand. At the time, the process was dominated by concerns with range and forest sectors with interest in prospective future oil and gas development, which then was limited to 83 active wells, averaging .18 ha in size. An important step was taken with this plan with the creation of a registered Notation of Interest by the Province in the UKRW, which ensured that attention was given to water management concerns in all land-use and development referrals. Upon completion of the plan, it was stated that "there are short-comings and gaps, notably a detailed set of resource management guidelines which set down measures and constraints to be followed

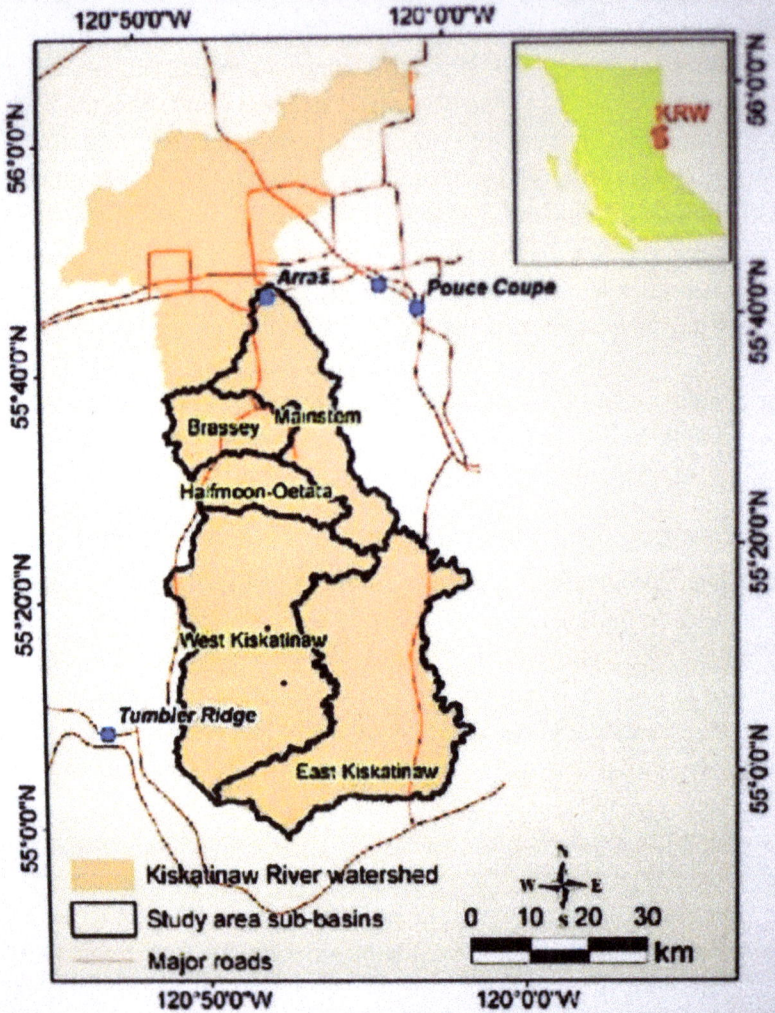

FIGURE 9.4. Map of the Kiskatinaw River Watershed. From Gopal Saha, Wilfred Laurier University.

by all resource users (to be prepared for future versions of the report)" (Government of BC, 1991, p. 1).

Subsequent land and resource management planning (LRMP) in the mid-1990s, and increased regulatory and oversight from passage of the Forest Practices Code, led to watershed assessments and the fostering of ecosystem-based forest-harvesting practices. In that plan, Dawson Creek's "Domestic Water Supply Area" was given recognition, but not as a "Community Watershed" since that status is only targeted for water-sheds less than 500 km^2 in area. The Bearhole Lakes Provincial Park and Protected Area was also created through the LRMP process to provide permanent protection for the Kiskatinaw River headwater and other sub-basins. Some additional management direction in the Dawson Creek LRMP provided for a 1000m3 Enhanced Management Zone within the lower Kiskatinaw River main-stem corridor, but no restrictions were set out regarding the type of industrial tenures that could be permitted within that zone (Government of BC, 1998). Some encroachment on this protected management area has occurred in response to management of Mountain Pine Beetle infestations. Figure 9.4 provides a map of the Kiskatinaw River watershed region.

First Nations were not engaged in these earlier watershed planning processes, but some limited involvement by the Saulteau First Nation did occur as part of the LRMP process. In the UKRW, further engagement focused primarily on development of the Bearhole Lake storage reservoir and maintenance of fish passage as part of the constructed level control weir. Recent studies have shown that Bearhole Lake indicates as being a viable long-term reserve water supply due to a net positive groundwater recharge to the Lake in the winter and spring (Kerr Wood Leidel, 2016). It is noted that Treaty 8 First Nations generally resisted participation in provincial land-use planning as there was an inadequate recognition of Treaty rights or an articulation of a government-to-government relation-ship. That situation has evolved in recent years, as the First Nations en-gage in different initiatives related to regional cumulative environmental effects and reconciliation agreements, including support for community watershed management objectives. In addition, annual reports are filed for public and First Nations review, along with other subsequent consulta-tions relating to the city's water management activities. Such impetus has been driven by independent reviews by the Forest Practices Board (2011) and more recently by the BC Auditor General (2015). Half of the eight priorities in that latter report recommended for immediate attention focused around water management related to aquatic ecosystems—watershed condition/risk, low flow/in-stream flow needs, water quality, and riparian objectives.

Notwithstanding a formal request by the mayor and council in 2014, the Province has not yet accepted the city's request to have it recognized as a "Designated Watershed" under Section 35 of the BC Oil & Gas Activities Act and specifically, the Environmental Management Protection Regulations (EMPR, 2016). Such a legal classification, if implemented, would raise the level of collaboration in reviewing development referrals. More importantly, it would further highlight issues where certain activities might need to be restricted in determined sensitive areas where the impact to water quality is a greater concern. Though the BC Oil & Gas Environmental Management Guideline (BCOGC) is an important planning tool, a Designated Watershed classification would ensure that "activities in such an operating area do not cause a material adverse effect" (2016, p. 13). Without such a shared decision-making mechanism, the city continues to be left with limited ability to influence water management, and only through incremental and site-specific land-use development referrals. A more formal role would serve to provide advance delineation of sensitive, protected, or enhanced management areas related to elevated water risk hazards such as shallow groundwater or vulnerable riparian and wetland areas, which might impact upon supply and/or quality.

By 2003, the city decided to update its watershed management plan with partial funding from the Peace River Watershed Council,[5] and embark on a process of re-engaging all stakeholders to identify watershed values, and creating a course for improved action ranging from education to enhanced watershed characterization and sediment source control by all land-use sectors (City of Dawson Creek, 2003). By this time, it had become clear that risks to water quality and flow from a rapidly expanding oil and gas development (wells, roads, pipelines, waste disposal facilities) led to increasing uncertainty of the UKRW as a viable long-term water source. Other sectors in agriculture (crops and range) also expressed interest in improved watershed management. It became apparent that a model approach could be pursued for collaborative watershed management to address issues of shared interest. Specific topics that would create a foundation for integrated watershed management[6] focused on the following areas of desired future outcomes:

- There is a partnership between the stakeholders with the goal to protect the water resource.
- Water quality (after treatment) continues to meet all provincial and federal drinking water requirements.
- Water supply and storage are adequate to meet the demands (both consumptive and non-consumptive).
- Raw water quality is protected from impacts from resource development activities.
- Integrated multiple resource use is compatible with the supply of safe drinking water, and the risk of water contamination from all activities is low or moderate in the watershed.
- Integrated and comprehensive plans are developed over time to address all watershed activities and development.

Concerns initially focused on elevated levels of parasites, bacteria, and pathogens traced to upstream land-uses, including ranching as well as natural sources. This issue provided impetus to a series of watershed characterization efforts (Government of British Columbia 2004; 2007; 2008). The city was strongly encouraged by the Northern Health Authority (Regional Drinking Water Team) to undertake development of a Source Water Protection Plan (SWPP) in 2006 to give impetus to a focus on water quality protection objectives. Funding was committed by the city with annual support from the Peace River Regional District to create the position of a watershed steward to oversee implementation of the city's watershed plans and research program. Although there are overlapping Métis and First Nations interests in the watershed, the SWPP process did not undertake any meaningful participation nor follow-up in the planning outputs, except as previously noted for the recommended prescribed water storage infrastructure project at Bearhole Lake. Continued public and First

Nations reporting is also required for that reservoir as part of its annual Management Plan, with a focus on protection of fish and riparian habitat.

Although both the 1991 and 2003 plans were aimed at promoting integrated watershed management (IWM) in concept, the approach did not gain the traction nor the support needed by the responsible agencies to ensure multiple industry sector compliance. The work did, however, provide impetus to addressing issues of available water supply and quality protection to support the City of Dawson Creek's needs as we elaborate in this paper. The gap in watershed characterization data, integrated management mechanisms, and adequate water legislation that addressed the complex challenges related to both ground and surface water management have all been critical considerations, which expanded the conversation. It was only when further droughts (2003, 2010, 2013), induced evidence of sedimentation, riparian habitat loss, and climate change issues became apparent in the past decade that there has been a growing awareness of the need to start recognizing formal IWM practice. This contrasts to experiences in other jurisdictions in southern BC and elsewhere in Canada, where greater attention has been given to the value of this approach (Fitzgibbon et al., 2006; Shrubole & Mitchell, 2007). Conservation Ontario, for example, has provided leadership through many decades of work by Conservation Authorities. That agency defines IWM as "the process of managing human activities and natural resources on a watershed basis. This approach allows us to protect important water resources, while at the same time addressing critical issues such as the current and future impacts of rapid growth and climate change" (Conservation Ontario, 2017). The challenge remains in trying to move from concept to practice in the UKRM and throughout north-east BC.

Building on Local Best Practice to Address Regional Water Management Challenges

Regional challenges remain related to water supply and flows in the general Upper Peace Basin, within which the UKRW is situated. As noted earlier, water quality and flow implications have long been known to exist in periods of low flow during drought and winter seasons. However, it is not yet known how groundwater flows affect the hydrological regime. Shallow groundwater areas, artesian formations, and numerous springs in

FIGURE 9.5. Water Management Issues Related to Industrial Development. Photo by Reg Whiten.

river headwall areas are known to exist at mid elevations in many watersheds and indicate potential risk from development activity. Related to this concern are potential risks to water quality from chemical additives used in hydraulic fracturing or from surface leakage during or after gas well development. Such issues were identified in various reports leading up to the peak period of activity (2005–2014) for shale gas exploration and development. Significant public and First Nations concerns were raised about potential impacts of shale gas development on drinking water supplies and other related human and ecosystem health considerations (Council of Canadian Academies [CCA], 2014; Campbell & Horne, 2011; Intrinsik, 2014). Issues related to industrial development in the watershed are illustrated by Figure 9.5.

FIGURE 9.6. Flow Gauge Installation on the Brassy Creek. Photo by Reg Whiten.

To close the information gap and improve oversight of development in its water supply area, the city has focused its efforts on watershed research and local capacity building. A three-year hydrology study, for example, was commissioned with the University of Northern BC to undertake baseline watershed characterization. This study included installation of eight hydrometric stations within the upper Kiskatinaw River to monitor surface and shallow groundwater flows as well as selected water quality parameters, while a second study component was aimed at detailed re-mote sensing analyses to investigate changing land-use patterns (Saha & Lee, 2014). The installation of a flow gauge on Brassy Creek is shown in Figure 9.6.

At the regional level, the Montney Water Project was also undertaken by the Province in partnership with several industry and the city. That initiative was aimed at understanding water resource in the major gas play region of the South Peace, including parts of the UKRW (GeoScience, 2011). Considerable impetus for this work was also drawn from challenges about large scale hydraulic fracturing operations by Treaty 8 First Nations and rural communities. This public attention led to the Provincial govern-ment and industry moving to disclose fracturing fluid constituents, intro-duction of a new water allocation and use reporting system, and improved hydrological modelling.

A national study by the Council of Canadian Academies (2014) provid-ed further direction towards improved water science research and mon-itoring related to shale gas development. These various studies highlighted the lack of groundwater information, monitoring and protection, and the pressing need for aquifer mapping. Additional research to characterize basin aquifer profiles using three-dimensional mapping of hydro-geology based on well water pressure gradients, and other groundwater research, has further helped to build the picture about shallow and overburden aquifers (as seen in BC aquifer maps, 2012, 2013, GeoScience BC, 2016). Another major effort involved airborne electro magnetic mapping in the region as a cost-effective method of mapping groundwater, and the in-itiative included extensive First Nations participation and collaboration (GeoScience BC, 2016)

Various interdisciplinary regional water workshops and field tours have helped to develop a shared research agenda, building partnerships for best practices projects, and setting new directions for more coordinated research and SWP implementation (Fraser Basin Council 2013; Lapp & Whiten, 2012). Other collaboration was initiated to improve climate monitoring for protection of wetlands in the watershed. A comprehensive water quality risk assessment focused on oil and gas activities further helped to identify potential surface and shallow groundwater contaminant pathways. Together this research has been increasing the city's ability to implement its watershed management and water-source protection plans as a model approach for other rural and First Nations. Lessons from this work were recognized by the province of British Columbia in developing its North-East Water Strategy.

Going Forward in Water Security Planning in the Upper Peace Basin

The City of Dawson Creek's work, combined with other regional water-related research, has demonstrated the potential of locally applied integrated watershed management in the Upper Peace basin and particularly where rural, urban, and First Nations communities have shared concerns about water security. In addition, it has focused understanding about the weak status of baseline information surface and water quality in the region that is now being addressed through various strategic stakeholder collaborations through the North-East Water Strategy (2015). This policy document is aimed at supporting implementation of the province's recent Water Sustainability Act (Government of BC, 2015), though the legislation does not provide explicit recognition of Aboriginal water use rights[7] (InterraPlan Inc. 2015).

Creating a foundation for greater local government involvement in water and land-use decision-making serves to provide impetus for considering other water-related environmental issues. Public and First Nations concerns, for example, about the acceptability of large-scale water diversions for multiple purposes (agriculture, shale-gas/LNG development or municipal) has not yet been undertaken, but such issues are likely to generate increasing scrutiny related to growing concerns about water availability in the western United States. With growing water demand in the Mid and Southwest United States, there is some speculation that existing water diversions, including industrial water pipeline infrastructure, may be considered by an international trade law as a "commodified resource" under a new or revised North American Free Trade Agreement. Such a legal challenge or negotiated terms by the federal government could enable large-scale water diversion as envisioned for decades under an updated North American Water and Power Alliance Scheme or other trade agreements (Lammers et al., 2013; Holms, 2016; Nelson, 2017). Concerns have been raised about all major water transfer infrastructure, such as regional inter-basin projects in the form of existing industry water developments, including water pipelines, storage facilities, or trans-basin diversion schemes. These issues include public investment costs, downstream hydro-ecological impacts, commercialization of water diversion through public/private partnerships, and legal questions related to Treaty resource use and water rights. With the expected completion by 2024 of the controversial Site C Dam on the Peace River, prospects remain for not only export of surplus power to Alberta, but potentially inter-basin water transfer to meet future long-term water security in drought affected regions.

Notwithstanding the major investment it made in water source protection for the UKRW, the city still operates primarily in a research and monitoring mode, and not as a full partner in integrated watershed management through a defined decision-making capacity. This is due in large part to the current BC regime of deregulation and complaint-based management, where a system of professional reliance for environmental assessments by industry proponents has shifted the extent of internal regulatory oversight by government regulatory agencies. An extensive 2015 review of professional reliance by the University of Victoria's Environmental Law Centre found, in fact, that "professional reliance" was undermining the public interest given numerous issues related to the rigour of management prescriptions, environmental monitoring, and potential conflicts of interest (Environmental Law Centre, 2015). An earlier report similarly suggested a growing number of major challenges on the professional reliance issue related to riparian protection in terms of public disclosure, system monitoring, and reporting (BC Ombudsman Office, 2014). In the fall of 2017, the government of BC's new Ministry of Environment and Climate Change launched a review of the professional reliance model with the objective of providing recommendations to inform: (a) professional

FIGURE 9.7. Managing Produced Water Upstream of Dawson Creek's Domestic Water Intake. Photo by Reg Whiten.

FIGURE 9.8. Managing Produced Water Upstream of Dawson Creek's Domestic Water Intake. Photo by Reg Whiten.

reliance use in the natural resource sector and in-house capacity; (b) government oversight of qualified professionals; and (c) development of an implementation plan with a timeline for tangible steps to increase public trust in government decisions (BC Ministry of Environment and Climate Change Strategy, 2017). Some of the challenges facing the management of produced water upstream of Dawson Creek's domestic water intake are shown in Figures 9.7 and 9.8.

While drinking water treatment and operations themselves are well supervised through strict operator training standards and oversight by the Northern Health Authority related to compliance with the BC Drinking Water Protection Act, source water protection may be more vulnerable on the issue of watershed monitoring and compliance under the current management system. A study on cumulative effects in the South Peace pointed to the need for critical attention for certain key watershed stewardship indicators, such as water use based upon over-allocation for the oil/gas sector, lack of reporting of other water use, and implications of climate change. For example, in certain winter months (November–March) such excesses were reported to range from 95 to 585% in the middle and east Kiskatinaw, despite efforts by the regulator to establish for that purpose a tracking system known as the North-East Water Tool. Another measure referred to as "riparian intactness," based on a maximum threshold of 10% incursion on Crown lands, was also being approached in the West Kiskatinaw sub-basin—an important indicator given that the province's Riparian Area Regulation for private lands does not apply and it is therefore difficult to control sedimentation on inadequately protected lands (Government of BC, 2014).

A significant tension for many local stakeholders and First Nations also exists with respect to water allocation and management in the region. As senior levels of government have advanced major regional resource development projects, including the Site C Hydro-Electric Dam and liquified natural gas (LNG) development, there have been several court actions and decisions seeking to clarify fiduciary obligations to Treaty 8 First Nations and landowner rights. Further impetus is also due to growing public and First Nation concerns about cumulative water quality and cumulative land-use impacts resulting from key industrial sectors like mining, forestry, and shale-gas development that produce contaminant waste by-products and fugitive methane gas emissions (Parfitt, 2017c). As earlier stated, concerns have also been raised about all major water transfer infrastructure (Parfitt, 2017 a, b). These issues highlight a need to consider broad public policy questions related to downstream hydro-ecological impacts, subsidized commercialization of water diversion through public/private partnerships, and legal questions related to Treaty resource use and water rights.

The highly controversial December 2017 decision of the BC NDP government to continue with construction of the earlier approved Site C Dam is also being shown to be closely linked to the future sale of power for shale-gas and LNG development, coupled with the extraction of water from BC Hydro's existing and recently approved water licences (Bell, 2014; Morgan, 2017). While being framed as a decision to maintain short-term fiscal management and climate change adaptation, critics argue that such a justification for continuing with the megaproject does not exist (Cox, 2017). Such opinions are based upon the conclusions of an independent review of the megaproject by the BC Utilities Commission, which provided a strong rationale for project cancellation tied to consideration of alternative energy supply and existing demand management strategies. The BCUC cited expert testimony that indicated flat current and foreseeable energy demand, inflated construction costs, and unmitigable impacts to highly valued prime agricultural land, critical fish and wildlife habitat, and First Nations resource-uses in both the upper and lower Peace River drainage system (BCUC, 2017). Still, a final decision was made after the BC government's re-election in 2020 to proceed to final construction, based on another Expert Panel's report that investigated financial cost and environmental issues (Milburn, 2020). In its findings, significant outstanding issues of massive project cost overruns and persistent geotechnical problems related to slippage of the underlying shale were underscored. This formation is also vulnerable to potential new seismic activity from oil and gas activity or possibly even the impacts from the weight of reservoir water (Wendling, 2021)

The Peel River Watershed – Making Progress Towards Ecosystem-Based Regional Planning

Much further north from the Kiskatinaw River on the Peace Region plateau lies the Peel River watershed of the northern Yukon, "a virtually intact landscape and the largest constellation of wild mountain rivers remaining in North America" (Peepre, 2010, p. 1). The Peel River watershed drains an area of approximately 70,600 km², and is located largely in the northern part of the Yukon Territory. There are six major tributaries within the Peel River watershed, including the Ogilvie, Blackstone, Hart, Wind, Bonnet Plume, and Snake Rivers. The lower reaches of the Peel River are in the Taiga Plains Ecozone, which is centered on the Mackenzie River valley. This part of the watershed is characterized by continuous permafrost, and extensive areas of low relief and low elevation peatlands. Summers are short and cool with average temperatures of approximately 10°C. Winters are long and cold and are typical of a high subarctic climate. Mean annual precipitation is approximately 300 mm/yr. and runoff is low relative to precipitation because of the low relief and relatively extensive wetlands. The headwaters are in the Taiga Cordillera Ecozone (Smith, 2004).

Unlike other resource planning regions in the Yukon, no permanent settlements exist within the Peel Watershed planning region, although scattered seasonal inhabitants along the Dempster Highway live in semi-permanent big game outfitting base-camps, scattered trappers' cabins, temporary mineral exploration camps, and some shut-in gas wells (Peel Watershed Planning Commission [PWPC], 2009). Four First Nations have traditional territory there and are still closely associated with the region: Na-Cho Nyak Dun, Tr'ondëk Hwëch'in, Teetł'it Gwich'in, and Vuntut Gwitch'in First Nations. In accordance with the negotiated Yukon Umbrella Final Agreement—UFA (1993), resource management in the planning region is shared between First Nations and the Yukon Territorial government through various agencies and boards. The Yukon manages non-settlement lands (both surface and subsurface rights) totaling 97.3% of the region. First Nations hold the remaining land either as fee simple settlement land that includes sub-surface rights, or otherwise as land designated with only surface rights. The UFA contrasts with the historical Treaty #8 (1899) that applies to north-east BC, but provides less definition for specific actions related to natural resource co-management and so relies on other negotiated implementation agreements to achieve mutually desired outcomes.

Though numerous judicial decisions over the past twenty years have reinforced the Crown's fiduciary responsibility to consult meaningfully on all aspects of resource management in both BC and the Yukon, First Nations continue to pursue Court action to seek remedy for protecting traditional resource-use and valued ecosystem resources. Perhaps the most significant environmental feature of the Peel Watershed is the natural or unregulated nature of the system with a full range of aquatic ecosystems and processes, high quality water, and intact hydrologic connectivity with globally significant biodiversity value for numerous focal species (Peepre 2010; Pojar 2006; Pringle 2001). Such intact river systems are considered unique and, according to Pojar, they are "fully functioning ecosystems with the greatest likelihood of accommodating climate change and maintaining ecological integrity. Over the long term, major undeveloped watersheds are regionally and globally significant conservation opportunities" (p. 12).

Pringle (2001) goes on to point out that in hydroscapes,

> Hydrologic connectivity must be carefully managed, both within and beyond the boundaries of biological reserves. Much of the landscape's surface configuration can be attributed to its drainage network of rivers that form a predictable structural pattern affecting watershed geochemistry, topography, climate, and vegetation. However, protection and management of hydrologic connectivity have not been given the attention that they deserve by either conservation biologists or resource managers. (p. 12)

The final stages of the Peel planning process thus give priority to the importance of conservation values within these hydroscapes; they also challenge land-use planning conventions that assign greater emphasis on resource access and development through mitigation rather than an application of hydro-ecosystem carrying capacities. Another important element of the Peel watershed management system are the Yukon-Northwest

Territories Bilateral Waters Agreement and the Gwich'in Transboundary Agreement, since both provide direction to the Peel land-use planning and decision-making process.

The water flow in the Peel Basin is controlled by bedrock and permafrost. Water flow peaks sharply in the early summer after spring snow melt and the region's few large lakes thaw and move from ground absorption to surface runoff. By contrast, winter groundwater contributions are small, given prolonged freezing conditions, so larger streams have lower late winter flows compared to southern streams, and smaller streams do not flow at all. Very high peak flows that occurred four times in prior periods (e.g., 1964–1982) have rarely occurred since that time. The size of peak annual flows (during spring freshet and large summer storm events) are important in shaping river channels, transporting sediment, and affecting plant and animal communities within the river and on the floodplain. However, it remains unknown if the reduced frequency of very high peak flows on the Peel River has affected the Peel River ecosystem. Such information is required to understand how climate change could affect river ecosystems through its impact on river flow (MRBBS, 2003).

Stantec (2012) reports that, over the past 40 years, there has been no significant change in the timing of the lowest flow rates in the lower reaches of the Peel River. In recent times, however, there have been significant changes to the timing and amount of winter base flow in the Peel River, with later seasonal onset and significantly greater and longer sustained fall flows. There has also been a significant increase in the annual minimum flow rate and the average rate of flow over the entire base-flow period. In the period from 2005 to 2010, although variable from year-to-year, the average rate of flow during the winter was about double what it was in the early 1970s. The increase in winter flow suggests that new hydrological flow-paths may have developed in recent years in association with warming permafrost. This suggestion is consistent with the observed decreases in flow rates during June; that is, as winter flow increases, there is perhaps less sustained flow during the late spring/early summer periods. Since there has historically only been two hydrometric stations maintained in the entire Peel watershed of the Yukon, much more flow and climate monitoring is required to establish stage-curve distributions in the headwater sub-basins to facilitate future planning and decision-making about resource use.

Water quality protection in the Peel watershed was also considered a critical issue and of particular interest to the Tetlit Gwichin First Nation (TGFN) on the Peel River at McPherson, who observe dramatic changes from winter to summer (MRBBS, 2003). Over a period of six years (2002–2008), the TGN collaborated with the federal government to sample for water quality. Data from water column and suspended sediment samples indicated high natural water quality in the Peel River and no concern for potable water use, based on both aquatic life and drinking water standards for metals, hydrocarbons, or organochlorines (Government of Canada, 2008). First Nation governments in the basin have insisted that all upstream land-use activities must not degrade the existing high natural quality of water in the Peel system.

Planning for Integrated Land Use and Watershed Stewardship in an Arctic Wilderness Region

In the fall of 2004, the Peel Watershed Planning Commission (PWPC) was formed to prepare a Regional Land-Use Plan (RLUP) for the Peel River Watershed region. Working under the legislative authority of the UFA, it was mandated under an arms-length arrangement as a planning body. In specific chapters of the UFA (Water Management, Special Management, and Land-Use Planning), there is provision to undertake a range of cooperative management and decision-making mechanisms related to settlement and non-settlement (Crown) lands. Though not explicitly stated in the UFA, an integrated approach to land-use planning and management is enabled thanks to the application of the UFA through its various Boards, Commissions, and Councils. For its part (and given our interest in this chapter), watershed protection is a specific objective that may be pursued through establishment of Special Management Areas as part of a Regional Land-Use Plan, and it was recommended by the PWPC for the Peel RLUP. While it is clearly stated that the Crown (YTG) holds authority concerning key aspects of watershed management (i.e., fish and wildlife habitats, water quality protection, and monitoring), it can be argued that the application of hydro-ecological information is a fundamental consideration to enable shared land or water-use planning and management

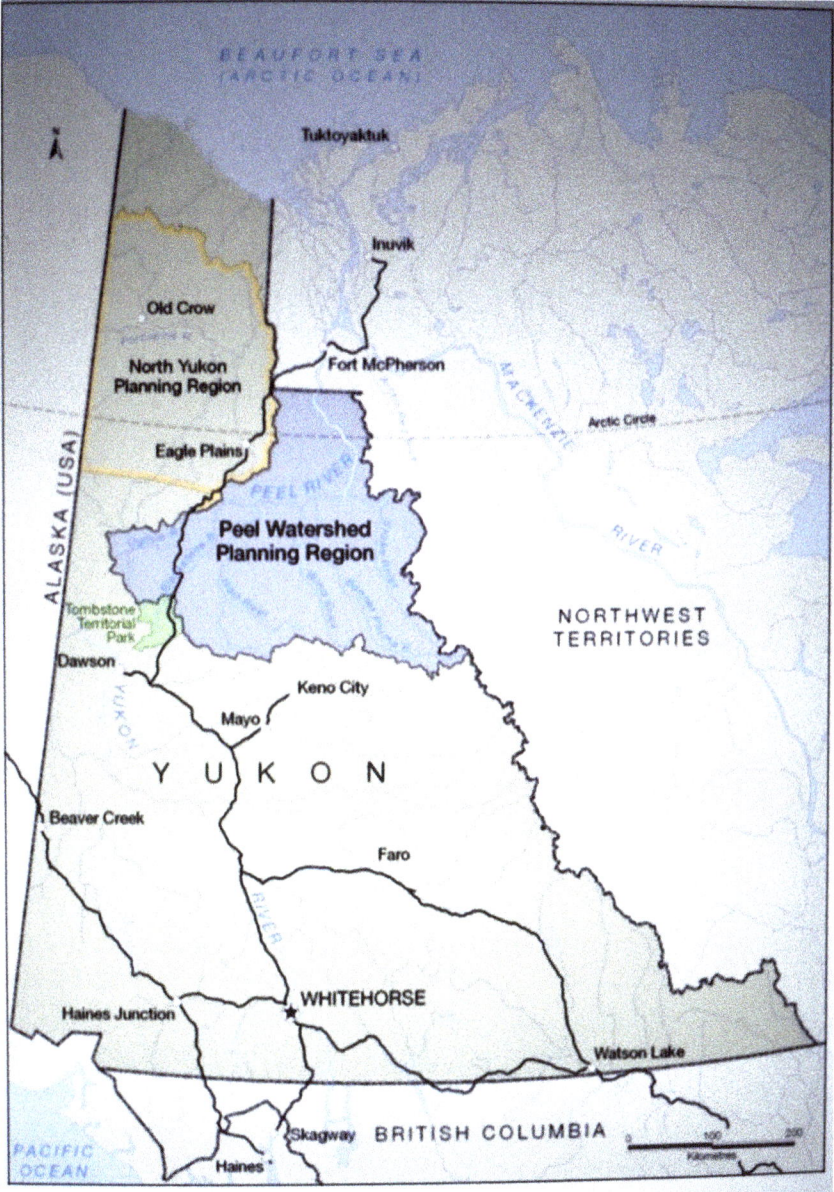

FIGURE 9.9. The Peel River Watershed. From Yukon Land Use Planning Council.

objectives to sustain First Nations resource uses. Figure 9.9 features the regions of focus in the Peel watershed planning process.

> **Statement of Intent:** The goal of the Peel Watershed Regional Land Use Plan is to ensure *wilderness* characteristics, wildlife and their habitats, cultural resources, and waters are maintained over time while managing resource use. These uses include, but are not limited to, traditional use, trapping, recreation, outfitting, wilderness tourism, subsistence harvesting, and the exploration and development of non-renewable resources. Achieving this goal requires managing development at a pace and scale that maintains *ecological integrity.* The long-term objective is to return all lands to their *natural state.*

With the support of the Yukon Land Use Planning Council, the first stage of planning focused on terms of reference, a statement of intent,[8] a principles document, and plan goals followed by baseline biophysical research. When considering the unique terms of the agreed foundation documents, and the context of a globally distinct eco-region, it was critical to commissioners that both the statement of intent and principles[9] would need to figure prominently in shaping the planning process and its outputs.

With the ongoing approval of the arties (via their representative Technical and Senior Liaison Committees), the research phase of the Commission's work resulted in a compendium of resource information analyses addressing all key economic sectors (mining, tourism/recreation, oil and gas), biophysical studies (fisheries and water resources), and analyses (global ecological significance, conservation assessment priorities, and economic development scenarios). Building upon the first phase of values and interests consultations, the planning team and commission were well equipped to move forward with the creation of multiple land-use planning scenarios. The sensitive hydroecology in the Taiga Cordillera regions (shown in Figure 9.10) underscores the need for such sophisticated building, prioritizing, and collaborative research.

FIGURE 9.10. Sensitive Hydroecology in the Taiga Cordillera. Photo from Peter Mather.

An extensive consultation and plan development process was undertaken over a one-year period. That work included multiple stakeholder meetings, technical focus groups and reviews, public and First Nations community workshops, and information sessions. These activities culminated in the preparation of a Recommended Land-Use Plan (Peel Watershed Regional Land-Use Plan [PWRLUP], 2009). Upon consideration of suggested modifications from all parties, a Final Recommended Plan was presented in July 2011 which retained the principal rationales for land-use management. While the affected First Nations agreed with the Final Plan, the Yukon Territorial Government was not satisfied that the Commission's Final Plan provided sufficient accommodation of access for extractive resource development and permanent resource roads. It chose not to reject the Plan, but rather to undertake a wholesale plan revision with very limited public review process, despite the objections of the other parties and a wide cross-section of the Yukon public.

Subsequent legal actions were launched in the Yukon Supreme Court and, from there, to the Supreme Court of Canada to consider questions primarily related to the interpretation of decision-making authority of the parties within the context of the UFA. In December 2017, the Supreme Court of Canada ruled unanimously in favour of the appellants with respect to the PWPC's efforts (2017). This precedent-setting decision recognized the need for the Crown to honour both the spirit and intent of the Yukon's 1993 Final Umbrella Agreement and all Treaties negotiated in good faith with Canada's Indigenous people and their governments. In presenting a framework for co-stewardship decision-making in the Recommended and Final Regional Land Use Plans, the Court decision inherently recognizes the importance of fully assessing hydro-ecosystem carrying capacities, biodiversity, and traditional resource use values as foundational for long-term planning.

During plan development, there was a focus on achieving wilderness protection and conservation objectives in accordance with the plan's agreed statement of intent to maintain those values, while striving to apply key principles related to sustainable development including consumptive resource use. Integrated watershed management objectives were applied in concept only to carefully consider hydro-ecosystem sensitivities and constraints in defining acceptable land-use (PWPC, 2009 and 2011). In weighing known information about specific watersheds/hydrological features versus what was available from base-line data (e.g., water quality and hydrometric data, aquifer delineations, groundwater-surface interactions), it became apparent that the Commission felt a need to strictly apply the "precautionary principle" in putting forth its Recommended and Final Plans for the Peel watershed. This was due in large part to the dearth of research on key issues such as climate change effects and environmental risk management related to extractive resource development in comparable arctic, alpine ecoregions.

Of interest in our discussion here are the results of research on Peel region water resources (Kenyon & Whitley, 2008). In that consultant's report, there were several important considerations that would shape how the Commission addressed land-use planning and management options for the Peel Watershed:

- Regulatory decisions would need to consider water/aquatic ecosystem objectives as identified in transboundary agreements, including the Gwich'in Final Agreement and Mackenzie River Basin Transboundary Waters Master Agreement,

- Several wetlands have been identified for their importance to international migrating waterbirds,

- No formal, spatially explicit wetland inventory existed,

- Benchmark water quality is naturally poor,

- Water availability is limited, particularly in winter,

- Up to 16 forms of permafrost degradation were identified as indicators of climate change, all causing some type of alteration to hydrology and occurring at various spatial scales,

- Future industrial demand for water and water availability for industrial activity were unknown,

- Industrial requirements may be more than the potential supply of available water,

- Water quality measures based on federal guidelines for aquatic life still remain at acceptable levels for drinking purposes for both traditional use and in downstream communities like Fort MacPherson and there was very strong interest in maintaining this standard,

- Water quantity had variable limited baseline data on the major river systems (period of records ranging from 1963 to 1984) and no reported information on groundwater or its surface interactions.

The dearth of information on watershed dynamics, water demand, and regulatory constraints flowing from transboundary agreements raised serious questions about realistic industrial development scenarios when viewed with known conservation, biodiversity, and hydro-ecological values. Given divergent public and stakeholder interests related to

FIGURE 9.11. Protests During Legal Actions on the Final Peel Watershed Recommended Plan. Photo from Reg Whiten.

development and conservation, it was apparent that any proposed development activities with inherently high environmental risk such as mineral development, processing, or transport would have to meet a very high standard of compliance with the agreed land-use scenario criteria and foundation plan documents cited earlier. When combined with consideration of constitutionally protected First Nation traditional use rights and resource co-stewardship provisions of the UFA, there was very limited capacity to ensure extractive resource development zoning designations. Advocacy and protest (seen in Figure 9.11) enabled collective effort to demonstrate the mounting evidence.

In other reports, it was claimed that the variability in Peel River Basin flows may pose challenges to industrial users in the future and would likely become a major consideration in any project assessment process for extractive resource development. These issues include high summer sediment loads, low and shifting winter base-flow patterns, and requirements for seasonal water storage and recycling (Peel Watershed Planning

Commission, 2009; Stantec, 2012). Environmental planning for mining and oil and gas requires an understanding of available winter water sources for exploration and development, including winter-road construction and various facility operations. Other concerns include fuel and other chemical storage, waste handling, and transport to address possible risks for soil and water contamination. Given emerging trends, likely related to climate change and permafrost melting, there appear to be significant hydrological constraints affecting the viability of any non-renewable resource developments in this region (PWPC, 2011). Continued research and monitoring of water and aquatic resources, along with knowledge of emerging industry water use needs and waste management technology, constitute a prerequisite to further consideration of these land-use options.

Efforts were made during earlier planning stages to apply an environmental mitigation framework for limited and conditional terms for extractive resource development in certain areas. This scenario process was essential to define the desired scope of land-use management options and compatibility. Unlike in other regional land-use planning processes, the parties did not commission a regional baseline socio-economic profile as recommended to assess various land-use scenario trade-offs. The result in the Recommended Plan was a strict adherence to the "precautionary principle" with emphasis on ecological, social, and cultural criteria, and less on economic considerations in considering sustainable development options. The resulting Recommended Plan included designation of Special Management Areas with a "watershed management" emphasis and other riparian units proposed for "land-use protection" (wetlands, lakes, and river corridors). The Final Plan presented a modified land-use zoning and management framework, but retained similar area-based rationales for land-use management based on specific terms of various inter-related provisions and terms of the UFA.

Lessons in Practice for Implementing Hydro-Ecosystem Based Land-Use Plans

When comparing northern British Columbia to the Yukon in terms of land-use planning and watershed management, some notable differences in planning practice emerge. The author's experience in the two regions provided insight in undertaking resources planning and management within source watersheds and hydroscapes. Although these sub-basins have starkly different biophysical features and land-use patterns, there is a shared experience in identifying the critical assessment and public engagement components for implementation of effective land-use and water management plans. Constitutionally protected Treaty and Indigenous rights and community reconciliation agreements must also be given full attention, along with other relevant water-related legislation to determine a compatible and sustainable level of land-use activity. Priority must be to continually assess and mitigate present and long-term risks for industrial development, drinking water supply, and sustainability of aquatic ecosystems. In both the Peel River and UKRW watersheds, affected resource communities, First Nations, stakeholders, and regulatory agencies have advocated for an interest-based approach in achieving these objectives based on a history of baseline research and planning efforts. Senior governments in both the Yukon and in BC, however, have not yet made the necessary commitments to enable full implementation of these plans. Provided that resources are put in place, there is great potential that sustainable water use and land management will address multiple objectives, further mitigating problems and supporting a low footprint.

Through a combination of watershed characterization,[10] integration of local/traditional knowledge, impact assessments, and monitoring regimes, it is possible to promote best management practices by all resource users. In this regard, collaboration for integrated resource management in both north-east BC and the Yukon may still be considered at a formative stage of formal adoption. Recent court rulings in both jurisdictions and ongoing legal challenges concerning Aboriginal land and water issues in both regions will likely provide impetus for developing a watershed co-stewardship framework which can be replicated in other areas. With sufficient support and mandate, the creation of regional or sub-basin water management boards can ensure effective dialogue and management oversight. At present, it remains unclear how or when meaningful watershed governance will be enabled in BC, but the necessary policy directions and legislative frameworks already exist or are forthcoming in both regions. Signatories on the arrangements are seen in Figure 9.12.

To assign priority for source water protection and achieve meaningful results, it will be necessary to consider cross-jurisdictional boundaries,

FIGURE 9.12. Signing of the Final Peel Watershed Regional Land-Use Plan, August 22, 2019. Photo by Yukon Land Use Planning Council.

water management agreements, and agency mandates. In both BC and the Yukon, attention was placed on identifying, characterizing, and managing risks to drinking water through the widely adopted, multi-barrier approach for source water protection (SWP). Nevertheless, only limited progress has been made in fostering effective operational models for SWP to consider a greater array of integrated resource management (IRM) approaches, including assessments of contaminant risk and hydro-ecological features and interactions. Present challenges lie in trying to foster preventative SWP objectives within the current regulatory context of results-based management and mitigation frameworks, where existing development permitting processes may not yet fully consider those objectives. Wetland protection, ground-surface water interactions, and cumulative land-use change are all key indicators of watershed health, yet these components remain only partially understood. Climate change and other landscape perturbations (drought, fire, mountain pine beetle, permafrost melting) are also now providing significant impetus to promote the IRM approach, including source water protection.

In both regions, senior levels of government are grappling at how best to advance major resource development projects (i.e., mining, LNG, and hydro-electric development) while also having to address court decisions regarding their fiduciary obligations to Indigenous governments. Gaps in watershed research, policy, and regulatory harmonization have been gradually filled for improved decision-making on water allocation and protection. Our planning process indicates, however, that it is a priority to further critical water research gaps to support meaningful land-use planning and watershed management. With growing public concerns about the water quality or supply impacts resulting from key industrial sectors, there are significant challenges in addressing cumulative effects in the UKRW related to both point, in addition to diffuse source water contamination from construction and management operations. In the case of the Peel watershed, the priority on conservation and protection goals was emphasized to avoid such cumulative impacts, given its significance as a globally unique ecoregion (Green et al., 2008).

By enabling collaborative watershed research and seeking formal designated community watershed status, the City of Dawson Creek is preparing a solid foundation for IRWM. Further impetus for water sustainability planning is provided by new provincial initiatives such as the North-East Water Strategy and Water Act (2014) with a new focus on groundwater management, attention to instream flow allocations, a shift to more demand rather than just supply-based management, and priority given to drinking water supply protection. In the Yukon, the Peel Watershed Regional Land-Use Plan placed critical attention on the importance of hydro-ecological functions and baseline water quality assessments to enable sustainable development and watershed stewardship within the context of the UFA and its transboundary agreements. With the clear definition given to water rights in the UFA and reinforced by the unanimous Canada Supreme Court decision of December 2017, an important precedent was set to recognize the importance of recognizing the honour and fiduciary responsibility of the Crown with respect to indigenous peoples as set-out in detail in its modern Treaty. The Court also validated its support of the Commission's process and directed the Yukon Government to conclude and ratify a Final Recommended Plan which occurred in August 2018. Such a rigorous framework of hydro-ecosystem based land-use planning is necessary to enable sustainable land-use management in a period of global biodiversity and adverse climate change impacts. With sound science, ongoing hydro-ecosystem monitoring, and effective public engagement tied to a commitment of indigenous Treaty implementation, our experience at two ends of the Mackenzie River Basin indicates watershed co-stewardship is not only a possible, but a necessary outcome.

NOTES

1   These include the Athabasca basin in Alberta and Saskatchewan, the Peace and Liard River drainage systems in British Columbia, the Peel River watershed in the Yukon, and both the Great Bear/Mackenzie and Great Slave basins of the North West Territories.

2   The term *hydroscapes* considers those units of land where key ecosystem interactions and biodiversity have been linked to human disturbance of key hydrological functions including—but not limited to—dams, associated flow regulation, groundwater extraction, water diversions, and point-source contaminants.

3   At the time of issuance for its original license, water supply for the city was limited to 400,000 Imp Gal/day. By the mid-1990s, it was increased to 3M Imp Gal/day or 0.183 m³/sec of river flow demand and 1.8% of mean annual flow. In a 2014 decision by the BC Water Comptroller, half of that largely unused license volume was made available for the city to transport its licenced supply out of province in response to demand for gas industry development.

4   Tenures for resource use are typically issued either as permits (short-term), as is the case for most shale gas water use, or as licences (long-term) for various other industry options, including domestic water supply.

5   The Peace River Watershed Council operated between the period 2000–2007 with participation of all levels of government, First Nations, and stakeholders, but lacked sufficient resources and mandate to continue operations.

6   *Integrated Watershed Management* is defined as "the process of managing human activities and natural resources on a watershed basis. This approach allows us to protect important water resources, while at the same time addressing critical issues such as the current and future impacts of rapid growth and climate change." (Conservation Ontario, 2012, p.1).

7   First Nations assert that water rights are of two classes: (a) on-reserve water rights; (b) legitimate expectations of the BC government to manage waters within Crown lands, so as to maintain the ecological integrity of fish and wildlife habitats in accordance with

their traditional resource harvesting practices. Various court cases in recent decades indicate that water rights are inherent in the exercise of aboriginal and Treaty resource use, and for water flow through reserve lands (Laidlaw & Ross; 2010, InterraPlan, 2014).

8   *Wilderness* is defined as any area in a largely natural condition in which ecosystem processes are largely unaltered by human activity, or in which human activity has been limited to developments or activities that do not significantly modify the environment, and this includes an area restored to a largely natural condition (Yukon Environment Act). *Ecological integrity* is defined as a concept that expresses the degree to which the physical, chemical, and biological components (including composition, structure, and process) of an ecosystem and their relationships are present, functioning, and capable of self-renewal. *Ecological integrity* implies the presence of appropriate species, populations, and communities, and the occurrence of ecological processes at appropriate rates and scales, as well as the environmental conditions that support these taxa and processes (U.S. National Park Service). *Natural state* in this context refers to terrestrial conditions and is elaborated in the surface disturbances. For example, a human-caused surface disturbance is considered recovered, or returned to its natural state, when it no longer facilitates travel or access by wildlife and people, when increased run-off and sediment loading is no longer significant, and when its contours roughly match the original contours.

9   Six principles governing the work of the PWPC were: (a) independence and impartiality; (b) sustainable development; (c) First Nations traditional and community resource use; (d) conservation; (e) adaptive management; and (f) precautionary principle (Peel Watershed Planning Commission, November 2008).

10   A watershed characterization is an overview of a watershed that includes a description of its geography and natural features, a summary of the drinking water systems, and a characterization of its water quality (based on the available data).

REFERENCES

Alberta Environment and Parks. (2017). *Alberta and the Mackenzie River basin.* http://aep.alberta.ca

BC Agriculture and Food. (2013). *Regional adaptation strategies – Peace Region, food climate action initiative.* Crown Publications.

BC Auditor General of BC. (2015). Managing the cumulative effects of natural resource development in BC.

BC Ministry of Environment. (2014). *Cumulative Effects Assessment for the South Peace Region Operational Trial Version 2.3.*

BC Ministry of Environment and Climate Change Strategy. (2017, October 3). *Review of professional reliance model to ensure public interest is protected* [Press Release].

BC Oil and Gas Commission. (2011). *Quarterly report on short-term water approvals and use.*

BC Ombudsman Office. (2014). Striking the balance: The challenges of using a professional reliance model in environmental protection – British Columbia's riparian area regulation (Public Report No. 50).

BC Provincial Health Officer. (2011). *Progress on the action plan for safe drinking water in British Columbia.*

BC Utilities Commission. (2017). *Site C inquiry final report.* Retrieved June 22, 2021, from http://www.sitecinquiry.com/

Bell, W. (2014). What the site C Dam is really for: An explosion of new fracking wells. *Vancouver Observer.* Retrieved August 11, 2014, from https://www.vancouverobserver.com/opinion/what-site-c-dam-really-explosion-new-fracking-wells

Campbell, K., & Horne, M. (2011). *Shale gas in British Columbia: Risks to B.C.'s water resources.* Pembina Institute.

City of Dawson Creek. (2007). *Kiskatinaw River water source protection plan.* Dobson Engineering Ltd.

City of Dawson Creek. (2014). *Sure water campaign information.* www.dawsoncreek.ca/water Dawson Creek.

Council of Canadians. (2012, November 10). Shell buys 10-years of water with funding of town's wastewater plant water. *NEWS.*

Council of Canadian Academies. (2014). *Environmental impacts of shale gas extraction in Canada.* The Expert Panel on Harnessing Science and Technology to Understand the Environmental Impacts of Shale Gas Extraction.

Cox, S. (2017). *NDP government's site C math a flunk, say project financing experts.* Retrieved December 15, 2017, from https://www.desmog.ca/2017/12/15/ndp-government-s-site-c-math-flunk-say-project-financing-experts

EDI Environmental. (2006). *Peel River watershed fisheries information summary report – preliminary assessment.* Peel Watershed Planning Commission.

Environment Canada. (2001). *Threats to sources of drinking water and aquatic ecosystem health in Canada* (NWRI Scientific Assessment Report Series No. 1). National Water Research Institute.

Fitzgibbon, J., Mitchell, B., & Veale, B. (2006). *Sustainable water management: State of practice in Canada and beyond.* Canadian Water Resources Association.

Forest Practices Board. (2011a). *Cumulative effects: From assessment towards management special* (Report FPB/SR/39). Forest Practices Board.

Forest Practices Board. (2011b). *Drinking water as a valued ecosystem component – A chapter in a cumulative effects assessment case study for the Kiskatinaw watershed* [Report FPB/SR/]. Victoria Forest Practices Board.

GeoScience BC. *Montney Water Project.* Retrieved June 22, 2021, from http://www.geosciencebc.com/s/Montney.asp

Government of British Columbia. (2015). *North-East water strategy*: Ensuring the responsible use and management of Northeast British Columbia's water resources.

Retrieved June 22, 2021 from https://www2.gov.bc.ca/assets/gov/environment/air-land-water/water/northeast-water-strategy/2015-northeast-water-strategy.pdf

Government of British Columbia Ministry of Forests Lands and Natural Resource Operations. (1998). *Recommended Dawson Creek land and resource management plan.*

Government of British Columbia Ministry of Forests and Ministry of Environment. (1991). *Kiskatinaw River integrated watershed management plan.*

Government of Canada Department of Aboriginal Affairs and Northern Development. (1993). *Umbrella final agreement between the Government of Canada, the Council for Yukon Indians and the Government of The Yukon.*

Government of Canada Indian and Northern Affairs Canada. (2006). *Report of the Expert Panel on Safe Drinking Water for First Nations.*

Government of Canada Indian and Northern Affairs Canada. (2008). Retrieved June 22, 2021 from https://www.enr.gov.nt.ca/sites/enr/files/peel_river_water_and_suspended_sediment_sampling_program_2002_-_2007.pdf

Government of Canada Water Resources Division, Indian and Northern Affairs. (2002). *Peel River Basin water quality report.*

Green, M.J.B, McCool, S., & Thorsell, J. (2008). *Peel Watershed, Yukon: International significance from the perspective of parks, recreation and conservation* (Report in coll. with UNEP-WCMC I. Lysenko & C. Besançon). Government of Yukon Parks Department of Environment.

Holmes, Dr. W. (2016). Personal communications.

InterraPlan Inc. (2014). *Towards a North-East BC water strategy: We drink the waters of the Peace – It is our life.* A gathering of input First Nations opinions concerning water stewardship in the Treaty 8 Region of BC (unpublished report for the Treaty 8 Tribal Association).

Intrinsik. (2014). *Detailed Human Health Risk Assessment of Oil and Gas Activities in Northeastern British Columbia* (Phase II. Report 10710). BC Ministry of Health.

Jacklin, J. (2004). *Assessment of the city of Dawson Creek drinking water supply: Source water characteristics.* BC Ministry of Environment.

Kalinczuk, J. (2014). City of Dawson Creek Water Manager citing letter from the BC Water Comptroller.

Kenyon, J. & Whitley, G. (2008). *Water resources assessment for the Peel watershed.* Peel Watershed Planning Commission, Yukon.

Kerr Wood Leidel. (2016). *Bearhole Lake water balance study* (Phase II Report). City of Dawson Creek, BC.

Laidlaw, D., & Passelac-Ross, M. (2010). Water rights and water stewardship: What about Aboriginal peoples? Canadian Institute of Law Resources. https://prism.ucalgary.ca/handle/1880/47784.

Lammers, R., & al. (2013). *Inter-Basin hydrological transfers – effects on macro-scale water resources.* University of New Hampshire.

Lapp S., & Whiten, R. (2012). *British Columbia/Alberta partnership for applied long-term watershed management research in the Peace River Region's Upper Kiskatinaw River.* Forum for Research and Extension in Natural Resources.

Mackenzie River Board. (2017). *Overview and history sections.* www.mrbb.ca

Mackenzie River Basin Board Secretariat. (2003). *Mackenzie River Basin state of the aquatic ecosystem* (Report).

Matscha, G. (2008). *Bacteria and parasite source identification in the Kiskatinaw River watershed.* BC Ministry of Environment.

Matscha, G., & Van Geloven. C. (2007). *Kiskatinaw watershed water quality assessment and management.* BC Ministry of Environment.

Milburn, P. (2020). Site C Project Review Report Prepared as Special Advisor to the Ministers of Finance and Energy, Mines and Low Carbon Innovation.

Mitchell, B., & Shrubsole, D. (2007). An overview of integration in resource and environmental management. In K.S. Hanna & D.S. Slocombe (Eds.), *Integrated resource and environmental management: Concepts and practice* (pp. 21–35). Toronto: Oxford University Press.

Morgan, G. (2017, October 4). BC Hydro says three LNG companies continue to demand electricity, justifying Site C. *Financial Post.* http://business.financialpost.com/news/bc-hydro-says-three-lng-companies-continue-to-demand-electricity-justifying-site-c

Nelson, J. (2017). *Site C and NAWAPA in The Watershed Sentinel.* Retrieved June 22, 2021 from https://watershedsentinel.ca/articles/site-c-nawapa/

Parfitt, B. (2017a). *A dam big problem.* Canadian Centre for Policy Alternatives. Retrieved June 22, 2021 from https://www.policyalternatives.ca/publications/reports/dam-big-problem

Parfitt, B. (2017b). *Fracking, First Nations and water.* Canadian Centre for Policy Alternatives, Retrieved June 22, 2021 from, https://www.policyalternatives.ca/protect-shared-waters

Parfitt, B. (2017c). *Newly disclosed data shows need for inquiry into fracking.* https://www.policyalternatives.ca/publications/commentary/newly-disclosed-data-shows-need-inquiry-fracking

Paul, S. & Lee, J. (2013). *Examining present and future water resources for the Kiskatinaw River – final report on land-use and land cover change analysis.* University of Northern BC.

Peel Watershed Planning Commission. (2009). *Peel watershed recommended regional land use plan.*

Peel Watershed Planning Commission. (2011). *Peel watershed final recommended regional land use plan.*

Peepre, J. (2010). *Scientific and professional findings supporting protection of the Peel watershed.* Canadian Parks and Wilderness Society.

Pojar, J. (2004). *Plants of the Pacific Northwest Coast.* Lone Pine Publishing.

Pringle, C. (2001, August). Hydrologic connectivity and the management of biological reserves: A global perspective. *Ecological Applications, 11:4*, 981–998.

Saha G., & Lee, J. (2012). *Examining present and future water resources for the Kiskatinaw River - final report on ground-water surface interactions and surface water quality sampling.* University of Northern BC.

Smith, C.A.S., Meikle, J.C., & Roots, C.F. (Eds). (2004). *Ecoregions of the Yukon Territory - biophysical properties of Yukon landscapes.* (Technical Bulletin 04-01, pp. 61 to 148). Agriculture and Agri-Food Canada.

Stantec. (2012). *Status and trends of flow, water quality and suspended sediment watershed.* Aboriginal and Northern Development, Yellowknife, NT.

Supreme Court of Canada. (2017). *First Nation of Nacho Nyak Dun, et al. v. Government of Yukon.* http://www.scc-csc.ca/case-dossier/info/sum-som-eng.aspx?cas=36779

Wendling, G. (2021). Webinar on Site C hosted by Raven Trust, April 10, 2021Whiten, R. (2012–2013). *Watershed program annual report.* City of Dawson Creek.

Yukon Courts. (2014). *The First Nation of Nacho Nyak Dun v. Yukon, Government of* (2014 YKSC 69: Date: 20141202 S.C. No. 13-A0142 Registry). Yukon Courts.

IV. INTERVENTIONS:
Thinking and Being with Water

Photo courtesy Robert Boschman

Introduction

We are aware of the movement of water, and move through it, even in dreams, the way a boat moves through its wake.

—Richard Harrison, Chapter 10

Consider building a boat.

—JuPong Lin and Devora Neumark, with Seitu Jones, Chapter 11

All over the world, major cities are trying to buy back their watersheds.

—Barbara Amos, Chapter 12

Recipient of the 2017 Governor General's Award for Poetry, Canadian poet Richard Harrison knows from experience what the rising waters of climate change can do to human homes and communities. His family home was inundated by the great flood of 2013 that took Calgary by complete surprise; but from this experience, Harrison did what artists do in crises: he allowed the emergency to inform his work—in this case, *On Not Losing My Father's Ashes in the Flood*. In this volume, Harrison's meditation on water contributes specifically to the ongoing historical conversation worldwide on the increasingly worrisome impacts of colonization on the environment. Calling himself a "child of the wheel," Harrison makes important connections between technologies, colonization, environment, and cultures. We, readers, are invited to reconsider in particular the wheel's impact on the waters of the Americas since 1492.

While Richard Harrison's chapter concludes with the image of a boat creating a wake, the chapter that follows invites readers to think about building a boat and provides blueprints for boat design and construction, courtesy of Seitu Jones, a co-contributor to the chapter by artists JuPong Lin and Devora Neumark. Their remarkable performance score constitutes a detailed, step-by-step program for bringing communities together to celebrate and acknowledge the core place that water holds for all humans. Their chapter sets forth a practice for any one at any time, now and into the future. Their forward-thinking model is also an inspiration, we hope, for others whose work takes them deeply into relationality and collaboration. Visual artist Barbara Amos engages in similar work, work that is relational, collaborative, and calls for direct action and participation. Her community work, shown here, exemplifies the crucial interventionist role that art and artists are taking relative to water. Amos' chapter also links readers to Sharon Meier MacDonald's subsequent chapter.

—Robert Boschman and Sonya Jakubec, editors

10

On Not Having Invented the Wheel: A Meditation on Invention, Land, and Water

Richard Harrison

1.

This morning I thought, "Read happy. Write sad."

Today is a day to write. Thales said, "Water is everything." He meant it, I'm told, in physical terms: the substance of the universe was singular, but I take it here in the sense that we say "love is everything," in terms of significance: water is life's greatest need. And it is the one we are destroying, the one whose relationship between give and take in the places where we have lived for millennia has been so distorted by consumption and waste that there is now desert where once there were rivers and lakes, and there is water or rock where there used to be ice. In my own neighbourhood, there was water where there used to be gardens and comfortable homes.

The other day I heard a terrible sentence about climate change, a sentence made more terrible because of how casually it was said: "Without changing our lives or careful geoengineering, we are in big trouble." It was part of the television news, spoken by someone superficially educated in what they are told to talk about from behind a desk, and then I heard its echo in a talk given by a world-renowned hydrologist, John Pomeroy. He stated that the Marmot Basin, flooded out because of logging, had been deliberately clear-cut to "engineer the watershed to increase flow." The lesson is there, yet the industrial world that some of us belong to and others have to live with has only gone farther with the idea of altering the planet to accommodate its own refusal to change.

In the news report, "geoengineering" meant putting reflective crystals into the atmosphere so the earth doesn't take in as much heat from the sun as it used to, and in that way, things will cool down. Imagine it: changing the entire atmosphere to adjust the temperature of the planet we are overheating from below. I never loved more the blue of that afternoon sky.

2.

One of the things I've heard said to prove the inevitability, if not the rightness, of European culture's displacement of the Indigenous peoples of the Americas is that when the Europeans got here, "the Indians didn't even have the wheel: that's how technologically limited they were."

The invention of the wheel: In my experience of being taught about the rise of humanity (though in those days it was the "rise of Man"), the invention of the wheel was one of those things, along with the discovery of fire, the making of clothes, and the domestication of animals that were the *sine qua non* of being human itself.

But no one addressed the corollary question: If you say that humanity invented the wheel, what are you saying about a people who didn't? And why didn't they? I know that a culture's invention or adoption of any technology is a complicated story, more often than not a cross between a gift and a collision, and the subject of much study and debate. I don't know if it's even possible to do the work to answer the question of why something *did not* happen. Or what that work would be. Perhaps the question is best used as a means to think about what has been done, but to think about it in a new and less triumphalist way.

3.

Inventing the wheel isn't about inventing the wheel, it's about inventing the axel, and the cart to carry much more than a sled, or a travois, or any person or animal on its own can carry compared to what it can pull. It's the device that makes the movement of people and material possible on huge and energy-efficient scales. It would have made migrations easier for everyone. It made Rome possible; the engine, the automobile, the railway. Transoceanic sailing ships big enough to carry sufficient settlers and soldiers to change a continent become possible when steered with the leverage provided by a wheel instead of the hands-on guidance of a rudder. And what is a propeller except a wheel that pushes sideways? Even airplanes: Wilbur and Orville Wright's plane is regarded as the first of its kind not because it was the first airplane to fly, but because it was the first to land intact, the way planes do now, carrying their wheels for thousands of miles across the sky just for that purpose. But the wheel is more than a device. The wheel doesn't just re-invent progress, it invents *for* progress a new way to measure and praise itself: not a better way to do something a person used to do another way, but a way to do something no person could ever do before.

4.

I used to teach composition for Trent University on a reserve in northern Quebec. I taught in the winter, so every couple of weeks, I'd drive from a temperate Ontario through the logging roads between Temiskaming and Val d'Or to meet my students, some of whom took four hour trips on snowmobiles to learn to write in the language of sanctioned Canadian education. This course was at once a testament to the resilience of the people of the reserve and to the condition of Indigenous life in Canada: The people were Algonquin, and at the time they did not officially exist, their tribe being said to have been wiped out. The people I was teaching to speak in one of the official languages of the country were, in that language, extinct. One of the elders told me, "We don't exist? Then they should change the map, and put "Memorial" between "Algonquin" and "Park.""

I also learned this from the elder: The Algonquin ideal of a person moving through the forest is that of someone who leaves no trace. The entire way of life outside the boundaries of human habitation was of being in the wider world in such a way that the wider world did not remember you. The example he gave me was that when you harvested mushrooms, no matter how hungry you were, you never took so many that the remainder couldn't grow back to replace what you'd taken. All the technologies of hunting, of harvesting, of building were designed to keep pace with the environment's ability to replenish what you took and take in what you left behind.

5.

Wheels and axels and carts are not the end of their own invention. They need roads—both the smooth asphalt kind and the kind made of strips of steel cross-braced with forests-worth of wood. The wheel alters the landscape to meet its needs: roads cut in with a permanence that can last for hundreds of years, because roads demand constant attention against natural erosion and decay caused by the thousands, maybe the millions of wheels for which they lay down and serve.

All travelers move in the present, but all roads run from past to future. The road is time expressed in motion: Whenever you stand in the road, you are standing in front of an oncoming car.

The road changes nature, and not just across its own width; the road's power stretches for miles either way, sometimes hundreds of them. Sometimes thousands. The image of passengers shooting buffalo from the moving train isn't only cruelty, and it isn't only congruent with the policy of a government determined to remove Indigenous peoples by destroying their source of food and shelter, it's the railway tracks removing the masses of animals that would get in the way of the progress of the train; those passengers are wheels making room for themselves.

The wheel hungers for space, and it thirsts for oil; oil is what gives the wheel its greatest travelling range and power, and the wheel makes possible oil's extraction at deeper and deeper levels beneath the earth—and at a greater and greater cost to the earth's supply of water. Not only is water used in immense quantities in the extraction of oil itself, the movement of water over both the ground and in the atmosphere is being changed by the wheel's conversion of oil into motion.

One gas tank at a time, wheels are burning the earth, melting the ice and displacing the world's water, burning it and pouring its ashes into the atmosphere, changing the way the weather works without regard to season, and we've seen the signs now three times here, where we thought, I think, we were immune, in the last three years: Canada's biggest flood, Calgary's most devastating snowfall, northern Alberta's most disastrous fire.

6.

Not only did the peoples of Turtle Island not invent the wheel, they seem never to have thought of it. I'm a settler, a child of the wheel, and not claimed enough by any Indigenous community to know enough about their stories, to know whether there's one, somewhere, about someone who "invented the wheel" and saw what it could do but realized what it would do and turned away.

But then another thought occurs to me in imagining such a story: The absence of the wheel is a void, but it's only a void in a world where the wheel is present. How could there be a story warning away from the wheel when there is neither the wheel nor the idea of one to avoid?

And why am I looking for a story at all? Isn't my longing for the existence of an Indigenous story that has more power than any story in my own culture, just me hoping that someone else has done what we could not? I may want to bring my own culture to what I think of as the Indigenous relationship between a people and their stories, but I can't do that by making that relationship the object of a Romance of my own.

The facts I have are these: Europeans had the wheel when they arrived in the New World and the Indigenous peoples here did not. Europeans have been busy making stories that have turned the world from an object of acceptance and awe into an object of investigation and control, and as far as I know, Indigenous stories hold fast to not just living with the mysterious, but preserving it. Stories may not change or limit a people's behaviour. Perhaps they only illustrate it, and we use them when we think that what we want to tell someone is best told through drama.

But now, in the dominant language of the age, and as much at ease with it as a conversation about a parade route, come words about re-engineering the atmosphere with the same purposes in mind that flooded out the Marmot Basin. This time it's the planet's relationship with the sun and the sky in order to cover over the consequences of a world driven by the wheel of progress.

Some things we cannot afford to invent. Either the Indigenous peoples never thought of the wheel, or they thought of it and realized that the best relationship between people and a disc with a hole in the middle was jewelry, so that to be human was to carry a wheel rather than be carried by it. The question about the absence of the signature device of European technology on Turtle Island isn't, Why not? but *How* not? How did you not even want what the wheel would bring? How did you not see the world as having an absence that the wheel would fill?

Thales said, "Water is everything." He meant it in the physical sense: everything is made of a single substance. In my earlier response to that interpretation of his sentence, I took it to be speaking about significance: "Water is everything" is like the sentence, "love is everything," meaning there's more than just that, but nothing more important. But contemplating worlds defined by the wheel and its absence, I think an answer to the question is closer than I thought; it's about the fundamental image of the world. The inventors of the wheel and all who live by it love the world as rock in which the things to count on are the things that last. The human place in this world is to change solid things—to move as wheels do over ground reshaped to their needs. But not to invent the wheel is to love the world as water, where it is patterns in motion, not objects, that stay the same, and the human place is to preserve the permanence that preserves us, to feel the stillness of the land the way we are aware of the movement of water, and move through it, even in dreams, the way a boat moves through its wake.

Instructions for Being Water: A Performance Score

JuPong Lin and Devora Neumark, in collaboration with Seitu Jones

Our world is in crisis; our collective home Mother Earth is at increasing risk of irrevocable change. We write as a team of artist-researchers, in synchrony with a team of climate scientists who have issued a warning that humanity has very little time to dramatically lower greenhouse emissions "or face the prospect of dangerous global warming."[1] They have stated that "entire ecosystems" are already beginning to collapse, while "summer sea ice is disappearing in the Arctic and coral reefs are dying from heat stress."[2] In our desire to contribute to a radical alternative to the widespread eclipse of the truth about interconnectivity, we — the Fierce Bellies collective — lean towards each other and again outward. We invite new kinships and invoke ways of living and being to counter the current patterns of destruction[3] stemming from the colonialist dualistic thinking that creates a sense of separation and otherness.[4]

The Fierce Bellies collective locates the launch of this composition in Musqueam, Squamish, and Tsleil-Waututh unceded and traditional First Nations territory, currently known as Vancouver, BC. We also acknowledge the Indigenous peoples of our current home places: Nonotuck and Nipmuc lands now called Massachusetts; Kanien'keha:ka — unceded Mohawk traditional territory — a place which has long served as a site of meeting and exchange amongst nations; Iqaluit (Inuktitut for "place of many fish") in the Inuit Nunangat; and the home of the Dakota, where the Twin Cities began at the confluence of two rivers, Oheyawahi or "a hill much visited."

We propose instructions for *being water*, instructions rooted in holistic thinking and oneness, in alignment with Chinese and Taiwanese, Jewish Kabbalistic, African American, and Indigenous traditions and practices.

NOTE TO READER: This is a live art performance score.[5] The authors invite you to adapt the instructions to suit your conditions. In this iteration of the score, we have incorporated excerpts from Lin's poem, *1000 Gifts of Decolonial Love*, and Neumark's collaborative epistolary projects, *Letters to the Water* and *Letters to the Ice*. We invite readers to replace these with their own community's creative voices, if and as desired.

1. **Study** the entire script, including the endnotes, before enacting this performance

2. **Find** at least three other people with whom you are willing to make kinship

3. **Gather** materials (print score on waterproof cloth)

4. **Make your way** to the nearest ocean, at low tide

5. **Acknowledge** the Indigenous Peoples of the place you choose

6. **Give thanks** to your ancestors whose migrations (forced or otherwise) have brought you to this place

7. **Step** into the water and open your senses

8. **Notice** the temperature of the water, the smell of the air, the touch of your feet

9. **Listen** with your entire being

   Voice #1: (sound of the water)

   Voice #2: (sound of your breath and heartbeat)

   Voice #3: (sound of winged, water-bound, and four-legged beings)

Voice #4: (sound of wind)

Voice #5: (all performers voice the question below)

Lín ê lâng án-tsuánn kiò hài-iûnn? (Taiwanese Hokkien)

How do your people call the ocean? (Non-English languages welcome)

All voices: (a chorus of above voices)

10. While in the water, someone from the group **speak** the following letter out loud (see free translation in English in Appendix A):

Bonjour Devora,

Je t'écris depuis le Nord du 50ᵉ parallèle.

Chaque jour, c'est l'eau du Golfe qui passe d'abord me saluer avant de te faire signe à toi qui samedi lira cette lettre, à 1 000 kilomètres du monde boréal dans lequel je vis depuis deux ans.

Samedi, comme promis, l'eau passera d'abord par ici.

Samedi, je mettrai ma ligne à pêche à l'eau, à l'embouchure de la Mishtashipu (prononcer : «michetachébo»), de la Grande (Mishta) Rivière (shipu), là où la rivière, la Moisie, se jette dans le Golfe du Saint-Laurent pour l'accompagner dans sa puissance.

Samedi, je me tiendrai à la pointe de ce territoire magnétique où se croisent les courants les plus contradictoires.

Les Innus sont les gardiens du Nitassinan (prononcer «nitassinanne»), de la Terre-Mère. Historiquement, la Moisie constituait le lieu de rassemblement des Innus, des derniers nomades qui venaient chaque été y camper pour pêcher et fumer le saumon, pour y récolter les petits fruits, en faire provision pour l'hiver.

Samedi, il y aura certainement sur la plage quelques familles de Uashat ou de Mani-utenam. Les Mamans s'assoiront sur leur glacière Canadian Tire avec leur café de chez Tim Horton et riront de bon cœur en attendant le moment propice pour lever le grand filet à saumon tendu à 500 mètres de l'embouchure. Samedi, il y aura plein de petits enfants bronzés qui pousseront des cris de joie en se baignant tout nus dans la Mishtashipu.

Samedi, je lancerai ma ligne dans cette eau nomade qui à chaque marée ramène vers ses grèves des épaves boisées qui font signe du Nitassinan: là où les épinettes noires sont la dentelle de la Terre.

Samedi, je me nourrirai de ce temps-là que j'aurai enfin à moi, pour moi, en regardant flotter ces dentelles d'eau douce qui bientôt deviendront salées, océaniques.

Samedi, l'omble de fontaine ou encore l'anguille décideront peut-être de faire mon souper.

Samedi, sur le bord de la Moisie, je me poserai et me reposerai. L'eau passe d'abord par ici.

(Valérie Gill, *Letters to the Water*, August 2015)

11. **Watch** for the changing tide

12. **Smell** the salt in the air

13. **Wade** deeper into the water

    I grew up fishing on weekends with my father and uncles in the Twin Cities lakes. I learned to appreciate the form, lines & functions of boats ... and studied wooden boat building with a focus on African watercraft.

    (Seitu Jones, January 2017)

14. **Share** stories about your first experience in a boat

15. While in the water, someone else from the group **speak** the following poem out loud:

    From across the ocean, and many miles of mountains

and valleys, I fold, unfold, refold, shrinking the divide
between
my home on Turtle Island and my birthplace —
Tâi-uân; between the Japanese empire and occupied Taiwan,
an island someone called "mudball in the sea"[6]
My mother called it a speck, a booger picked from the
nostril of China.

(JuPong Lin, *1000 Gifts of Decolonial Love*, April 2020)

16. **Immerse** yourself fully

17. **Taste** the salt on your lips

18. **Spot** for bald eagles and other birds of prey

19. **Pay homage** to the lives lost at sea

Voice #1: (bonded through the Middle Passage)

Voice #2: (while yearning for safe harbour)

Voice #3: (extinguished by swallowed plastic or covered in oil)

Voice #4: (displaced by the rising seas)

Voice #5: (choked off from water by imperial expansion)

All voices: (a chorus of above five voices)

20. Someone from the group **speak** the following letter out loud:

Dear Water: The Blackfoot word *Kiitohksin* means "that
which sustains us." Not just the things that sustain us but
the relationships & everything intangible we rely on (&
that rely on us). We haven't lived up to this vision of the
world; we have abused you & our relationship with you.
But this is not an apology; it's a promise. In this time of
reconciliation, mending partnerships starts with you —
that which sustains us & binds us & creates us.
We are water & we must heal ourselves.

(Liam Haggarty, *Letters to the Water*, October 2016)

21. **Retreat** back to shore

22. **Sit** facing the open sea, a foot from the water's edge

23. **Be present** to the changing tide

24. When the water washes over your knees, someone else from the group **speak** the following poem (or another one of the group's choosing) out loud:

> Black-tipped, wide-spread wings,
> Spread wide as the wings of the lost Siberian crane
> that landed in the fields of farmer Huang Jheng-jun
> one lazy June day,[7] first sighting ever
> in Taiwan. The farmer named his rice in honor
> of this snail-eating helper friend — "Jin Ho."
>
> Fold, unfold, refold a prayer for the
> Siberian crane, one of the most critically endangered
> of the 11 sister cranes, pushed closer to extinction
> every warming year,
> their marshy homes drained for farming,
> their existence made precarious by the rising heat
> of our extractive habits, by our insatiable pumps sucking
> black gold out of sacred soil
> and water — the bluest gold — from our earthly commons.
>
> (JuPong Lin, *1000 Gifts of Decolonial Love*, April 2020)

25. **Wade** along the water's edge

26. **Find** a place where the water licks your hips

27. With your mind, **draw up** qi[8] from the water through your legs, lower *dantyan*, *mingmen*, upper *dantyan*, head, and into the sky

28. With your mind, **draw down** qi from the sky through your legs, lower *dantyan*, *mingmen*, upper *dantyan*, head, and into the water

29. **Dive** into deeper water, immersing your body fully, facing down

30. **Float** and **hold your breath** for as long as you can

31. When everyone has re-surfaced, **listen** to each other **breathe**

32.   Below the surface, **form** a qi ball between your hands

As you would on a cold day to warm your hands, rub them together while resting your attention on the feeling of your qi or life force. Feel the energy in each of your hands and also the connection between them. This may be subtle at first so your awareness may need to be heightened. Once you feel that your hands are warm and you can sense the qi, slowly begin creating space between them, keeping your palms, fingers, and thumb parallel to each other in a relaxed gesture. Alternate bringing your hands closer and further apart in a slow and steady rhythm to further awaken your sensitivity to the qi (but don't let your hands touch when you bring them together). Notice if you feel heat or an energetic flux between your palms.

33.   **Expand** the qi ball and send it across the water to find where it connects with the shore nearest your heartland

34.   While in the water, someone from the group **speak** the following letter out loud:

35.   Ice is--

> For me ice is something good.
> I will relate to one of our communities: we believe that
> God resided in the ice in one of our mountains -- in Mt.
> Kenya, where the ice was, where the first man and the first
> woman were created.
> So, I feel like ice is a kind of a god, is kind of a nature. It
> controls the world -- like destiny. It's connected -- if you
> see the ice in the north pole, when it melts the sea rises.
> It controls everything. So, ice I feel like for me, it's God.
> It's water. It's life. It's healing. It quenches your thirst. It's
> something really, really, really powerful. And from here we
> relate with ice -- like up in the mountain -- the highest
> place ... and ice is situated in a place where we also try to
> relate in terms of problems. Like we say "You are as tall as
> the mountain you climb"; and you find ice is there. So, ice
> is ... it's life. Here we are excited about ice. I remember a
> few years ago it iced in one area of Nairobi -- in the out-

side of Nairobi: it's a spectacle that we are wowed with. It's something that we've never seen here, so we really treasure it. We treasure it. Even my first relationship with ice, I remember it was in Scandinavia. Ice was melting and I was out in the snow, in the ice, in the place of ice. And, also, sometimes it used to rain like hailstorms, whereby it was ice, and we were fascinated about it. But it no longer rains the hailstorms –– the ice pebbles. So, there is a danger within our climate, and we need to restore our world, and we need to restore our ice.

(John Titi Namai, *Letters to the Ice*, 2021)

36. When the water rises above your waist, someone else from the group **speak** the following poem out loud:

> And we resist, we fold, we hold onto
> ancestral memory, manual memory, muscle knowledge,
> plant medicine, animal relations, interbeing, sun-moon,
> yin yang[9] cycles, always moving like salty waves, falling
> rising, folding-unfolding into infinite timelessness.
> Folding a beak is an act of resistance,
> a reversal of space and time.
> We can make flesh of cultural memory, and release
> a revolutionary chorus of all beings.
> …
>
> I fold for Bikini Atoll forever scarred by US nuclear weapons
>   testing,
>   Pu'uloa, Oahu, renamed Pearl Harbor by U.S.
>   occupiers,
> Turtle island where Indigenous resurgence sings of
>   decolonial love
> …
>
> I fold for our children, for water, for life
>   And call us to rise up, spread wings and fly

(JuPong Lin, *1000 Gifts of Decolonial Love*, April 2020)

37. **Immerse** yourself fully in the water a third time

38. **Follow** the tide to shore

39. **Consider** building a boat

FIGURE 11.1. Seitu Jones building the *Lutra* with Goddard College MFA in Interdisciplinary Art advisees at Fort Worden, WA, 2011. Photo by MFAIA at Goddard College.

FIGURE 11.2. *Lutra* ceremonial launch with Goddard College staff and students and first outing in Puget Sound, 2011. Photo by MFAIA at Goddard College.

FIGURE 11.3. *Lutra* ceremonial launch with Goddard College staff and students and first outing in Puget Sound, 2011. Photo by MFAIA at Goddard College.

FIGURE 11.4. *Lutra* ceremonial launch with Goddard College staff and students and first outing in Puget Sound, 2011. Photo by MFAIA at Goddard College.

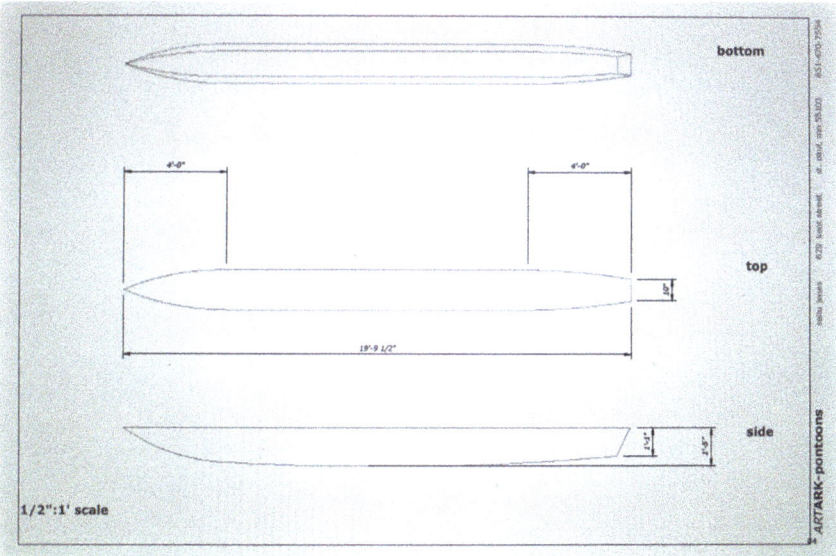

FIGURE 11.5. Seitu Jones, *Art*Ark design. Photo by Seitu Jones.

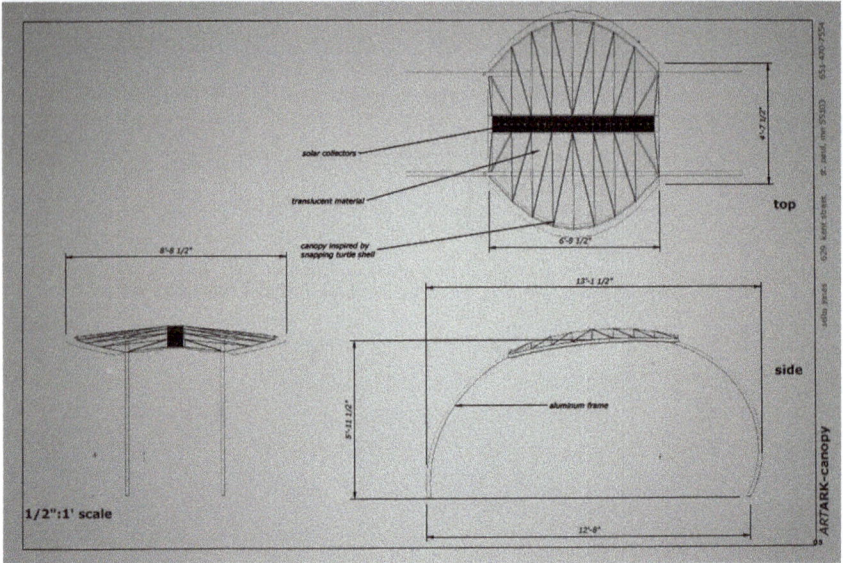

FIGURE 11.6. Seitu Jones, *Art*Ark design, canopy. Photo by Seitu Jones.

FIGURE 11.7.[10] Test launch of the *ARTark* on Lake Phalen, St. Paul, built by Seitu Jones with boat apprentices from Urban Boatbuilders, May 31, 2017. Source: http://urbanboatbuilders.org.

40. **Link** arms and face the open shore

41. **Listen** to each other breathe

42. **Follow** the breath in and out of your body, breathing into each other's bodies

43. **Open** your pores

44. **Teach** one another how to save a life

45. **Retreat** to shore

46. **Sit** at water's edge

47. **Speak** the following letter out loud (see free English translation in Appendix B):

    Chère eau,

    Je t'aime. Je t'aime parce que tu es mon symbole de résistance. Tu t'infiltres, tu t'enrages, tu te calmes, tu résistes, tu aspires, tu propulses, tu nourris, tu abreuves, tu nettoies, tu transportes, tu protèges, tu coules, tu tombes et tu t'élèves.

    Tu es puissante et indomptable, je t'aime.

    (M.-A. Poulin, *Letters to Water*, August 2015)

48. **Draft** a letter of gratitude to the water and **read** it out loud

49. **In repose, sense** your openings, your pores

50. When the skin on your neck feels dry, someone **speak** the following letter out loud:

    Thanks to a gathering of molecules most extraordinary. A delicate balance of two tiny atoms dancing around a larger one. Millions of groupings moving and changing and holding together. An attraction that makes life possible. Thank you for your movement.

    (Andrea Mackay, *Letters to the Water*, August 2015)

51. **Study** this image in Figure 11.8[11]

FIGURE 11.8."Water is Life," by the Onaman Collective. Photo with permission.

52. **Consider** the Standing Rock Sioux Reservation's fight against the Dakota Access Pipeline. Nick Estes wrote, in 2016, "Camp Oceti Sakowin, Red Warrior Camp, and Sacred Stone Camp, the various Native-led groups standing in unity against DAPL, have brought together the largest, mass-gathering of Natives and allies in more than a century, all on land and along a river the Army Corps of Engineers claims sole jurisdiction and authority over."[12] As the fight against the pipeline continues to this day, an important lesson needs to be acknowledged that the pressure must be maintained across all sectors of society to protect water.

53. **Ask** yourself: What is your lifelong commitment to, "Water is Life"?[13]

Repeat as necessary.

NOTES

1   Ian Johnston, "World Has Three Years to Prevent Dangerous Climate Change, Warn
     Experts," *The Independent*, June 29, 2017. http://www.independent.co.uk/environment/
     world-climate-change-save-humanity-experts-global-warming-rising-sea-levels-
     food-a7813251.html.

2   Christiana Figueres, Hans Joachim Schellnhuber, Gail Whiteman, Johan Rockström,
     Anthony Hobley and Stefan Rahmstorf, "Three Years to Safeguard Our Climate,"
     Nature News, 546 (June 29), 2017, https://www.nature.com/articles/546593a.

3   Colonizers accentuated divisions between privileged and non-privileged. "They created
     boundaries that divided colonized groups from one another and from their lands in
     ways that guaranteed a legacy of conflict and violence long after the colonial rulers
     departed," Val Plumwood, "Colonization, Eurocentrism and Anthropocentrism," in
     Decolonizing Nature: Strategies for Conservation in a Post-Colonial Era, ed. Martin
     Mulligan and W. M. Adam (London: Earthscan Publications, 2003), 51.

4   "The ideology of colonization, therefore, involves a form of anthropocentrism that
     underlies and justifies the colonization of non-human nature through the imposition
     of the colonizers' land forms and visions of ideal landscapes in just the same way that
     Eurocentrism underlies and justifies modern forms of European colonization, which
     see Indigenous cultures as 'primitive,' less rational and closer to children, animals and
     nature," Plumwood, "Colonization, Eurocentrism and Anthropocentrism," 53.

5   "I saw scores as a way of describing all such processes in all the arts, of making process
     visible and thereby designing with process through scores. I saw scores also as a way of
     communicating these processes over time and space to other people in other places at
     other moments and as a vehicle to allow many people to enter into the act of creation
     together, *allowing* for participation, feedback, and communications," Lawrence
     Halprin, *The RSVP Cycles; Creative Processes in the Human Environment* (New York: G.
     Braziller, 1969), p. 1.

6   This expression is from Keliher Macabe and Yonghe Yu, *Out of China or Yu Yonghe's
     Tale of Formosa: A History of Seventeenth-Century Taiwan* (Taipei: SMC Publishing
     Inc., 2004).

7   "Rare Crane a Boost to Taiwan's Troubled Wetlands," *Phys.org*, accessed August 28,
     2016, http://phys.org/news/2016-04-rare-crane-boost-taiwan-wetlands.html.

8   "Qi is simultaneously what makes things happen in stuff and — depending on context
     — stuff that makes things happen or stuff in which things happen," Richard J. Smith,
     The "I Ching": A Biography. Lives of Great Religious Books (Princeton: Princeton
     University Press, 2012), 44.

9   "It is worth noting here that the moon also signifies water, the yin. Water bears live-
     giving power. Several myths describe women who become pregnant by touching water,"
     Robin Wang, *Yinyang: The Way of Heaven and Earth in Chinese Thought and Culture*.
     New Approaches to Asian History 11 (Cambridge: Cambridge University Press, 2012),
     28.

10   http://urbanboatbuilders.org.

11   Christi Belcourt (Michif/Métis) and Isaac Murdoch (Ojibway), "Water is Life," Onaman Collective, 2016, http://onamancollective.com/murdoch-belcourt-banner-downloads/.

12   Nick Estes, "Fighting for Our Lives: #NoDAPL in Historical Context." *The Red Nation* (blog), September 18, 2016. http://therednation.org/fighting-for-our-lives-nodapl-in-context/.

13   The Hebrew phrase *mayim chayim*, or "living waters," means forever flowing water and represents energy, health, and fuel for the soul.

REFERENCES

Belcourt, Christi, and Isaac Murdoch. "Water is Life," Onaman Collective, 2016. http://onamancollective.com/murdoch-belcourt-banner-downloads/.

Estes, Nick. "Fighting for Our Lives: #NoDAPL in Historical Context." *The Red Nation* (blog), September 18, 2016. http://therednation.org/fighting-for-our-lives-nodapl-in-context/.

Figueres, Christiana, Hans Joachim Schellnhuber, Gail Whiteman, Johan Rockström, Anthony Hobley, and Stefan Rahmstorf. "Three Years to Safeguard Our Climate." *Nature News* 546 (June 29), 2017. https://www.nature.com/articles/546593a.

Halprin, Lawrence. *The RSVP Cycles; Creative Processes in the Human Environment.* New York: G. Braziller, 1969.

Johnston, Ian. "World Has Three Years to Prevent Dangerous Climate Change, Warn Experts." *The Independent*, June 29, 2017. http://www.independent.co.uk/environment/world-climate-change-save-humanity-experts-global-warming-rising-sea-levels-food-a7813251.html.

Macabe, Keliher, and Yonghe Yu. *Out of China or Yu Yonghe's Tale of Formosa: A History of Seventeenth-Century Taiwan.* Taipei: SMC Publishing Inc., 2004.

Plumwood, Val. "Colonization, Eurocentrism and Anthropocentrism." In *Decolonizing Nature: Strategies for Conservation in a Post-Colonial Era*, edited by Martin Mulligan and W. M. Adam, 51-78. London: Earthscan Publications, 2003.

"Rare Crane a Boost to Taiwan's Troubled Wetlands," *Phys.org*. Accessed August 28, 2016. http://phys.org/news/2016-04-rare-crane-boost-taiwan-wetlands.html.

Smith, Richard J. *The "I Ching": A Biography.* Lives of Great Religious Books. Princeton: Princeton University Press, 2012.

Wang, Robin. *Yinyang: The Way of Heaven and Earth in Chinese Thought and Culture.* New Approaches to Asian History 11. Cambridge: Cambridge University Press, 2012.

Appendix A

Letters to the Water, August 2015, by Valérie Gill (free translation)

Hello Devora,

I am writing from north of the 50th parallel.

Saturday you will read this letter: every day it is the water of the Gulf, which first passes to greet me, that will come your way, 1,000 kilometers from the boreal world in which I've lived for the past two years. Saturday, as promised, the water will pass first through here.

Saturday, I will put my fishing line at the mouth of the Mishtashipu (pronounced "michetachébo"), from the Grande (Mishta) River (shipu), where the Moisie River flows into the Gulf of St. Lawrence to accompany its power.

Saturday, I will stand at the tip of this magnetic territory where the most contradictory currents cross.

The Innu are the guardians of Nitassinan (pronounced "nitas-sinanne"), of Mother Earth. Historically, the Moisie was the gathering place of the Innu, the last nomads who came here every summer to camp, to fish and smoke the salmon, to harvest the berries, to stock up for the winter.

Saturday, there will most certainly be some families from Uashat or Mani-utenam on the beach. The Moms will sit on their Canadian Tire coolers with their Tim Horton coffees and laugh heartily while waiting for the great salmon net stretched 500 meters from the mouth of the river. Saturday, there will be plenty of tanned little children who will shout for joy while bathing naked in the Mishtashipu.

Saturday, I will launch my line in this nomadic water, which at each tide brings back wooden wrecks, which signal Nitassinan: where the black spruce is the lace of the Earth.

Saturday, I will feed on that time that I will finally have to myself, and only for me, watching these bits of floating lace of fresh water that will soon become salty, oceanic.

Saturday, the brook trout or the eel may decide to make my supper.

Saturday, on the edge of the Moisie, I will self-reflect and rest. The water first passes through here.

Appendix B

Letters to Water, August 2015, by M.-A. Poulin (free translation)

Dear Water,

I love you. I love you because you are my symbol of resistance. You infiltrate, you enrage, you calm, you resist, you aspire, you propel, you nourish, you quench thirst, you clean, you transport, you protect, you flow, you fall, and you rise.

You are powerful and indomitable; I love you.

The Red Alert Project

Barbara Amos

The Context

A small community in Southern Alberta was confronted with the possible effects of resource extraction (logging the forests) along a beloved watershed, the headwaters of the Castle River in Southern Alberta. Located in Crowsnest Pass, Alberta, this is the area where tributaries come into the Oldman Reservoir then travel up to Saskatoon and out into Hudson's Bay. Decades of effort had gone into protecting this area located along these eastern slopes of the Rocky Mountains, the headwaters for Western Canada. In 2012, a lawsuit against the legitimate claims of the local community citizens had been filed by the resource extraction company. While the lawsuit was dismissed by the courts, new charges were laid by another resource extraction company that wanted to clear-cut an area of forest. They sought to arrest protesters who were holding placards at the side of a road. They succeeded by finding an old outdated bylaw to arrest and block protesters. They served writs to a number of people, effectively preventing them from being on public land. This meant that people could not use the roads, sidewalks, or public parks, they could not observe or protect the land and water.

Letters were written, government officials were engaged, and public opinion was supportive, yet little progress was made to address environmental protection in the area. Despair and anxiety were high. The Red

Alert Project (Figures 12.1 to 12.12) is a story of intimidation and resistance that took place during the protest and the succeeding years of other ways and means of community mobilization for the watershed.

Another Way

Exhausted, the community asked, how do we go forward when we feel such intimidation and despair? It was difficult to believe that this was happening in Canada.

As an artist who recently moved into the area, I invited the community to consider that creativity is a regenerative force and to seek creative ways to advocate for these environmental issues. We needed to mitigate despair and thereby restore energy to this crucial cause. We met in my studio. We engaged with shared intent and creativity. We discovered a creative process that was intrinsically satisfying. While there were no funds or grants to rely upon, over the next seven years, people were consistently involved with intentional non-partisan advocacy. Most of the participation was local, but a few travelled from urban centres and other provinces.

The first event held was titled "Artworks for Wild Spaces." A request went through the small surrounding communities to gather donated and recycled crocheted afghan blankets. Geometric patterns were selected to create good visual compositions. These handmade items spoke intuitively about the care and the nurturing of our lands. They were potent metaphors for this project. Thirty-three people living or otherwise closely connected to the proposed clear-cut site were wrapped in the afghans. Photographs documented the event and were posted online. Every post was accompanied by a clear, simple statement that these watersheds needed legislated protection.

In these early days of social media, a photograph went viral and generated significant publicity. The photograph and an accompanying article appeared in various print publications—a magazine, online press, and a CBC interview—engaging communities across southern Alberta and in the larger urban centres. Attention to the issue was our goal, but now, in light of legal push back against protesters and their arrests, participants were concerned about being identified and lost a sense of personal safety. Sadly, one realized, it was wiser for the residents to remain anonymous.

Outcomes of Our Work

Initially, the community was divided about how to advocate to protect the watershed. Varying approaches were identified and discussed. It was finally decided that water was the issue that encompassed all others. A focus on protecting the watersheds became central and embraced all concerns.

These events then moved the issues to a wider circle and this proved valuable. One image made the cover of a magazine,[1] while others were included in daily news articles, both in print or online,[2] or presented at public lectures.[3] Some were referenced in academic publications on public discourse.[4] The community of Castle River grew in numbers and purpose, proceeding to mount a court case against the provincial government.

Attention shifted and focused on resource extraction on the watershed as a result of multiple, sustained connections and renewed energy of members of the community and beyond. While the efforts of many others grew, all concentrated on the same purpose. Over the next few years, I worked with small groups to create the images for the press and online social media postings. Each image was accompanied by a simple statement. The intent was three-fold: to restore and engage the community, to create awareness of the issues, and to bring the outlying urban populations into the discussion.

Part of a much larger forty-year effort to protect the headwaters of the Castle River in Southern Alberta, this project enabled a place to hold tensions alongside companions; it provided comfort, celebration, grief and anger, and vigilance. A new provincial government of 2015 passed legislation to create a new provincial park called the Castle Provincial and Wildlands Park. Heeding the red alert signaled by so many, this offered protection to remote areas of the Castle River watershed and managed use of the accessible areas. The wider project is not over.

We need to continue our vigilance, and continue to revisit what we value and the lines we must draw to protect it.

The Red Line Images

This series of images document the Red Alert Project, and is about the questions that we need to consider. What is the bottom line? What are our limitations? Figures 12.1 to 12.6 introduce the overall project. Figures 12.7 to 12.12 depict the wider story explored within the Red Alert Project with a spotlight on the insights and questions raised as the lines were drawn.

Figure 12.1. THE WATCH

Figure 12.2. THE GUARDIANS

Figure 12.3. GRIEF AND ANGER

Figure 12.4. VIGILANCE

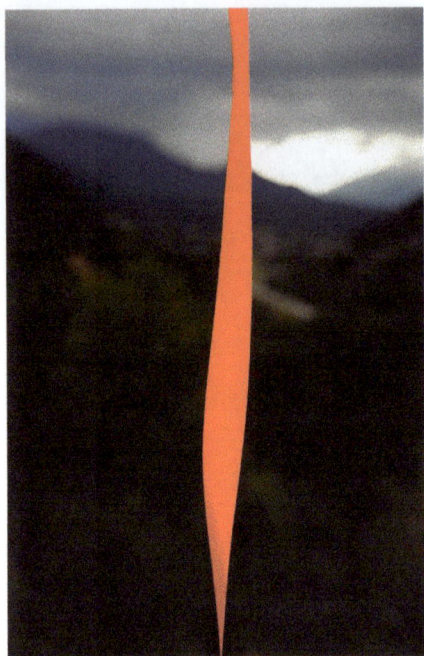

FIGURE 12.5. TENSION

FIGURE 12.6. THE RED LINE

Drawing With Survey Tape

Survey tape in a forest means that dramatic change is about to occur. I draw with survey tape. It is like a red felt marker. Instead of making a drawing of nature, I make a drawing with nature. The riverbed is my page. I draw a line. The water or the breeze shifts the line. It is a collaboration that fascinates me. We all know that enormous changes are on the way. This moment of collaborating with nature as illustrated in Figure 12.7 restores me, brings inspiration and hope.

FIGURE 12.7. DRAWING WITH SURVEY TAPE

Line of Clarity

A sharp line of survey tape (see Figure 12.8) in the water notes purity and clarity. When did you last see a river like this? What is the line of clarity? How do we hold on to it?

FIGURE 12.8. LINE OF CLARITY

Limitations

Sometimes we do not know natural limitations until they have been reached. Then it is too late. Figure 12.9 depicts this truth. All over the world, major cities are trying to buy back their watersheds. It is expensive. It takes time. Our waterways are vulnerable. Legislation would protect them. We need public will to create that legislation.

FIGURE 12.9. LIMITATIONS

Change

Water creates everything. It changes everything. Water is an essential to life. It is limited. It is viewed by many as a resource. Resources are viewed as commodities in our present world. Resources are regulated, permitted, bought, and sold. We need a different approach for water. We need to protect our water. It is so beautiful (see Figure 12.10). It makes me wonder. Can we change in a way that brings us hope?

FIGURE 12.10. CHANGE

Ice Petroglyph

What will those in future generations think of our era? Figure 12.11 invites the question.

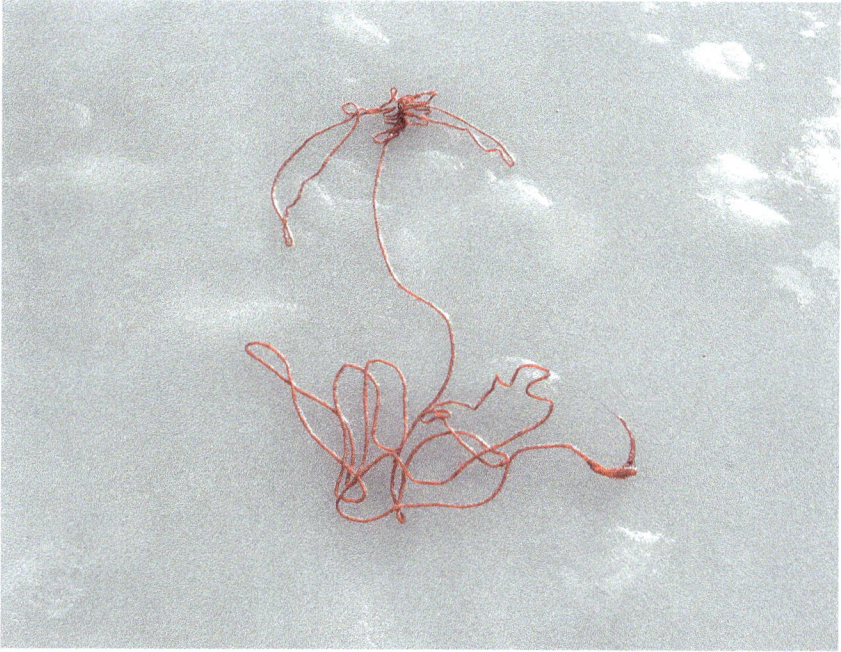

FIGURE 12.11. ICE PETROGLYPH

New Horizons

There is uncertainty as we look to new horizons (see Figure 12.12). We need to remember that change might bring us a better world.

FIGURE 12.12. NEW HORIZONS

NOTES

1   *Wild Lands Advocate* 20, no. 5 (Oct. 2012).

2   Such as, The Calgary Herald Regional Section Front Page; The Lethbridge Herald; The Pincher Creek Echo; The Prairie Post; The Crowsnest Pass Promoter; CTV News; CBC News; CBC Radio One, The Noon Hour; Alberta Views, "Eye on Alberta", and Pincher Creek Journal.

3   Guest lectures at the Visual Arts Alberta Association (CARFAC) Annual Conference, 2014; the Calgary Association of Life Long Learners, Speakers Series 2016; the Under Western Skies Panel, 2016; the University of Calgary, Nickle Arts Museum Curators Selections, 2019; and the Alberta Eco Trust Gatherings, 2020.

4   Maureen Daly Goggin, "Yarn Bombing: Claiming Rhetorical Citizenship in Public Spaces," in *Contemporary Rhetorical Citizenship*, eds. Christian Mock and Lisa Villadsen Lisa (Leiden University Press, 2014), pp. 93-116, https://muse.jhu.edu/book/46337.

REFERENCES

Goggin, Maureen Daly. "Yarn Bombing: Claiming Rhetorical Citizenship in Public Spaces." In *Contemporary Rhetorical Citizenship*, edited by Christian Mock and Lisa Villadsen Lisa, 93–116. Leiden University Press, 2014. https://muse.jhu.edu/book/46337.

Wild Lands Advocate 20, no. 5 (Oct. 2012). https://albertawilderness.ca/wp-content/uploads/2015/08/20121115_wla_v20n5.pdf.

V. RESPONSES:
Two Canadian Community Models

Photo courtesy Robert Boschman

Introduction

At this time, anything is possible.

—Sharon Meier MacDonald, Chapter 14

The new perspective is a blend of both views.

—Bill Bunn and Robert Boschman, Chapter 15

Signs of water exist in our communities in relationship to people in places—places and relationships drenched in sensory experience. As explained in the preceding sections, signs and practical responses to issues of water stewardship arise from the aesthetic, philosophical, historical, and cultural attunement to water. Immersed in sensation of sights, sounds, and scents, people and communities called to intervene may take on the solidity of a mountain, or the stillness or motion of water, as they respond to changes and challenges in their midst. Like the performances showcased in Harrison's meditative poetry, Lin and Neumark's stunning score, and Amos' Red Alert piercing art project, different communities embody their attunement in locally relevant ways that signal more universal political and social relations of power. As this phenomenon is currently studied by those seeking to understand ecological grief and responses to climate emergencies, we ask ourselves how is it that some people and communities respond to the challenges before them, while others seemingly freeze, hoping instead that by not responding the troubles in the waters will simply float on by. How is it that communities and people turn away from the practical responses that will support their own survival?

These questions, and other important contexts rich in community experiences, are explored through two Canadian case studies. The Ghost River story by Sharon Meier MacDonald is filled with descriptions of everyday qualities and characters found in any good ghost story: the community regrouping various protagonists ready to face the ghost of clear-cut logging at a crucial headwaters site. Bunn and Boschmann go on to showcase the impact of resource extraction on the waters of Uranium City, through powerful sensory experiences in the story-telling traditions of knowledge-keepers and photographic accounts. In both these cases, we are brought into the slow, unglamorous muddy work of learning and listening, which is essential for communities to respond to water stewardship—and the opportunities only available therein.

—Robert Boschman and Sonya Jakubec, editors

13

Ghost Story: A Community Organizing Model of Changemaking

Sharon Meier MacDonald

Fifty kilometres northwest of Calgary, the Ghost Valley is a critical watershed for the over-allocated Bow River, the water source for 1.6 million Albertans, and three irrigation districts in a flood- and drought-prone area. The Ghost Valley encompasses rangelands, lush wetlands, forested foothills, and majestic mountains. Approximately five hundred Albertans call this beautiful area home. Thousands of recreational users visit the Ghost Public Lands every weekend, a landscape subjected to multiple overlapping land uses.

And so it Begins

Despite the area's beauty, all was not well with the Ghost in the spring of 2014. Like much of southern Alberta, the Ghost Valley community was recovering from the previous year's unprecedented flood. Eight homes had been destroyed, and those families were still displaced. Heavy trucks hauling aggregate to rebuild berms and bridges opened several dozen sizeable potholes in Highway 40, the Ghost Valley's main transportation corridor, adding to the community's sense that the valley had become an unsafe place. Lack of information regarding project timelines or safety precautions further eroded community confidence.

Rumours began to swirl: "Did you know they're going to frack twenty gas wells?"; "I hear they're building a dry dam on the Ghost River"; "Did you hear about the clear-cut logging that's coming later this year?" No one seemed to have concrete information. When it came to industrial land uses in the Ghost Valley, residents were often the last to know. We were a danger-oriented people, viewing changes thrust upon us as crises, threatening, and even victimizing. We felt we had no choices. We just had to adjust.

A community elder noted the profound unease within the community and determined that we must come together. He enlisted my help because I had previously hosted many community social events and I had contact information for most residents. I naively said yes, never imagining where the next three years would take me and the Ghost Valley community.

Propelled to Act

We came together at the community hall on March 19, 2014, a group of sixty-five neighbours sharing information and offering support to one another. We spoke of how we seemed to be the last to know about local land use decisions. We were determined to change this, believing people have the right to be involved in decisions that affect their lives.

Our process of community organizing was extremely organic. Only eighteen months later did we find the time to reflect on our process of changemaking, realizing we had intuitively incorporated key elements for successful community activism. In times of crisis, communities find their way forward not because they have a good strategy, but because they begin to act (Weick 2000).

We quickly gathered information and received reassurances related to the dry dam and fracking plans. However, the timber harvest planned for a settled portion of our valley alarmed us. The Ghost Valley is part of Spray Lake Sawmill's Forest Management Agreement and quota areas. Spray Lake Sawmill's online maps seemed to indicate that the South B9 Quota area along Richards and Jamieson Roads in the Municipal District of Bighorn would be harvested over twenty years, something the community felt it could live with. Then, at an April 2014 meeting focused on proposed log haul routes, residents questioned why so many truckloads of timber were leaving the valley in such a short timeframe. The answer was that timber harvest would be compressed into only three short years.

Shock ran through the community. Within eight months, vast clear-cuts as large as 285 hectares (seven hundred acres) would open between legacy properties. Trucks would haul more than fifty-three hundred loads of timber over narrow, winding residential roads. Timber harvest would alter wildlife habitat. Highly visible clear-cuts and cutover trails would negatively impact the local tourism economy. Residents feared that the speed and scale of the proposed timber harvest could potentially endanger water resources and reduce the flood mitigation capacity of this critical watershed upstream of Calgary. As well, clear-cut harvest plans would impact the Traditional Land Use area of our Stoney Nakoda neighbours.

Spatial Harvest Sequence, an Alberta forest planning standard, is meant to ensure that forest health, ecological services, and socioeconomic values of the surrounding community are preserved. Spatial Harvest Sequence refers to the way in which timber harvest is scheduled to take place in five-year quadrants over a twenty-year period, pacing harvest in a way that allows the landscape and its inhabitants to gradually absorb the changes. To compress this harvest into three years was too much and too fast for the community to accept. None of it made sense until a government spokesperson revealed that favourable timber prices were a deciding factor (Fedeyko 2015).

Defining the Crisis

Land and people are inextricably linked. We are neighbours on a shared landscape and what we do on the landscape matters. Land use planning decisions are in essence decisions about people and their way of life. Throughout history, land use decisions have often caused conflict and suffering. With the flood fresh in our memories, we worried that clear-cut logging in the upper watershed could increase the risk of downstream flooding. This particular timber harvest had been approved in principle years before. There seemed no mechanism by which to bring new realities such as burgeoning population, a tourism economy, and the 2013 flood to bear on this timber harvest. We determined that as a community, we must challenge both the clear-cut logging and the lack of meaningful public consultation because of their negative impact upon two things essential for sustaining the humanity: water and community. The urgency of the situation propelled us to act.

Forging Identity

Our community is made up of country residential dwellers, fairly new arrivals who love the landscape and who plan on making it a permanent home; ranchers, long-term land stewards whose families arrived a century ago; and First Nations, whose families have lived on this landscape for generations, sustained by its plants, animals, and waters.

In other words, we each possess a deep love for this landscape. It is not simply a commodity. It is our heritage passed down from those whom the land sustained before us, and it is our legacy, what we will leave to sustain those who come after us. The land is the constant, not us. We come and go but this land remains. We are bound together through history by this landscape.

The Ghost Valley's prior reputation for strong opinions and strong emotions led some to doubt we could work together long enough to achieve anything. Yet from day one, we experienced surprising synergy. We constantly reminded ourselves of our identity and purpose: "Together we are the Ghost Valley community and we are trying to be good neighbours to one another. We are simply asking industries that operate in the Ghost Valley to also be good neighbours, showing respect for people and for the land."

Building Trust and Friendship

Community implies relationships, typically relationships between people within the same geographical area. In the case of Ghost Valley residents, lived experience upon the landscape and profound love for it made our relationship with the land a powerful driver in our community's process. In fact, it was largely our shared love for the Ghost Valley landscape that opened us, reclusive country folks, to the possibility of forming strong relationships with one another.

Community meetings became a tool for building trust and understanding. Sitting in a circle, we each shared where we lived and why we cared. Long-term residents distrustful of new arrivals heard in their introductions a deep dedication to their new home. Newer residents who thought some of the long-term residents were odd or standoffish realized the great wealth of knowledge they possessed through decades of lived experience upon the landscape.

Conversation Among Equals

Before we knew it, we had built the foundation for respectful dialogue. Every person in attendance was assured the chance to speak and to be heard. Deep love for the land and a sense of urgency leveled the playing field. Participants checked their status and their egos at the door, articulating that any hope of success depended upon our standing together to create change before it was too late.

In our quest for better-managed forests, we were launched on a journey of discovery. We realized that all water is connected. Water connects us all. We are neighbours on this shared landscape. We soon realized that our greatest strength was in the community of relationships we possessed with the land and with each another. The stronger and healthier our relationships, the more successful our work would be. Healthy relationships require communication, trust, common goals, and maintenance through time (Homan 2016). Prioritizing these things was essential to our success.

Grounding in a Unified Purpose

We had plenty of different ideas and lots of differences between us. How could we possibly agree long enough to get anything done? We had to dialogue and listen closely to one another. Intuitively we kept notes on what community members said in meetings. Certain themes kept being repeated. Sometimes a community member expressed one of these themes especially well and we captured the wording on paper.

Soon we were able to create a values statement, the "why" of our community action:

> We know that we need water for life, that water is life.
>
> We know that all water is connected, that water connects us all.
>
> We are neighbours on a shared landscape and everything we do on the landscape matters.

We believe that we must show respect for people and for the land.

People have the right to be involved in the decisions that affect their lives.

Species that call this landscape home have the right to continue to exist.

We make space for them.

We refrain from unnecessary violence to the landscape, even though we use its resources for our needs.

When the effects of our actions on the landscape are not fully understood, we err on the side of caution by waiting until more complete data becomes available to inform our actions.

We know that the landscape sustains us.

It provides air, water, food, shelter, and belonging.

We do our work from a place of gratitude and humility, acknowledging what the land gives us for life and acknowledging what the land needs from us so that it can continue to provide for us.

We believe that preserving this landscape depends upon a strong community, working together for the common good.

We have found that trust and friendship are the most certain means by which we can orchestrate lasting change.

As a caring community, as a community of people who care—for one another, for our shared landscape—we can find joy and purpose in uncertain times.

We are not alone. We are grounded in the landscape and in each other. We are home.

Reading this values statement and making time for a few moments of silence at the beginning of each meeting provided opportunity for participants to quietly reaffirm within themselves their dedication to furthering the common good (Joy 2011). Our values statement grounded us in what we knew to be true, including the importance of conducting ourselves in meetings with the respect, transparency, and humility necessary to maintain right relationships with one another (Joy 2011). Remembering what we knew to be true enabled us to bring our best selves.

Valuing Interdependence

We found ourselves referring to the principles within our values statement when we needed to make tough decisions. At times, outgoing community members were eager to speed ahead with various initiatives, while more cautious community members sought to slow things down, citing reasons of credibility or ethics. Remembering that "trust and friendship are the most certain means by which we can orchestrate lasting change," our more outgoing members willingly put several schemes on hold in order to preserve trust between community members. In some cases, deferring action avoided what could have been a terrible mistake. In other cases, the more cautious members of the community realized they could trust their outgoing colleagues to listen respectfully and to slow things down, until the more cautious members had enough time to become comfortable with the proposed course of action.

Unleashing Capacity

At first, we hoped for a simple solution. Maybe a conservation group like Yellowstone to Yukon would help us. Perhaps Alberta Wilderness Association would take up our cause. Some resident could have quiet words with government officials or with mill managers and decision makers would make the desired changes. But when no miracle materialized, we realized that we had to do this for ourselves. Not only did we have the right to a good life together in this place, but we also had the responsibility to make it so (Homan 2016). We had to shed passivity and self-doubt to see ourselves as actors, changemakers, and way finders.

Realizing our shared responsibility for our community's future, we took stock of what we could each contribute to further our common goals and we were astounded by the resources that existed within our community—within us! We ourselves were our greatest assets. Once in motion, we grasped the scope of the problem and identified necessary tasks and those with the resources to accomplish these tasks. Each action generated other possibilities, involving additional community members with the necessary skill sets. In the words of Deng Xiaoping, we would "cross the river by feeling for stones."

Overnight, a small group of neighbours pledged their skills in hydrology, geology, archeology, photography, marketing, technical writing, social media, graphic design, environmental management, and firsthand knowledge of the landscape. The group chose the name Stop Ghost Clearcut to indicate its opposition to clear-cut forestry in this critical watershed. Seven core participants provided information and raised awareness through a website and a Facebook page. The group researched ways to advocate for the Ghost Valley landscape and provided options to the broader Ghost Valley community. The Stop Ghost Clearcut team's value to the broader community was well recognized, even by those who found its name too radical. This group of neighbours became the leadership team of the community action, forwarding me information to disseminate via the Ghost Valley community's bi-weekly email news update.

Open Systems and Egalitarian Structure

To be a true community movement, power must be shared as equally as possible. Community members who possess expert knowledge or influential status must use these forms of power for the good of the whole (Joy 2011). So too must community leaders who have access to unseen forms of power, such as access to information, control of the flow of information, access to power (e.g., invited to meet with high-level decision makers), and the ability to provide or withhold a platform for the voices of other community members.

From the outset, our leadership team tried to practice an open information flow. Information was put into the hands of community members as often as possible through website links, information briefs, and cloud files. In this way, community participants could determine what level of information they desired without becoming overloaded. Community members were invited whenever possible to attend high-level meetings and educational opportunities. Notes from these meetings were shared openly whenever possible. To our surprise, we observed that the open information flow calmed the anxiety palpable within the community, even while the open information flow facilitated increased participation from neighbours who wished to contribute to the community effort.

Connecting People With one Another

Soon community members were getting together between meetings to gather information, walk the land, and engage in projects they designed. For eighteen consecutive months, thirty neighbours dedicated multiple hours gathering information, writing letters, taking pictures, making videos, managing social media, monitoring maps, walking cut blocks, spreading the word, booking special speakers, organizing educational opportunities for the community, and meeting with decision makers. Their findings and connections were shared back with the leadership team. This new information was collated and communicated back out to the community, a positive feedback loop generating new activities and new connections. This just seemed to happen as people stepped forward to offer what they could. Later we discovered that this method of social change is characteristic of a community-organizing approach.

Each of us had a unique contribution to make, ensuring our individual role as a valued member of the Ghost Valley community. Deep appreciation for one another's contributions resulted. Several community members specifically commented that they had always felt as though they did not fit in socially, but now for the first time, they felt as though they had something valuable to offer and as though they belonged to a community. These experiences furthered trust and friendship between community members, which in turn facilitated the flow of resources.

A Leader who Loves us

While change can be led by the grassroots, a leader will eventually be required to facilitate meetings, to coordinate communication, and to manage projects. These roles come with unseen power, giving a leader greater influence upon the leadership team and gradually upon community members participating in the action. For this reason, a community must carefully choose its leader, selecting a person who truly grasps that facilitation is leadership without taking the reins.

Essentially a community-organizing model requires what Alice Walker terms "a leader who loves us" (Walker 2008). A leader who loves us knows how to listen and how to pay attention. A leader who loves us sees the positive potentialities already within us and can hold up, to us, an image of what we could be if we so decided. A leader who loves us continually shifts our focus to what is strong and what is good, for whatever we focus on will grow to squeeze out old ways that no longer serve ourselves or the community well.

A leader who loves us also recognizes that we are often fearful people. An underlying fear of loss frequently accompanies a community's experience of crisis. Some participants may be paralyzed by this fear. Other participants may turn fear into anger, with a propensity to use a language of violence, even harming relationships with other community members. Many people have not learned skills for appropriately expressing fear, sadness, or anger. Inappropriate expression runs the risk of cementing the separation between "us and them," reducing or even eliminating options for resolution of differences. A skilled facilitator works to calm participants' underlying fear of loss, ideally guiding participants to realize that they are capable of more adaptive responses than language tinged with violence.

Within the Ghost community, we intentionally worked to shift our language of anger and violence towards more effective responses. We built calming strategies into our meetings, taking an early coffee break once the opening circle finished and the evening's topic had been introduced. People found comfort in refreshments and in conversation with supportive community members. As facilitator, I circulated, connecting with those who might find the topic challenging and urging others with expertise or insight to share with the community. Public speaking is terrifying for many people, even more so in a large group or when discussing a stressful topic, so index cards and pens were provided for those who preferred to write either speaking notes for themselves or notes for the facilitator to read to the group. The facilitator's own inner work is foundational to an ability to remain grounded and thereby have a calming effect on others.

Despite a facilitation role, the leader should blend back into the group whenever possible. Community members are capable of letter writing, media interviews, meetings with external networks, and numerous other tasks. Others should be empowered to represent the community, diffusing leadership and ensuring continuity of the community action even if something should happen to the identified leader.

Even if the group facilitator becomes the face of the organization or coordinates the many pieces into a cohesive whole, the leader must always conduct herself so that community members say, "Look what we did," rather than, "Look what she did." A community's capacity for change-making must always reside within as many community members as possible acting for the common good.

External Networking

The Ghost Valley community had some early successes. Public pressure convinced Municipal District of Bighorn councillors to refuse the forestry company access to municipal roadways for a year. Other access options over private land were also refused. The Ghost Valley landscape gained one year of grace.

In December 2014, a team of community members created a press release documenting the pair of Trumpeter Swans nesting on the Ghost Valley's Kangienos Lake, the shores of which were slated for clear-cut within the year, even though forestry's Operating Ground Rules prescribed buffers. The press release received wide media coverage and mobilized over one hundred people, many of them grade four students using art, music, theatre, and letters to the editor, government, and mill managers to secure adequate buffers for the swans of Kangienos Lake.

From January through October 2015, a speaker series with such notables as Robert Sandford, Kevin Van Tighem, and Karsten Heuer enlisted the support of people from Bragg Creek, Calgary, and Cochrane. These friends supported the Ghost community's actions through financial contributions, letter writing, and spreading the word to their contacts.

When Albertans surprised the world on May 5, 2015 by electing a New Democratic provincial government, we hoped timber harvest plans would be reconsidered. We had little success in reaching our previous government decision-makers. Now maybe change would come.

Highlighting Strengths

From November 2014 through August 2015, ever-expanding circles of the Ghost community became aware of the clear-cut plans and joined the community action, contributing fresh ideas and energy. By September 2015, nearly four-hundred of the Ghost Valley's five-hundred residents had indicated their support for the Ghost Valley community's actions, many attending community meetings or participating openly, but others phoning or emailing to indicate their support while explaining credible reasons why they could not attend community meetings. In the spirit of trust and friendship, we did not question one another's level of participation.

In September 2015, fearing their business Saddle Peak Trail Rides might lose clients after clear-cut logging changed the landscape, community members Dave and Jacquie Richards offered neighbours trail rides and a free roast beef dinner. At a time when most people would retreat privately into legitimate sorrow, their generous hospitality in the face of adversity was profoundly moving. Only the most courageous people supported by a caring community could conduct themselves as the Richards family did on that day. We gathered to enjoy this beautiful intact landscape one last time, reminding ourselves that we were grounded in the landscape and in each other, and knowing with certainty that our community includes the best people to be found anywhere.

Dialogue Across the Divide

From July through October 2015, we advocated tirelessly with our new government, attending meetings with Alberta Agriculture and Forestry staff and hosting a town hall with our new Member of the Legislative Assembly, Cameron Westhead. We submitted our petition with the names of nearly fifteen hundred Albertans calling for a reconsideration of timber harvest plans.

We were relieved when the new government directed that the 285-hectare cut block be divided into several smaller blocks with greater retention patches for wildlife cover and some wet areas protected from harvest. In addition, the erosive bluff block overlooking the Ghost River was removed from harvest plans. Back in 2014, a community member had funded legal action to stall final approval for this particular block. His bold risk was rewarded when the new government conclusively removed this block from harvest.

The new government required the forestry company to perform an exercise in "meaningful consultation." A company forester was to walk some of the most concerning cut blocks with residents. Though the exercise did not achieve much change, we appreciated this forester's willingness to dialogue with us, share sandwiches and cookies, and return later to help fix a neighbour's fence impacted by logging. This forester's presence in our community reminded us that despite being on opposite sides of an argument, we were all just human beings in a community trying to find a new way forward together. We needed to continue to make changes to the system rather than attacking those who found themselves actors within it.

Giving up the Ghost

On Tuesday, October 20, 2015, three of us met on behalf of our community with Minister of Forestry Oniel Carlier, urging him to reconsider timber harvests approved years before by Alberta's previous government. Minister Carlier seemed dismissive, advising us to take future concerns to Forestry staff.

Tragically, as we spoke with the Minister, the cell phone set up to help us keep time flashed up a text. Simultaneously in the Ghost Valley, Saddle Peak outfitter Dave Richards and conservationist Kevin Van Tighem planning to ride Lesueur Ridge were shocked to find the area being clear-cut when they arrived, the recreational trail up the ridge impassable. Kevin Van Tighem poignantly documented this heartbreaking experience in a Facebook post that went viral and included it in his book *Our Place: Changing the Nature of Alberta*. Media broadcast the story throughout Western Canada.

Stepping Outside our Comfort Zone

The Minister's seeming lack of interest coupled with clear-cut harvest of the area's most scenic viewpoint were huge blows to the community. On October 31, 2015, seventy-five Ghost Valley community members and supporters rallied against the government's decision to give up the Ghost. One year earlier, we could not have imagined ourselves as protesters. Now there seemed no other choice. People gathered with their banners and signs at the intersection of Highway 1A and Highway 40. The media was out in force, helping us spread a message of care for ecosystems and communities.

November 10, 2015 dealt the Ghost another blow. Under great pressure, the Council of Municipal District of Bighorn offered Spray Lake Sawmills a Road Use Agreement for hauling logs out over Jamieson Road. Residents made a strong case for their belief that public safety would be endangered by ten-foot wide logging trucks on this narrow, winding residential road with lanes only nine feet wide in places. Protest rallies on November 14 and 21, 2015, again saw community members waving signs.

Developing Empathy for the Broader Community

During January and February 2016, neighbours living along Jamieson Road saw logging trucks travel this narrow hilly roadway. In a blunt reminder of the interconnectedness of all things, the community noted that not only were the trees expendable, but public safety also seemed to come second to an industry's right to extract natural resources. Several community members courageously used the experience to develop empathy for Indigenous communities worldwide, which endure far worse treatment without the recourse to democratic process, white privilege, and various other advantages.

Public pressure impressed government and industry with the need to find another log haul option. Due to unrelenting pressure by community members who wrote regular letters, made presentations to Council, and monitored daily the enforceable conditions of the Road Use Agreement, the forestry company was motivated to strike a deal with a private landowner to haul logs out by another route, restoring a sense of safety to Jamieson Road residents, even as they watched the trees come down on crown lands adjacent to their private land holdings.

In December 2016 through February 2017, the remainder of the Ghost Valley harvest was cut. In only two short years, the forestry company completed a government-approved timber harvest seemingly mapped out over twenty years as per Alberta's Forests Act, Section 19. The environment was unable to weigh in, but over the next decades, its recovery will begin to inform the wisdom of this particular land use decision. The local outfitter also had limited options to weigh in on the impact that an unsightly environment may have on his tourism-based business. Only time will tell whether his business can indeed survive.

Mitigating Harm

Since we did not save the trees, what did we actually achieve? As Joanna Macy outlines, we must work on three fronts to care for the environment:

1. Mitigate harm caused by our politics and our economy.
2. Change practice to new environmentally sensitive ways of doing things.
3. Change ourselves. (Macy 2017)

We, in the Ghost Valley, have slowly become an opportunity-oriented people. We have learned that there is no magic wand to make all things right. Instead, many of us realize that we are actually taking on the elephant in the room—a global economy premised on continual growth through resource exploitation while overlooking the limits that can be borne by an ecosystem and by those directly dependent upon it. The only way to eat an elephant is in small bites. We have cleverly found ways to make small differences for our landscape, our wildlife, and ourselves, mostly by working together in relationships of trust and friendship to magnify our impact a hundredfold.

What did we accomplish? Not nearly enough. Mitigating harm is an incomplete response to the challenges that our ecosystems face, but for those life forms dependent on the small corner that is spared, it means the world. Securing buffers for the nesting swans, saving the bluff block, preserving a greater number of wet areas and retention patches, highlighting a First Nations ceremonial site which was then left standing—these are some of the small ways in which the Ghost Valley community managed to mitigate harm in the face of widescale clear-cut timber harvest.

Changing Practice

The Ghost Valley community has only just begun its efforts to change current practice for managing our Eastern slopes headwaters. The Ghost Valley community has shown government and industry that doing things the same way they have always been done is no longer good enough. Albertans have come to expect decision-making that reflects the public's values. Citizens are finding their voice and co-creating their future together. The impacts of these shifts have not yet been fully felt. At this time, anything is possible.

Since the clear-cut, Alberta Agriculture and Forestry staff have shown increased management and oversight of the forestry industry as practiced in the Ghost Valley. Alberta Environment and Parks staff have been increasingly responsive to public requests for enforcement and care for clear-cut landscapes now accessed by recreational users. The Ghost Valley community is encouraged by the positive differences these changed practices are making for the Ghost Public Lands.

On December 12, 2016, our elected representative Cameron Westhead presented Motion 511 in the Alberta Legislature, calling upon the government of Alberta to manage public lands in Alberta's Eastern slopes headwaters with a view to optimizing water resources. He specifically mentioned the Ghost Valley community, listing several community members by name, as he credited those instrumental in shaping this motion. While the motion is non-binding, it signals positive possibilities for Alberta's landscapes.

Changing Ourselves

When we organize as a community, we make tremendous strides in changing ourselves because we quickly come to see our connections to each other and to the natural world lead to changes in our behaviours. Trust, connection, and honest relationships are the fastest routes to changing ourselves.

Advantages of the Community-Organizing Model

We, Westerners, tend to believe that change comes through power. We also tend to believe that power equals force. Both assumptions are limiting, and taken together, they imply that change comes through force. In fact, force is often the crudest instrument available to us when it comes to changemaking.

Change can also come through love, kindness, trust, friendship, connection, conversation, collaboration, negotiation, persistence, knowledge, new experiences, new ideas or new energy into a system, epiphany moments, positive peer pressure, community cohesion, a sense of belonging, a feeling that one is at home, and numerous other things. If true power is the ability to create change, then the things listed above could be regarded as types of power.

Here is something to consider: Love, kindness, trust, friendship, connection, conversation, collaboration, and a sense of belonging are at the heart of what it means to be human. As humans, we have free access to these powers of the human spirit. Changemaking need not require money or external resources; rather, the capacity for changemaking resides within each of us. Most often, what is needed to unleash this changemaking potential is a strong community grounded in trust, friendship, and a common goal.

Grief

During these past seasons of clear-cut timber harvest, Ghost Valley community members have been filled with sadness and anger. These difficult emotions come from our sense of connection to the land. We do not apologize for our passion or our grief. Grief is the price of love and there is nothing wrong with love.

We know what it is to pour ourselves into something when success is not guaranteed. We went into this with our eyes open, knowing we were not likely to save that which we love, but that did not stop us from trying. We know it would have been an even greater failure on our part if we had not tried. We will look our children and our grandchildren in the eyes, and say, "We tried our very best."

Other communities affected by clear-cut logging warned us that the stress of dealing with entrenched government and corporate cultures can play havoc with one's physical and emotional health and can divide a community. From the start, we strategized how we would safeguard against this by building a strong community. We speak publicly about watershed values and watershed actions, but running parallel to watershed protection endeavours is a quiet story of which this community can be immensely proud: the strength of this community's practical care for one another.

Over the past years, community members performed countless acts of practical care for neighbours enduring various struggles. Meals were delivered to those with health struggles. A furnace was fixed free of charge. Grocery cards were gifted to those with financial struggles. A young person received a substantial college bursary. Community members shut in by age or illness were visited. Endless pots of soup were shared. Listening ears comforted those in the midst of grief and loss.

A Cochrane resident who attended one of our meetings for the first time spoke up as the evening ended, saying, "I see what you are doing in the Ghost. This group is held together with love." Our love for the land brought us together, and it somehow enabled us to care for one another long enough to build the goodwill required for working across differences. Many of us joked that we may not have saved the trees, but perhaps we saved ourselves by creating a safe and caring community, the kind of community many of us have always dreamed of. We may not have gone where we intended to go, but we may have ended up exactly where we needed to be. Our community will now be the medicine for disappointment, grief, and anger.

Building Bridges

At times of grief related to clear-cutting, we came together across cultural lines. A most memorable gathering occurred December 4, 2015, when Stoney Nakoda elders led our community in ceremony to make peace with that season's clear-cutting. Coming together across cultures was facilitated by courageous community members within each culture stepping out in front of their peers to show us the way into uncharted territory.

That day, on the strength of relationship built between a community member and the forester cutting the trees, that forester moved his feller buncher away from the ceremony site so that the community could access the site. As well, Spray Lake Sawmills management and staff travelled to the site to escort community members safely to the stand of trees in which the ceremony was to occur. After the deeply moving ceremony, the stand of trees was left uncut in recognition of its enduring value as a sacred site. It is a sacred site in more ways than most of us will ever know.

On May 26, 2016, Driftpile First Nation travelled to the Ghost Valley to join with Stoney Nakoda elders in ceremony to honour the two nations' common clear-cut experience, recognizing that the exploitation model of resource extraction may lead to yet another wave of losses for northern

Indigenous peoples dependent on an intact forest in order to maintain cultural practices.

On May 6, 2017, Stoney Nakoda elders led our community in a process of blessing the land and ourselves to heal, now that timber harvest in our area has concluded. We must build a bridge back to wholeness. Our ongoing work on behalf of the landscape and on behalf of our community must be powered by trust, friendship, love, and gratitude, for these energize the human spirit in a way that anger and fear never can.

Moving Beyond Adversarial Confrontation

Changemaking within the context of community provides frequent opportunity for building bridges and for honouring what is best within one another. On a regular basis, we look into the faces of those whom we suppose to be on the other side of our struggle. When we realize the Minister of Agriculture and Forestry shares a birthday with one of our community leaders, when the wife of a mill manager interacts in the kindest way possible with our young children, or when we share a laugh with the government biologist at the grocery store, we grasp the future we must somehow co-create across the divide. No rationale remains for the designations of "us and them." It is only "we" now.

Compelling and Credible

In the spring of 2016, we realized our community had pressing needs in addition to forestry concerns. Significant public safety risks existed on the Ghost Public Lands. An increasing number of recreational users were engaging in target practice at informal shooting ranges. Explosive targets had ignited four fires in the Ghost Valley. Community members drafted a press release and composed a letter to government ministries. Media interest in the story persisted throughout the summer. Due in part to the Fort McMurray fire, most of our suggestions for reducing fire risk in the Ghost were enacted by government by summer's end. Our request for change was so compelling that it could not be ignored by media, government, or the public.

We then realized that we needed to get our hands dirty for the landscape we love. The Ghost's TransAlta Road was littered with derelict vehicles, old mattresses, and living room furniture. Enviros Wildness

School and Ghost River Rediscovery, two nonprofits operating in the Ghost, offered to organize a cleanup day, with the financial contributions of Centrica, Spray Lake Sawmills, and TransAlta. On June 11, 2016, fifty people showed up to pick up forty cubic yards of trash. This waste had littered the Ghost for two years, signaling to visitors that dumping and burning were acceptable. No law enforcement body or government agency seemed to have the ability to address this problem, but on June 11, people brought torches to cut up five derelict vehicles, hauling the metal away for recycling. On that day, we realized that we, the people, were truly the leaders, the ones we had been waiting for (Walker 2008).

Change is contagious, beckoning others to join in. Passersby were inspired and asked to help with future cleanups. Another derelict vehicle was removed in October 2016. The Minister of Alberta Environment and Parks sent the Ghost Valley community a letter of thanks for significant contributions to the care of Alberta's Public Lands. Alberta Environment and Parks stepped up enforcement in the area, particularly on long weekends.

By the time the community returned to clean up the same area in June 2017, our Member of the Legislative Assembly Cameron Westhead with us, there was hardly any trash to be found. Our practical care for the land has just slightly shifted everything. With government and a broad cross-section of the Ghost community working together, the culture of the Ghost Public Lands is beginning to change. It started with us.

Sustaining our Community Capacity for Changemaking

Clear-cut timber harvest has wrapped up in the Ghost for the foreseeable future. While most in the community feel relief, we know this is not the time to rest. Our community possesses new learning, new skills, and new abilities to work together and to work across ideological divides. We are most likely to maintain these capacities by occasionally taking on new challenges. New opportunities to enhance our quality of life together in this place are on the horizon. The Ghost Valley community is now recognized as a stakeholder in the upcoming consultations related to the Ghost-Kananaskis sub-regional land use planning process taking place in 2018.

As the Ghost Valley community moves through an intentional path of closure in relation to our clear-cut forestry experience, an odd set of circumstances put another changemaking opportunity directly in our path.

On March 23, 2017, the Ghost Valley community hosted Yellowstone to Yukon's Stephen Legault to speak on forestry's future. Our speaker caught the interest of the off-highway vehicle community, with 115 people from both sides of the off-highway vehicle debate attending. Our meeting was more peaceful and respectful than most in the conservation community expected, with leaders now contemplating ways to build bridges between our communities. We do not know where this might lead. The Ghost Valley community's reality is that we share this landscape with others. We must engage in dialogue to figure out how to make it work. Our first joint event, working together to pick up trash in the Ghost and sharing a barbecue lunch, went well. We will look for other opportunities to work together in hopes of furthering our dialogue on behalf of the landscape we share.

Reflecting on the Journey

I have been called a tree-hugger, but I do not actually consider myself an environmentalist, beyond the grief I feel—as all humans should feel—when standing in the presence of violence and death. Why then have I spent years in what appears to be an environmental struggle? The answer is that I care about my neighbours. They identified clear-cut timber harvest as negatively impacting our community's well-being together in this place. Therefore, addressing clear-cut timber harvest became the work of our community's changemaking.

Sometimes life is simple. When we care about people in our community, we get to work to make our lives better together in this place. As the saying goes, "This is not rocket science." It is not science at all. It is just plain old-fashioned compassion. The fierce untamable goodness of my neighbours is unparalleled. My children and I are fortunate to live among the best people I know in the community of which I have always dreamed.

Confidence in Community

While things have not yet worked out as we hoped, we ended up with each other and with the sense that we are part of something bigger than ourselves. We proved that when people come together in trust and friendship, they find ways to address the community's shared concerns, working together to magnify their individual efforts a hundredfold. We know that preserving this landscape depends upon a strong community, working together for the common good. This is the essence of a community-organizing approach to changemaking: We the people are truly the leaders. We are the ones we have been waiting for (Walker 2008).

REFERENCES

Fedeyko, Marni. "Ghost Valley residents concerned about condensed logging plans." *Discover Airdrie*, https://www.discoverairdrie.com/index.php?option=com_content&acview=araticle&id=11860%3Aghost-valley-residents-concerned-about-condensed-cutting-plans&catid=1%3Alocal-news&Itemid=136. Accessed June 30, 2017.

Homan, Mark S. *Promoting Community Change: Making It Happen in the Real World*. 6th ed., Boston: Cengage Learning, 2016.

Joy, Leonard. *How Does Societal Transformation Happen?* Caye Caulker: Quaker Institute for the Future, 2011.

Macy, Joanna. "Three Dimensions of the Great Turning," http://www.joannamacy.net/three-dimensions-of-the-great-turning.html. Accessed June 30, 2017.

Walker, Alice. "What our country desperately needs is leader who loves us," *The Guardian*, September 20, 2008, https://www.theguardian.com/commentisfree/2008/sep/20/uselections2008.barackobama.

Weick, Karl E. *Making Sense of the Organization*. Madden: Blackwell Publishing Ltd., 2001.

The New Thunderbirds: The Waters of Uranium City, Saskatchewan

Bill Bunn and Robert Boschman[1]

This chapter is dedicated to the memory of Patrick Deranger

In front of us on a battered couch sits Patrick Deranger, a Dene man who was born on the north shore of Lake Athabasca (Figure 14.1). He is an elder. His long grey hair is pulled back. After he receives the tobacco we bring, his dark eyes spark as the stories he's about to tell inhabit him. He is uniquely qualified to speak about the water of Uranium City: as a child, he and his family lived on the land that would hold that community. They were removed from the site in order to make way for this mining town, planned and built by Eldorado Mining, a Crown Corporation, in the mid-twentieth century. As an elder, Patrick Deranger knows the stories of water from the old people; the Dene have occupied these Treaty 8 lands from time immemorial.

As we meet, he pulls a barnacled abalone shell from the shelf near the front door. The shell is the size of an ashtray and brims with cinder. He's backlit by the morning sun pouring in the front room picture window. He takes a pinch of tobacco from a cigarette and places it in the middle of the abalone shell and lights it with a lighter. Smoke, glowing with light, snakes into the still air.

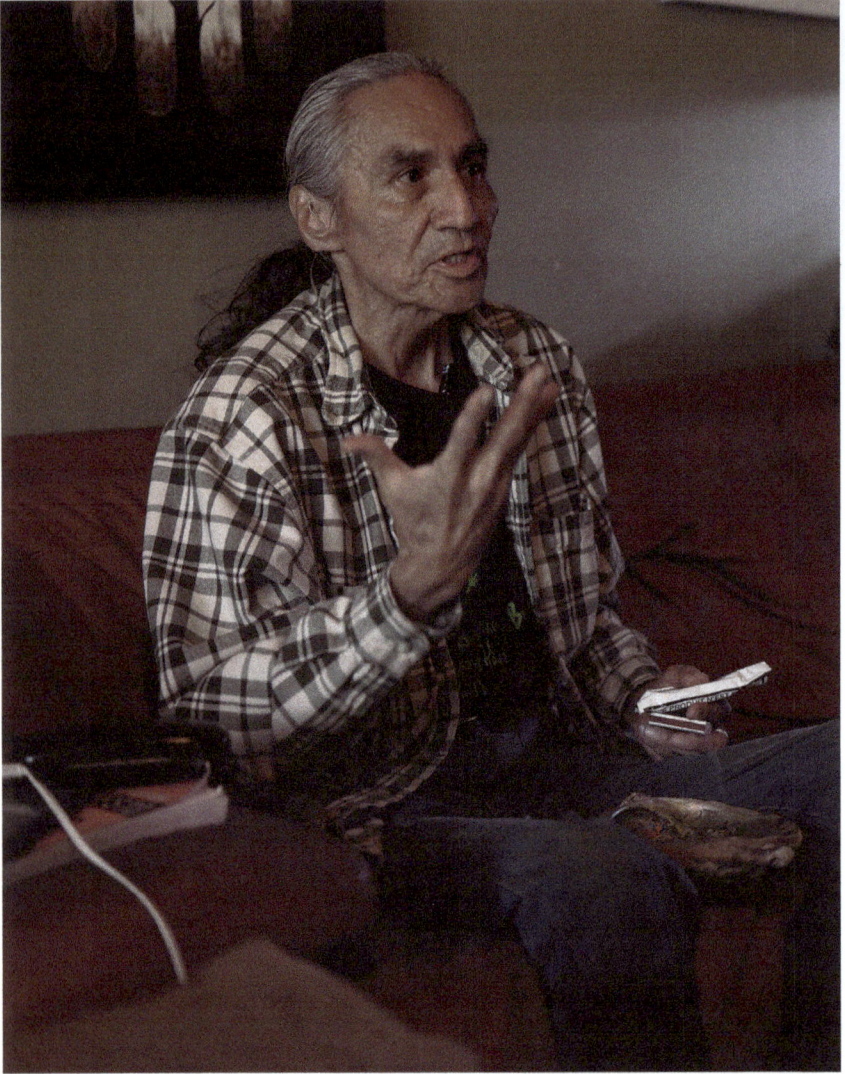

Figure 14.1. Dene Elder Patrick Deranger, 2019. Photo courtesy Robert Boschman.

The old people say any time you're going to be talking about things having to do with the land, you have to acknowledge the things you're going to discuss. It has to do with spirits; it has to do with the lay of the land. The Creator put things there. We're inviting dignitaries here, we shake hands, and we thank them. We do this with the smoke. The old people always say be careful what you talk about and how you talk about it, that you don't make mistakes and you don't make it up. You work to keep the original story intact as to how it was presented in the past. I offer some tobacco, so I don't upset what was put into place. These ancient spirits are very powerful, so it's important that these protocols are kept.

With that, he gently grabs two handfuls of smoke and smooths them into his hair. Another handful he pats to his chest, over his heart. He invites us to do the same, and we do. He pinches some smudge herb from a braid on the coffee table and places it on the burning tobacco.

The fire has to do with the Mystery, the Creator, the mystery. The smoke is the breath of this mystery. Some of these stories are imbued with a lot of power. Telling stories in the summer can also affect the weather. There is a time and place for storytelling. Usually, we tell stories in the winter.

He explains that it is not wise to jump straight into a story.

A story, in itself, is a spirit. Physics tells us that energy can neither be created nor destroyed. Knowledge is a form of energy. So we're talking about sets of powers, interrelated. So we invite these dignitaries, these spirits, and they are stories. We are greeting a moving entity, a life, a spirit. A story is a tangible life form. So we recognize and acknowledge that this spirit exists. Just like my dog, when he comes up to you and wants an exchange.

When I was young, going to school, I read about these creatures. These creatures were large creatures of all different kinds and shapes, big and small. At one time, they roamed the country. These creatures were ferocious. At one time they numbered in the millions. But they all disappeared. I'm learning this from teachers and books. But behind me, I hear whisperings of the old people. The old people said "Look, these creatures are still around. We've seen them. They have emerged from the land." The old people say one time, these large creatures were causing too much of a problem for people. So this mystery that created life realized it was a serious problem because people were getting killed. It was decided that they would not kill off these creatures. We will change how they live on the earth. We're going to send them into the earth. That's where they are to remain. Life is not stationary; it moves. So sometimes they come up. Then it becomes dangerous for us, as human beings. The majority of times we see them in the water. Anywhere there is water, the ground underneath that water is soft. It's easier for the creatures to come out. Most of the time this happens in the summertime. The Thunderbird is to round up these creatures and herd them back into the earth using its powers, and its powers have to do with the thunder and lightning. Its eyes have to do with the lightening. Its voice has to do with the thunder. So when they start to emerge, and the old people are travelling the land, and you see these huge cumulous clouds forming, the old people say there is a chance something tried to emerge. (Deranger, 2019)

The Uranium City site, set close to the eastern shores of Lake Athabasca, has an abundance of water (Figure 14.2). Striated stone bowls carved into the Canadian Shield cradle thousands of lakes. This abundance of water made the area a rich territory for the Cree and the Dene peoples. Patrick's people wandered this territory for thousands of years, depending on water for life, food, hygiene, and transport. Thus, the Dene's creation story bears strong connections to water.

FIGURE 14.2. Uranium City Ruins, 2018. Photo courtesy Bill Bunn.

The Dene creation story involves giant beaver and strong water elements (Deranger, 2017). The giant beaver stories may seem, at first glance, to be a fanciful narrative element. In our research, we learned that giant beaver are a matter of archeological fact, the last ones roaming the area between ten and fourteen thousand years ago (Guthrie, 2006). These beaver, or *castoroides*, weighed between 198 and 300 pounds, about the size of a black bear. Ethnologist Jane Beck notes the presence of the large beaver in a host of Indigenous stories from many times and places, and her one conclusion is that the presence of these creatures in multiple Indigenous cultures suggests the approximate age of the stories. In Beck's words, "When it can be established that a folktale is anchored in fact it may very well be as revealing about a people's past as any archaeological discovery" (1972, p. 109). The prevalence of the giant beaver in Indigenous stories, taken together with carbon dating, suggests that these stories are at least 10,000 years old.

The beaver's connection with water is evident. The beaver and the Dene people, in their ancient stories, live in conflict: beavers alter watercourses, tip canoes, attack, and even eat humans. The beavers act in many cases as agents of aquatic control, and in the Dene recounting of their stories, beaver are the enemy of the people.

FIGURE 14.3. Lake Athabasca, 2018. Photo courtesy Robert Boschman.

The beaver, in all these stories, live underground. So when Dene heroes Hachoghe, Yamôôzha, or Yamōria defend their people against the beaver, it involves digging underground, digging into a beaver lodge, and attacking the beaver where it lives. The beaver is associated with water, but also lives underground. Part of the Thunderbird's duty, then, is to keep an eye out for the beaver, an underground and waterborne threat.

The manifestations of these stories still exist in the Uranium City area. Ironically, the site of one Eldorado mine is Beaverlodge mountain, the storied home of a family of giant beaver, where a Dene hero entered and fought with the beaver he found there, and prevailed, turning the soil and rock red with the beavers' blood. On a nearby island on Lake Athabasca (Figure 14.3), there is a huge, naturally occurring hole in the ground. According to the locals, this is the hole from which some of the giant beaver emerged.

The centrality of water to the Dene expresses a theme carried through many ancient cultures and religions. The role of water in human existence was and is so critical that most ancient world cultures and religions regard water as sacred. Our foundational need for drink and hygiene is one of the reasons water has often played a sacred role in religion and culture. Water met these twin needs, and in response, people held it as sacred. Why does water play a central role in these ancient cultures? Terje Oestigaard notes that

> Water is a medium for everything—it has human character because we are humans; it is a social matter but also a spiritual substance and divine manifestation with immanent powers; and, still, it belongs to the realm of nature as a fluid liquid. The hydrological cycle links all places and spheres together, and water transcends the common categories by which we conceptualize the world and cosmos. (2011, p. 38)

As a practical cultural centre, water absorbs and holds a social significance. Water, as Oestigaard notes, forms the heart of ancient cultures, their view of the world, and their culture:

> The pervasive role of water-worlds in society and cosmos unites micro and macrocosmos, creates life, and legitimizes social hierarchies and religious practices and beliefs. Water is a medium which links or changes totally different aspects of humanity and divinities into a coherent unit; it bridges paradoxes, transcends the different human and divine realms, allows interactions with gods, and enables the divinities to interfere with humanity. (p. 38)

Water, in Oestigaard's view, played a unifying and legitimizing role in ancient cultures. In a sense, it helped to structure and govern ancient cultures. This seems true of the Dene, and their stories of the world's beginning.

The Dene's view of water is one that historian J. L. Manore would argue is "organic." Manore suggests that

> When Europeans first made contact with the aboriginal nations in what was to become Canada, an "organic" view

prevailed within aboriginal cultures. For many of the First Nations, the rivers of Turtle Island, as they called North America, were and are the veins of Mother Earth. As such they give the Earth its life-blood, they function as the earth's circulatory system, transporting waste and nutrients from one area to another, and participating in the circulation of vital materials. (2006, p. 233)

As Dr. Manore points out, original peoples exhibited an "organic" attitude towards water. These cultures honoured and respected water as "the source of individual and collective life" (p. 231). In their world view, water is a living thing, autonomous and free to act. The job of the human was to respect the water, track it as though it were any other living thing. Water is sacred, organic, autonomous, and self-governing.

The Birth of Canada: Water Flows in a New Light

Water was central to the Dene culture, and it was and continues to be crucial in connection to the abandoned mines and town of Uranium City. The centrality of water did not change when the mining companies explored and commandeered the land. Water of the new world was to play as central a role as it had in Indigenous cultures. It was the heart of what was to become Uranium City. It was the core of what made mining in that remote region possible. It endures as the critical feature of what remains of Uranium City and the area. What changed was the attitude towards water. The mining community displaced the original peoples and their "organic" world view with what Dr. Manore calls a "mechanistic" one.

The mechanistic view of water has origins as far back as Macedonian culture, 6,000 BCE. Humans then learned that water was a powerful tool and could be used as a machine, a medium, and for transport (Kornfield, 2009). And that attitude eclipsed the reverence for water, the "organic" view, and replaced it with an engineering view: water should be used, manipulated, and controlled. This mechanistic view meant that water had

no value except in terms of cash flow. [Waters are] … not divine; not a means of creating and recreating life. They are commodities to be bought and sold … [Water] (and nature) cannot be allowed to run their course; their integrity as natural systems are not respected. (Manore, 2006, p. 239)

The mechanized possibilities of water intensified in the late 16th century, as the options for human control increased in terms of scale (Manore, 2006). Oxford Civil Engineer Leveson Francis Vernon-Harcourt dedicated his 1882 volume, *A Treatise on Rivers and Canals*, to "the control and improvement of rivers." He distilled mechanistic thinking to this:

> Rivers are not always suitable for navigation, in their natural condition, even in the lower portions of their course; and, owing to the continual changes they tend to produce in their channels and at their outlets, they are liable to deteriorate if left to themselves. Accordingly, the maintenance, control, and improvement of rivers constitute one of the most important, and at the same time one of the most difficult branches of civil engineering. (p. 1)

In Canada, mechanized thinking concerning water was in place from the outset as European traders learned from First Peoples the economic possibilities of this vast land; they realized that the easiest way to move goods and services across the continent was to use its bodies of water, flowing or frozen. For traders and colonials, water was not part of a venal, life-sustaining flow but rather a useful commercial distribution system. Harold Innis, the mid-twentieth-century Canadian historian and geographer, notes the importance of the First Nations technologies in early Canada, particularly in transportation (Figure 14.4). The canoe allowed for the transportation of goods, primarily furs: "It was their transportation technology, most notably the birch-bark canoe, that allowed for the shipment of furs and goods over great distances" (1930/2017, p. 234).

In 1833, William Dunlop in a book offering advice to would-be immigrants said this of Canada's water systems: "No country under heaven is so completely adapted for internal navigation" (p. 58). Wayland Drew, a popular Canadian writer and teacher, went so far as to declare,

FIGURE 14.4. Canoe, Uranium City, 2017. Photo courtesy Robert Boschman.

> The canoe is to Canada what the horse is to the United
> States—the prime vehicle by which the land was first ex-
> plored and first grasped imaginatively. American myths in-
> volve heroic rides, but the great Canadian journey is a canoe
> trip. (n.d.)

Drew's point implies the centrality of water to the foundation of Canada.
For the Canadian context in general, water is a key part of its founding.
John Ralston Saul notes that

> The canoe … was to be used as our principal means of trans-
> portation—personal, governmental, military and commer-
> cial—for several centuries. Why? Because the First Nations
> had developed the appropriate means of transport for our
> road system, that is, our rivers and lakes. (2009, p. 38)

Finally, the economic uses of water corresponded precisely with the rise in the political uses of water. Innis notes, "It is no mere accident that the present Dominion coincides roughly with the fur-trading areas of northern North America" (Innis, 1930/2017, p. 392). Business interests, as always, were bound, inextricably, to politics, to governments who exploited the new territories and the waters they required to harvest resources and bring them to global markets.

Thus, the Dene's organic conception of water was replaced by a mechanized one (Figure 14.5). The mechanization of water was understood as "'lines of power and time carrying empires from source to expansive breadth'. ... [Waters] became symbols of imperial power ... they were no longer the source of individual and collective life; they were vehicles or transporters of nationalist identities" (Innis, 1930/2017, p. 231). Nearly thirty years after Canada was formed, the young government claimed ownership of all water. In 1894, the *North West Irrigation Act* vested all water rights in the Federal Crown. Rights were transferred to individual provinces. In Saskatchewan's case, water rights were assigned by the *Water Rights Act* of 1931. As the *Water Rights Act* of Saskatchewan declares,

> the property in and the right to the use of all water at any time in any river, stream, watercourse, lake, creek, spring, ravine, canyon, lagoon, swamp, marsh or other body of water shall ... be deemed to be vested in the Crown. (p. 5)

These acts codified the new tide of thought: where one finds water, one finds colonial government.

From a literary perspective, we note an interesting genre shift here. Whereas for thousands of years before, water lore and information were carried and passed through the medium of story, water information under colonial governmental control was now transferred through law and policy. The organic story of water was passed through narrative moments from old to young. The mechanized view suppressed and displaced narratives and worked with courts and enforcement instead. Narrative was durable, effective, emerging from deep time, having lasted millennia. Law and policy are not nearly as durable and require constant adjustment and

FIGURE 14.5. Water Line, Fredette R, 2018. Photo courtesy Robert Boschman.

enforcement as the context changes. Colonial settler law and policy require colonial settler government.

This new view of water, mechanized and governmentalized, informed prospectors as they explored, surveyed, claimed, and mined the Athabasca region at the tail end of the gold rush that had already impacted the Canadian north. These water systems had indeed also transported the fish and fur of earlier booms. Gold and uranium reflected commercial concerns of the new era. Prospectors in floatplanes and small boats swarmed through the area looking for anything of value (Figure 14.6). The Gold Rush established an idea, a metaphor, that fueled the ambition to explore and exploit northern lands, which led to the discovery and recovery of uranium and the founding of Uranium City.

Uranium City's Place in the Uranium Prospecting Narrative

Uranium City's conception and construction could almost be viewed as inevitable, as a confluence of world events and a series of mining attempts created the circumstances for its seeming necessity. Such circumstances

FIGURE 14.6. Uranium City Region Boat, 2017. Photo courtesy Robert Boschman.

depended on water's presence, on its being mechanized and government-alized. Decisions made in the mid-twentieth century continue to impact the waters of Uranium City and its area to this day.

Canada has a very long history of prospecting and mining. Uranium mining began to be established thirty years after the end of the Klondike Gold Rush from 1896 to 1899. This intense event brought an estimated 100,000 prospectors to the Yukon. Decades after its close, the gold rush, fresh in the world's collective mind, became a pattern and a metaphor that would shape and drive the approach to Canada's uranium. Canada's northern region, especially in the province of Saskatchewan, became a prospecting frontier and the parent of many a mining fortune.

Uranium City begins its history at the half-way point of the uranium boom in Canada. Surveyors noticed uranium's presence as early as the summer of 1900, when James McIntosh Bell and Charles Camsell, on be-half of *The Geological Survey of Canada*, recorded evidence of uranium among other useful resources as they toured the Canadian north. Using the observations of the Geological Survey of Canada, prospector Gilbert LaBine staked the first major discovery of uranium, or pitchblende, in early 1930. LaBine opened the Eldorado Gold Mines operation to extract uranium from Cameron Bay, later renamed Port Radium, North West Territories in 1932. The ore he transported to Port Hope, Ontario, where it was milled into "radium salts," was used to treat cancer. At that time, Belgium had a monopoly on the making of radium salts, which sold for $70,000 per gram. Port Radium closed in 1940.

Closer to where Uranium City would eventually be built, prospectors Tom Box and Gus Neiman struck gold in 1934 and built a mine, which was followed by the creation of a town to support the mine two years later. To power the mine and the new townsite of Goldfields, their mining company built a small run-of-the-river hydroelectric station. The Wellington Power Station commissioned its first unit in 1939 to service the mine and townsite. Goldfields was located twenty-four kilometres to the south of where Uranium City would subsequently be built. At first, Goldfields and its box mine glowed with promise. For a few years during the 1930s, it was thought that Goldfields would become an important hub for the north, but the numbers reporting the ore body size and concentration had been fudged, and the mine and town were abandoned in 1942 (Figure 14.7). However, the war effort and the atomic bomb development put a new and urgent value on uranium. In 1941, the United States and the United Kingdom asked Canada to furnish uranium for the war. At the time, Canada was the only known source of uranium not under German control (Edwards, 2014).

Port Radium reopened in late 1941 in utter secrecy; at this point, the only operational uranium mine in Canada was LaBine's Eldorado Mine. Within two years, the Canadian government expropriated and nationalized it as Eldorado Mining and Refining Limited. All prospecting activity was strictly limited, except on behalf of the federal company or the Geological Survey of Canada. The top-secret 1943 Quebec Agreement on the Atom Bomb Project meant that Canada agreed to supply uranium to the Allied war effort and that it would mine that uranium from Canada's north. Ironically, the Agreement was signed by President Roosevelt and Prime Minister Churchill alone. The uranium was to be milled at Port Hope, Ontario, and a secret lab in Montreal would be used to study the

FIGURE 14.7. Gold Smelters, 2018. Photo courtesy Robert Boschman.

making of plutonium (Edwards, 2014). These events, and the agreements struck to meet the challenges they presented, had a large impact on the waters in the Uranium City area. The Quebec Agreement also led to Canada's first experimental Nuclear Reactor at Chalk River, Zero Energy Experimental Pile (or ZEEP), when it began operating in September 1945 (Edwards, 2014). ZEEP was a prototype for the CANDU line of reactors. As one of the earliest reactors, the ZEEP created another potential use for uranium: electrical generation. Wartime demand, combined with the emerging possibility of power generation, meant that the world wanted more uranium than it had.

Eldorado prospectors located and staked the Beaverlodge site in 1945, which was developed slowly into a mineable site over the next four years. In 1950, the company built a modern town, also called Eldorado, to service the 350 miners and mill workers employed there. Following the war, the Canadian government lifted the ban on uranium prospecting, and prospectors returned to the area. Gilbert LaBine, now head of the nationalized Eldorado Mining and Refining Limited, realized there was still room for increasing the uranium supply and thus resumed looking for other sources of uranium once the prospecting ban was lifted. While prospectors continued to search and stake their claims, they weren't welcome in Eldorado, which only had room for its own employees. As early as 1948, a tent community had begun at the site of what is now Uranium City. Once the Goldfields mine closed, the town of Goldfields quickly declined, and on April 1, 1950 its incorporated status was revoked. Given the Uranium City site's then remoteness, its new residents began to visit Goldfields to find and even move its resources. Entire homes would eventually be moved to the new townsite dedicated to uranium extraction.

The new townsite was also the traditional ancient homeland of the Dene. The Deranger family lived here, and Patrick Deranger, interviewed at the outset of this chapter, was born here at about this time. As the growing group of prospectors and miners began to populate the area, the Derangers, along with other Indigenous families, were relocated to an area south of town, an area that became known as Saskatchewan Government Airlines Hill, or SGA Hill. SGA Hill was cut off from the new town with its resources and emerging infrastructure. By removing the Dene from the heart of the town, indeed from the place where even today a sign remains for the Uranium City Hotel on an empty lot, the "organic" view of the world and its waters was also removed to the margins of the settlement, away from the uranium extraction business (Figure 14.8).

In 1952, one of LaBine's prospectors, Albert Zeemel, found himself on the Crackingstone Peninsula, not far from the Beaverlodge find. Zeemel was to send a radiogram immediately if he found anything. And he did. According to the well-known story, he radioed this message: "Come quick, I've shot an elephant" (Schiller, 1954, p. 12). Zeemel was, of course, referring to an enormous uranium discovery, the Gunnar strike. He called it an elephant, unaware of the Dene creation myth with its idea that huge living forces lived in the ground and could emerge threateningly, accompanied by widespread harm to humans. Zeemel's strike caught the world's attention. Robert Schiller, a reporter for *Mclean's Magazine*, noted,

> News of the discovery set off reactions around the world. In many parts of Canada and the United States, and as far away as Saudi Arabia and South Africa, mining men

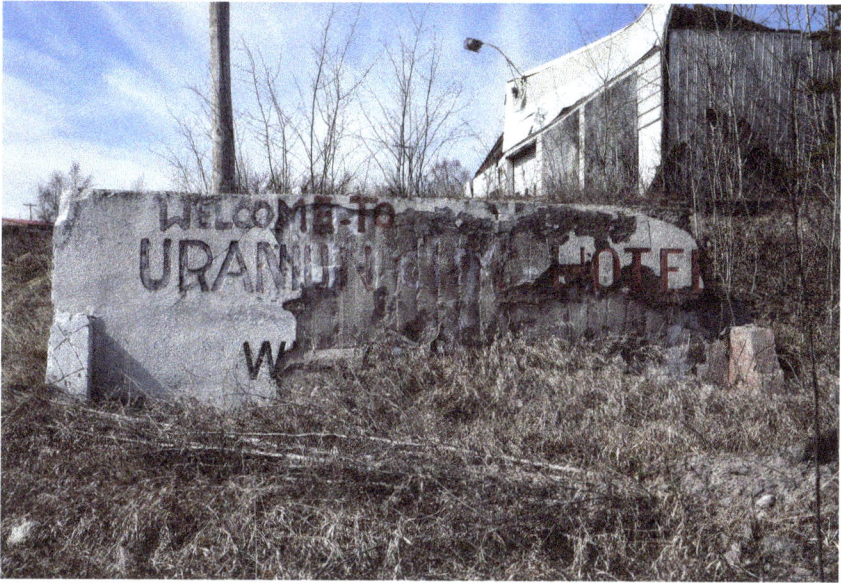

FIGURE 14.8. Deranger Family Site, 2017. Photo courtesy Robert Boschman.

dropped what they were doing and bought plane tickets north. (1954, p. 12)

The swell of prospectors further altered the landscape:

The Gunnar strike swelled what had been a mere trickle of prospectors to Athabaska into an avalanche. Undiscouraged by geologists' warnings that the chance of making a successful find was only one in a thousand, storekeepers, salesmen, clerks, farmers, accountants, cooks, even a Polish count and countess swarmed into the bush. They laid claim to every rock and gully for a hundred miles around. To keep the prospectors alive and supplied, the Saskatchewan provincial government laid out the townsite of Uranium City, eight miles from the Eldorado company's community at

FIGURE 14.9. Uranium Adit [horizontal entrance to a mineshaft], 2017. Photo courtesy Robert Boschman.

Beaverlodge. The first two buildings erected were the claim recorder's office and a liquor store. (p. 12)

The boom drove people to plunder the Goldfields townsite. Goldfields' permanent homes had been abandoned to the elements. In the winter of 1952, however, many houses were moved to Uranium City.

The abandoned components of Goldfields supplied some of the essential infrastructure and created momentum for the building of Uranium City. For one thing, electrical power from the Wellington Station was diverted to Uranium City. A number of the Goldfields buildings were moved over: "A movie theatre, hospital, police station and iron-barred jail were dragged over the ice from the nearby ghost town of Goldfields" (Schiller, p. 51).

Just as with the gold rush, there was a booming market serving uranium prospectors, too. The prospector would make a find, stake the claim, and mine the uranium (Figure 14.9). Uranium City newspapers would often announce news and regulation changes to help facilitate the prospector culture in the area. By 1957, prospectors could stake as many claims as they liked, but the first nine cost five dollars apiece while additional claims were ten dollars each (Mining Regulations, 1957). From time to time, when claims would lapse, prospectors would disappear in a shroud of secrecy to re-stake their claims (Mining Regulations, 1957). Current Uranium City residents tell stories of mom and pop miners and prospectors driving their pickups loaded with uranium ore to one of the mills in the area. They would be paid for the load by the mill.

Water, Please. Mine first.

If water facilitated the exploration and exploitation of the Canadian North, many uranium discoveries were fortuitously positioned because they were close to water. In the case of Uranium City, mining concerns were expeditiously outfitted for water long before citizens received it. The uranium mining and milling processes use huge quantities of water. Water is one of the great problems at other uranium mine and mill sites around the world. In Australia, for example, conservation groups object to the amount of water that uranium mines require: "BHP Billiton's Olympic Dam uranium mine has been for years taking 35 million litres of water each day from the underground aquifer" (Wise International, 2012). The staggering amount of water used in Australia, the article notes, is "one that has been taken for granted for decades. In the past, groundwater supplies were treated as an infinite resource, and subject to an 'out of sight, out of mind' attitude" (Wise International). In the case of Uranium City and its environs, remoteness allowed for an "out of sight, out of mind" attitude. In Uranium City's case, there was an ample supply of water. More than enough to do the job. The remoteness of the location meant that accountability, especially in the early days, was almost non-existent.

At the height of uranium extraction in the Uranium City area, there were numerous mines operating, ranging in size and approach. There were three major mill sites operating as well: Gunnar, Lorado, and Beaverlodge. The water use in the area was enormous. The uranium mill sites drew their water from the nearby lakes where they were built: Laredo Mill, Nero Lake; Eldorado Mill site, Beaverlodge Lake; Gunnar, Lake Athabasca. The mill sites drew water from these lakes to make their slurries; the slurry was dumped into tailing ponds where the water could evaporate. In the case of the Gunnar and Eldorado mill sites, slurry was pumped directly back into the environment until regulatory bodies required tailings ponds instead.

At the Beaverlodge uranium mill near Uranium City, vast quantities of radioactive waste were dumped into Fookes Lake via an outlet pipe, ultimately converting the lake into a tailings reservoir (Figure 14.10). This tailings reservoir lies in the Fulton Creek watershed (Prebble & Coxworth, 2013). During an inquiry into the mine's practices, Eldorado staff noted that "the site operated without an effluent treatment process for approximately 25 years" (p. 9). Proper water treatment was finally installed in 1977 to adhere to the federal Metal Mine Liquid Effluent Regulations (Prebble & Coxworth). In the latter case, as in numerous others, the mechanized, governmentalized waters of Uranium City were certainly put to use. The Gunnar, Eldorado, and Laredo mill sites serviced the numerous smaller mines prospected and dug by individual prospectors.

Given the growing power needs of the mines and mills in the Uranium City region during the early years of extraction and refining, additional hydroelectric projects near the 1939 Wellington Power Station were constructed and came online. A hydroelectric generating unit was added to Wellington in 1959, while Waterloo Power Station was commissioned in

FIGURE 14.10. Fookes Lake. Photo courtesy Simon Enoch.

1961, adding eight megawatts. Charlot River Power Station was commissioned in 1980, just two years before Eldorado shuttered its operations, and supplemented a final 10 megawatts to the pool. All three power stations continue to operate as run-of-the-river type stations, meaning that not much water is stored to generate energy. Sixteen percent of Saskatchewan's total electrical power generation is produced by hydroelectric means. These three dams generate approximately .03 percent of the province's total electricity (SaskPower, n.d.).

Water Please. Citizens Second.

Though the environmental dangers surrounding uranium mining weren't as well understood as they clearly are today, the mining community knew enough to keep the town and mill water systems as separate as possible. The general water flow in the region is east to west; mining and mill operations would contaminate western waters, so it was decided to use Fredette Lake, northeast of the townsite, as the source for Uranium City's potable water. City planners believed Fredette's waters would remain unaffected by uranium production. Still, once this water source had been designated, Uranium City's progress towards modern water and sewage systems was incremental. Indeed, it continued to depend on barreled water, as it had from its earliest period when it was a tent town. Water delivery, though it functioned as a system, could never seem to keep up with residents' demand (Good, 1954).

Ronald Schiller expressed disappointment when he visited the area early in 1954. Uranium City was, he wrote, "a raw drab-looking pioneer settlement that stands like an open gash in the bush. There is neither plumbing nor a water system; drinking water, hauled up from the lake, sells for a dollar a barrel." For Schiller, one mark of a dignified town had to do with its water. By contrast, he much preferred the small community of Beaverlodge, a company town five miles away that had been installed to service Eldorado Mine and Mill, for its "hot and cold running water" (p. 13).

Early in 1954, around the time of Shiller's visit, the administration of Uranium City promised improvements to the water supply situation. The town pledged to install "street taps at intervals through the town supplied with chlorinated water pumped from Fredette Creek." The tap system was to be installed during the summer of 1954 and was to "enable the residents to haul their own water by the bucketful and alleviate the overburdened water delivery system" (Good, 1954, p. 4). The tap system also meant that the town could install a hydrant system to help protect the city from the threat of fire. In 1957, the town was finally able to install a water and sewage system at a cost of almost $500,000 CAD. This new system included a series of fire hydrants (Figure 14.11) to better protect buildings and the growing investment in the area (The Municipal Corporation of Uranium City and District, 1957).

Water's role in the community was not simply industrial and connected with the functions of living. Given water's centrality in Uranium City life, it is also not surprising that recreational boating played a huge part in the leisure activities in the area. Uranium City was a temple of water recreation. Boating, swimming, fishing, anything and everything connected with water became part and parcel of the Uranium City lifestyle. There was even a scuba diving club.

Though the potable and industrial water systems were separate, the latter nevertheless intruded on some of the best recreational waters in the

FIGURE 14.11. Hydrant, 2018. Photo courtesy Robert Boschman.

area. Beaverlodge Lake, for example, is a large lake good for recreation. Nero Lake, the dumping site for some of Laredo Mill's tailings, wasn't used for recreation when the Lorado Mill site was operating and is still not used for recreation now. But Nero also flows into Beaverlodge and that lake is often used for fishing, boating, and even swimming and diving. Though there are many smaller lakes to the east of Uranium City, the preferred boating lakes tended to be the ones on the west side: Beaverlodge Lake, Martin Lake, and Lake Athabasca, lakes where citizens could encounter mine or mill contaminants.

Transport

As it always had, water meant transportation, both by barge and amphibious plane in spring, summer, and early fall, and by means of ice road and ski plane during the winter. The region's westerly side offered the best access to transportation opportunities. This side also offered the largest volumes of water for mining and milling and provided the best access to Lake Athabasca.

The region's extensive aquatic transportation system, especially from the west, is noted by geologist L. P. Tremblay in a 1963 report:

> The area can … be reached by rail from Edmonton to Mc-Murray and from there by boat or barge from Waterways to Bushell, where a dock and hangars for storage space have been installed at the north end of Black Bay on Lake Athabasca in the southwest corner of the map-area. The train part of the trip is 305 miles and the boat part 260 miles. There are also winter roads from McMurray and Lac La Ronge. Most of the heavy freight, such as food, equipment for the various mines, and building material, is carried by barge during the summer when Athabasca River is navigable, or by tractor trains on the winter roads in cold weather. (1963/1972)

Most of the processed uranium was flown from Uranium City to points where it could be shipped by rail. Lisa Piper notes that sometimes lakes were used to land planes to transport uranium to rail points like Waterways, Alberta. From there, it could be shipped using the Northern Transportation Route, a route built and used to move uranium from Port Radium to Port Hope (2010).

Current Waters

In our two field trips to Uranium City in May 2017 and May 2018, we noted water as a powerful and ubiquitous presence across the land (Figure 14.12). Flying north from Saskatoon via Prince Albert, Point's North, and Fond du Lac, we could see thousands of rivers, creeks, ponds, sloughs, and lakes. Saskatchewan boasts around 100,000 lakes and most of these are located in the top half of the province, between Prince Albert and Uranium City, on the north shore of Lake Athabasca, which by itself takes up about 3,000 square kilometers.

On our first field trip to Uranium City in early May 2017, we arrived at break up, the moment the ice road is too soft to offer a viable driving surface. The decomposing ice forms long pencil-like crystals called candles that stand crowded and upright. As the ice rots, the candles break away in

FIGURE 14.12. Approaching Uranium City, 2018. Photo courtesy Robert Boschman.

small clumps, creating a sound like chimes as the thin ice crystals knock together before falling into the water. The candles chime when the water moves as well (Figure 14.13).

Break up means that the cheapest form of transport to and from this region is now over. There are no permanent roads to Uranium City; in 2019, one can drive in all seasons as far as Fond du Lac, on the far eastern end of Lake Athabasca, where the winter road begins. Dean Classen, the town's mayor, makes several major hauls during winter in order to provision himself and the city for the following year. He makes trips south with an empty truck and trailer, then back again with both loaded to the limit.

Uranium City Water Today – the Struggle is Water

The water system installed in the summer of 1957 is the same system Uranium City relies on today. Water flows from Fredette Lake, down Fredette Creek, and empties into a small reservoir where it is drawn to a pump house and piped to a treatment facility before being distributed to homes and businesses in town. At its peak population, Uranium City

FIGURE 14.13. Break Up, 2017. Photo courtesy Robert Boschman.

was home to as many as 5,000 people. At 342 litres per person per day, the town's total possible water usage would amount to approximately 1,710,000 litres per day. In a year, 624,150,000 litres, or 137,293,806 imperial gallons, were used.

Luis-Enrique Arrazola quotes Ian Brewster on the struggle facing Uranium City: "What is left of the city is threatened by the discontinuation of water and hydro services but, according to Brewster, the remaining residents are committed to keeping the area alive" (2012, p. 12). The current Uranium City residents know the importance of water to the survival of their community. The infrastructure is old; it works because the community's sole employee, Wayne Powder, attends to it full time. Powder monitors and maintains the pump house and water purification plant as well as the distribution system (Figure 14.14).

Of the 630 plus homes and forty-two commercial buildings that once made up Uranium City, only about 40 homes and 11 commercial buildings still require water today. Homes that remain viable are close to the water

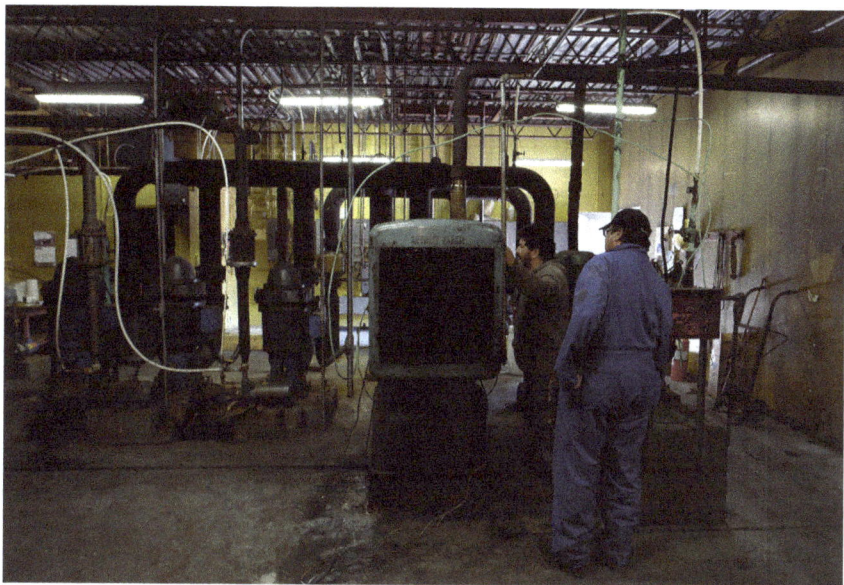

FIGURE 14.14. Tending Infrastructure, 2018. Photo courtesy Robert Boschman.

works. Remaining homes, condominiums, and apartment blocks have been salvaged for copper and fixtures (Figure 14.15). Uranium City's water supply is currently under a boil water advisory in addition to a precautionary drinking water advisory. The latter has been in effect since 2001, the longest running precautionary drinking water advisory in the province (Schick, 2019). According to the provincial government, Uranium City received about $695,000 for drinking water projects between 2002 and 2009. However, the community is still under the advisory, along with a more recent boil-water order.

According to Mayor Classen, most residents drink from their taps anyway. The town did install a bottle filling station, which issues good quality drinking water, but no one uses it (Schick, 2019). "Honestly, to meet provincial and federal standards, somebody has to pump a couple million dollars into the water treatment plant here," said Classen. There are other things which need attention first, such as repairs to water and sewer lines. The federal and provincial governments have run grant programs, and

FIGURE 14.15. Abandoned Homes, 2017. Photo courtesy Bill Bunn.

Classen has applied for funding, but the $2 million needed exceed those grant allocations. At this point, the mayor seems resigned to the advisory staying in place (2019).

Signs of the old water systems are everywhere in Uranium City (Figure 14.16). The numerous abandoned homes confirm their former water connections. Indeed, the townsite is haunted by Freud's sense of the "uncanny," which he described as "nothing new or foreign, but something familiar and old—established in the mind that has been estranged only by the process of repression" (1919, p. 13). In Uranium City's case, the repression expresses itself through a combination of silence, decay, and the forces of nature slowly consuming the townsite.

In addition to Uranium City's fight to maintain its water and sewer systems with water from Fredette Lake to the east, there is the continued presence of 14.8 million tonnes of contaminants threatening the water systems to the west (Figure 14.17). Canada's mechanized governmental view of water has brought Uranium City to a crisis point. The Sierra Club of Canada includes it as one of its "Toxic Thirteen sites," stating that "Uranium City is a city living with what Ralph Klein once called one of Canada's worst environmental nightmares" (Sierra Club of Canada and

FIGURE 14.16. The Uncanny, 2018. Photo courtesy Robert Boschman.

MiningWatch Canada, 2005). They note that the "Local communities are left to deal with the toxic legacy, or, frequently, to cope and live with the contamination and its impacts on their health and the health of their children." The Sierra Club criticizes the government's Federal Contaminated Sites Inventory, which currently lists 778 contaminated sites in Canada requiring attention (Government of Canada, n.d.). Uranium City, the Club notes, is conspicuously absent from that list (Sierra Club of Canada and MiningWatch Canada, 2005). Billions of litres of water were used in the mining process, some of which ended up in tailings ponds, isolated from the freshwater systems. Slurry and sludge were piped to the tailing pond; then the water evaporated, separating itself from the contaminants and leaving them behind. Tailings can easily leach into the system and some in this region have never been processed at all. During the earlier period of uranium mining and milling here, most mine waste was piped straight into freshwater systems until the practice was finally banned. Much of this contamination settled to the bottom of the lakes. There are

Figure 14.17. Warning, 2017. Photo courtesy Robert Boschman.

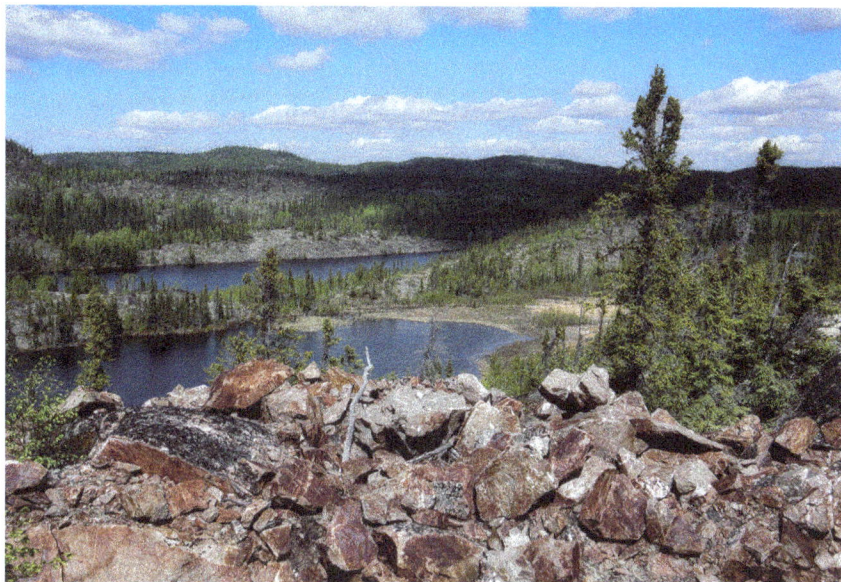

FIGURE 14.18. Goldfields, 2018. Photo courtesy Robert Boschman.

also legacy tailings from mining operations other than uranium in the area. For example, the box mine at Goldfields was abandoned in 1942, leaving the tailings from its gold extraction near Lodge Bay on Lake Athabasca (Figure 14.18). The gold mining process, like the uranium process, also relied heavily on water. As one study optimistically observed, the presence of these tailings "might provide an opportunity for future comparison of abandoned uranium tailings with gold tailings" (Swanson & Abouguendia, 1981).

The uranium mining and milling processes "produce very large amounts of waste rock, and contaminated waters and sludges" (Nuclear Decommissioning Authority, 2014). According to Dr. Gordon Edwards, President of the Canadian Coalition for Nuclear Responsibility, of the more than 250 million tonnes of uranium mining tailings in Canada, approximately 14.8 million tonnes of tailings are buried or submerged in the Uranium City area. The tailings cover approximately 89 hectares or 220 acres (Swanson & Abouguendia, 1981). The submerged tailings are at the bottom of Fookes Lake, a lake that eventually flows into Beaverlodge lake (Figure 14.19), where Eldorado Nuclear poured tailings directly into the lake from the opening of the Eldorado mine until 1977 (P. Prebble & A. Coxworth, 2013). Gunnar Mine's tailings lie at the bottom of Lake Athabasca, while Lorado's are located in Nero Lake.

The strategy for remediating tailings is to leave them in place precisely because they are so toxic. As the Saskatchewan Research Council has conducted remediations, accessible tailing ponds have been buried, though many in the community want the toxicity moved. The SRC argues that to dig up the tailings and move them would create further damages.

The consequences of mining and milling activity in the area is difficult to estimate. Peter Prebble and Ann Coxworth note that

> Both the Ace Creek and Fulton Creek watersheds drain into Beaverlodge Lake, a water body with a surface area of 57 square kilometres, and water depths commonly in the 40 to 60 metre range. Beaverlodge Lake suffered the consequences of Eldorado Nuclear Ltd.'s decision not to install a proper effluent treatment system for the first 25 years of its mining and milling operation. (2013, p. 4)

The outlet pipe from the uranium mill at Beaverlodge dumped "vast quantities of radioactive waste ... into Fookes Lake, converting it into a tailings reservoir. The tailings reservoir lies in the Fulton Creek watershed" (p. 4). Fookes Lake flows into Beaverlodge Lake and

> under normal conditions, the large size of Beaverlodge Lake would quickly dilute pollution. However, Beaverlodge Lake has been so badly contaminated by the polluted discharge from the Ace Creek and Fulton Creek watersheds that concentrations of uranium in surface waters in Beaverlodge Lake are now 7 times higher than Saskatchewan Municipal Drinking Water Quality Objectives. Depending on sampling locations within the lake, uranium concentrations in surface waters are 8 to 9 times higher than Saskatche-

FIGURE 14.19. Beaverlodge, 2017. Photo courtesy Robert Boschman.

wan Surface Water Quality Objectives for the Protection of
Aquatic Life (p. 4, 5).

The overall 14.8 million tonnes of contaminant must sit in place. Some
of it is buried. Some of it sits where it settled at the bottom of lakes. Some
still lies where it was placed many years ago, open and exposed. The net
result is this: this area now needs constant monitoring. In most cases, the
tailings do tend to sink to the bottom of any bodies of water. Uranium
itself is 1.6 times denser than lead. When it settles, it doesn't tend to move.
But it can, and sometimes it does. Because water circulates, because it has
access to some of the deepest toxicities buried in the area, there is always a
chance it will waken some disaster, allowing these buried beasts to emerge
again. Into the future, indefinitely, and for as long as human cultures exist,
this area, with its numerous surface and subsurface toxicities, will require
vigilant monitoring.

A New Thunderbird

The role of thunderbird, the job of keeping buried things buried, has been taken up by many, including most notably the Saskatchewan Government. Like the thunderbird, the provincial government now keeps a weather eye out. Water consultants, ornithologists, biologists, and other scientists regularly visit the area to monitor the environment. The Saskatchewan Research Council (SRC) is one such government group; it contracts with various scientists to monitor water and wildlife throughout the Uranium City region on the north shore of Lake Athabasca.

Additionally, the Athabasca Working Group also monitors water in the area. The Athabasca Working Group is an arm of Canada North Environmental Services, "a private environmental consulting company that is 100% owned by Kitsaki Management Limited Partnership, the business arm of the Lac La Ronge Indian Band." They began monitoring the environment in the Uranium City area in 1999. Their "focus … is to monitor certain parameters related to uranium operations that are of concern to human and environmental health. These include: copper, lead, nickel, molybdenum, zinc, radium-226, uranium, selenium, and arsenic." They provide "residents with opportunities to test the environment around their communities for parameters that could come from uranium mining and milling operations." Their main focus is the area's water system, because contaminants can "spread by water flowing from lakes near the uranium operations" (http://cannorth.com). As we already state in this chapter, waterflows move east to west in the area; following this, the Athabasca Working Group compares samples between Fredette Lake, to the east of most operations, and Black Bay on Lake Athabasca, west of operations and the townsite. Wayne and Sandy Powder, two current Uranium City residents, have collected samples for this program. Ken Mercredi is very active in the area, guiding scientists and other visitors as well as monitoring watersheds as a citizen scientist.

All of these individuals and organizations reflect a new, hybrid view of nature aptly described by David Suzuki:

> The way we see the world shapes the way we treat it. If a mountain is a deity, not a pile of ore; if a river is one of the

veins of the land, not potential irrigation water; if a forest is a sacred grove, not timber; if other species are biological kin, not resources; or if the planet is our mother, not an opportunity—then we will treat each other with greater respect. This is the challenge, to look at the world from a different perspective. (Parry, 2016)

If the ancient thunderbird kept an eye out for threats rising out of the earth, particularly the water, the new thunderbirds are concerned with much the same thing. But, the new thunderbird views water differently than the old people did, and differently again from the geologists and prospectors who came here. It is not a return to the ancient view of water, nor is it a mechanized view, entirely. The new perspective is a blend of both views. It is a view that relies heavily on the ancient perspective, one that sees the interconnectedness of all things, that respects water and cares for it, that remembers its sacredness. At the same time, it also relies on a mechanized view that accounts for the molecular composition of the water, tests and measures chemicals, and monitors water systems. In the post-uranium mining world found not only in the region described here but also throughout the world, both are needed. Both views have roles to play in the restoration of place.

And both understandings of water are in the eye of the new thunderbirds. The new thunderbirds respect the water and understand it is the mother of all things, that water is interconnected to all things. But this new thunderbird also watches thresholds met and exceeded through water samples, animal counts, and physical inspections. If these underground beasts rise, it might not be their physical threat that we see. Instead, we might note elevated selenium levels and abnormal gamma activity. This is the new threat brought on by the governmental, mechanized use of water in Uranium City in the mid-twentieth century.

In a more forward-thinking plan, the Saskatchewan Research Council has outlined a monitoring program for the next 100 years (MacPherson, 2019). But this falls short of the true monitoring window needed for Uranium-234. Some of these nuclear contaminants mean that monitoring should continue for the next 24,000 years, mirroring, in some ways,

Chernobyl's fate. And monitoring is the cost of exploiting this business opportunity, of unleashing this force of nature from the ground.

Likely, Canadian federal and provincial law and policy regarding Uranium City will not be sufficient. Policy and law continue to reflect the mechanized view, although we can hope that the 2015 Truth and Reconciliation Commission Report (TRC) will engender change in the underlying views that support policy and law. Policy and law need to be managed and, of course, imply a government working to maintain these things. But to be fair, a 24,000-year monitoring program is unrealistic; story might be a better way to pass on the knowledge, and story is a value inherent in Indigenous ways of knowing and outlined as such in this book as well as in the TRC Report.

Hence, like the Dene story of creation described at the outset of this chapter, the watching of these waters needs to continue both as governmental policy, for as long as our governments last, and as story so that those living in the area, when Canada perhaps no longer exists, continue to act as the new thunderbirds and keep their watchful diligence.

NOTE

1   The authors wish to acknowledge the Social Sciences and Research Council of Canada
     (SSHRC) for supporting their research on uranium extraction communities through
     an Insight Development grant. Without the assistance of Mount Royal University's
     Institute for Environmental Sustainability, the Office of Research, Scholarship, and
     Community Engagement, and Dr. Jennifer Pettit, the Dean of Arts, the authors could
     not have begun this work. Bunn and Boschman proceed under the clearance of the
     Human Research Ethics Board. They acknowledge the peoples and lands of Treaty
     8 and wish to thank especially the good folks of Uranium City. Thank you, Patrick
     Deranger and Ken Mercredi, our mentors and guides.

REFERENCES

Arrazola, L.-E. (2012, March 12). Uranium City is small-town Canada taken to the extreme. *National Post.*

Beck, J. (1972). The Giant Beaver: A Prehistoric memory. *Ethnohistory, 19*(2), 109–122.

Canadian Nuclear Association. (2010). *History of Uranium Mining in Canada.* https://web.archive.org/web/20120216100517/http://www.cna.ca/curriculum/cna_can_nuc_hist/uranium_hist_mining-eng.asp?bc=History%20of%20Uranium%20Mining%20in%20Canada&pid=History%20of%20Uranium%20Mining%20in%20Canada

Drew, Wayland. (n.d.). Fur Brigades — Brigades de Fourrures. *Canadian Primary Sources in the Classroom.* Retrieved June 22, 2021, from http://www.begbiecontestsociety.org/furbrigade.htm

Dunlop, W. (1833). *Statistical sketches of Upper Canada.* John Murray.

Edwards, G. (2014). *Nuclear waste governance in Canada.* Canadian Coalition for Nuclear Responsibility. 19th REFORM Group Meeting.

Freud, S. (1919). *The uncanny.* Retrieved July 20, 2019, from https://web.mit.edu/allanmc/www/freud1.pdf

Good, D. A. (1954, January 15). Of things to come. *The Uranium Times.*

Government of Canada. (n.d.). *Federal contaminated sites inventory.* Retrieved September 2019, from https://www.tbs-sct.gc.ca/fcsi-rscf/home-accueil-eng.aspx

Government of Canada. (2017, March 10). *Residential water use.* https://www.canada.ca/en/environment-climate-change/services/environmental-indicators/residential-water-use.html

Guthrie, R. D. (2006). New carbon dates link climatic change with human colonization and Pleistocene extinctions. *Nature: International Journal of Science,* 207–209.

Innis, H. (2017). *The fur trade in Canada.* University of Toronto Press. (Original work published in 1930)

Kornfield, I. E. (2009). Mesopotamia: A history of water and law. In J. W. Dellapenna & J. Gupta (Eds.), *The evolution of the law and politics of water* (pp. 21–36). Springer.

MacPherson, A. (2019, June 4). "There is life after remediation": Gunnar mine reclamation forging ahead despite legal battle. *Saskatoon Star-Phoenix.*

Manore, J. L. (2006). Rivers as text: From pre-modern to post-modern understandings of development, technology, and the environment in Canada and abroad. In T. Tvedt, E. Jakobsson & T. Oestigaard (Eds.), A *History of water: Vol. 3. The world of water* (pp. 229–253). I.B.Tauris.

Mining Regulations. (1957, January 14). *Northland News,* 8.

Municipal Corporation of Uranium City and District. (1957, April 13). Notice. *Northland News.*

Nuclear Decommissioning Authority. (2014). Factsheet: Uranium mining and milling. http://ukinventory.nda.gov.uk/wp-content/uploads/sites/2/2014/01/Fact-sheet-uranium-mining-and-milling.pdf

Oestigaard, T. (2011). Water. In T. Insoll (Ed.), *The Oxford handbook of the archaeology of ritual and religion* (pp. 39–50). Oxford University Press.

Parry, B. (2016, November 29). Why land rights for indigenous peoples could be the answer to climate change. *The Guardian*. https://www.theguardian.com/commentisfree/2016/nov/29/land-rights-indigenous-peoples-climate-change-deforestation-amazon

Piper, L. (2010). *The industrial transformation of subarctic Canada*. UBC Press.

Prebble, P., & A. Coxworth. (2013). *The government of Canada's legacy of contamination in northern Saskatchewan watersheds*. Canadian Centre for Policy Alternatives - Saskatchewan Office.

Ralston SAUL, J. (2009). *A fair country*. Penguin Canada.

SaskPower. (n.d.). *System map*. Retrieved September 2019, from https://www.saskpower.com/Our-Power-Future/Our-Electricity/Electrical-System/System-Map

Schick, L. (2019, March 5). Murky water: Sask. settlement under water advisory for nearly 18 years. *980 CJME*.

Schiller, R. (1954). Athabaska's atom boom. *Mclean's Magazine*, 12–13, 51–54.

Sierra Club of Canada and MiningWatch Canada. (2005, August, 11). Environmentalists decry "Arthur Anderse." Approach to toxic accounting. https://miningwatch.ca/news/2005/8/11/environmentalists-decry-arthur-andersen-approach-toxic-accounting

Swanson, S., & Z. Abouguendia. (1981). *The problem of abandoned uranium tailings in Northern Saskatchewan: An overview*. Saskatchewan Research Council.

Tremblay, L. P. (1972). *Geology of the Beaverlodge mining area, Saskatchewan*. Geological Survey of Canada. (Original work published 1963).

Wise International. (2012). Uranium mining and water. *Nuclear Monitor, 743*.

World Nuclear Association. (2010). *Brief history of uranium mining in Canada*. Retrieved July 12, 2019, from https://www.world-nuclear.org/information-library/country-profiles/countries-a-f/appendices/uranium-in-canada-appendix-1-brief-history-of-uran.aspx

VI. IMPLEMENTATION:

An Engineering Application for Global Climate Change

Introduction

We are on the brink of endless opportunities to learn more by consolidating science instead of breaking it apart into traditional silos.

—Anna Frank, Chapter 15

The science of implementation invites us to investigate individual, organizational, political, and social ecologies that interact with, facilitate, or create barriers to practical applications of knowledge. Even with the most refined tools and technologies and engaged communities, implementation of best practices or best evidence does not always go according to plan. We know this well as community-engaged scholars: there is so much more that influences decision-making than research.

Effective implementation demands a broad ecological approach. As the previous section on community responses illustrates, competing interests, political maneuvering, lack of communication, limited cultural diversity and knowledge, fear, denial, fatigue, apathy, and poorly designed change management can all interfere with even life-sustaining and positive action. How then can the complex global systems be taken into account for effective water management practices? Through this complexity, how can the philosophical immersions, social and cultural formations, connected histories, aesthetic expressions, and storied community responses converge wide-reaching ecologies with global applications?

This final section provides a practical solution to water being at the centre of the global climate crisis, through management change and its application at both human and global scales. In her chapter, engineer Anna Frank highlights a new cycle of hydrology that takes into account multiple levels of implementation to address the crucial hydro-climatic, agricultural, industrial, and water management concerns of our times. Through the exploration of water cycles around the world, Frank's presentation of a global model concludes this book with material and practical matters at hand, allowing us to consider solutions for understanding and stewarding our water—and ourselves—in the Anthropocene.

—Robert Boschman and Sonya Jakubec, editors

Large-Scale Water Harvesting: An Application Model in the Time of Accelerating Global Climate Change

Anna Frank

Water is vital to all living organisms, environments, and economies. Freshwater is a major strand of the Canadian national identity and a crucial resource for all other countries. Unfortunately, there is not enough systematic and joint talk about water issues from the federal and provincial perspectives, even though there has been a lot of environmental talk centered on global warming. The irony here is obvious because water and climate change are interconnected (Scarpaleggia, 2017). One of the major causes and drivers of climate change is water. Water state (solid, liquid, or gas), distribution through the spheres, usage, and quality highly influence the temperature regime of the atmosphere and surface. Similarly, water affects soil quality, erosion, wind patterns, the movement of weather systems, and the life cycle of everything on the planet. Climate change influences dry and wet spells with greater intensity creating extremes we have not seen before, while, at the same time, our coping capacity for either extreme is still low in many countries, including developed ones such as Canada.

Climate change also brings up some crucial questions:

1. How will the hydro-climatic conditions of watersheds react to global climatic and environmental changes, particularly to the aforementioned new extremes?

2. What will be the future of water quality in response to hydro-climatic changes, agricultural activities, industrial developments, land use change, and water management?

3. How can basin-wide water management and decision-making processes be improved under the new hydro-climatic and water quality conditions, where areas/regions/countries are impacted by vast social, economic, and environmental issues (Pomeroy, 2017)?

Adaptation to inevitable change and threat mitigation requires new science to understand the changing Earth system and new approaches (Wheater, 2017), a different rhetoric, and acceptance of new ideas and long-term projects that influence structural improvement in water resources and the water hydrological cycle. Humanity has already influenced all natural processes; it is now a question of whether we can remain in control and engineer a sustainable environment or not. In this chapter, I will address our ability to influence large-scale hydrological processes.

Hydrological Cycle

Human society depends on natural resources for every segment of our existence. Air, water, land, mineral resources, plants, and animals are crucial for our own survival. Unfortunately, even while as a civilization we do not possess complete knowledge of how everything in nature is connected, we destroy, shape, and forever change the environment that we are so dependent on. Above all, we still cannot foresee the whole spectrum of the influence of our actions and how the changes we initiate will evolve under future environmental conditions.

The hydrological cycle is the most fundamental principle of hydrology (Maidment, 1992). It influences climate and weather patterns, land characteristics, biosphere development, and human lifestyle. Practically, the Earth as we know it is shaped by water. Unfortunately, we still teach the classic model of the hydrological cycle, which does not exist anymore. The extensive influence of human factors on the hydrological cycle has been recorded for thousands of years. Every aspect of human living changes the water ways and shapes the hydrological cycle. In the vast majority of countries, ground waters are highly depleted, which of course influences the amount of water on the surface and in the atmosphere.

Structurally the "humanized" hydrological cycle influences the stability of all interrelated processes. The water cycle, today, is ruled by a domino effect that spreads through all spheres of existence. It is time to revisit the rhetoric about climate change and realize that humans have already reengineered the earth. With the transformation of the earth's surface and the hydrological cycle, we have forever altered weather patterns and the water regime.

Nevertheless, there is an opportunity to build a sustainable society, resistant to future alterations with a respectful approach to the environment. A "new" hydrological cycle can be reconstructed, and it could provide sustainability through rain and flood water harvesting. The water cycle is the key factor that we can influence to unlock the full potential of supervised geoengineering and make things, hopefully, better.

The hydrological cycle is the true connector of each segment of the earth system. Water is everywhere. The amount of water in each segment of the hydrological cycle influences the speed of change and the timeline of the processes. Tapping into the power of the hydrological cycle is crucial to stop, reverse, or redirect the climate (weather) pattern changes unfavorable to humans and the environment in general. Moreover, control of the hydrological cycle would provide a significant headstart in the second stage of geoengineering: reforestation, reshaping of desert into fertile land, enhancing sustainable urbanization, conservation of more natural spaces insisting on exclusion, and returning nature to true wild life away from human influence.

Even though this sounds like science fiction, water harvesting and redirection are already taking place in humanized zones and already changing environments. Planning for those actions on a large scale would increase our environmental capacities to cope with negative human impacts. Rain water harvesting and flood water harvesting are not new concepts; they have existed for thousands of years. Unfortunately, in our continuous growth, economically driven decision paradigm, economic and political interests see the uncertainty of weather-dependent sources as a liability. Thus, science and engineering have focused for centuries on slow-pass water resources, such as ground waters and big surface-water bodies.

Today, after thousands of years of exploiting "invisible," once-thought-to-be infinite ground water resources, we need to learn the role ground-water will play in defining water security. Groundwaters are worryingly depleted, while all the water ever released into the atmosphere influences the intensity and frequency of weather events. Higher concentrations of water in the atmosphere, combined with an elevated level of pollutants, indicate higher probabilities for weather extremes, such as torrential rain and extreme drought. In simple terms, the more water we place into the atmosphere, the more this changes the weather patterns that we notice. Moreover, in addition to the high rate of global groundwater exploitation, a high rate of evaporation and widespread Arctic and Antarctic ice melting adds to the seriousness of induced changes on the hydrological cycle.

To be able to focus on solutions, we have to stop separating ground-water and surface water in water management, and acknowledge that the air-soil-groundwater-surface water interface is the very essence of how the hydrological cycle works (Sandford, 2015). Only then can we notice a couple of spots within the hydrological cycle on which we can act to induce positive change and model climate back towards a life-supporting one. Considering water quality, quantity, and importance for life, water harvesting could be safely and sustainably conducted from the atmosphere, flood waters, and oceans. Each segment needs to be planned and interconnected with the other systems for water allocation and exploitation already in place. Harvesting deposition of rain and flood waters in underground systems of reservoirs would provide a significant enough delay in evaporation and mimic natural replenishment of ground waters and natural water flow.

In this chapter, large-scale water harvesting only considers organized and controlled rain water and flood water collection and the redistribution of rain and flood waters. Large-scale rain and flood water management is a radical change from the status quo, with long-term impacts and a long-term need for investments, but it is highly relevant and feasible in ameliorating our current environmental situation. It is worth consideration, discussion, improvement and, in the end, investment and realization.

Most importantly, it is possible and—if properly done—it would provide benefit to all life.

Non-Urban Large-scale Rain and Flood Water Harvesting Systems Implications and Use

To properly manage water, we have to understand its dual nature:

1. Water is a constituent, initiator, and catalyst of all natural processes crucial for the maintenance and creation of life on the planet.

2. It is an irrepressible resource and base for economic and social development.

As majestic as it is, still, water is vulnerable and dependent on the soil quality and chemistry of the atmosphere; and it is very susceptible to anthropogenic influence (pollution and overuse). Sustainable water management considers both roles and aspects of building resilience of water supply and the social resilience to water-related hazards. Environmental design is about working with water flow. At this moment, we already have many systems in place: urban elements (buildings, infrastructure, transit ways, parks, wastelands); rural communities, protected areas, designated areas for special purposes (mines, oil and gas, military); Indigenous lands; and border areas. It is impossible to ignore existing systems while designing an efficient and sustainable water redistribution and protection system. However, as water flow is all about energy, it is energy efficient to take into account the flow of water as the starting point of sustainable design. Blocking water flow causes stagnation, raises the risk of flooding and loss of biodiversity. Open water sources in stagnation are of lower quality than the ones with a steady and regular flow. Considering the appearance of water in nature, at first glance it is not most obvious that the best place to let water flow and redistribute is underground. More than 60% of fresh water lies in the ground, ice, and permafrost, while the other 40% is distributed within the atmosphere, rivers, swamps, and marshes, soil moisture, lakes, and living things. Accounting for two crucial things—water flow and underground (or in soil) storage—a sustainable water harvesting system can be designed.

An example of such a system is over 3,000 years old. Qanat is the generic term for an ancient environmentally sustainable water harvesting method and conveyance technique believed to have originated in Persia in the early millennium B.C. (Guliyev & Hasanov 2012; Middle East Institute, 2014). This amazing technology—known as *falaj* in Oman, *khettara* or *foggara* in North Africa, *karez* or *kanerjing* in the northwestern desert of China, and *karez* in Afghanistan, Pakistan, and Central Asia—continues to provide reliable supplies of water for human settlements and irrigation in hot, arid, and semi-arid climates. In fact, qanat technology exists in more than thirty-four countries. In Iran alone, there are an estimated 50,000 qanats, nearly three-quarters of which are still working. In Oman, there are more than 3,000 active qanats (aflaj). The qanat system (Wessels, 2014; Lightfoot, 1996) consists of a network of underground canals that transport water from aquifers in highlands to the surface at lower levels by gravity.

Qanats are classified according to the following criteria: length and depth of the qanat, topography, and geographical situation, type of aquifer, qanat discharge, and source of qanat flow. Classification according to the source of qanat flow is the most interesting one, as this indicates that the use of the qanat should be restricted to harvesting ground waters. However, the reality is that the water flow through the qanat may not be due to ground water seepage into the qanat's gallery, but to other sources such as a nearby spring or river, or could be fed by rainwater (Semsar Yazdi & Labbaf Khaneiki, 2010). By this criterion, we can classify qanats in four types:

A. Normal qanat: a normal or simple qanat drains groundwater, which directly enters the qanat production section.

B. Qanat-spring: when, in addition to ground water, spring water enters and feeds a qanat's water.

C. Qanat-river: this qanat resembles the spring type, except that it receives a surface stream (whether permanent or temporary created by storm water). In most cases, it is used in situations when it is impossible to transfer river water to the desired lands by gravity flow through open trenches, because the river bed is lower than the irrigated land on either side. Therefore, digging an underground conduit is helpful to sort out the topographical problem. The structure of this conduit resembles that of a typical qanat, but its water has nothing to do with harvesting an aquifer.

D. Qanat-well: is a hybrid combination of pumped well and qanat. In cases where the groundwater table drops down below and does not feed the mother well, the mother well in that case is deepened and equipped with a pump to deliver the water up to the gallery.

The rapid depletion of ground waters, as well as decline in their quality, is becoming a problem of great priority to be solved. In Canada, for example, the vast majority of rural areas are dependent on local wells and there is no continuous or appropriate monitoring of availability of ground water. Besides, the sheer size of Canada represents an obstacle to implement a continuous and centralized water supply to all inhabited areas. As many small communities are located between forests and green belts, traditional water supply systems would be costly and unsafe. But implementing traditional qanat knowledge in remote areas would ensure water supply in dry periods, in addition to drainage in periods of intense rainfall and flooding. Contemporary structures usually usurp the habitats of animals and affect biodiversity of local flora. Allowing water to flow underground while still being accessible for extraction would create a better and safer environment. Considering recent natural disasters in Canada, such as Alberta's fire in 2016, access to water on the spot would ensure timely reaction and the prevention of future disasters. As a qanat system could be adapted and supplemented with an underground reservoir, as well as open surface reservoirs, the system could provide a continuous flow of water through remote areas and re-direct water from one watershed to another without interrupting life on the surface.

Indigenous knowledge of water collection and living with the moody character of water should also be incorporated in sustainable water management and planning. Resilience is part of sustainability. Water is a major attribute of many disasters and should be considered more as a character than as a resource. It has its life, its ways, and its rhythm. Listening and following water ways would allow us to visualize the invisible network underground, which can be wisely modified into a system that we can actually see and use.

Humanity has already gone far along the path of engineering the Earth. We cannot just simply sit and say no more. Infrastructure that cuts through the veins of Earth leaves deep scars and changes all that ever was. Now it is time to humbly consider how we can work with water, ground, and sky with the aim of preserving life on the entire planet. And water is the best place to start.

Remote areas of the globe hide risks of great magnitude, as was learned from recent events in Alberta. Those risks will not be avoided in any other place on Earth. Disasters await the right circumstances. To anthropomorphize this thought, we could say they are patient and will uncover themselves when and as they see fit, if we do not bridge the gap between nature and people and start working with nature. Cities and all human infrastructure, along with the exploitation of natural resources, change environment with every second of the day and every breath we take. We at least should embrace the idea that by allowing water to flow and by reconnecting watersheds, we are ensuring that we will have water when there is no rain, and that by building protected underground reservoirs, we will at least raise our resilience to the inevitable change that is coming.

Underground Reservoirs and Dynamic Flow Re-Distribution Systems

Water has a high need to move in order to preserve its natural characteristics. Systems that provide water movement, but prevent excessive evaporation, are a crucial element for water conservation and protection. By protecting water, one protects society (Neill, 2016). By allowing water to be available in current zones of human occupation, one prevents migration and confrontation over the most important resource after clean air.

In 2008, the USA National Research Council gave a detailed overview of underground water systems that could resolve a future water crisis (Committee on Sustainable Underground Storage of Recoverable Water, National Research Council 2008). Even though concepts and practices of sending rain and surface water to underground systems have existed for thousands of years, the terms used to describe them vary widely and have changed over the years. As described by the Committee, Managed Underground Storage (MUS) refers to the deliberate placement of water into an underground location through a recharge method. With an intention for future reuse, this method could include surface infiltration and percolation through the vadose zone to a saturated aquifer or placement directly to an underground location.

Despite obvious benefits from MUS, there are also questions about consequences of the use of such systems at large scales. Since 2008, there have been no visible global commitments to research the implications and impact of interconnected managed underground water storages on a large scale. Questions of water quality, ground stability, implications of landslides and earthquakes due to change of ground saturation in percolation zones are just some of the technical issues to resolve. Other more human-induced issues include the price of such water in case of reuse, water rights, and water security including intentional threats to water quality. Understanding the effects of the underground aquifers can indicate whether the consequences of MUS, either beneficial or detrimental, will be long term, and whether it will have a significant environmental effect. Nevertheless, the need for managed underground "rivers" will only grow in time of great extremes such as more frequent floods and droughts. With plans for sustainable development and more coherent urban planning, urban zones will be even more dependent on proper, timely, developed, and efficient underground systems.

The aim of water harvesting is to collect urban runoff, surface runoff, and/or flood water surplus, and to store it and make it available when and where there is water shortage. This can be achieved by either

1. Impeding and trapping water in maximised individual

   storage units, or

2. Developing a water transit network among optimised individual reservoirs.

Harvested rain water and flood waters have a tremendous potential for meeting both indoor and outdoor water demands. With advanced landscaping that is both beautiful and functional, a significant amount of water can be collected, saved, and redistributed. We can capture rainfall when and where it lands. Currently, most of the harvested rain water is stored in sets of water tanks or rain barrels. Statistics Canada projects a 140 billion litres per year savings in the Great Lakes basin with introduction of water conservation strategies like rain water harvesting (RWH) (Adamaley, 2011; Statistics Canada, 2010). Unfortunately, RWH is still an untapped potential across the globe. The reason may be simple: those who have a significant amount of rain water to harvest have the least need.For that reason, a large-scale interconnected RWH system would ensure that water is diverted from areas where surplus is raising the risk of flooding to those areas in need of water.

Considering the need for urban space and the change of hydrology within urban zones, an underground network of water storage provides a solution for more than one issue. In crowded urban zones, the acquisition of the land for the purpose of flood or drought protection is quite problematic. In order to provide security and build resilience to natural hazards such as floods and droughts, an underground discharge system of channels and reservoirs is an adequate solution for the twenty-first century. Moreover, it is quite achievable as well.

An example from Japan shows that urban runoff can be successfully collected and relocated. A huge underground storm water drain system saves billions of dollars in flood-caused damages and prevents fatalities. Tokyo is shaped heavily by water. It is a densely populated area crisscrossed by rivers and channels that is geologically challenging; and it is situated on a flat floodplain of soft alluvial soil in a monsoon climate, with frequent typhoons on an active earthquake and volcanic belt. Not that long ago, in the mid-1900s, Tokyo's suburbs recorded a set of heavy typhoons and severe wet seasons followed by floods that destroyed large parts of the low-lying old downtown. Floods, back then, were a regular part of life. Over the last decades, Tokyo has built a new resilience against the forces of nature (Yu-Shou, 2016). A coordinated system of massive underground structures keeps the mega-city safe from the inevitable floods. There is high awareness that Tokyo has to be prepared and become resilient to the threats of global warming, floods, earthquakes, and a variety of other disasters. With an already very vulnerable geological position, more than a hundred square kilometres of the city basin is below sea level. Rapid industrialization made it even lower, and in the 1960s and 1970s the situation became more prone to disastrous floods.

Tokyo has an average annual rainfall of 1,530 mm, which is significantly more than most Canadian cities, with the exception of Vancouver (1,457mm), St. John's (1,534mm), and Halifax (1,468mm). But still none of these Canadian cities is experiencing pressure on its infrastructure as does Tokyo with 30 million people. In addition to the issues of dense population and vulnerable geographical predispositions, rising average temperatures and the additional heat island effect of the city are changing patterns of rainfall, adding to the complexity of the flood protection problem. Intense localized showers regularly deliver more than 100 mm of rain per hour. The occurrence of these heavy rainstorms has increased by around fifty percent over the last century. The traditional flood prediction approach, based on historical occurrence of floods, has been abandoned and due to the onset of sudden heavy rains, flooding is expected to occur at any time.

Tokyo's flood protection system originates from the early 1920s. An artificial waterway was constructed in 1924 in a junction with the Arakawa River. Its purpose was to divert flood waters away from eastern Tokyo which was a planned city growth area. Since the original design of the flood protection system, the flood discharge has doubled. Due to urbanization, the need for rapid drainage of storm water continues to grow with time. Lack of available land and repeated emergency situations led Tokyo to build an underground discharge channel. The surge tank is just the tail end of a flood control system that stretches another six kilometers underground, bypassing a low-lying basin. It collects water from five water courses, connecting all in one stream fifty meters under the surface of the city. Four modified aircraft turbines power the system, allowing two-hundred cubic meters per second discharge. The whole system is designed to withstand a once in two-hundred-year flood. The main objective of the facility is to reduce the damage caused by regular flooding. The sheer size of the structure is an engineering wonder. The cathedral-like chamber acts as a buffer in a flood emergency (see Figure 15.1)

Five stories deep, the surge tank is the length of two football fields. The purpose of the surge tank is to break the momentum of the water as it comes down from the tunnels. This giant system is designed so the

FIGURE 15.1. Water Chamber. Inside the 248,508 cubic feet water chamber, are five-dozen 60-foot high pillars, each reinforced by five hundred tons of concrete. Released under the GNU Free Documentation License.

tank never fills up and always discharges to the Eda River. On average, the facility experiences overflow to the chamber about seven times a year.

It took three billion dollars and thirteen years for Tokyo to build this system that saves astronomical amounts of money in damages. The Alberta floods alone will take over ten years of recovery with a projected cost of five billion dollars. There is a sound economic reason for implementing such a system in Canada. Due to its significant difference in geological as well as climatic characteristics, Canada has an advantage over Japan in availability of land, but on the other hand colder winters would require building the system below the frost line.

In as many cases as possible, a rain water harvesting system (RWH) should be combined with a flood water harvesting system (FWH). The early harvesting of water within a river bed results in lowering the risk of high peaks and overflow. It ensures an early stage of control of floods, with acting at the source of the problem and not just mitigating consequences. When the crown of the flood wave is reaching the peak, instead of allowing overflow and flooding, water could be collected in the river bed with systems based on sinkhole physics, bathtub overflow mechanism, and highway drainage systems. If we observe rivers as highways, we notice that accumulation is happening gradually but steadily like a traffic jam. Most of the solutions rely on releasing pressure through surface channels. But as land is as much a precious resource as water, there is not much space left to build more discharge channels. An underground system would allow the creation of many kilometers of pipes and tunnels in all directions without disturbing the surface. At the end of the system, there would be a reservoir to collect and store water for dry periods or discharge excess water to the most eligible river system or ocean.

As flood water is rising along the river bed, we can redirect that water to underground passage ways to avoid high water levels and overflows. The positioning of collectors at an optimal maximal water level would ensure enough water downstream for natural processes. Strategic positioning of these collectors at an adequate distance along the river would ensure steady drainage of flood waters as they accumulate into the river from rain, surface runoff, or tributaries. Collected water would not be wasted and instead be used for the regulation of water levels in river basins, drought preparedness, forest fire controls, or replenishment of ground waters.

Urban RWH is already implemented throughout Canada and the U.S. The City of Guelph, Mississauga, and McMaster University are some examples of good practice and long-term sustainable planning. Unfortunately, the approach to issues of rain water harvesting, flood water harvesting, water rights, and water redistribution is not coherent across Canada and the U.S. Opinions differ from province to province, as well as policies and rules.

Challenges of Implementation of Large-Scale Rain and Flood Water Harvesting Projects

The United Nations have already recognized the importance of rainwater harvesting as an environmentally sound approach for sustainable urban water management. Marginally larger rainwater harvesting and utilisation systems exist in the Changi Airport, Singapore, as well as Tokyo and Berlin. Storing rainwater from rooftop run-off in jars is an appropriate and inexpensive means of obtaining high quality drinking water in Thailand. Recognising the need to alter the drainage system, the Indonesian government introduced a regulation requiring that all buildings have an infiltration well. The regulation applies to two-thirds of the territory, including the Special Province of Yogyakarta, the Capital Special Province of Jakarta, West Java, and Central Java Province. In the Philippines, a rainwater harvesting programme was initiated in 1989 in Capiz Province with the assistance of the Canadian International Development Research Centre (IDRC) (United Nations Environmental Programme, 2017). Rainwater harvesting on a large scale is becoming increasingly important in the UK and the government has included legislation ensuring that new buildings now have to take into account how they deal with run-off water. The Code for Sustainable Homes, UK (Department for Communities and Local Government, 2014), also actively encourages the fitting of underground water tanks. The federal government in Canada, through the National Research Council and the Canadian Commission on Building and Fire Codes, produced the model National Building Code and the model National Plumbing Code. This document provides guidance for designing, constructing, and managing rainwater harvesting systems based on the minimum safety requirements established in these model national codes. It is important to note, however, that the provisions of the 2010 NPC have no force unless adopted by the applicable province or territory.

In Canada the applicable rainwater harvesting requirements are those set or referred to by the province or territory. This means the legality of rainwater harvesting differs from province to province. While in Ontario, as of the publication date of *Federal Guidelines* (Canada Mortgage and Housing Corporation, 2012), applicable provincial codes and regulations permit the use of rainwater for flushing toilets and urinals, as well as for sub-surface irrigation and below ground irrigation systems, in British Columbia the legality of rainwater collection is uncertain.

Kate Duke's (2014) inquiry into the right to capture rainwater is divided into four parts. Part one considers the nature of rainwater harvesting, its benefits, and its potential impacts. While rainwater harvesting has many benefits, it also has the potential to adversely affect instream flows and other water uses. Part two relates to the statutory framework of water allocation in the province and whether it affects the legality of rainwater harvesting. Although the legislation is not unambiguous, the right to collect rainwater does not appear to be affected by the Water Act or the Water Protection Act. Part three concerns the historical common law position on water-related rights. While there is some support for the proposition that a landowner has a proprietary interest in rainwater before it is captured, the most likely common law position is that rainwater is common property and subject to the old common law concept of the law of capture. Since this common law framework provides no redress to those who are adversely affected by rainwater harvesting, Duke's fourth point briefly addresses possible avenues for legal reform of the right to capture rainwater.

Water Balance Models

Besides the legal aspects of RWH and FWH systems, there is the issue of their impact on local wildlife, biodiversity, communities, economy, and climate change. To provide answers on these matters, water balance models (WBM) must be consulted in consideration of all possible scenarios. Good planning systems depend on continually updated WBM, great data mining, and assimilation of results generated from forecast models with on-site measurements and monitoring of the system in real time.

Water balance models have the aim of preserving an ecosystem's stability that redistribute excessive waters or give an alarm in case of water deficit for system. WBMs are a base for good dimensioning of water harvesting systems. WBMs are developed in order to understand the water cycle, protect and exploit water resources, and mitigate the negative impact of water resources on human infrastructures. WBMs have to consider in detail the water balance equation on five different levels (starting at Level 0 as shown in the formula to follow) and various time scales in order to create a full introspective in water "flow" through the hydrological cycle:

$$\text{Level 0: } AV_0(t + \Delta t) = AV_0(t) + S \cdot \int_t^{t+\Delta t}(P(t) - ET(t))dt \qquad (1)$$

$$\text{Level 1: } AV_1(t + \Delta t) = AV_1(t) + \int_t^{t+\Delta t}(Q(t) - N_q)dt \qquad (2)$$

$$\text{Level 2: } AV_2(t + \Delta t) = AV_2(t) + S \cdot \int_t^{t+\Delta t}(H(t) - N_H)dt \qquad (3)$$

$$\text{Level 3: } (-)Biological\ processes\ BM(t + \Delta t) = BM(t) + S \cdot \int_t^{t+\Delta t} Growth(t)dt \qquad (4)$$

$$\text{Level 4:}(-)\ Anthropogenic\ influence\ - water\ consumption. \qquad (5)$$

Components of the water balance are (1) atmospheric, (2) surface waters—visible water, (3) underground water—hidden waters, (4) biosphere, and (5) anthropogenic activities not reflected in either of the other four levels of equation. Each level 0-4 has a different spatial and temporal scale. Hydrological processes can take anywhere from seconds to hundreds of years. For example, on a null level happen instant processes such as evaporation on a hot summer day when one can see the shimmer in the air from water being pulled out from the surface by hot air. These processes feed the next level and are the leading water routes between spheres (bio-lito-hydro-atmo). The scale on which one observes the process changes the details that are accounted. On a grand scale, the hydrological cycle consists of a multiverse of small-scale systems contributing to global patterns. Changes on these levels contribute to weather pattern change, formation of drought, or torrential rains. Ultimately cumulative changes on a micro scale lead to climate change. Each equation's level consists of billions of participants—plants, soil types and ground structures, rivers, animals, and humans. Different plant types have different growth dynamics and need for water, various soils transport water differently, and people across the globe use water in numerous ways, often unmonitored. Each level is characterized by a different dynamic of internal change, mature plants vs. young plants, population migrations and growth—humans and animals, industrial processes, river meanders, ice cap melting or growth, tectonic movements and change in underground storage. The multilevel equation becomes even more complex when considering the time scales of multiple hydrological processes.

Each WBM has to:

1. provide information regarding how systems will change under specific influences and be a reliable tool in planning and infrastructural development;
2. predict and forecast at various times and spatial scales movement and distribution of water within the system;
3. reproduce the variability of hydrological processes;
4. have the ability to close water balance considering a full water balance equation.

Water balance models rely on many assumptions and categorically and intentionally neglect processes on lower time scales. Considering the time scale of different water hazards and processes, there is no unique model that we can use. We require a composite of different scale modelling to see the big picture. Uncertainties related to algorithms, approximations, and representativeness of observations exist in each model. Modelling purposes, target area, calculation method, temporal and spatial boundaries, available data and facilities, all these drive the accuracy of water balance results. Generally, the degree of accuracy of WBMs is determined before any computations (Ghandhari & Alavi Moghaddam, 2011). To achieve better results, the following four considerations in the modelling or in selection of the WBM should be included:

1. appropriate parent model;
2. avoidance of any unnecessary details in calculations;
3. using all available data and facilities; and
4. allowing for new scientific findings.

Prior to the design of any water harvest system, a reliable WBM should be applied for long-term planning. The aim of using WBMs is to provide adequate advice for infrastructural planning on a large scale that will ensure that built flood and rain water harvest systems will last at least 100 years and more.

We have to be aware that for all of these considerations we need time, with the realization that nature does not take a break. Each segment of the large-scale projects depends on

1. proper preparation and research of resources under impact of climate change;
2. environmental impact assessment of designed structures;
3. communication between communities, decision makers, academia, and all other stakeholders;
4. the existence of adequate policies and timely, proper implementation of these;
5. the willingness and readiness to take long-term risks and invest in the projects;
6. maintenance of long-term investments;
7. control of economic, social, health, and environmental risks;
8. investment in continuous education of future users and managers of the system, once built.

All of this and much more depends on the projections and advice based on WBMs. Furthermore, various software tools exist to provide water balance or hydrological modeling (SANTINEL-3, MODIS, TRMM, GPM, GRACE, SMOS, SWAT, HEC-HMS, DELFT-3D, MIKE, and others). Realizing that each and every WBM has its own uncertainties, we have to acknowledge that WBMS alone are not enough. Context is needed. Good WBMs are only the beginning. An example of good practice is the Global Water Future program, which focuses its scientific pillars beyond plain hydrological modelling and includes layers upon layers of crucial elements that run the Earth system and, within it, the hydrological cycle.

We are on the brink of endless opportunities to learn more by con-solidating science instead of breaking it apart into traditional silos. Once WBMs have proper and detailed input data on a variety of scales, then we will have a reliable support system for long-term decision making and infrastructural planning. There is a great awareness that models depend on our overall knowledge of the system. By acknowledging the complexities of Earth's processes, and by including traditional knowledge and experience as well as incorporating system vulnerabilities, models will be better able to follow water through the hydrological cycle.

Conclusion

"Water in the end is the universal healer. Having it in any inadequate supply, either too much or too little, we expire at every level of our being" (Neill, 2016, 357). Redistribution of harvested water leads to change in all sectors of human society: health, education, and economy, as well influencing environmental change. The legality of the reuse of rain and flood water should be targeted on the community level, where the joint benefit of the community and environment would be the priority. Large-scale systems could provide enough technical space to locally generate energy applying small turbines on sections where water flow changes elevation. The standard method of operation is that a large reservoir of water is created by damming a river and then allowing a tunnel or pipeline of water, at the bottom of the dam, to flow past turbines on generators to turn those turbines and create electricity. Stauffer has invented an alternative method to create a pipeline of water that turns the turbines of the hydroelectric power generator and does not require a dam or a reservoir of water behind a dam. Instead, the powerful flow of water can be created by gravity in a submerged pipeline that flows from a higher elevation to a lower elevation (Stauffer, 2014).

Rain water management consists of three interconnected activities: harvest, recycle, and reuse. Benefits would outweigh any investment needed. The environmental price, if we do not invest in large-scale application of RWH and FWH, is the continuous and cumulative effects of floods and droughts, with impacts to environment, health, economy, development, and security. Financial losses caused by floods and droughts are counted in billions of dollars. The insurance industry will have a hard time covering all the damage to come, which will necessarily create greater policy costs. Arguably, the insurance industry may take first place in a long list of stakeholders who would benefit from large scale RWH and FWH systems, but many others would of course also benefit.

By intervening with water levels, we are influencing climate, land, and ecosystems. Canada, for instance, has a great opportunity to become a leader in this crucial sector for human survival. Having rich water resources constitutes a robust opportunity in research and development. Hydrologists and atmospheric scientists from across the country have clear evidence that Canada's climate is changing, and that these changes are being reflected in the timing and type of precipitation and in other factors that could affect water security (Sandford, 2015). Saving should start now.

REFERENCES

Adamaley, M. (2011). An inquiry into residential water conservation in Canada. *Inquiry Paper*. McMaster University.

Canada Mortgage and Housing Corporation. (2012). *Guidelines for residential rainwater harvesting systems handbook*. CMHC.

Committee on Opportunities in the Hydrologic Sciences. (1991). *Opportunities in the hydrologic sciences*. The National Academies Press.

Committee on Sustainable Underground Storage of Recoverable Water. National Research Council. (2008). *Prospects for managed underground storage of recoverable water*. The National Academies Press.

Department for Communities and Local Government. (2014). *Code for sustainable homes technical guide*. Department for Communities and Local Government.

Duke, K. (2014). Ownership of rainwater and the legality of rainwater harvesting in British Columbia. *APPEAL, 19*, 21–41.

Fang, W. (2009). *Karez technology for drought disaster reduction*. Disaster Reduction Hyberbase.

Freez, A. R., & J. A. Cherry. (1979). *Groundwater*. Prentice-Hall.

Ghandhari, A., & Alavi Moghaddam, S.M.R. (2011). Water balance principles: A review of studies on five watersheds in Iran. *Journal of Environmental Science and Technology 4* (5), 465–479. doi:10.3923/jest.2011.465.479

Guliyev, A., & A. Hasanov. (2012). Azerbaijani Kahrizes (Qanats). In S. Yazdi Semsar, A. Bahri & E. Yazdi Ahmadieh (Eds.), *Abstracts - International conference on traditional knowledge for water resources management* (p. 49). UN Education, Scientific and Cultural Organization.

Lightfoot, D. R. (1996). Syrian qanat Romani: History, ecology, abandonment. *Journal of Arid Environments, 33*, 321–336.

Maidment, D. R. (1992). *Handbook of hydrology*. McGraw-Hill.

Middle East Institute. (2014, January 18). *Harvesting water and harnessing cooperation: Qanat systems in the Middle East and Asia.* Accessed March 2017, from http://www.mei.edu/content/harvesting-water-and-harnessing-cooperation-qanat-systems-middle-east-and-asia

Neill, P. (2016). *The once and future ocean.* Leete's Island Books.

Pomeroy, J. (2017). Global water future - National water modelling and observation strategy. *Canadian Water Resources Association Workshop.*

Sandford, R. W. (2015). *Storm warning - water and climate security in a changing world.* Rocky Mountain Books Ltd.

Scarpaleggia, F. (2017). What should a national water strategy look like and how do we get there? *Canadian Water Resources Association Workshop.*

Semsar Yazdi, A. A., & Labbaf Khaneiki, M. (2010). *Veins of desert. A review on the technique of qanat / Falaj / Karez.* Iranian Ministry of Energy Publications.

Statistics Canada. (2010). *Canada's water supply - stocks and glows.* Accessed 2017. http://www.statcan.gc.ca/pub/16-201-x/2010000/part-partie2-eng.htm.

Stauffer, David. (2014). *River bottom siphon for hydro-electric generation and irrigation.* United States Patent US 2014/0193201 A1. July 10.

U.S. Department of Energy. (2017). *Building catalog: Case studies of high performance buildings.* https://buildingdata.energy.gov/

United Nations Environmental Programme. (2017). *An environmentally sound approach for sustainable urban water management: An introductory guide for decision-makers.* http://www.unep.or.jp/ietc/publications/urban/urbanenv-2/index.asp.

USBR Provo Area Office. (n.d.). *Qanats.* http://www.waterhistory.org/histories/qanats/.

Wessels, J. (2014). *Qanats and water cooperation for sustainable future.* Accessed 2017, January 19, from http://www.mei.edu/content/qanats-and-water-cooperation-sustainable-future

Wheater, H. (2017). Global water futures: Solutions to water threats in an era of global change. *Canadian Water Resources Association workshop.*

Yu-Shou, S. (2016). Urban flood resilience in New York City, London, Randstad, Tokyo, Shanghai, and Taipei. *Journal of Management and Sustainability, 6*(1), 92–108.

Contributors

BARBARA AMOS holds her degree from the University of Waterloo. She is an interdisciplinary artist who has developed creative projects that address multicultural issues and environmental concerns. Her commissions include a 90-foot sectional painting about creating community in a recreation centre; a photographic commission about multiculturalism in a hospital covering 45 linear feet; and a steel scope about environmental fragmentation with a handmade lens on a city street. She was also invited to create a scope for the International Sculpture Garden in Burlington, Ontario. In 2017 she worked with a school to empower young people to ask questions about migration and a changing climate. The project culminated in new curriculum and the completion of a 12x16 foot painting for an outdoor learning centre. She exhibited one of her sketchbooks at the Whitney Museum and The Los Angeles County Museum of Modern Art. She was invited to become a member of the Trico Changemakers Studio at Mount Royal University. Her work is featured in more than 20 publications. Her paintings are in many collections and she is represented by Abbozzo Gallery at 401 Richmond in Toronto and Gibson Fine Art, Calgary. For more information: www.BarbaraAmos.com.

ROBERT BOSCHMAN is professor and chair of English, Languages, and Cultures at Mount Royal University in Calgary, Alberta. He is co-founder of Under Western Skies, a biennial conference series on the environment held at Mount Royal from 2010 to 2016. His first book, *In the Way of Nature* (McFarland), was published in 2009. *Found in Alberta: Environmental Themes for the Anthropocene* (Wilfrid Laurier University Press) appeared in 2014, followed by *On Active Grounds: Agency and Time in the Environmental Humanities* (WLUP) in 2019, both coedited with

Mario Trono. He also collaborates with Bill Bunn and Sarah Elizabeth Howden in documenting abandoned uranium extraction communities, with funding from the Social Sciences and Humanities Research Council of Canada. In 2020, he contributed to *Critical Zones: The Science and Politics of Landing on Earth* (ZKM and MIT Press), coedited by Bruno Latour and Peter Weibel. Boschman's *White Coal City: A Memoir of Place and Family* (University of Regina Press) was published in February 2021. His environmental photography can be viewed at robertboschman.com.

BILL BUNN is an associate professor at Mount Royal University. He teaches composition, creative writing, and writing pedagogy. He is currently engaged in a SSHRC research project with Robert Boschman and Sarah Elizabeth Howden to investigate the impacts of uranium extraction on five mining communities around the world. He co-published an article with Boschman, titled, "Nuclear Avenue: 'Cyclonic Development,' Abandonment, and Relations in Uranium City, Canada," in *Humanities*, 2018. His recent novel for young adults, *Out on the Drink*, was published by Bitingduck Press in 2017.

DENISE L. DI SANTO is a water resources planner with a passion for connecting water and people through collaboration and inclusive watershed-based processes. She holds a Master of Science degree in renewable natural resources from the University of Arizona, a bachelor of science degree in geography from the University of Calgary, and a bachelor of education degree from Lakehead University in Thunder Bay, Ontario. With broad watershed management experience, Denise takes a systems approach to water management, identifying enabling conditions for ecosystem protection and recovery toward enduring solutions for resilient watersheds and communities. From her research on groundwater contamination and community impacts in the U.S. desert Southwest, she continues to seek out new learning in the Pacific Northwest and Western Canada. A water protector, Denise appreciates the knowledge and perspectives presented to her by people and communities throughout western North America, and the lessons that come from the sharing of stories. She believes that water resources management is about *managing us* as inhabitants of watersheds.

Anna Frank provides expert consulting in Regulatory Affairs, Environmental engineering science, risk assessment, water resource management and protection, and all issues related to sustainability, hydrology, and climate change adaptation. With over a decade of research and teaching experience in the Faculty of Technical Sciences at the University of Novi Sad, Serbia, and at the Water Institute at the University of Waterloo, Dr. Frank has contributed to many papers and conference presentations. She also provides consulting services to the industry since 2011, such as Dufferin Research's environmental studies until 2020, and currently she offers her expertise and scientific support for decision-making for the international consulting company, YORDAS Group. In addition, she has managed several multi-country projects funded by the European Union.

Maria Elisa de Paula Eduardo Garavello is a senior professor at the University of São Paulo. She conducts research on the environment and society, focusing on "otherness" and "dialogue of knowledge" in relation to the following themes: traditional and local communities, food security and sovereignty, environment, sustainability and autonomy, development and public policies.

Andrea Garcia is a biologist with a background in ecology and remote sensing/GIS related to the Cerrado (Brazilian Savannah). With a Master's degree in applied ecology, specializing in economics, her PhD is in applied ecology from the University of São Paulo, Brazil. Published in several journals, her work focuses on modeling changes in land cover and land use in the Amazon Basin and elsewhere, in order to shed light on processes shaping landscapes and how they relate to ecological and developmental theories.

C. R. Grimmer, who also goes by Chelsea Grimmer and uses she/her and they/them pronouns interchangeably, is the author of the award-winning poetry collection *The Lyme Letters* (Texas Tech University Press) as well as *O-(ezekiel's wife)* (GASHER Journal and Press). They completed their PhD in literature and cultural studies at the University of Washington with support from The Simpson Center for the Humanities' Andrew

W. Mellon Foundation Public Humanities Fellowship and The Harlan Hahn Disability Studies Fellowship. C. R. created and hosts *The Poetry Vlog (TPV)*, has published poems in *Poetry Magazine, FENCE Magazine,* and *[PANK]*, in addition to articles in journals such as *The Comparatist.* Their current scholarly book project, *Poetry as Public Scholarship: Activist Poetics in the Time of Social Media,* combines research analysis and practitioner discourses to examine the relationships between racial capitalism and poetry's circulation on social media. For more information, visit crgrimmer.com.

SHIRLEY ANNE SWELCHALOT HARDMAN, a PhD candidate, is a Stó:lō ascendant living in Shxwha:y Village. She earned a Master's degree in Indigenous Education at Simon Fraser University and is completing her doctoral work at the University of British Columbia in Educational Studies. Shirley participates in the Indigenous resurgence, listening deeply and learning from storytellers and Indigenous knowledge keepers. She is Senior Advisor on Indigenous Affairs at the University of the Fraser Valley. Ey Si:yam Hoych'ka Si:yam.

RICHARD HARRISON is the winner of the 2017 Governor General's Award for English Poetry for his book *On Not Losing My Father's Ashes in the Flood.* As his contribution to this volume of essays underscores, the intersection of technology and myth is one of his principal concerns. Along with six other well-received and award-winning books of poetry, Richard is the co-author of *Secret Identity Reader: Essays on Sex, Death, and the Superhero* and the co-editor of *Now is the Winter: Thinking About Hockey.*

SONYA L. JAKUBEC is a registered nurse and professor in the School of Nursing and Midwifery at Mount Royal University (MRU) in Calgary, Alberta. Her research is concerned with the interconnection of supportive environments and wellbeing across the lifespan and currently focuses on aspects of the Healthy Parks-Healthy People movement. Committed to knowledge mobilization for social and environmental benefit, Sonya contributes to research, knowledge synthesis, and dissemination for students across health and community practice disciplines, for decision makers at all levels of program delivery, management and policy-making, and for general scholarly and public learning.

MICHAELA KECK received her PhD in American Studies at Goethe University in Frankfurt/Main, Germany. She teaches literature and cultural studies at the Institute for English and American Studies at Carl von Ossietzky University of Oldenburg. She also taught undergraduate and graduate courses at National Sun Yat-sen University in Taiwan (2006–2009) and in the American Studies program at the University of Groningen in Holland (2011–2012). Her research interests are at the intersections of literature and the environment as well as literature and visual culture. She is the author of *Walking in the Wilderness: The Peripatetic Tradition in Nineteenth-Century American Literature and Painting* (2006) and, more recently, *Deliberately Out of Bounds: Women's Work on Myth in Nineteenth-Century American Fiction* (2017). She has published several articles about ecocritical readings of nineteenth-century American nature writings and landscape painting, among them "Thoreau's Walden and the American Dream" in *Bloom's Literary Themes*. With an additional interest in women's fiction, she has written a number of book chapters and journal articles about women writers ranging from Louisa May Alcott to Margaret Atwood. Other research foci are Afro-American fiction and visual culture as well as captivity narratives. For more information, see https://www.uni-oldenburg.de/en/michaela-keck/.

MARCELLA LAFEVER, PhD (University of New Mexico, 2005) is an associate professor in communications at the University of the Fraser Valley. Marcella's research focuses on the social exclusion that results from public dialogue and decision-making where cultural ways of speaking are outside the norms expected in dominant Canadian culture. Her 9P Planning model posits a process that builds intercultural relationships to increase social inclusion in public dialogue. Dr. LaFever's current work investigates use of Indigenous storytelling as a form of dialogic participation.

JULIE LAPLANTE is a full professor of anthropology in the School of Sociological and Anthropological Studies at the University of Ottawa and has been working on human-plant entanglements in healing since the early 1990s. At first, she directed her attention to the intersections in-between indigenous and bio-scientific/humanitarian plant and molecule based medicine in the Brazilian Amazon; later, she focused on both ancestral and clinical bodily, visual, and sonorous abilities in healing with plants at two edges of the Indian Ocean (South Africa, Java Indonesia) and more recently in Cameroon. Dr. Plante was a senior research fellow at the Max Planck Institute for Social Anthropology (2006–2010). She has published in numerous journals and is the author of *Pouvoir Guérir: médecines autochtones et humanitaires* (Presses Université Laval, 2004), as well as *Healing Roots: Anthropology in Life and Medicine* (Berghahn Books, 2015); recently, she co-edited *Search After Method. Sensing, Moving, and Imagining in Anthropological Fieldwork* (Berghahn Books, 2020). Other publications include *Becoming-Plant in Indian Ocean Worlds: Lines, Flows, Winds, and Water (2015) and* the production of an anthropological film, *Jamu Stories* (2015).

JuPong Lin is a Taiwan-born interdisciplinary artist, writer, and educator. JuPong's installations and community performances blend paper-folding, poetics, and contemplative movement. Impelled by the existential threat of climate catastrophe, JuPong reclaims ancestral traditions to activate deep, personal, and systemic transformation for a just transition. JuPong has exhibited and performed nationally; her poetry has been published in *Dark Matter Women Witnessing* and *Honoring Nature* (2021). JuPong has been a faculty member in the Master of Fine Arts in Interdisciplinary Arts (MFAIA) program at Goddard College since 2005. As the Director of the program, she led an initiative to establish a concentration in decolonial arts.

Sharon Meier MacDonald, MA in counselling, is a registered social worker whose work as mental health educator focuses on the importance of enlisting community members as change agents. When her community of Ghost Valley, Alberta, faced the challenge of clear-cut logging, neighbours asked her to fill a leadership role. MacDonald's story of the Ghost Valley's initial experiences was published as "Taking Action for the Ghost" in the December 2015 issue of *Wild Lands Advocate*. She thereafter led the Ghost Valley Community to produce the film *Forests, Fins & Footprints:*

Clearcutting a Community, screened by several film festivals, including the 2018 International Wildlife Film Festival.

Arivalagan Murugeshapandian is an assistant professor, Department of Folklore, St. Xavier's College, Palayamkottai, Tamil Nadu State, South India. He earned his doctoral degree at the Madras Institute of Development Studies, Chennai, Tamil Nadu, South India and conducted doctoral research on the topic of Forests, Environmental Change and Tribal Communities in Colonial Tamilnadu. Between 2008 and 2011, he was an international SEPHIS doctoral fellow at the International Institute of Social History, in The Netherlands. In his current research, Arivalagan specializes in environmental history and tribal studies. In 2016, he was invited to deliver a talk for the Series on Tamil Worlds at the University of Toronto. His paper, "Beyond Colonialism: Towards a New Environmental History of India," was published in *Environmental History in the Making, Volume 1: Explaining* (Springer, in 2017). Another contribution, "'Self' rather than the 'Other': Towards a Subjective Ethnography of Kani Community," was published in *Rethinking Social Justice* (Orient Black Swan, 2020).

Devora Neumark, PhD, is a second-generation Holocaust survivor born to refugees from Russia and Poland. They are an interdisciplinary artist-researcher, educator, and community-engaged practitioner. Devora taught in the Goddard College Master of Fine Arts in Interdisciplinary Arts program from July 2003 to May 2021 and is a Yale School of Public Health-certified Climate Change Adaptation Practitioner. Their SSHRC-funded research-creation dissertation, titled *Radical Beauty for Troubled Times: Involuntary Displacement and the (Un)Making of Home* (Concordia University, 2013), is an inquiry into the relationship between the traumas associated with forced dislocation and the deliberate beautification of home. Devora is currently developing two related bodies of contemplative artwork: one engages wellness and the cultivation of joy as radical practice; the other is focused on environmental trauma and mainstreaming climate justice.

Pearl Penner holds a Masters degree in Community and Regional Planning with an Indigenous Community Planning focus from the University of British Columbia. Pearl was born and raised in Abbotsford, BC, and grew up around the teachings of the Medicine Wheel. She learned from Elder Mary Uslick, who brought the vision of the Medicine Wheel to the Stó:lō Nation Territory. Pearl has dedicated her career to working with Indigenous people and communities.

Fernanda Viegas Reichardt, a graduate of law, holds a PhD in sciences (applied ecology) and concluded her postdoctoral research at the University of São Paulo, Brazil. She also served as a researcher at the Institute of Advanced Studies at the University of São Paulo and at the MARE Research Center of the Portuguese Foundation for Science and Technology. Her research adopts a trans-interdisciplinary approach and emphasizes the human and environmental rights of the traditional peoples of the Cerrado (Brazilian Savannah), including the Xavante peoples.

Bob Sandford is the Global Water Futures Chair, Water & Climate Security at the United Nations University Institute for Water, Environment and Health. He is the co-author of the UN *Water in the World We Want* report on post-2015 global sustainable development goals relating to water. In his work, Bob is committed to translating scientific research outcomes into language decision-makers can use to craft timely and meaningful public policy, and to bringing international example to bear on local water issues. Bob is Senior Advisor on water issues for the Interaction Council, a global public policy forum composed of more than thirty former Heads of State including Canadian Prime Minister Jean Chrétien, U.S. President Bill Clinton, and the former Prime Minister of Norway, Gro Brundtland. Bob is a Fellow of the Centre for Hydrology at the University of Saskatchewan and a Fellow of the Biogeoscience Institute at the University of Calgary. He sits on the Advisory Board of Living Lakes Canada and is a member of the Forum for Leadership on Water (FLOW), a national water policy research group centred in Toronto. In addition to many other books, Bob is the author of a number of high-profile works on water, including *Cold Matters: The State & Fate of Canada's Snow and Ice* and *Saving Lake Winnipeg*. Bob co-authored with Kerry *Freek*,

Flood Forecast: Climate Risk & Resilience in Canada. His book, *Vanishing Glaciers: The Snows of Yesteryear and the Future Climate of the Mountain West,* won the 2017 Lane Anderson Prize for the best science writing in Canada.

HENRY BIKWIBILI TANTOH is a geographer by training with a PhD in geography and environmental studies from the University of the Witwatersrand, South Africa; he also holds a Bachelor's and a Master's degree in Geography and Environmental Planning from the University of Dschang, Cameroon. Dr. Tantoh is a lecturer and a researcher. His research explores the social, economic, and political aspects of natural resource management and environmental governance and their relationships to wider societal change. Much of his recent work has been concerned with the politics of natural resource management in sub-Sahara Africa, with a particular focus on co-management of water resources and systems that promote stakeholder participation, community development, political ecology, climate change and sustainability.

REG WHITEN, M.E.Des, RPP, P.Ag is a watershed stewardship agrologist and an experienced consultant in land-use planning and management through northern Canada. He has served as Land-Use Advisor to Treaty 8 First Nations, as Senior Planner to the Peel Watershed Planning Commission (2008–2009), and as Watershed Steward to the City of Dawson Creek (2010–2014). Reg continues to consult on land-use and watershed management with specialization on rural and First Nations community engagement. Currently, he serves also as Sustainability Facilitator with the Boreal Centre for Sustainability, which he founded in 2000. Last year, he was appointed by the BC government to serve as a Member of the BC Environmental Appeal Board, Forest Appeals Commission and Oil & Gas Appeals Tribunal. He has travelled extensively, and now maintains a homestead property practicing northern permaculture.